DISCARD

Cloud and Virtual Data Storage Networking

Your journey to efficient and
effective information services

Cloud and Virtual Data Storage Networking

Your journey to efficient and
effective information services

Greg Schulz

CRC Press
Taylor & Francis Group
Boca Raton   London   New York

CRC Press is an imprint of the
Taylor & Francis Group, an **informa** business
AN AUERBACH BOOK

CRC Press
Taylor & Francis Group
6000 Broken Sound Parkway NW, Suite 300
Boca Raton, FL 33487-2742

© 2012 by Taylor & Francis Group, LLC
CRC Press is an imprint of Taylor & Francis Group, an Informa business

No claim to original U.S. Government works

Printed in the United States of America on acid-free paper
Version Date: 20110726

International Standard Book Number: 978-1-4398-5173-9 (Hardback)

Visit the Taylor & Francis Web site at
http://www.taylorandfrancis.com

and the CRC Press Web site at
http://www.crcpress.com

Contents

Preface

Since I wrote *The Green and Virtual Data Center* (CRC Press, 2009), I have had the opportunity to meet and speak with thousands of information technology (IT) professionals around the world, both in person and virtually via different venues. Even as that last book was being printed, the ideas to be found in this new book were coming together, as I refined my premises and identified new industry trends. One of those trends is the result of hype and FUD (fear, uncertainty, and doubt) about material from various sources. However, there is a gap between the hype and the FUD, addressed by a theme of this book: *Don't be scared of clouds and virtualization, but do look before you leap.* What this means is that you should do your homework, prepare, learn, and get involved with proof of concepts and training to build the momentum and success to continue an ongoing IT journey to enable agility, flexibility, scale, and productivity while reducing costs and complexity.

Another notable trend today is that the amount of data being generated, moved, processed, and stored for longer periods of time shows no signs of decreasing. Even during the recent global economic crisis and recessions, there were few, if any, signs of a data or information slowdown. In fact, there was evidence to the contrary: While financial institutions were being plagued with record-breaking negative economic impacts, they were also generating, moving, and processing record amounts of data that had to be preserved. The only thing that has changed is that we need to do even more with less—or more with what we currently have—to support and sustain business growth. This means leveraging existing and new or emerging technologies and techniques to stretch available resources, including budgets, people, floor space, and power, to support business growth, new applications, and even more data and information.

To sustain business growth while enabling new functionalities or services, providers of information services need to look at various options for becoming more efficient. Becoming more efficient means more than cost avoidance; it also includes boosting productivity while streamlining information services delivery. This means stretching resources (people, processes, budgets, hardware, software, energy, facilities, and services) further while enabling better business agility and productivity. This book picks up where

The Green and Virtual Data Center (Intel recommended reading for developers) ended and considers how IT or other providers of information services can do more with available resources (people, processes, products, and services) while reducing per-unit costs and maintaining or enhancing quality of service and customer satisfaction.

Beyond Buzzwords, Hype, and FUD

There are those who think that cloud technology is all about building from the ground up, or at least establishing new protocols, interfaces, management standards, and reference models. Not surprisingly, these tend to be engineers, technical marketers, investors, entrepreneurs, or just fans of the latest "shiny new toy." Then there are those who believe that cloud and virtualization techniques and their associated technologies can be used to complement or enhance existing environments.

This book looks at clarifying "cloud confusion" and expanding the discussion of virtualization beyond consolidation for enabling agility, flexibility, and ease of management. For some, this will mean private clouds or traditional IT approaches leveraging some new technologies; for others, it will mean public clouds used completely or in a complementary manner. Some moving to public clouds will use technology that is still emerging, perhaps rebuilding or rip-and-replace, and others will see the move as a green-field or clean-sheet opportunity.

Who Should Read This Book

This book cuts across various IT data technology and resource domains to provide a single source that discusses the interdependencies that need to be supported to enable a virtualized, efficient, effective, and agile information services delivery environment. Do you need or want a cloud? Do you have to have or would you like a virtual environment? Do you feel compelled to have a converged data and storage network, or is there a particular business opportunity or challenge? What is the business case, demand, challenge, or opportunity for addressing or enabling clouds, dynamic infrastructure, and virtual technology? This book looks at these and other questions, providing answers, ideas, and insight to stimulate thinking about where, when, why, and how to deploy cloud, virtualization, and data storage networking resources on a public, private, or legacy IT basis. The book is about convergence in terms of technologies, techniques, and various best practices that pertain to cloud, virtualization, dynamic infrastructure, and traditional environments' delivery of information services.

Audiences that will benefit from reading this book include IT purchasing, facilities, server, storage, networking, database, and applications analysts, administrators, and architects, as well as CIOs, CTOs, CMOs, and CFOs. Also, manufacturers and solution partners (vendors), value-added resellers, consultants, sales, marketing, support, and engineering specialists, public relations, investment communities, and media professionals associated with IT technologies and services can all find something of interest.

The book looks at the changing role of data and storage networks to support and sustain resilient and flexible, scalable virtual and cloud environments, and how to leverage those techniques into existing environments to achieve great efficiency, boosting service while reducing per-unit costs. If this resonates or if you want to learn more, then this book is a must-read for real-world perspectives and insight to address server, storage, networking, and other infrastructure resource management topics to support current and next-generation public or private virtual data centers that rely on flexible, scalable, and resilient data storage and networks. This could be the starting point on your cloud or virtualization journey, but also a great resource for use in traditional environments. It is short on hype and FUD; instead, it focuses on what you need to determine where various technologies and techniques can be applied.

How This Book Is Organized

This easy-to-navigate book is divided into four parts. Part I, "Why Cloud, Virtualization and Data Storage Networks Are Needed," includes Chapters 1 and 2 and covers the background and basics of information service delivery and clouds; Part II, "Managing Data and Resources: Protect, Preserve, Secure, and Serve," includes Chapters 3 through 6 and looks at common management tasks along with metrics for enabling efficient and effective data infrastructure environments. Part III, "Technology, Tools, and Solution Options," includes Chapters 7 through 13 and explores the various resource technologies (servers, storage, and networking) and techniques. Finally, Part IV, "Putting IT All Together," comprising Chapters 14 and 15, brings together the previous parts and provides a glimpse into the future of cloud, virtualization, and data storage networking.

Is It a Nonstop Flight or a Journey with Intermediate Stops and Layovers?

A major theme of this book is that IT has been on a journey for several decades to get to a place where more can be done with available resources while maintaining or enhancing quality of service, feature functionality, and cost reduction. Challenges of journeys include departing too soon, before proper preparations have been made, or waiting too long and missing an opportunity. On the other hand, rushing in too quickly may lead to surprises that result in less than pleasant experiences. So, don't be scared of clouds, dynamic infrastructure, and virtualization, but look before you leap. Learn the benefits as well as the caveats of clouds, and understand where the gaps are, so that you can work around them while leveraging what is available to expand your horizons for the long haul.

As you read the chapters in this book, you will discover a mix of existing and emerging technologies; to some this will be review, while for others it may be new. The main idea is that cloud and virtual environments rely on physical or fundamental resources, processes, and people operating collectively and collaboratively in a more efficient, effective, and agile manner. Whether you are going all in with clouds and virtualization or are simply looking to expand your awareness while continuing with business as usual for your environments, the technologies, techniques, and best practices laid out in these pages apply equally to cloud, virtual, and physical data and storage networking environments of all sizes.

For some environments, there have been numerous intermediate stops during the journey from mainframe to distributed to client server to Web-based to consolidated, virtualized, and cloud computing paradigms, with various initiatives, including service-oriented architectures (SOAs), information utilities, and other models along the way. Some organizations have transitioned "nonstop" from one era to another, whereas others have had clean-sheet or green-field (starting from scratch) opportunities.

For some, the journey is to the cloud (public or private), while for others the cloud is a platform to enable a transition through an information continuum journey of years or decades. For example, despite being declared dead, the mainframe is very much alive for some organizations, supporting legacy and Linux open systems providing SOAs and private or public cloud capabilities. The trick is finding the right balance of old and new, without clinging to the past or rushing into the future without having an idea of where you are going.

An important part of the journey involves measuring your progress, determining where you are and when you will get to where you are going while staying within your budget and on schedule. Keeping resources safe during transition, for business continuance, disaster recovery, or data protection in general, is also important.

When you go on a trip for business or fun, your vehicle, medium, or platform may be foot, bicycle, automobile, plane, train, or some combination. You decide on the method based on performance or speed, capacity, and comfort; space, reliability, and schedule availability; effectiveness, personal preferences, and economics. Often the decision is made entirely on economics, without factoring in time and productivity or enjoyment. Sometimes, an airplane ride from the U.S. West Coast to the Midwest is more productive because of the time saved, even if the cost is higher than traveling by car.

Having said all of that, it is now time to stow your items, place your seat back and tray table in the upright and locked position, and secure your seat belt as we prepare for takeoff. I hope you enjoy your journey through the following chapters and pages.

Greg Schulz

Acknowledgments

Writing a book is more than putting pen to paper or, in this case, typing on a computer: It involves hundreds of hours working behind the scenes on various activities. Writing a book is similar to a technology development project, whether hardware, software, or a service, in that it includes an initial assessment of the need. Having established the need for this project, I chose to write the book myself. Other behind-the-scenes activities in any project include research, design and validation, actual content generation, edits, reviews or debugging, more edits, working with text as well as graphics, project management, contracts, marketing, and production, among others.

Thanks and appreciation to all of the vendors, value-added resellers, service providers, press and media, freelance writers, venture capitalists, bloggers, consultants, twitter tweeps, and IT professionals around the world I have been fortunate enough to talk with while putting this book together. I would also like to thank others who were directly or indirectly involved with this project, including Andy Fox, Mike Connor, Corey Donovan, Rob Dombrowsky, Jim Dyer, Chris Foote, Rich Lillis, Ed Haletky, Mike Hall, Greg Knieriemen and Marc Farley of Infosmack, Keith Norbie, Bruce Ravid, Drew Robb, Hubert Smith, Eric Siebert, Stanley Stevens, the Nelsons and Schoellers, as well as George Terwey.

Special thanks to Tom Becchetti, Greg Brunton and Kay Wylie, Gert Brouwer, Georgiana and Alex Comsa, Preston Deguise, David Marshall, Dr. "J" Metz, and Sherryl Savage. Thanks to John Wyzalek, my publisher, with whom I formalized this project over a great lunch in New York City while watching the St. Patrick's Day parade at a restaurant in Grand Central Station (one of the best burgers ever!), Chris Manion and everyone else at CRC/Taylor & Francis/Auerbach, as well as a big thank you to Theron Shreve of Derryfield Publishing Services and his crew, including Lynne Lackenbach and Marje Pollack. Very special thanks to Damaris Larson, who continues to push and challenge me in support of this and countless other writing projects: You are the best!

Finally, thanks to my wife, Karen, and to "Big Babe" and "Little Leo," for having the patience to support me while I worked on yet another book project!

To all of the above and to you the reader, thank you very much.

Greg Schulz

About the Author

Greg Schulz is an independent IT industry advisor, author, blogger (http://storage-ioblog.com), and consultant. Greg has over 30 years of experience across a variety of server, storage, networking, hardware, software, and services architectures, platforms, and paradigms. He brings the rare perspective of having been a IT professional working in various business sectors (e.g., as an IT customer), a vendor, and a value-added reseller, in addition to having been an analyst and advisory consultant across servers, storage, networks, hardware, software, virtualization, and cloud services.

After spending time as a customer and a vendor, Greg became a Senior Analyst at an IT analysis firm covering virtualization, SAN, NAS, and associated storage management tools, techniques, best practices, and technologies in addition to providing advisory and education services. In 2006, Greg leveraged the experiences of having been on the customer, vendor, and analyst sides of the "IT table" to form the independent IT advisory consultancy firm Server and StorageIO (StorageIO). He has been a member of various storage-related organizations, including the Computer Measurement Group (CMG), the Storage Networking Industry Association (SNIA), and the RAID Advisory Board (RAB), as well as vendor and technology-focused user groups. Greg also speaks frequently at conferences, seminars, and private events around the world.

Greg has received numerous awards and accolades, including being named a VMware vExpert and an EcoTech Warrior by the *Minneapolis-St. Paul Business Journal,* based on his work with virtualization, including his book, *The Green and Virtual Data Center* (CRC Press, 2009). In addition to his thousands of reports, blogs, twitter tweets, columns, articles, tips, pod casts, videos, and webcasts, Greg is also author of the SNIA-endorsed study guide, *Resilient Storage Networks—Designing Flexible Scalable Data Infrastructures* (Elsevier, 2004). Greg is regularly quoted and interviewed as one of the most sought-after independent IT advisors providing perspectives, commentary, and opinion on industry activity. Greg has a B.A. in computer science and a M.Sc. in software engineering from the University of St. Thomas. Learn more at www.storageio.com.

Chapter 1

Industry Trends and Perspectives: From Issues and Challenges to Opportunities

There is no such thing as a data or information recession.

– Greg Schulz

In This Chapter

- Moving beyond the hype
- Navigating the maze of cloud and virtualization stories
- The business demands of IT and data storage
- IT issues and challenges involving data storage
- The business benefit of cloud and virtual data storage networking
- Opportunities to address data storage issues and challenges
- The role of virtualization, cloud, and storage networking
- Maximizing IT resources without compromising quality of service
- What defines a public and private cloud service, product, solution, or paradigm
- The importance of information access, data consistency, and availability

1

This chapter looks at the big picture of business issues and demand drivers that set up the need for cloud, virtualization, and data storage networking. Key themes and buzzwords covered include cloud computing, cloud storage, public and private clouds, information factories, virtualization, business issues or challenges, barriers to productivity, technology tools and techniques, along with best practices. Additional themes and topics discussed include enabling agility, flexibility, scalability, resiliency, multitenancy, elasticity, managed service providers (MSPs), converged networks, Infrastructure as a Service (IaaS), Platform as a Service (PaaS), Software as a Service (SaaS), and IT optimization.

1.1. Getting Started

You probably didn't wake up this morning thinking, "I need to have someone buy or implement a cloud, virtualization, or storage networking solution." Granted, if you are a vendor or a consultant, that may be your job (assessing, designing, selling, installing, or supporting data storage, networks, virtualization, or clouds). However, if you are not a vendor, consultant, analyst, or journalist, but rather someone responsible for information technology (IT)–related solutions for your organization, typically the need to buy and deploy a new solution is tied to solving some business issue or capitalizing on an opportunity.

A common challenge in many organizations is exploding data growth along with associated management tasks and constraints, including budgets, staffing, time, physical facilities, floor space, and power and cooling. Before going further into why you need or do not need a cloud, virtualization, or a storage network, let's take a step back and look at what is driving data growth and the consequent need to manage it more effectively.

1.2. The Importance of Data and Storage

We live in an information-centric world. As a society, we have a growing reliance on creating and consuming data (Figure 1.1), which must be available when and where it is needed. Data and related information services are enabled or provided via information technology services combining applications, facilities, networks, servers, storage hardware, and software resources.

More data can be stored in the same or smaller physical footprint than in the past, thus requiring less power and cooling per gigabyte (GB), terabyte (TB), petabyte (PB), or exabyte (EB). However, data growth rates necessary to sustain business activity, enhance IT service delivery, and enable new applications are placing continued demands requiring more processing, network, or input/output (I/O) bandwidth and data storage capacity.

As a result of this increasing reliance on information, both for home and personal use along with business and professional needs, more data is being generated, processed, moved, stored, and retained in multiple copies for longer periods of time. The net result is that IT organizations of all sizes are faced with having to do more with what they have (sometimes with less), including maximizing available IT resources while overcoming common footprint constraints (available power, cooling, floor space, server, storage and networking resources, management, budgets, and IT staffing).

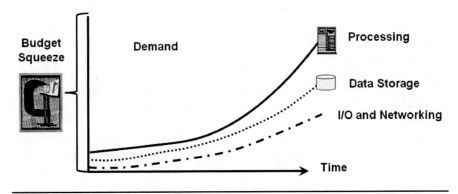

Figure 1.1   IT and data storage demand drivers.

1.2.1. The Business End of IT Data Storage Impact

Just as we live in an information-centric society which extends from home to the office, from the small office/home office (SOHO) to the remote office/branch office (ROBO), small/medium-size business (SMB), small/medium enterprise (SME), to ultra-large organizations or enterprises, there is another common theme, and that is economics. Economics are a constant focus, whether it is costs or expense, profits and margins, return on investment (ROI), total cost of ownership, or some other business specific measurement.

On the one hand, there is a need or reliance on having more information; on the other, there are the constants of economics, cause and effect, and supply and demand. You need or want information, but there is a cost to supporting or managing it. Yet information can also directly or indirectly drive profits, so a balancing act is necessary. Thus, to support or sustain economic (business) growth or manage the data necessary to maintain daily activity, there are associated costs (hardware, software, people, facilities, power, etc.) that need to be managed.

Innovation is doing more with what you have: supporting growth and enhancement of services without negatively impacting service-level objectives (SLOs), including quality of services, while reducing per-unit cost for service delivery (as shown in Figure 1.2). The trick is to find the balance among boosting productivity, reducing costs, and maintaining or enhancing customer service delivery.

Figure 1.2 sums up the balancing act of maximizing use of available IT resources while supporting growing business demands in a cost-effective manner. IT resources include people, processes or best practices, time, budgets, physical facilities, power, cooling, floor space, server, storage and networking hardware, along with software and services. All too often, the approach has been to drive cost down by increasing utilization at the expense of quality of service (QoS) and SLOs. An example is leveraging consolidation or migration to a cloud service based on a lower-cost model that trades QoS and SLO for price.

Another variation is to boost QoS and SLOs along with performance to meet demand at the expense of cost or less effectively utilized resources. In other words, it's relatively easy to improve in one area while causing issues or aggravation in another. Innovation occurs when all three categories shown in Figure 1.2 are positively impacted.

Figure 1.2 identifies constraints or barriers to cost-effective service delivery while maintaining or enhancing the service delivery experience including QoS and SLOs. Cloud, virtualization, and data storage networking are tools and techniques that, combined with best practices, can be used to enable innovation and meet the objectives of Figure 1.2.

Clouds, virtualization, and data storage networks can be used to enable cost reduction and stretching of resources by supporting consolidation initiatives. However, these same tools and techniques can also be used for enabling agility, flexibility, and enhanced services that can improve both top- and bottom-line business metrics. For some environments or applications the focus may be on cost reduction while supporting little to no growth, while for others it may mean working with the same or a slightly increased budget while supporting business demand and SLOs. In some organizations this also means reducing costs or stretching available budgets and resources to do more with what they have.

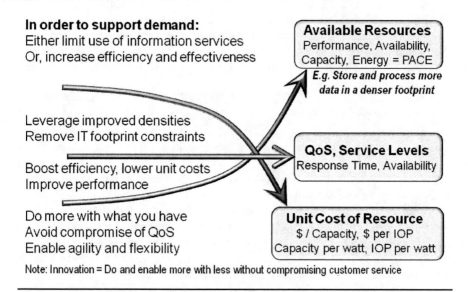

In order to support demand:
Either limit use of information services
Or, increase efficiency and effectiveness

Available Resources
Performance, Availability,
Capacity, Energy = PACE

*E.g. Store and process more
data in a denser footprint*

Leverage improved densities
Remove IT footprint constraints

QoS, Service Levels
Response Time, Availability

Boost efficiency, lower unit costs
Improve performance

Do more with what you have
Avoid compromise of QoS
Enable agility and flexibility

Unit Cost of Resource
$ / Capacity, $ per IOP
Capacity per watt, IOP per watt

Note: Innovation = Do and enable more with less without compromising customer service

Figure 1.2 Supporting demand, maintaining quality of service (QoS), while reducing costs.

1.2.2. Addressing Business and IT Issues

Clouds, virtualization, and storage networks are tools, techniques, and best practices to help support or sustain growth while reducing per-unit costs, removing complexity, enabling flexibility or agility, and also enhancing customer experiences. Clouds, virtualization, and storage networks are not the objective themselves; rather, they are tools, vehicles, or mechanisms that can be used to help achieve broader business and IT objectives. They can be used for new, start-from-scratch environments; they can also be aligned with existing IT service delivery as well as help with a transition-over-time evolution of IT.

Thus, taking a step back from the technology, tools, and techniques, and keeping the bigger picture in focus, helps to understand what to use when, where, and why, as well as how to go about it in a more effective manner.

1.2.3. What Is Driving Data Growth and Information Reliance

The popularity of rich media and Internet-based applications has resulted in explosive growth of unstructured file data, requiring new and more scalable storage solutions. General examples of unstructured data include spreadsheets, PowerPoint, slide decks, Adobe PDF and Word documents, Web pages, video and audio, JPEG, MP3, and MP4, photos, audio, and video files.

Examples of applications driving continued growth of unstructured data include:

- Gaming, security, and other surveillance video or security
- Unified communications including Voice-over-IP (VoIP)
- Rich media entertainment production and viewing
- Digital archive media management
- Medicine, life science, and health care
- Energy including oil and gas exploration
- Messaging and collaborations (email, IM, texting)
- Internet, Web, social media networking, video and audio
- Finances, marketing, engineering, and customer relations management (CRM)
- Regulatory and compliance requirements

While structured data in the form of databases continues to grow, for most environments and applications the high-growth area and expanding data footprint along with associated performance bottlenecks is centered on semistructured email data and unstructured file data. Unstructured data has varying I/O characteristics that change over time—for example, data starting out with a lot of activity, then going idle for a time, followed by extensive reads, as in the case of a video or audio file becoming known and popular on a media, entertainment, social networking, or a company-sponsored website.

Data footprint is the total data storage needed to support your various business application and information needs. Your data footprint may, in fact, be larger than how much actual data you have. A general approach to determine your data footprint is to simply add up all of your on-line, near-line and off-line data storage (disk and tape) capacity.

1.3. Business Issues and IT Challenges

I commonly get asked if virtualization and clouds are a passing fad, full of hype, or if they are real and being attacked by fear–uncertainty–doubt (FUD). Granted, and unfortunately, there is a lot of hype along with FUD, leading to confusion about both cloud and virtualization—tending to set them up as popular fads, much as compliance, "green" IT, information lifecycle management (ILM), client server, and storage networking were initially viewed.

Common business issues, challenges, and trends pertaining to IT include:

- Increased reliance on information services being accessible when needed
- Competitive and other market dynamics causing financial constraints and focus
- Regulatory compliance and other industry or corporate mandates
- Stretched resources (staffing levels, skill sets, budgets, facilities)
- The need to reduce costs while increasing services and productivity
- A shift from cost reduction or avoidance to efficiency and effectiveness models

How often do you use data storage or information services? Perhaps you use data storage without realizing it, at home, at work, and elsewhere. Data storage is in play all around us, used for different purposes and in various forms. Some might say that data storage is the most important IT resource compared to servers or computers, networks, desktop, laptops or workstations, or application software tools. On the other hand, some would say that networks are the most important, or servers, or whatever is that individual's specialty. For the sake of argument I will position data storage as equal to servers, networks, hardware, and software, as all are needed to be effective.

Common IT issues, challenges, problems, and trends include:

- More data to process, move, manage, store, and retain for longer periods of time
- Increased reliance and expectation that information services be available 7×24
- Limited or strained resource constraints causing bottlenecks or barriers
  - o People or staffing and applicable skill sets
  - o Hardware, software, and networking bandwidth
  - o Budgets (capital and operating)
  - o Power, cooling, floor space
  - o Time for backup or data protection windows
- Regulatory, compliance, and other regulations
- Demand causing performance, availability, capacity, and energy (PACE) impacts
- Software or hardware licensing and maintenance, support as well as service fees
- Aging IT infrastructures along with related interoperability and complexity
- Time involved in aligning IT resources to business or service needs
- Speed and accuracy of IT resource provisioning

When I talk with IT professionals or customers, I ask them if they have a mandate to reduce costs, which is a common industry messaging or rallying theme. Surprisingly, a majority of them indicate that it is not costs per se that they have to reduce (though some do). Rather, they have to do more with what they have with their current budget to support business growth, new applications, and functionality.

1.4. Business and IT Opportunities

Now, back to the question you woke up with this morning: "Do I need to have someone buy or implement a cloud, virtualization, or storage networking solution?"

Or maybe you woke up wondering how you are going to support business growth, demands for more data, flexibility, reduce cost, and enhance service delivery. Or perhaps you need to figure out how to defend your environment or market your environment to the rest of your business as opposed to the business going to external resources.

For some, efficiency and optimization can be avoidance or simply increasing utilization to reduce or spread costs over more work being done. However, another form of efficiency and effectiveness is stretching resources to do more while boosting productivity or removing barriers and constraints.

1.4.1. Traditional Information Services Delivery/Model

Delivery of information services continues to evolve. As this evolution of techniques, technologies, best practices, and new products continues, there are decades of legacy applications and data that need to be supported.

The basics of any information services delivery model can be summarized (Figure 1.3) as users accessing business applications running on a server with information stored somewhere, all accessed via some device over a network. The device could be a dumb terminal cabled or networked to the server with dedicated direct attached disk storage or a smart phone via a wireless connection.

Similarly, the server could be virtualized or nonvirtualized with an operating system, database, and other tools to support and manage the applications and storage. From these basic information services delivery models, additional deployment scenarios can be established, including dedicated or shared applications, services, time sharing, or what we call today cloud and managed services, among others. Likewise, there can be different types of tiered servers, storage, and networks, which will be discussed in more detail over the next several chapters.

A common expression is that what is old is new and what is new is old. In the case of cloud and virtualization, for some these are new or perhaps repackaged open variations of what they have seen, heard, or read about previously. For example, IBM mainframes have had propriety virtualization for several decades. Those same platforms—which have been declared dead or dinosaurs—with their tenets of being highly optimized, metered or instrumented with metrics and reporting, scalable, and resilient—are what some cloud attributes seek to emulate from an open perspective. This has led to some interesting discussions about why not keep things on the mainframe (clinging to the past) versus moving everything to the cloud (racing to the future).

Depending on the types of applications, the answer may be to move some or all to the cloud. On the other hand, leveraging a cloud managed service provider, hosting, or outsourcing can be the answer for other applications to coexist with your environment. For example, if you still have the need for an IBM zOS class mainframe, but it has become a small part of your environment, then outsourcing it or leaving a hosted or managed service can be an option.

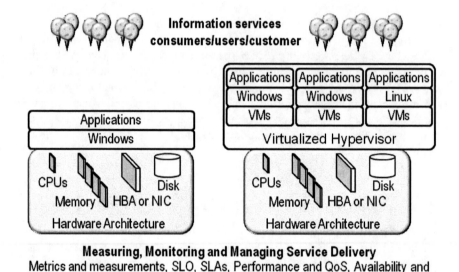

Figure 1.3 Information services delivery basics.

1.4.2. Information Factories

Most IT organizations or infrastructures exist to support the business applications and information needs of an organization. In some cases, the business applications services provided by IT include supporting factories, accounting, marketing, and engineering, among others. However, IT or information providers also often suffer from "shoemaker's children" syndrome in that they may not have adequate insight or management tools for themselves. For example, an organizations may have accounting and tracking systems supported by IT, but does IT have accounting or metrics on performance, availability, capacity, configuration, energy, and economics for a given service delivery?

Traditional factories (Figure 1.4) leverage different tools, techniques, metrics, measurements, best practices, resources, and people skill sets to build and deliver goods or services to a prescribed service level and price point. Factories can be dedicated or

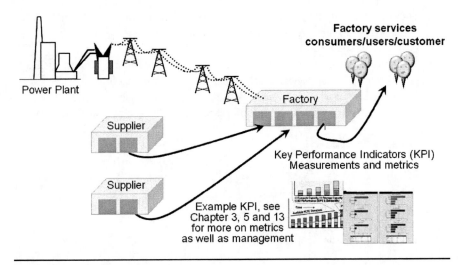

Figure 1.4   Traditional factory.

private, they can be shared or supplier-based, or they can be hybrid, similar to how IT services can be sourced, used, and delivered. An organization may have its own factory, or its factory could be a virtual or third-party jobbing or other service. Goods/services may be produced by someone under contract. IT services may be delivered via an organization's own factory, via a third party, or virtualized.

Basic characteristics of factories include:

- Reliable, to meet demand, avoid downtime, avoid mistakes and rework
- Scalable, to meet changing workload demands
- Efficient, reduce waste, customer SLOs met in an economical manner
- Work is done quickly, yet reliably, with good quality
- Flexible capacity and ability to retool to meet changing needs
- Factories may be wholly owned, shared, or owned by a third party
- Factories consume materials and resources to create/deliver goods and services
- Those goods and services may in turn be consumed by other factories
- Factories produce product to a blueprint, template, or run book specifications

The notion of the information factory (Figure 1.5) sets up the discussion around cloud, virtualization, and storage networks on either a public, private, or hybrid basis.

For some, the idea of an information factory and cloud may bring *déjà vu* experiences of the information utility model of the late 1980s and early 1990s.

Additional characteristics of factories include:

- Rely on suppliers or secondary and tertiary factories (subs)
- Have bill of materials, metrics and measurements, costing information
- Quality assurances programs to ensure that QoS and SLOs are being met

- Focus on reducing defects and waste while boosting productivity to reduce cost
- Build templates for optimized information service delivery
- Best practices, processes, policies and procedures
- Balance of productivity, cost control, waste reduction, utilization, meeting SLOs
- Leverage new technologies that have good payback for enabling goals
- Cost-effective habitats for deploying and using technologies
- Efficiency gained with repeatable processes, and increased workload activity

Information factories can be

- Private
- Public
- Hybrid

Information factories (or clouds) should be or enable:

- Multitenancy, measurability, and accountability
- For service providers, this can include chargeback
- Secure, flexible, dynamic, scalable, and resilient
- Able to relocate services as needed
- Rapid deployment and provisioning of resources
- Efficient, cost-effective resource usage that meets QoS and SLAs
- Automate and guide users or customers to best-fit services selection

The similarities between factories, information factories, clouds, and information services delivery should be clear.

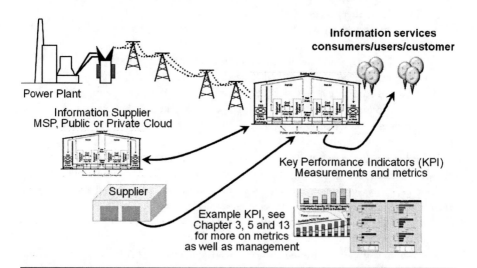

Figure 1.5 Information factory.

1.5. Opportunity for Cloud, Virtualization, and Data Storage Networking

Like a physical factory, some of an information factory's work is done on the premises and some off-site at other locations, including those of subcontractors or suppliers. In the case of information factories, the product being produced is information services, with the machinery being servers, storage, and I/O networking managed with software, processes, procedures, and metrics. Raw materials include data, energy to power and cool the physical facility, and technologies, all operating to deliver the services at a low defect or error rate while meeting or exceeding QoS, performance, availability, and accessibility requirements in a cost-effective manner.

For some cloud compute or storage providers, the value proposition is that they can supply the service at a lower cost than if you use your own capabilities. Similar to service bureaus, out-sourcing, managed service, or hosting facilities of the past, cloud-based services are a means of shifting or avoiding costs by moving work or data elsewhere to be processed or stored.

However, it is a mistake to consider clouds for just for their cost-saving abilities while ignoring performance, availability, data integrity, ease of management, and other factors that can impact service delivery and expenses. Clouds should be looked at not as a replacement or competing technology or technique, but rather as a complementary approach to existing in-house resources.

Cloud computing and storage are simply additional tiers of servers and data repositories that may have different performance, availability, capacity, or economics associated with them to meet specific business and/or application needs. That is, cloud computing and cloud storage coexist and complement what is currently being done, with the objective of boosting quality of service, availability, or customer satisfaction while supporting more data being processed, moved, and stored for longer periods of time at a lower unit cost.

1.5.1. IT Clouds and Virtualization: Not If, Rather When, Where, Why, and How

There are many different types and definitions of clouds, including those of the National Institute of Standards and Technology (NIST) and the Data Management Task Force (DMTF). Cloud computing is a paradigm, and thus its definition is still evolving along with use cases and the underlying technologies, techniques, and best practices.

Some see clouds as the wave of the future, even if they're not sure what that future may be. To others, a cloud is a cloud if, and only if, it is outside of what you currently are doing or have done with IT. Some will argue that a cloud is only a cloud if new hardware or software is involved, while others will assert that a cloud is only a cloud if your applications and data exist outside your location.

Consequently, different people will have different thoughts or perspectives about clouds, depending on their perception or definition. For example, in Figure 1.6, thoughts and opinions based on an ongoing StorageIO blog research poll of a mix of vendors, IT professionals, and others shows at two extremes; those who see clouds as the solution to everything, and those who see no chance or place for a cloud whatever it happens to be. In the middle are about 81–82% (the poll is ongoing, so results may vary) of the respondents, who vary from seeing a place for clouds depending on the definition or use case to others who are skeptical but want to learn more about what to use when, where, and why.

It's about delivering information services in a cost-effective manner that supports demand while meeting service objectives (Figure 1.2). Figure 1.7 shows various information services delivery models that rely on different techniques, technologies, and best practices that can be competitive or complementary. Cloud metaphor has been used in and around IT for decades as being a means to abstract underlying networking details or an applications architecture.

A key attribute of clouds is that of abstracting or masking underlying complexities while enabling agility, flexibility, efficient, and effective services delivery. This leads to some confusion, which for some creates opportunities to promote new products, protocols, standards, or services while for others it means repackaging old initiatives. For example, some may have a *déjà* moment when looking at a cloud presentation back to the late 1980s during the information utility wave that was appearing with the advent of the x86-based PCs along with client servers. For others, that moment could be time sharing or service bureau, and for others the cloud's Web-based and highly abstracted virtualized environments.

What are IT clouds? Where do they fit? How does tape coexist with clouds? Like many IT professionals, you may already be using or leveraging cloud-based computing or storage techniques, either as a product or as a service, without realizing it.

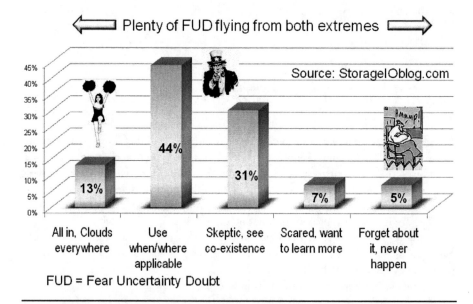

Figure 1.6   IT cloud confusion and opportunity. (*Source:* StorageIOblog.com.)

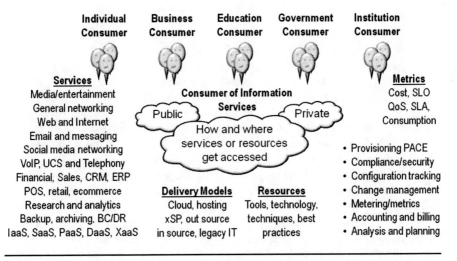

Figure 1.7   Various information services delivery and resource models.

Common cloud-based functions or services include:

- Remote or off-site backup, replication, vaulting, or data copy
- Remote or off-site storage on-line, near-line, or off-line
- Email and messaging services including social media networking and Web 2.0
- Archive, fixed content, and other reference or look-up data
- Website, blog, video, audio, photo, and other rich media content hosting
- Application hosting (e.g., salesforce.com, concur expense, social media)
- Virtual server or virtual machine (VM) hosting (Amazon, VCE, etc.)
- General on-line storage or application-specific storage such as Google Docs

Does this mean that if backup, business continuance (BC) or disaster recovery (DR), or archive data is sent off-site to a storage or hosting facility, it has been sent to the cloud? Some say no unless the data were transmitted electronically to on-line disk at a service provider location leveraging programmatic interfaces and other cloud ware (technology, services, or protocols developed, optimized, or packaged for public and private clouds). That might also be a product- or services-based definition. However, in theory, the concept is not that far off, as clouds, in addition to being a product or service, are also a management philosophy or paradigm to do more with what you have without negatively impacting service delivery.

Characteristics of clouds include:

- Ease of service access (self-service)
- Ease of service deployment or provisioning
- Elasticity and multitenancy
- Safety, security, with data integrity

- Flexibility, scalability, and resilience
- Cost effectiveness and measurability
- Abstraction or masking of underlying complexities
- Can move or change the focus and presentation
- Leverage repeatable processes, templates, and best practices
- Efficiency as a result of scale and increased workload or usage

Confusion exists in that there are many different types of clouds, including public and private, products and services, some that use familiar interfaces or protocols with others using different technologies. Clouds can be a service or a product, an architecture, or a management paradigm, similar to previous generations such as the information utility or service-oriented architectures (SOA), client server computing, and others.

What this means is that some of the tenets of cloud storage and computing involve shifting how resources are used and managed, thus enabling the notion of an information factory. They can be external or internal, public and private, housed at a hosting or co-location facility as well as at traditional out-sourcing or managed service providers. Thus a hosting site may or may not be a cloud, and a cloud can leverage hosting services but does not require them. Various information services delivery models are shown in Table 1.1.

1.5.2. Private Cloud: Coexistence vs. Competing with Legacy IT

Clouds and virtualization should be seen for what they really are as opposed to what they are often portrayed to be so that a solution can be sold. In other words, take a step back, look at the business issue, then apply the applicable technology or task at hand to the situation. Instead of clouds being a solution looking for a problem, they become a tool and technique that can be used in different complementary ways. Cloud computing and storage are another tier of traditional computing or servers providing different performance, availability, capacity, economic, and management attributes compared to traditional technology delivery vehicles.

If IT is a core piece of the business, it probably makes more sense to retain tighter control. For example, a manufacturing company may out-source or rely on suppliers for key components, or perhaps even provide contract-under-supervision manufacturing, leveraging proprietary processes and techniques. Than if the related IT functions are also essential, they too would be retained and kept close to the vest while other functions might be out-sourced or sent to the cloud.

1.6. Common Cloud, Virtualization, and Storage Networking Questions

Does cloud storage require special hardware or software, or is it a matter of how those resources are used, deployed, and managed? As with many things, the answer is, "It

Table 1.1 Information and Data Services Deployment Models

Model	Characteristics and When to Use	Examples
Co-location ("colo")	Shared facilities with dedicated space for your equipment. Power, cooling, security, networking, and some monitoring or other optional services provided. Primary or supplemental space for your hardware.	iphouse, Rackspace, Sungard, Timewarner, visi, and many others
Hosting services	Services and or application hosting. These could be email, Web, or virtual machines. In addition, these could be Applications as a Service (AaaS). Many colos provide application hosting services. Instead of renting space for hardware, you rent time and use of software.	VCE, ADP, Amazon, Bluehost, Google, HP, IBM, iphouse, Oracle, Rackspace, Salesforce, and others
Legacy IT	Hardware (servers, storage, and networks) plus software (applications and tools) are bought or leased, operated, and managed by IT staff.	Hardware and software in your existing environment
Managed service provider	Similar if not the same as a hosting service. Provides some service, which might be applications, archiving, backup, storage space, backup, replication, email, Web, blogs, video hosting, business continuance/disaster recovery, among others. Instead of you running or hosting the application, you use a service provided to you that runs on someone else's shared infrastructure. Some may have *déjà* with service bureaus or time sharing.	Amazon, AT&T, Carbonite, Campaigner, EMC Mozy, GoDaddy, Google, Iron Mountain, Microsoft, Nirvanix, Seagate i365, Sungard, Terremark, Wells Fargo vSafe, among others
Out-sourcing	Could be on- or off-site, where you either move your applications and possibly equipment to a third party who operates and manages to specific service-level objectives (SLOs) and service-level agreements (SLAs).	Dell/Perot, HP/EDS, IBM, Lockheed/Martin, SunGard, Terremark, Tata, Xerox/ACS, and Wipro, among others
Private cloud	Dedicated to an organization need. Could be managed by IT staff or third party on-site or off-site. May use cloud-specific technologies or traditional technologies managed with cloudlike premises or paradigms. May be called in-source or IT 2.0.	Instrumented or metered IT environment for effective service delivery. Many different products available
Public cloud	An IT infrastructure that supports shared computing, storage, and or application services provided by an organization. The services may be available free or for a fee. They can be used to replace or complement existing IT capabilities. Access shared applications such as salesforce, email, backup or archive destination, virtual servers, and storage, among others. Buzzwords include applications as a service (AaaS), infrastructure as a service (IaaS), storage as a service (SaaS), and platform as a service (PaaS), among many other XaaS variations.	AT&T, VCE, Amazon E2C or S3, Google, Iron Mountain, Rackspace, Salesforce, Terremark, HP, and IBM, among many others

depends." For example, a vendor of a particular product will try to convince you this product is needed, and that a deployment must incorporate this solution.

Are clouds real, or just hype? Certainly there is a lot of hype from vendors and the industry in general, as is often the case with new or emerging technologies, techniques, paradigms, or movements. Likewise, some solutions or vendors trade more on hype and FUD compared to others. However, there are also plenty of real and viable techniques, technologies, products, and services that organizations of all sizes can be leveraging today as well as planning for in the future. The trick is sifting through the fog of cloud fodder, FUD, and hype to determine what is applicable for your environment today and into the future.

Of course, your definition of a cloud will also have a bearing on the above; however, I hope that after reading this book, you will also see that there are many different approaches, technologies, techniques, services, and solutions that can be applied to different situations. In other words, let's move from a solution looking for a problem to problems that need solutions, and what to use when, where, why, as well as how.

What is virtualization life beyond consolidation? The next major wave (trend) of virtualization, including from applications to desktop, servers to storage and networking, will be an expanded focus on agility. What this means is that there will continue to be an expanding market capability for consolidation, which is the current focus of the virtualization wave.

However, the next wave shifts to expand in another dimension that is less focused on how many virtual machines (VMs) there are per physical machine (PM) and instead around agility, flexibility, as well as ease of management. In other words, for those servers or storage systems that cannot be consolidated and hence are thought to be unsuited to virtualization, break down those myths and virtualize for agility instead of consolidation.

Should everything be consolidated? Generally speaking, I would say no. However, many, if not most, things can be virtualized, assuming that for some servers or storage there may be fewer VMs per PM or even a single VM per PM. Some might wonder why you would virtualize with only one VM per PM, as this seems to defeat the purpose of virtualization. This is only the case if your view of virtualization is that of consolidation. However, many things can be virtualized for agility, emulation, transparency, or abstraction, keeping performance, quality of service, and other constraints or concerns in mind.

Virtualization of Windows and x86 environments is understood, but what about UNIX and other systems or environments? Some UNIX as well as Linux distributions that rely on or support x86 platforms can run on popular hypervisors such as vSphere, Hyper-V, and Xen. However, for other UNIX systems, such as HP-UX, Solaris (non x86), and AIX, those systems have features as part of the operating system or underlying hardware platforms for virtualization. Examples include Logical Domains (LDOMs) for Solaris, HP-UX partitions, and hypervisor in the IBM pSeries that supports AIX, among other systems.

Do clouds have to be physically off-site and hosted by a third party? No, clouds can be implemented internally (known as a private cloud) at your premises using existing technologies as well as leveraging off-site or third-party-provided services.

Do you have to start from scratch to leverage clouds or virtualization? Generally speaking, you do not have to start with a fresh sheet to leverage clouds and virtualization. In some cases you can leverage different technologies or services to coexist and complement what you have, while others may require changes. You may also want to leverage the opportunity to change the way things are done as part of deploying cloud and virtualization technologies.

Are clouds, virtualization, and storage networks only for large environments? No, those are common myths in that many solutions, services, or products are marketed toward higher-end environments. However, there are also solutions applicable across different size organizations, with some, such as cloud-based backup, available all the way down into the consumer space. Cloud-based backup is a market "sweet spot" for small to mid-sized businesses, given the relatively smaller amount of data that can be moved along with opportunities to leverage cloud or managed service providers.

Are clouds a replacement for traditional IT? Depending on what you believe or want to believe defines a cloud, the answer is maybe or no. Some cloud services are aimed at replacing all or portions of traditional IT, while others are positioned to complement existing IT. Likewise, there are cloud services and products that can be used in either public or private that coexist with traditional IT.

Is chargeback a requirement for having or using a cloud? For public cloud and other fee-based service models, some form of invoicing, charging, and billing is needed. However, it is a popular myth that all private clouds need chargeback. What they do need is instrumentation, metrics, and measurement, including bill-of-material (BOM) information about the cost to deliver a given level of service. For some organizations that currently implement formal chargeback with real or virtual invoices, it would make sense to be continued candidates for chargeback. The important thing is that there are metrics to show how resources are being used and accounted for. If your view of accounting, merging, measuring, and reporting is chargeback, then yes, you need chargeback. However, for many other scenarios, the emphasis should be on accounting and metrics that matter.

Do clouds and virtual environments automatically guide users or customers where to place data? Various cloud services, along with some products, have tools and wizards to help guide users or customers to what resources are best for a given need. Some solutions also help to automate or support scheduled polices to perform recurring tasks or functions. Automation and tools can help shift recurring tasks from having to be performed by IT staff, enabling skilled workers to focus on service enhancement, analysis, and other value-adding functions.

1.7. Cloud, Virtualization, and Storage Networking: Bringing It Together (for Now)

Additional examples of technologies to use for addressing various problems or enabling opportunities are shown in subsequent chapters. Figure 1.8 shows as an example of how clouds, virtualization, and storage networking technologies and techniques combine in complementary manners for different IT and business purposes. For example, server and storage virtualization are shown for both consolidation as well as to enable agility, simplified management, and emulation to bridge old technologies to new roles.

Other items shown in Figure 1.8 include leveraging public cloud-based backup and archive services along with solutions for enabling private cloud and virtualized environments. Various types of I/O networking technologies are used to attach servers (physical and virtual) to local and remote storage. Different types of storage including high-performance on-line or primary, secondary, near-line as well as off-line and removable technologies are also shown.

Although not shown explicitly, various management tools, protocols, and interfaces also combine in Figure 1.8 for enabling high availability and business continuance/disaster recovery, including routine backup as well enabling data footprint reduction (DFR). Also shown in Figure 1.8 are metrics for gaining situational awareness of resources, including cost of service delivery and service-level objectives, among others. These and other topics, technologies, tools, and techniques will be discussed in more detail in subsequent chapters.

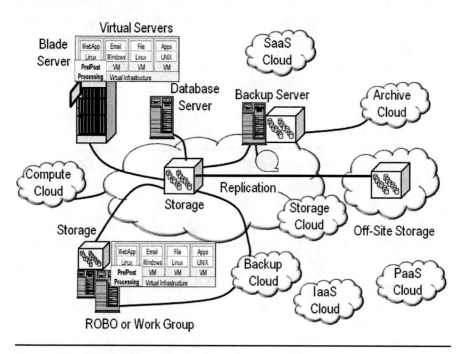

Figure 1.8   Public and private cloud products as well as services can coexist.

1.8. Chapter Summary

Don't be scared of clouds: Learn to navigate your way around and through the various technologies, techniques, products and services, and identify where they might complement and enable a flexible, scalable, and resilient IT infrastructure. Take some time to listen and learn, and become educated about the different types of clouds (public, private, services, products, architectures, or marketecture), their attributes (compute, storage, applications, services, cost, availability, performance, protocols, functionality), and their value propositions.

Look at how cloud technologies and techniques can complement your existing environment to meet business objectives. You might find there are fits, or you might find there are not, but it's important to do the research and know where you stand.

The subsequent chapters will look at the what, why, where, when, and how to use various techniques to address or enable business and IT objectives. Given the diversity of readers' backgrounds, feel free to jump around different chapters as you see fit. Likewise, I need to put in a shameless plug to read my other books, *The Green and Virtual Data Center* (CRC) and *Resilient Storage Networks: Designing Flexible and Scalable Data Infrastructures* (Elsevier), as companions to this book, as well as my blog and website.

General action items include:

- Avoid simply moving problems or bottlenecks—find and fix them instead.
- With clouds and virtualization, the question is not if, but rather when, where, with what, and how.
- Prepare for next wave of virtualization: Life beyond consolidation enabling agility.
- Cloud services, products, and solutions are complementary to existing IT infrastructures.

Chapter 2

Cloud, Virtualization, and Data Storage Networking Fundamentals

The more space you have, the more it seems to get filled up.

– Greg Schulz

In This Chapter

- Storage (hardware, software, and management tools)
- Block, file, direct attached, networked, and cloud storage
- Input/output, networking, and related convergence topics
- Public and private cloud products and services
- Virtualization (applications, desktop, server, storage, and networking)

This chapter provides a primer and overview of major IT resource components as well as how information is supported by them. Key themes and buzzwords discussed include block, file, object storage, and data sharing, along with public and private cloud products and services. Additional themes and buzzards include file systems, objects, Direct Attached Storage (DAS), Network Attached Storage (NAS), storage area networks (SANs), and virtualization.

Chapter 1 provided the big picture of why there is a need for clouds, storage, and networking, along with virtualization, to address business and IT challenges. For those already familiar with storage, input/output (I/O) networking, virtualization, and cloud fundamentals, feel free to skip over or just skim this chapter.

2.1. Getting Started

Data storage is taken for granted by many people while not being really understood, particularly when there is no more room to save files or photos. Then storage becomes frustrating, if not a nightmare, when you cannot find the file or document that you need. Even worse is after a disaster (fire, flood, hurricane, virus or data corruption, theft or accidental deletion), when you realize what should have been preserved was not adequately protected. Cost is also a concern, whether it is how much you have to pay to park your files, videos, or other data somewhere, or to have it backed up or to purchase more disk storage devices.

As was pointed out in Chapter 1, there is no such thing as a data or information recession. As a society we have become addicted to information-related services at home, at work, as well as when in transit. If you do not believe me, try this simple test: See how long you can go without checking your email, texting, using your cell phone or PDA, looking at a website, listening to satellite radio or watching TV (regular, HD, or IP), accessing your bank account, or shopping on-line. Even this book depended on lots of data storage resources for backups, copies, revisions, artwork, and other items.

Many resources are needed to support information services, including applications and management software. Also necessary are I/O and networking for connectivity between servers and data storage, infrastructure resource management (IRM) tasks, processes, procedures, and best practices. These items apply whether your information services are being deployed or accessed from a traditional IT, virtualized, or kept in a cloud environment.

2.2. Server and Storage I/O Fundamentals

Servers, also known as computers, are important in a discussion about cloud, virtualization, and data storage networking in that they have multiple functions. The most common—and obvious—function is that servers run the applications or programs that deliver information services. These programs are also responsible for generating I/O data and networking activity. Another role that servers play in cloud and virtualized data centers is that of functioning as data or storage appliances performing tasks that in some cases were previously done by purpose-built storage systems.

Servers vary in physical size, cost, performance, availability, capacity, and energy consumption, and they have specific features for different target markets or applications. Packaging also varies across different types of servers, ranging from small hand-held portable digital assistants (PDAs) to large-frame or full cabinet-sized mainframe servers. Another form of server packaging is a virtual server, where a hypervisor, such as Microsoft Hyper-V, VMware vSphere, or Citrix Xen, among others, is used to create virtual machines (VMs) from physical machines (PMs). Cloud-based compute or server resources can also leverage or require a VM.

Computers or servers are targeted for different markets, including small office/home office (SOHO), small/medium business (SMB), small/medium enterprise (SME), and ultra-large-scale or extreme scaling, including high-performance computing (HPC). Servers are also positioned for different price bands and deployment scenarios.

General categories of servers and computers include:

- Laptops, desktops, and workstations
- Small floor-standing towers or rack-mounted 1U and 2U servers
- Medium-sized floor-standing towers or larger rack-mounted servers
- Blade centers and blade systems
- Large-sized floor-standing servers, including mainframes
- Specialized fault-tolerant, rugged, and embedded processing or real-time servers
- Physical and virtual along with cloud-based servers

Servers have different names—email server, database server, application server, Web server, video or file server, network server, security server, backup server, or storage server, depending on their use. In the examples just given, what defines the type of server is the type of software being used to deliver a type of service. This can lead to confusion when looking at servers, because a server may be able to support different types of workloads, thus it should be considered a server, storage, part of a network, or an application platform. Sometimes the term "appliance" will be used for a server; this is indicative of the type of service the combined hardware and software solution are providing.

Although technically not a type of server, some manufacturers use the term "tin-wrapped" software in an attempt to not be classified as an appliance, server, or hardware vendor but still wanting their software to be positioned more as a turnkey solution. The idea is to avoid being perceived as a software-only solution that requires integration with hardware. These systems usually use off-the-shelf, commercially available general-purpose servers with the vendor's software technology preintegrated and installed, ready for use. Thus, tin-wrapped software is a turnkey software solution with some "tin," or hardware, wrapped around it.

A variation of the tin-wrapped software model is the software-wrapped appliance or a virtual appliance. Under this model, vendors use a virtual machine to host their software on the same physical server or appliance that is being used for other functions. For example, a database vendor or virtual tape library software vendor may install its solution into separate VMs on a physical server, with applications running in other VMs or partitions. This approach works in terms of consolidating underutilized servers, but caution should be exercised to avoid overconsolidating and oversubscribing available physical hardware resources, particularly for time-sensitive applications. Keep in mind that cloud, virtual, and tin-wrapped servers or software still need physical compute, memory, I/O, networking, and storage resources.

2.2.1. Server and I/O Architectures

Generally speaking, servers (see Figure 2.1), regardless of specific vendor implementation, have a common architecture. That architecture consists of a central processing unit (CPU) or processor, memory, internal busses or communication chips, and I/O ports for communicating with the outside world via networks or storage devices. Computers need to perform I/O to various devices, and at the heart of many I/O and networking connectivity solutions is the Peripheral Component Interconnect (PCI) industry-standard interface.

PCI is a standard that specifies the chipsets that are used to communicate between CPUs and memory with the outside world of I/O and networking device peripherals. Figure 2.1 shows an example of a PCI implementation including various components such as bridges, adapter slots, and adapter types. PCIe leverages multiple serial unidirectional point-to-point links, known as lanes, compared to traditional PCI, which uses a parallel bus–based design.

The most current version of PCI, as defined by the PCI Special Interest Group (PCISIG), is PCI Express (PCIe). Backwards compatibility exists by bridging previous generations, including PCIx and PCI, off of a native PCIe bus or, in the past, bridging a PCIe bus to a PCIx native implementation. Examples of PCI, PCIx, and PCIe adapters include Ethernet, Fibre Channel, Fibre Channel over Ethernet (FCoE), InfiniBand Architecture (IBA), SAS, SATA, Universal Serial Bus (USB), and 1394 Firewire. There are also many specialized devices such as analog-to-digital data acquisition, video surveillance, medical monitoring, and other data acquisition or metering (e.g., data collection) devices.

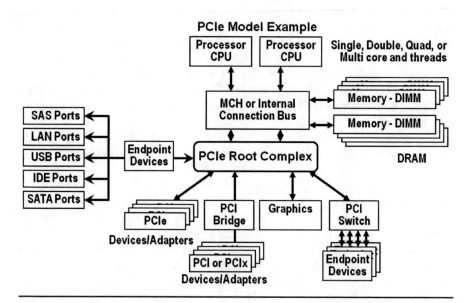

Figure 2.1 Generic computer or server hardware architecture. (*Source:* Greg Schulz, *The Green and Virtual Data Center,* CRC Press, Boca Raton, FL, 2009.)

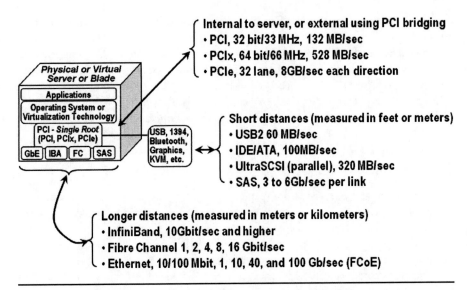

Figure 2.2   General computer and I/O connectivity model. (*Source:* Greg Schulz, *The Green and Virtual Data Center*, CRC Press, Boca Raton, FL, 2009.

While the specific components and the number of components will vary depending on the server, in general, servers have one of more of the following:

- Compute or CPU chips or sockets
- One or more cores per CPU socket or chips capable of single or multithreading
- Internal communication and I/O buses for connecting components
- Some main memory, commonly dynamic random access memory (DRAM)
- Optional sockets for expansion memory, extra CPUs, and I/O expansion slots
- Attachment for keyboards, video, and monitors (KVM)
- I/O connectivity for attachment of peripherals including networks and storage
- I/O networking connectivity ports and expansion slots such as PCIe
- Optional internal disk storage and expansion slots for external storage
- Power supplies and cooling fans

Figure 2.2 shows a generic computer and I/O connectivity model, which will vary depending on specific vendor packaging and market focus. For example, some computers have more and faster processors (CPUs) and cores along with larger amounts of main memory as well as extensive connectivity or expansion options. Other computers or servers are physically smaller, lower in price and with fewer resources (CPU, memory, and I/O expansion capabilities), targeted at different needs.

In Figure 2.2, the component closest to the main processor has the fastest I/O connectivity; however, it will also be the most expensive, distance limited, and require special components. Moving farther away from the main processor, I/O still remains fast with distance—measured in feet or meters instead of inches—but is more flexible and cost-effective.

In general, the faster a processor or server, the more prone to a performance impact it will be when having to wait for slower I/O operations. Fast servers need lower latency and better-performing I/O connectivity and networks. Better performing means lower latency, more input/output operations per second (IOPS), as well as improved bandwidth to meet various application profiles and types of operations.

2.2.2. Storage Hierarchy

The storage hierarchy extends from memory inside servers out to external shared storage, including virtual and cloud accessible resources. Too often, discussions separate or even distance the relationship between server memory and data storage—after all, one is considered to be a server topic and the other a disk discussion. However, the two are very much interrelated and thus benefit as well as impact each other. Servers need I/O networking to communicate with other servers, with users of information services, and with local, remote, or cloud storage resources.

In Figure 2.3, an example of the storage or memory hierarchy is shown, ranging from fast processor core or L1 (level 1) and L2 (level 2) on-board processor memory to slow, low-cost, high-capacity removable storage. At the top of the pyramid is the fastest, lowest-latency, most expensive memory or storage, which is also less able to be shared without overhead with other processors or servers. At the bottom of the pyramid is the lowest-cost storage, with the highest capacity while being portable and sharable.

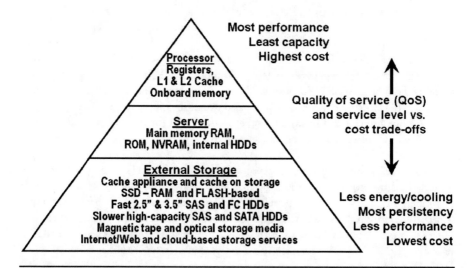

Figure 2.3 Memory and storage pyramid. (*Source:* Greg Schulz, *The Green and Virtual Data Center*, CRC Press, Boca Raton, FL, 2009.)

The importance of main or processor (server) memory and external storage is that virtual machines need memory to exist when active and a place on disk to reside when not in memory. Keep in mind that a virtual machine is a computer whose components are emulated via data structures stored and accessed via memory. The more VMs there are, the more memory is required—and not just more, but faster memory is also important.

Another demand driver for increased memory capabilities on servers are applications such as database, video rendering, and business analytics, modeling, and simulations, for which large amounts of data are kept in memory for speed of access. As a result, more memory is being installed into denser footprints in servers along with more sockets for processors. An example is the IBM Power7-based Power 750, with 512 GB of DRAM and 32 cores (4 sockets, each with 8 cores).

Why are there all these different types of storage? The answer, with all technology points set aside, comes down to economics. There is a price to pay for performance. For some applications this can be considered the cost of doing business, or even a business enabler, to buy time when time is money and using a low-cost storage could have a corresponding impact on performance.

Storage can be tiered, with the applicable memory or storage technology applied to the task at hand. At a lower cost (and slower) than RAM-based memory, disk storage, along with NVRAM and FLASH-based memory devices, are also persistent. As noted in Figure 2.3, cloud is listed as a tier of storage to be used as a tool to complement other technologies. In other words, it is important from both cost and performance perspectives to use the right tool for the task at hand to enable smarter, more intelligent, and effective information services delivery.

2.2.3. From Bits to Bytes

Storage is an extension of memory, and cache is a convergence of memory and external media. Digital data at a low level is stored as 1's and 0's, binary bits indicating on or off, implemented using different physical techniques depending on the physical media (disk, tape, optical, solid-state memory). The bits are generally grouped into bytes (1 byte = 8 bits) and subsequently organized into larger groups for different purposes.

The gibibyte is an international system of units (SI) measure (see Table 2.1) used for data storage and networking in base 2 format, where 1 GiBi 2^{30} bytes or 1,073,741,824 bytes. Another common unit of measure used for data storage and servers as well as their operating systems is the gigabyte (GB) in base 10 (decimal) format. A GB, also sometimes shown as a GByte, represents 10^9 or 1,000,000,000 bytes.

Computer memory is typically represented in base 2, with disk storage often being shown in both base 2 and base 10. For example, the 7200-RPM Seagate Momentus XT Hybrid Hard Disk Drive (HHDD) that I used in my laptop for writing this book is advertised as 500 GB. The HHDD is a traditional 2.5-in. hard disk drive (HDD) that also has an integrated 4-GB flash solid-state device (SSD) and 32 MB of DRAM. Before any operating system, RAID (redundant array of independent disks), or other formatting and overhead, the HHDD presents 500,107,862,016 bytes based on 976,773,168

(512-byte) sectors or 500 GB. However, a common question is what happened to the missing 36,763,049,984 bytes of storage capacity (e.g., 500 × 2^30 base 2).

The Seagate Momentus XT (ST95005620AS) 500-GB HHDD guarantees 976,773,168 (512-byte) sectors. Seagate is using the standard of 1 GB = 1 billion bytes (See Table 2.1). Note that accessible storage capacity can vary depending on operating environment and upper-level formatting (e.g., operating system, RAID, controllers, snapshot, or other overhead).

The common mistake or assumption is that a 500-GB disk drive has 1,073,741,824 (2^30) × 500 or 536,870,912,000 bytes of accessible capacity (before overhead). However, in the example above, the disk drive presents only 500,107,862,016 bytes, leaving some to wonder where the other 36,763,049,984 bytes went to. The answer is that they did not go anywhere because they were never there, depending on what numbering base you were using or assuming. This has led to most vendors including in their packaging along with documentation what the actually accessible capacity is before environment overhead is subtracted. As an example, in a Windows environment, after formatting overhead, the empty disk shows as having a capacity of 465.74 GB.

The importance of the above is to understand that if you need a specific amount of data storage capacity, get what you expect and need. This means understanding the various ways and locations of where as well as how storage capacity is measured. Factor in overhead of controllers, RAID, spares, operating and file system, and volume mangers, along with data protection such as snapshots or other reserved space, as part of storage capacity.

Table 2.1 shows data standard units of measures in both base 2 and base 10. Some of the capacities shown in Table 2.1 may seem unimaginably large today. However, keep in mind that 10 years ago a 9-GB disk drive spinning at 7200 (7.2K) revolutions per minute (RPM) was considered to be large-capacity and fast. By comparison, in late 2010, fast, energy-efficient SAS and Fibre Channel 15.5K-RPM 600-GB disk drives were shipping along with high-capacity 7.2K SAS and SATA 2-TB drives and some 3-TB consumer drives, with even larger drives soon to be appearing on the market. We will talk more about hard disk drives (HDDs), solid-state devices (SSDs), and other related technologies as well as trends in later chapters.

Table 2.1 Storage Counting Numbering and Units of Measures

		Base 2			Base 10
kibi	ki	2^10	kilo	k, K	10^3
mebi	Mi	2^20	mega	M	10^6
gibi	Gi	2^30	giga	G	10^9
tebi	Ti	2^40	tera	TB	10^12
pebi	Pi	2^50	peta	P	10^15
exbi	Ei	2^60	exa	E	10^18
zebi	Zi	2^70	zetta	Z	10^21
yobi	Yi	2^80	yotta	Y	10^24

2.2.4. Disk Storage Fundamentals

Figure 2.3 shows the basics of storage hierarchy, core or primary memory to external dedicated and shared storage. Storage can be dedicated internal Direct Attached Storage (DAS) or external shared DAS in addition to being networked and shared on a local or remote or cloud basis.

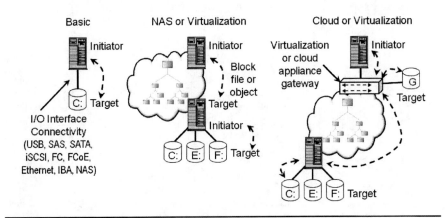

Figure 2.4   Initiator and target examples.

2.2.5. Initiators and Targets

A fundamental storage and I/O networking concept is that of the initiator (client or source) and target (server or destination) as shown in Figure 2.4. There is as initiator and a target in all types of storage and access mechanisms across physical, virtual, and cloud technologies. The topologies, underlying implementations, and specific functionality will vary with vendor-specific products.

Servers or other initiators initiate I/O requires (reads, writes, and status inquiries) of targets that then respond to the requests. Initiators are either taught (configured) targets or discover them at boot or start-up. These targets can be block, file, object, or some other service-based destination providing and responding to storage I/O requests. For example, a server with an initiator identifier or address makes a request to a block storage device using the SCSI command set (e.g., SAS, iSCSI, Fibre Channel, FCoE, or SRP on InfiniBand), where the target is a SCSI logical unit (LUN).

Building on the previous example, the same server can initiate I/O activity such as a file read or write request using NFS or CIFS over TCP/IP on an Ethernet-based network to a NAS target. In the case of a file request, the initiator has a mount point that is used to direct read and write requests to the target which responds to the requests. Servers also initiate I/O requests to cloud targets or destinations. While the protocols can differ for block, file, and object or specific application programming interface (API), the basic functionality of initiators and target exists even if referred to by different nomenclature.

While initiators are typically servers, they can also be storage systems, appliances, or gateways that function both as a target and an initiator. A common example of a storage system acting as both a target and an initiator is local or remote replication. In this scenario, a server sends data to be written to the target device that in turn initiates a write or update operating to another target storage system.

Another example of a target also being an initiator is a virtualization appliance or a cloud point-of-presence (cPoP) access gateway. These devices that are targets then initiate data to be copied to another physical, virtual, or cloud device.

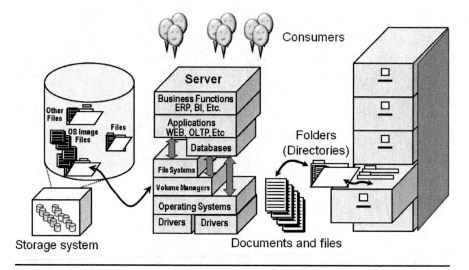

Figure 2.5   How data and information is stored.

2.2.6. How Data Is Written to and Read from a Storage Device

In Figure 2.5, an application creates a file and then saves it—for example, a Word document created and saved to disk. The application—Word in this example—works with the underlying operating system or file system to ensure that the data is safely written to the appropriate location on the specific storage system or disk drive. The operating system or file system is responsible for working with applications to maintain directories or folders where files are stored.

The operating system, file system, or database shown in Figure 2.5 is responsible for mapping the file system where the folder or directories are located to a specific disk drive or LUN or a volume on a storage system. A storage system that receives data from a server via file access—as in the case of a NAS device or file server—is, in turn, responsible for mapping and tracking where blocks of data are written to on specific storage devices.

Data is accessed on the disk storage device (Figure 2.6) by a physical and a logical address, sometimes known as a physical block number (PBN) and a logical block number (LBN). The file system or an application performing direct (raw) I/O keeps track of what storage is mapped to which logical blocks on what storage volumes. Within the storage controller and disk drive, a mapping table is maintained to associate logical blocks with physical block locations on the disk or other medium such as tape.

When data is written to disk, regardless of whether it is an object, file, Web database, or video, the lowest common denominator is a block of storage (Figure 2.6). Blocks of storage have been traditionally organized into 512 bytes, which aligned with memory page sizes. While 512-byte blocks and memory page sizes are still common, given larger-capacity disk drives as well as larger storage systems, 4-K (e.g., 8 × 512 bytes) block sizes are appearing.

Larger block sizes enable more data to be managed or kept track of in the same footprint by requiring fewer pointers or directory entries. For example, using a 4-K block size, eight times the amount of data can be kept track of by operating systems or storage controllers in the same footprint. Another benefit is that with data access patterns changing along with larger I/O operations, 4 K makes for more efficient operations than the equivalent 8 × 512 byte operations for the same amount of data to be moved.

At another detailed layer, the disk drive or flash solid-state device also handles bad block vectoring or replacement transparently to the storage controller or operating system. Note that this form or level of bad block repair is independent of upper-level data protection and availability features, including RAID, backup/restore, replication, snapshots, or continuous data protection (CDP), among others.

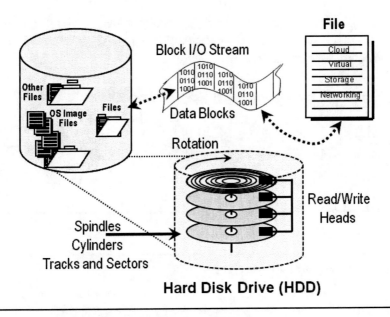

Figure 2.6   Hard disk drive storage organization.

2.2.7. Storage Sharing vs. Data Sharing

Storage and data sharing may sound like the same thing, and the phrases are often used interchangeably; however, they are quite different and not at all interchangeable. Sharing *storage* means being able to have a disk drive or storage system accessible by two or more initiators or host computer servers. By being shared, only portions of the disk device or storage system is accessible to specific servers or initiators, as seen in Figure 2.7.

For example, the C: E: and F: storage devices or volumes are only accessible to the servers that own them. On the right side of Figure 2.7, each server is shown with its own dedicated storage. In the middle of Figure 2.7 a shared storage device is shown, with each server having its own LUN, volume, or partition. Data sharing is shown with different servers having access to the D: volume, where they can access various documents, objects, or VM files with applicable security authorization.

With shared storage, different servers can initiate I/O activity to the portion of storage to which they have access, which might be a partition, logical drive or volume, or LUN. For high-availability (HA) clustering, shared storage can be accessed by multiple servers running software that maintains data integrity and coherent access to the device.

Shared *data,* on the other hand, involves multiple servers being able to read or write to the same file via file serving and sharing software. File serving or sharing software is typically found in most operating systems as well as within NAS that support common protocols including Network File System (NFS) and Common Internet File System (CIFS).

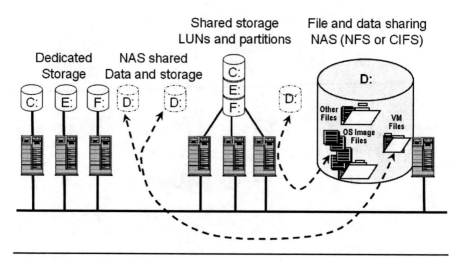

Figure 2.7   Storage and data sharing.

2.2.8. Different Types of Storage: Not All Data Storage Is the Same

There are many different types of storage (Figure 2.8) for different application requirements and various usage scenarios. Some storage is performance-oriented for bandwidth (throughput), measured in megaytes or gigabytes per second, or in terms of response time (latency), or as the number of I/O operations per second (IOPS). Storage can be optimized or targeted for on-line active and primary usage, near-line for idle or inactive data, or off-line, where the focus can be high capacity at low cost.

On-line or active applications are those for which data is being worked with, read, and written, such as file systems, home directories, databases, and email. Near-line or applications with idle data include reference material or repositories, backups, and archives.

Some general categories of storage include:

- Shared or dedicated, internal or external to a server/computer
- Local, remote or cloud, block, file, or object
- On-line active or high-performance primary
- Inactive or idle, near-line or off-line

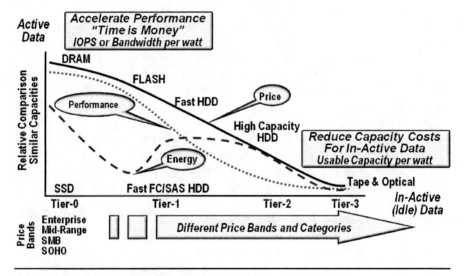

Figure 2.8   Types and tiers of storage media.

2.2.8.1. Structured, Unstructured, and Meta Data

Some applications store and access data in highly structured databases (e.g., databases or application-specific organization) such as IBM DB2/UDB, Intersystem's Caché, Microsoft SQLserver, MySQL, Oracle 11g, and SAP Sybase, among others. Other applications have their own predefined stores or pools where storage is allocated either as a LUN or as a volume in the case of block access. In the case of block-based access, the application, database, or file system works with applications to know what files to access. In other scenarios, applications access a file by name in a folder or directory that is part of a mount point or share in a file system, either locally or on a remote file server or NAS device. Another means of data access is via an applications program interface (API), where a client requests information from a server via a defined mechanism.

In the case of a database, applications only need to know the schema or how the database is organized to make queries with tools including Structured Query Language

(SQL), while the database handles read or writing of data either in a block or file system mode. For block mode the database is assigned LUNs or storage space where it creates its files or datasets that it manages. If using a file system, the database leverages the underlying file system to handle some of the storage management tasks.

Structured data has defined attributes, making searching or other functions relatively easy. This structure, however, can make adding or changing the organization more complex or costly. As a result, there is the growing category of unstructured data, also known as file-accessed data. The value proposition of unstructured data is that there is no formal organization other than files stored in a folder or directory in a file system. File names can vary depending on the specific file system or operating system environment, with attributes—including creation and modification dates, ownership, and extension—that can usually indicate what application it is associated with along with security and file size.

Some file systems and files can support additional meta data (data about the data) or properties. The flexibility of unstructured data causes challenges when it comes to being able to search or determine what the files contain. For example, with a database, the schema or organization makes it relatively easy to search and determine what is stored. However, with unstructured data, additional meta data needs to be discovered via tools including eDiscovery (search) and classification tools. Additional meta data that can be discovered and stored in a meta database or repository includes information about the contents of files, along with dependencies on other information or applications. The use of structured or unstructured data depends on preferences, the performance of the specific file system or storage being used, desired flexibility, and other criteria.

In general, storage is accessed locally, remotely, or via a cloud using:

- Application Programming Interface (API)
- Block-based access of disk partitions, LUNs, or volumes
- File-based using local or networked file systems
- Object-based access

In early generations of computers, back when dinosaurs roamed the earth (maybe not quite that far back), in an era before file systems and volume managers, programmers (aka the user) had to know physically where files or data were saved and to be read. Fast forward a few decades and a few computer generations, and saving a file has become fairly transparent and relatively easy. Granted, you still need to know some form of an address or directory or folder or share where the data is located, but you do not have to worry about knowing what starting and stop locations on the disk or storage system to access.

2.2.8.2. Block Storage Access

Block-based data access is the lowest level of access and the fundamental building block for all storage. This means that block-based data access is relevant for cloud and virtualized storage as well as storage networks. Regardless of whether applications on servers (initiators) request data via an API, object, file, or via a block-based request from a file system, database, email, or other means, it ultimately gets resolved and handled at the lowest layers as blocks of data read from or written to disks, solid-state disks, or tape-based storage.

For those who see or access data via a file system, database, document management system, SharePoint, email, or some other application, the block-based details have been abstracted for you. That abstraction occurs at many levels, beginning at the disk drive, the storage system, or controller, perhaps implementing RAID to which it is attached as a target, as well as via additional layers including virtualized storage, device drivers and file systems, and volume managers, databases, and applications.

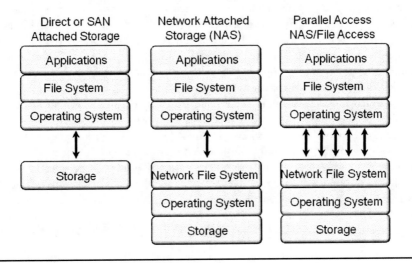

Figure 2.9   File access examples.

2.2.8.3. Files Access, File Systems, and Objects

File-based data access of unstructured data (Figure 2.9) is seeing rapid growth due to ease of use and flexibility for traditional environments as well as for virtual and cloud data infrastructures. File-based data access is simplified by abstracting the underlying block-based components, enabling information to be accessed via filename.

File system software provides the abstraction of file-based access on a local or remote basis. Instead of knowing where the physical data is located on a disk or storage system, meaningful file names are used, along with directory structures or folders, for organization purposes. With file sharing, the client or initiator makes requests to the filer (target or destination) to process I/O requests on a file basis. The filer of the file system software presents (serves) data from the storage device to other host servers via the network using a file-sharing protocol while maintaining data coherency.

NAS filers can have dedicated HDD or SSD-based storage, external third-party storage, or a combination of both. NAS systems that leverage or support attachment of third-party storage from other vendors are known as gateways, NAS heads, routers, or virtual filers, among other marketing names. For example, NetApp has vFilers that support attachment of their own storage as well as systems from HDS, IBM, and many others. The advantage of using a NAS gateway such as those from Dell, BlueArc, EMC, HP, IBM, NetApp, Oracle, and others is the ability to reuse and repurpose existing storage systems for investment protection or purchasing flexibility.

NAS systems with integrated or dedicated storage across different market segments include BlueArc, Cisco, and Data robotics, Dell, EMC, Fujitsu, HP, IBM, Iomega, NetApp, Overland, Oracle, and Seagate. NAS software, in addition to propriety solutions from those mentioned and others, includes that from Microsoft (Windows Storage Server) and Oracle (ZFS), as well as others.

Some examples of data or information access protocols are shown in Table 2.2; others include HTTP (HyperText Transfer Protocol), FTP (File Transfer Protocol), WebDAV, Bit Torrent, REST, SOAP, eXtensible Access Method (XAM), and Digital Imaging and Communications in Medicine (DICOM), among others. Table 2.3 shows examples of software and solutions, including a mix of general-purpose, specialized, parallel, and clustered file systems.

Note that products shown in the Product column of Table 2.3 are software-based and may or may not be currently available as a software-only solution. Some of the vendors, particularly those who have acquired the software from its developer, have chosen to make it available only as a bundled preconfigured solution or via original equipment manufacturers (OEM) to other solution partners. Check specific vendors' websites and supported configuration for additional details or limitations. Other file systems and clustered file systems software or bundled solutions include, among others, SGI XFS and CXFS, Panasas PanFS, and Symantec/Veritas file system and clustered file system.

Table 2.2 Common File Access Protocols

Acronym	Protocol Name	Comment
AFP	Apple File Protocol	Apple file serving and sharing
CIFS	Common Internet File System	Microsoft Windows file serving and sharing
NFS	Network File System	File sharing for Unix, Linux, Windows and others
pNFS	Parallel NFS	Part of NFS standard supporting parallel file access suited for reading or writing large sequential files

2.2.8.4. Object and API Storage Access

Object-based storage, or content-addressable storage (CAS), is continuous building on the block and file storage access models. As previously discussed, file systems store files in a hierarchy directory structure mapped onto an underlying block storage device. Instead

Table 2.3 Common File System Software Stacks or Products

Product	Vendor	Comment
Exanet	Dell	Software bundled with Dell hardware as a scale-out or bulk NAS
GPFS	IBM	Software bundled with IBM hardware (SONAS) for scale-out NAS
IBRIX	HP	Software bundled with HP hardware as scale-out or bulk NAS
Lustre	Oracle	Scale-out parallel file system software
Polyserve	HP	Software bundled with HP hardware as scale-out or bulk NAS
SAM QFS	Oracle	Software integrated with Storage Archive Manager for hierarchical storage management
SFS	Symantec	Scale-out file system software sold by Symantec and others
WSS	Microsoft	Windows Storage Servers is used in many entry-level NAS products
ZFS	Oracle	Oracle bundled solution as 7000 series storage or by original equipment manufacturers

of a storage system reading and writing blocks of data as required by a file system, object-based storage works with objects. With block- and file-based storage, applications coordinate with file systems where and how data is read and written from a storage device with the data in blocks and with little meta data attached to the stored information.

In the case of object storage, instead of as a group of blocks of data, data is stored as an object that contains meta data as well as the information being stored. The object (Figure 2.10) is defined by an application or some other entity and organized in such

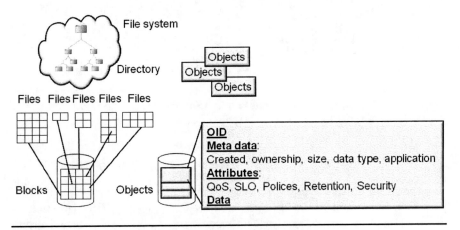

Figure 2.10   Block-and-file vs. object-based storage access.

a way that information about the data (meta data) is also attached to the data being stored, independent of the file system, database, or other organizational mechanisms.

Instead of a server or file system retaining the information about the data in a file system directory and inode (directory entry), CAS stores and retrieves information using unique key identifiers that are derived from the contents of the data being stored. If the data being stored is changed, the identifier also is changed. While there are variations in how CAS is implemented, the common approach is to add a level of abstraction as well as preserve data uniqueness for compliance and other retention applications.

Vendors with CAS and object-based storage solutions include Amazon, Clever-safe, Dell, EMC, HDS, HP, IBM, NetApp, Oracle, Panasas, and Scality. An emerging International Committee for Information Technology (INCITS) and an ANSI specification, the T10 Object Storage Device (OSD), is also evolving to formalize object storage and associated technologies. It is also worth mentioning that the ANSI T10 group (www.t10.org) is responsible for the SCSI command set found in open-system block storage solutions. Another, related group is ANSI T11, which focuses on Fibre Channel matters.

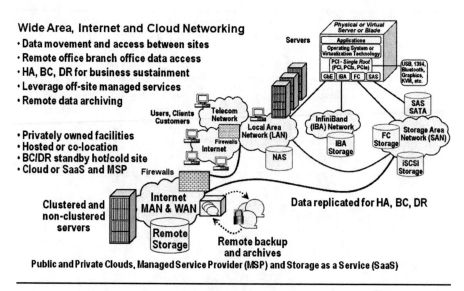

Figure 2.11 I/O and data storage networks. (*Source:* Greg Schulz, *The Green and Virtual Data Center*, CRC Press, Boca Raton, FL, 2009.)

2.3. I/O Connectivity and Networking Fundamentals

There are many different types of I/O and networking protocols, interfaces, and transport media, as shown in Figure 2.11. While networks and storage I/O interfaces support different aspects of computing, they both support moving information between computing and I/O interfaces. Over time, storage I/O interfaces have become specialized to support the needs and characteristics of moving data between servers and storage as well as between storage devices.

Local area networks (LANs) and wide area networks (WANs) are used for:

- Accessing and moving data to or from public/private clouds
- Data movement, staging, sharing, and distribution
- Storage access and file or data sharing (NAS)
- High-availability clustering and workload balancing
- Backup/restore for business continuance and disaster recovery
- Web and other client access, including PDAs, terminals, etc.
- Voice and video applications including Voice-over-IP (VoIP)

The term *networked storage* is often assumed to mean network attached storage (NAS) as opposed to a storage area network (SAN). In a general context, networked storage can mean storage that is accessed via some form of I/O network.

SAN and NAS are both part of storage networking. SAN is associated with Fibre Channel block-based access and NAS with LAN NFS or CIFS (SMB) file-based access. Each has its place to address different business needs. A SAN can also provide high-speed backup of NAS filers using Fibre Channel to access shared tape devices. Similar to the benefits of host servers, NAS filers also benefit from storage and backup sharing for resiliency. With a SAN, unless concurrent access software such as HACMP, Quantum Stornext, or some other clustered shared access tool is used, the LUN, device, or volume is owned by a single operating system or virtual machine guest at a time. In the case of NAS, data can be accessed by multiple servers, as the owner of the data, which provides concurrency as well as integrity, is the file server.

Some storage networking benefits include:

- Physically removing storage from servers
- Improved server resiliency and clusters
- Diskless servers using shared resources
- Storage and data sharing and consolidation
- Improved backup and recovery resource sharing
- Improved distance, capacity, and performance
- Simplified management via consolidated resources
- Lower total cost of ownership (TCO) from resource sharing

A storage network can be as simple as a point-to-point connection between one or more servers attached to and sharing one or more storage devices including disk and tape. A storage network can also be as complex as multiple subnets (segments or regions) spanning local, metropolitan, and global sites and using multiple topologies and technologies.

There are many different types of servers optimized for various applications, performance, capacity, and price points (e.g., tiered servers), with various tiers of storage, Similar to storage tiers, there also different tiers of I/O connectivity and networking (Figure 2.11). Storage and I/O interconnects (Figure 2.11) have also evolved from various vendors' proprietary interfaces and protocols to industry-standard Fibre Channel, InfiniBand, Serial Attached SCSI (SAS), and Serial ATA (SATA) as well as Ethernet-based storage.

With the exception of IBM legacy mainframes that utilize count key data (CKD) or extended count key data (ECKD) protocols, open systems-based computers, networking, and storage devices have standardized on the SCSI command set for block-based I/O. Physical traditional parallel SCSI cabling has given way to serial-based connectivity for block storage access. For example, SAS, iSCSI (TCP/IP on Ethernet), Fibre Channel, and SRP (InfiniBand) all rely on the SCSI command set mapped onto different transports.

Looking at Figure 2.12, one might ask why so many different networks and transports are needed: Why not just move everything to Ethernet and TCP/IP? The simple answer is that the different interfaces and transports are used to meet different needs, enabling the most applicable tool or technology to be used for the task at hand. An ongoing trend, however, has been toward convergence of protocols, transports, and networking cabling, as shown in Figure 2.12. In fact, the number of protocols has essentially converged to one for open-systems block I/O using the SCSI command set [SAS, Fibre Channel, and Fibre Channel over Ethernet (FCoE), iSCSI or SRP on InfiniBand (native SCSI on InfiniBand vs. iSCSI on IP on InfiniBand)].

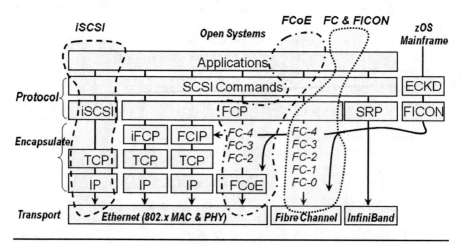

Figure 2.12   Data center I/O protocols, interfaces, and transports. (*Source:* Greg Schulz, *The Green and Virtual Data Center*, CRC Press, Boca Raton, FL, 2009.)

2.4. IT Clouds

There are many different types of clouds (public, private, and hybrid), with different types of functionalities and service personalities (e.g., storage of objects, backup, archive, generator file storage space, application-specific using various APIs or interfaces). There are cloud services to which you move your applications or whose software you use as a service, those to which you move your data and use cloud applications that reside in the same or a different location to access that data, and those in which your data is accessed via a cloud gateway, router, cloud point of presence (cpop), software, or other agent. Then there are products that are located at your site that enable cloudlike operations or management, and some that can be considered private clouds.

Many cloud definitions are based on a particular product or product focus area where more than one vendor aligns around common themes. For example, several vendors use the public cloud services model in which you can have your own private or shared space using a specific API such as REST, DICOM, SOAP, or others. Some solutions or products are designed for building services that, in turn, can be sold or provided to others. There is no one right cloud approach; rather, there are various approaches to align with your specific needs and preferences.

Cloud functionality varies by public, private, or hybrid cloud as well as for a fee or free, depending on the specific model or how it is deployed. Products can be turnkey off the shelf, custom, or a combination, including hardware, software, and services. Functionality can vary based on cost, service-level agreement, or type of service or product. Some services are based on shared infrastructure, whereas others are dedicated or isolated as well as having the ability to specify in what geographic region the data is parked for regulatory compliance, encryption for security, import/export capabilities for large volumes of data, along with audit and management tools.

Clouds can be a product, technology, or service as well as a management paradigm. They can leverage various technologies, including storage (DAS, SAN, and NAS, along with disk, SSD, and tape), servers, file systems along with various types of networking protocols or access methods, as well as associated management tools, metrics, and best practices.

Services provided by public or private clouds include application-specific software (Salesforce.com, ADP/payroll, concur expense reporting tools), archiving and data preservation, backup and restore, business continuance/disaster recovery, business analytics and simulation, compute capabilities, database and data warehousing, document sharing (Google Docs), email, collaboration and messaging, file sharing or hosting, along with object storage, office functions (word processing, spreadsheet, calendaring), photo, video, audio storage, presentations, slide content sharing, SharePoint and document management, video surveillance and security, and virtual machines.

From the xSP nomenclature, where "x" is replaced with various letters representing different themes—such as "I" for Internet or Infrastructure—"x as a Service" is now being used in a similar manner, as "xaaS," for example, Archive as a Service (AaaS), Application as a Service (AaaS), Backup as a Service (BaaS), Desktop as a Service (DaaS), Disk as a Service (DaaS), Infrastructure as a Service (IaaS), Platform as a Service (PaaS), Software as a Service (SaaS), and Storage as a Service (SaaS), among many others.

Some consider the only XaaS categories to be AaaS, PaaS, and IaaS, and that everything else must be included under those umbrellas. The reason for this is that those are the models that line up with the product or service they are selling or supporting, so it makes sense to keep conversations focused around those themes. In those instances it makes sense, but, realistically, there are other categories for the more broadly focused aspects of public and private cloud products, services, and management paradigms.

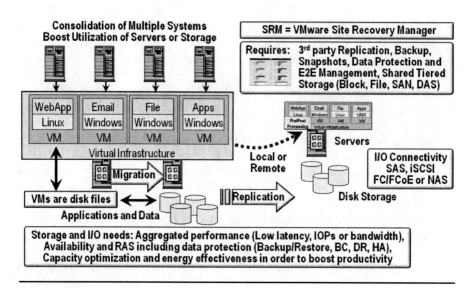

Figure 2.13   Various forms of virtualization, storage, and I/O.

2.5. Virtualization: Servers, Storage, and Networking

There are many facets of virtualization (Figure 2.13). Aggregation has become well known and a popular approach to consolidate underutilized IT resources including servers, storage, and networks. The benefits of consolidation include improved efficiency by eliminating underutilized servers or storage to free up electrical power, cooling requirements, floor space, and management activity, or to reuse and repurpose servers that have been made surplus to enable growth or support new application service capabilities.

Figure 2.13 shows two examples of virtualization being used, with consolidation on the left side and transparency for emulation and abstraction to support scaling on the right. On the consolidation side, the operating systems and applications of multiple underutilized physical servers are shown being consolidated onto a single or, for redundancy, multiple servers in a virtual environment with a separate virtual machine emulating a physical machine. In this example, each of the operating systems and applications that were previously running on their own dedicated server now run on a virtual server to boost utilization and reduce the number of physical servers needed.

For applications and data that do not lend themselves to consolidation, a different form of virtualization is to enable transparency of physical resources to support interoperability and coexistence between new and existing software tools, servers, storage, and networking technologies, for example, enabling new, more energy-efficient servers or storage with improved performance to coexist with existing resources and applications.

Another facet of virtualization transparency is to enable new technologies to be moved into and out of running or active production environments to facilitate technology upgrades and replacements. Virtualization can also be used to adjust physical resources to changing application demands such as seasonal planned or unplanned workload increases. Transparency via virtualization also enables routine planned and unplanned maintenance functions to be performed on IT resources without disrupting applications and users of IT services.

2.6. Virtualization and Storage Services

Various storage virtualization services are implemented in different locations to support various tasks. In Figure 2.14 are shown examples of pooling or aggregation for both block- and file-based storage, virtual tape libraries for coexistence and interoperability with existing IT hardware and software resources, global or virtual file systems, transparent data migration of data for technology upgrades and maintenance, and support for high availability (HA) and business continuance/disaster recovery (BC/DR).

One of the most commonly talked about forms of storage virtualization is aggregation and pooling solutions. Aggregation and pooling for consolidation of LUNs, file systems, and volume pooling, and associated management, are intended to increase capacity utilization and investment protection, including supporting heterogeneous data management across different tiers, categories, and price bands of storage from various vendors. Given the focus on consolidation of storage and other IT resources along with continued technology maturity, more aggregation and pooling solutions can be expected to be deployed as storage virtualization matures.

While aggregation and pooling are growing in popularity in terms of deployment, most current storage virtualization solutions are forms of abstraction. Abstraction and technology transparency include device emulation, interoperability, coexistence, backward compatibility, transition to new technology with transparent data movement and migration, support for HA and BC/DR, data replication or mirroring (local and remote), snapshots, backup, and data archiving.

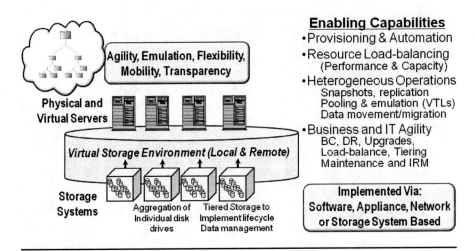

Figure 2.14   The many forms of storage virtualization.

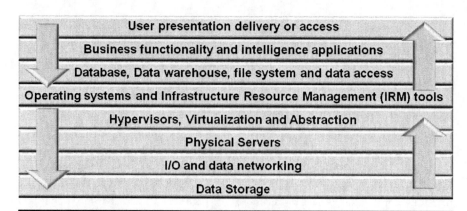

Figure 2.15 Data infrastructure stack and relationships.

2.7. Data and Storage Access

Figure 2.15 brings things together in terms of the topics covered in this chapter. In general, different layers and protocols interact to support information services delivery. Looking at Figure 2.15, storage is at the bottom and the tenants of data infrastructure components are farther up the stack. Data infrastructures needed to support information factories involve more than just disk or storage devices on a local or remote basis. The delivery of information services also relies on infrastructure resource management (IRM) tools, file systems, databases, virtualization, cloud technologies, and other tools and technologies.

The items or layers in Figure 2.15 can be consolidated or increased for additional detail, including middleware and other component items. To help put things into perspective, let's take a moment to look at where servers and storage have been, currently are at, as well as where they are going. Figure 2.16 shows from left to right how servers

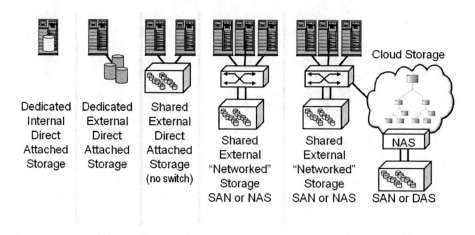

Figure 2.16 The server and storage I/O continuum.

and storage have evolved from being closely coupled as well as propriety to unbundled, open, and interoperable. Also shown is the evolution from dedicated to shared Direct Attached Storage (DAS) to networked along with local and remote, physical, virtual, and cloud.

2.7.1. Direct Attached Storage (DAS)

Figure 2.16 shows different storage access scenarios, including dedicated internal DAS, dedicated external DAS, shared external DAS, shared external networked (SAN or NAS) storage, and cloud-accessible storage. DAS is also called point-to-point storage, in that a server attaches directly to storage systems adapter ports using iSCSI, Fibre Channel, or SAS without a switch. It is important to keep in mind that DAS does not have to mean dedicated internal storage; it can also mean external shared direct accessible storage using SAS, iSCSI, or Fibre Chanel.

While a general industry trend is toward increased use of networked storage, that is, either block SAN using iSCSI, Fibre Channel, or FCoE as well as NAS using NFS and CIFS, there is still a strong if not growing use of DAS for deploying virtualization and clouds.

For example, storage and data services, including backup/restore, data protection, and archive solutions may present their functionality to clients or initiators (e.g., servers) via SAN block or NAS; however, the back-end storage may in fact be DAS-based. Another example is a cloud-based storage solution that presents iSCSI LUNs or virtual tape, HTTP, FTP, WebDav, or NAS NFS or CIFS access to clients, while the underlying storage may be DAS SAS (Figure 2.16).

2.7.2. Networked Storage: Network Attached Storage (NAS)

Four examples of NAS are shown in Figure 2.17. Shown first, on the left, is a server sharing internal or external storage using NFS, AFP, or Windows CIFS, among other software. The next example is a high-availability NAS appliance that supports various file- and data-sharing protocols such as NFS and CIFS along with integrated storage. In the middle of Figure 2.17 is shown a SAN with a NAS appliance without integrated storage that accesses shared storage. At the far right of Figure 2.17 is a hybrid showing a NAS system that also has access to a cloud point of presence (cPOP), gateway, or appliance for accessing cloud data. The cloud-based storage in the lower right-hand corner of Figure 2.17 is a NAS server with external DAS storage such as a shared SAS RAID storage system.

2.7.3. Networked Storage: Storage Area Network (SAN)

Storage area network (SAN) examples are shown in Figure 2.18, with a small or simple configuration on the left and a more complex variation on the right. On the left side of

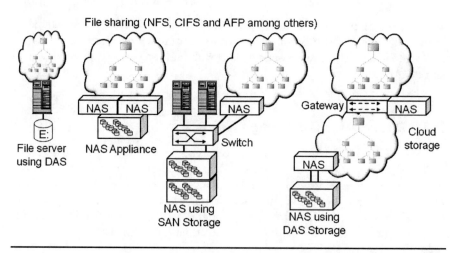

Figure 2.17   Network Attached Storage (NAS) examples.

Figure 2.18, multiple servers attach to a SAN switch, which in turn attaches to one or more storage systems. Not shown would be a high-availability configuration in which a pair of switches is used to connect servers and storage via redundant paths.

The SAN interface or protocols that can be used include shared SAS with a switch, iSCSI using Ethernet, Fibre Channel, and Fibre Channel over Ethernet or InfiniBand. The example on the right side of Figure 2.18 shows multiple blade servers along with traditional servers and a NAS gateway appliance attached to a SAN switch or director (large switch). Also attached to the switch are multiple storage systems that support deduplication, virtual tape libraries (VTLs), NAS, and other functionalities for backup/restore along with archiving. The example on the right in Figure 2.18 could be a pair of switches in a single location, across a campus, or across a metropolitan or wide area basis.

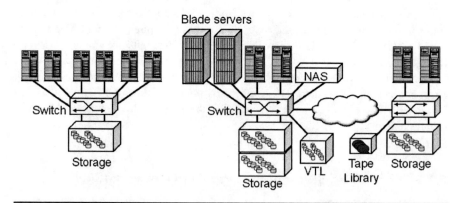

Figure 2.18   Storage area network (SAN) example.

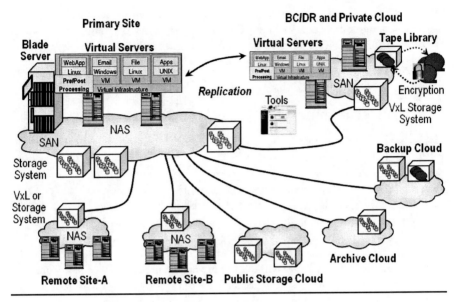

Figure 2.19   Cloud storage example.

2.7.4. Networked Storage: Public and Private Clouds

Figure 2.19 shows various cloud products and services supporting public and private capabilities combined with DAS, SAN, and NAS storage access for local as well as remote locations. Also shown are physical machines (PM) and virtual machine (VM) servers, primary on-line storage, and technologies for data protection. To support data protection, replication between locations along with backup/restore using disk to disk (D2D) as well as tape for long-term archiving or data preservation is also provided.

2.8. Common Questions

Do virtual servers need virtual storage? While virtual servers can benefit from features found in many virtual storage systems, generally speaking, virtual servers do not need or require virtual storage. However, virtual servers do need access to shared storage such as external SAS, iSCSI, Fibre Channel, FCoE, or NAS.

Do clouds need cloud storage? The answer depends on your definition of a cloud. For example, private clouds can use traditional storage products combined with additional management tools and best practices. Private clouds can also leverage cloud-specific solutions as well as external, third-party-provided public clouds. Public clouds often include storage as part of their solution offering or partner with cloud storage services providers.

Doesn't DAS mean dedicated internal storage? DAS is often mistaken for meaning dedicated internal attached storage inside a server. While this is true, DAS can also refer to external shared storage that is directly attached to one or more servers without using switches over interfaces including SAS, iSCSI, and Fibre Channel. Another name for external shared DAS is point-to-point storage, such as where iSCSI storage is connected directly to a server via its Ethernet ports without a switch.

2.9. Chapter Summary

Not all data and information is the same in terms of frequency of access and retention, yet typically it is all treated the same. While the cost per unit of storage is decreasing, the amount of storage that can be managed per person is not scaling at a proportional rate, resulting in a storage management efficiency gap. Information data can be stored in different formats using various interfaces to access it.

General action items include:

- Fast servers need fast storage and networks.
- You cannot have software without hardware, and hardware needs software.
- Clouds and virtual environments continue to rely on physical resources.
- There are many types of storage and access for different purposes.

Unless you are in a hurry to keep reading to get through this book, now is a good time to take a break, relax, and think about what we have covered so far, before moving on to the next section. Also visit my website at www.storageio.com and my blog at www.storageioblog.com, where you will find additional details, discussions, and related content to the material discussed here and in subsequent chapters.

Chapter 3

Infrastructure Resource Management

Reduce waste and rework to boost resource effectiveness.

– Greg Schulz

In This Chapter

- What is infrastructure resource management (IRM)?
- Why is IRM important for cloud, virtual, and storage networks?
- What is the role of service categories and capabilities?

This chapter looks at managing IT resources to enable an efficient, effective cloud, virtual or physical storage, and networking environment. Key themes, buzzwords, and trends addressed in this chapter include infrastructure resource management (IRM), storage and systems resource management (SRM), systems resource analysis (SRA), service classes and categories, along with end-to-end (E2E) management. Note that while in the context of this chapter SRM means systems (or storage) resource management, the acronym also has another meaning. In the context of server virtualization with VMware, SRM means site recovery manager for managing data protection, business continuance/disaster recovery (BC/DR), and availability.

3.1. Managing Data Infrastructures for Cloud and Virtual Environments

Information services need to be delivered in a timely, efficient, flexible, reliable, and cost-effective manner. Figure 3.1 shows common IT resources including servers, storage, and

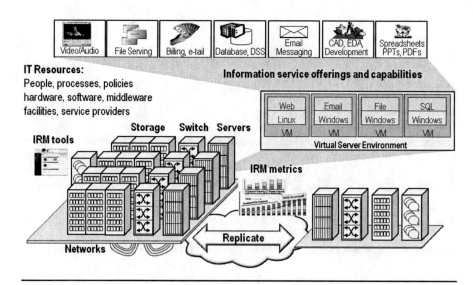

Figure 3.1   Delivering information services via resources and IRM.

input/output (I/O) network hardware along with people, processes, best practices, and facilities. Also shown in Figure 3.1 are metrics and tools for performing common IRM tasks, including data protection and management for different applications or services. Hardware and software along with external provided services combine with IRM tasks to enable flexible, scalable, and resilient data infrastructures to support cloud, virtual, and traditional environments.

Resources that support information services delivery include:

- Hardware—servers, storage, I/O and network connectivity, desktops
- Software—applications, middleware, databases, operating systems, hypervisors
- Facilities—physical structures, cabinets, power and cooling, security
- People—internal and external staff, skill sets, and experience
- Services—network bandwidth, managed service providers, clouds

Cloud, virtual, and networked data storage environments need to be

- Flexible, scalable, highly resilient, and self-healing
- Elastic, multitenant, and with rapid or self-provisioning of resources
- Application and data transparent from physical resources
- Efficient and effective without loss of performance or increased cost complexity
- Environmentally friendly and energy efficient yet economical to maintain
- Highly automated and seen as information factories as opposed to cost centers
- Measurable with metrics and reporting, to gauge relative effectiveness
- Secure from various threat risks without impeding productivity

Table 3.1 contains various IRM-related terms, their acronyms, and brief descriptions, which will be used in this as well as following chapters.

Table 3.1 IRM-Related Terms

Acronym	Term	Description
CMDB	Configuration management database	IT management repository or knowledge base
DPA	Data protection analysis	Analysis of data protection activities
DPM	Data protection management	Management of data protection activities
E2E	End-to-end	From resource to service delivery
IRM	Infrastructure resource management	Management of IT resources and service delivery
ITIL	IT infrastructure library	Processes and methodologies for IT service management
ITSM	IT service management	IRM functions including service desk
MTTM	Mean time to migrate	How quickly a migration can be done
MTTP	Mean time to provision	How quickly resources are provisioned for use
MTBF	Mean time between failures	Time between failures or downtime
MTTR	Mean time to repair/recover	How fast a resource or service is restored to use
KPI	Key performance indicators	IT and IRM service metrics
PACE	Performance availability capacity energy or economics	Common application and services attribute characteristics
PCFE	Power, cooling, and floor space EH&S (environmental health & safety)	Green IT and facilities attributes
PMDB	Performance management database	Capacity and performance repository
RPO	Recovery-point objective	Time to which data is protected
RTO	Recovery-time objective	Time until service or resources will be ready for use
SLA	Service-level agreement	Agreement for services to be delivered
SLO	Service-level objective	Level of services to be delivered
SRA	Storage/system resource analysis	Analysis, correlation, and reporting tools
SRM	Storage resource management	May also mean system resource management or VMware Site Recovery Manager tool

3.2. Introduction to Infrastructure Resource Management

Infrastructure resource management (IRM) is a collection of best practices, processes, procedures, technologies, and tools along with the people skill sets and knowledge used to manage IT resources effectively. While there can be areas of overlap, the aim of IRM is to deliver application services and information to meet business service objectives while addressing performance, availability, capacity, and energy (PACE) requirements in a cost-effective manner. IRM can be further broken down into resources management (e.g., managing servers, storage, I/O and networking hardware, software, and services) and managing services or information delivery. IRM is focused on processes, procedures, hardware, and software tools that facilitate application and data management tasks. There is some correlation with data management in that many IRM tasks are associated with serving, protecting, and preserving data. For example, data management involves archiving, backup/restore, society, and enabling business continuance (BC) as well as disaster recovery (DR), just as IRM does.

With reference to the idea of an information factory that was introduced in Chapter 1, IRM is a corollary to enterprise resource management (ERM) and enterprise resource planning (ERP) along with their associated tasks. For a traditional factory to be efficient and support effective business operations, there needs to be planning, analysis, best practices, polices, procedures, workflows, product designs, tools, and measurement metrics. These same ideas apply to information factories and are known collectively as IRM. For those who like the "working smarter" philosophy, IRM can also mean intelligent resource management, whereby business agility and flexibility are enabled while reducing per-unit costs and boosting productivity without compromising services delivery.

Typically, industry messaging around efficiency is centered on consolidation or avoidance, which is part of the effectiveness equation. However, the other parts of becoming more effective—that is, doing more with what you have (or less)—are to reduce waste or rework. The most recent focus of efficiency has been on hardware waste in the form of driving up utilization via consolidation and server virtualization, or data footprint reduction (DFR) using archiving, compression, and deduplication, among other techniques. The next wave of efficiency shifts to boosting productivity for active data and applications, which is more about performance per watt of energy or in a given amount of time or footprint. This also means reducing waste in terms of complex workflow, management paperwork, and the amount of rework, along with out-of-band (exception-handling) tasks that lend themselves to automation.

For example, a factory can run at a high utilization rate to reduce the costs of facilities, hardware or software tools, and personnel by producing more goods (e.g., more goods produced per hour per person or tool). However, if a result of that higher utilization is that the defect and rework rate goes up or measurements are ignored leading to customer dissatisfaction, the improved utilization benefits are negated. This translates to cloud, virtualization, and data storage networking environments in that the associated resources can be driven to higher levels of utilization to show reduced costs, but their effectiveness also needs to be considered.

Traditional IRM has had a paradigm based on hardware and application affinity (dependencies and mappings). Affinity has meant that hardware and software resources may be dedicated to specific applications, lines of business, or other entities. Even in shared networked storage (SAN or NAS) environments, resources may be dedicated while leveraging common infrastructure components. The result can be pockets of technologies, including SAN islands, where some applications may be lacking adequate resources. At the same time, other applications may have surplus or otherwise available resources that cannot be shared, resulting in lost opportunity. Consequently, effective sharing for load balancing to maximize resource usage and return on investment may not be obtained.

The evolving IRM paradigm is around elasticity, multitenancy, scalability, and flexibility, and it is metered and service-oriented. Service-oriented means a combination of being able to rapidly provide new services while keeping customer experience and satisfaction in mind. Also part of being focused on the customer is to enable organizations to be competitive with outside service offerings while focusing on being more productive and economically efficient.

Part of the process of implementing cloud, virtual, or storage networking is to remove previous barriers and change traditional thinking such as hardware vs. software, servers vs. storage, storage vs. networking, applications vs. operating systems, and IT equipment vs. facilities. A reality is that hardware cannot exist without software and software cannot exist or function without hardware.

While specific technology domain areas or groups may be focused on their respective areas, interdependencies across IT resource areas are a matter of fact for efficient virtual data centers. For example, provisioning a virtual server relies on configuration and security of the virtual environment, physical servers, storage, and networks, along with associated software and facility-related resources. Similarly, backing up or protecting data for an application can involve multiple servers running different portions of an application, which requires coordination of servers, storage, networks, software, and data protection tasks.

There are many different tasks and activities along with various tools to facilitate managing IT resources across different technology domains. In a virtual data center, many of these tools and technologies take on increased interdependencies due to the reliance on abstracting physical resources to applications and IT services.

Common IRM activities include:

- Audit, accounting, analysis, billing, chargeback
- Backup/restore, business continuance/disaster recovery
- Configuration discovery, remediating, change validation management
- Data footprint reduction (archiving, compression, deduplication)
- Data protection and security (logical and physical)
- Establishment of templates, blueprints, and guides for configuration
- Metering, measuring, reporting, capacity planning
- Migrating data to support technology upgrades, refresh, or consolidation
- Provisioning of resources, troubleshooting, diagnostics
- Service-level agreements, service-level objectives, service delivery management
- Resource analysis, resolution, tuning, capacity planning

IRM tasks also include configuration of physical resources, for example, server and operating systems, applications, utilities, and other software. IRM also is involved in networking and I/O connectivity configuration, along with associated security, high availability, backup/restore, snapshots, replication, RAID, volume groups, and file system setup. Other IRM tasks include creation or provisioning of virtual entities out of physical resources, including virtual machines (VMs), virtual networking and I/O interfaces, and virtual desktops, along with associated backup/restore capabilities.

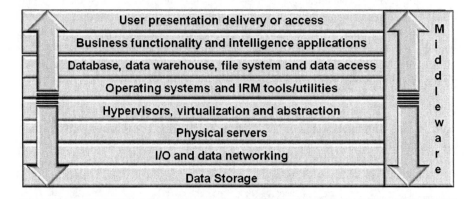

Figure 3.2   Information services delivery and IRM stack.

3.3. Understanding IT Resources

Figure 3.2 shows various information services delivery and IRM layers along with middleware (shown on the right). It is important to understand a few terms, some of which have been used already and some that will appear in future discussions.

Application. The definition of application will vary. For example, if your focus is SAN, LAN, MAN, or WAN networking protocols and interfaces, applications might be things such as file sharing, email, virtual servers, or whatever is being transported over the network. If your area of focus is farther up the technology stack, applications might be the servers and their operating systems, file systems or volume managers, databases, or associated IRM tools such as backup/restore, snapshots, replication, and storage resource management (SRM).

Your idea of applications might instead be more related to business function or information services, utilizing underlying middleware, databases, file systems, operating systems or hypervisors, SAN, LAN, MAN, and WANs. In this context, applications, such as those seen along the top of Figure 3.1, include messaging or collaboration (email, texting, VoIP), computer-assisted design (CAD) , enterprise resource planning (ERP), financials, patient picture archiving systems (PACS) or lab systems, video surveillance and gaming, entertainment, Web services, social media, etail, or office functions, among many others. The importance here is that there are different types and layers of applications that have various interdependencies on IRM functions and resources.

Cross domain and convergence. This encompasses techniques, best practices, polices, or IRM activities that span two or more technology areas—for example, server and storage, storage and networking, networking and servers, hardware and software, virtual and physical. Cross-domain or cross-technology management involves performing IRM and related activities on virtual servers that rely on physical servers, storage networks, and associated hypervisors, operating systems, and related middleware or software tools. If you are involved, interested, or exploring converged technologies and techniques, then you are by default interested in cross-technology domain activities. As an example, converged networking combines storage and servers I/O along with general networking, from a technology standpoint thus involving cross-domain management.

Elastic or elasticity. Traditional information services delivery resources (servers, storage, networks, hardware and software) tend to be deployed in fixed scenarios. By being fixed, even with shared SAN or NAS storage, applications have an affinity or association with specific devices or pools of physical or virtual resources. Being elastic, resources can be stretched or contracted to meet changing business or information services resource needs along with load balancing in a flexible or agile manner.

Federated. Applications and servers along with databases or storage systems can be federated as resources as well as their management federated. Federation can apply to management along with use of autonomous or heterogeneous (e.g., separate) resources in a seamless or transparent manner. For example, a federated database relies on middleware or other transparency tools or appliances to abstract the underlying different databases from their accessing applications. Federated management can provide a virtual management interface to different technologies. The lines or definitions between federated, cloud, and virtualized can be blurred in that they all provide layers of abstraction across different technologies. Multiple different technologies can be federated for access or management. Similarly, different virtual servers or storage can also be federated from an access use or management perspective.

Guest. Guest can mean different things from an IRM standpoint. One is that of an operating system and associated applications deployed and running on or in a virtual machine (VM). Another meaning of guest is a customer or consumer of information services, a trend that many businesses in different industries from retail to transportation to lodging are using.

IaaS. In the context of cloud conversation, IaaS usually refers to Infrastructure as a Service (IaaS). IaaS means that instead of having your own dedicated infrastructure comprised of hardware, software, IRM, and related techniques, technologies, and processes, it is provided to you or your application by a service provider. Depending on what infrastructure services are delivered or supported via a particular vendor's tool, precise definition of IaaS will vary.

Middleware. Middleware can be thought of as an abstraction or transparency layer to facilitate interoperability between different software tools and technology layers. Similar to the different types and layers or categories of applications, which vary depending on area of focus or experience, middleware can also vary. In Figure 3.2, middleware is shown generically on the right-hand side spanning across the different services and IRM tasks. There are different middleware layers that can sit between business applications and databases or Web services or at a lower level in the stack shown in Figure 3.2.

Various protocols and interfaces can be used to implement or facilitate middleware functionality, including SOAP and XML. Examples of middleware include Apache, EMC RSA authentication client, IBM, Linxter, Microsoft.NET, Oracle Fusion, GlassFish, WebLogic, Red Hat, SNIA CDMI, VMware Springsource, and many others.

Multitenancy. Multitenancy is the IT resource equivalent to having multiple tenants in a shared housing environment, each with its own quarters or habitat. Multitenancy can apply to servers such as virtual machines, where guest operating systems and their applications share underlying physical resources yet are logically isolated from each other. For storage, multitenancy enables applications or data consumers to share resources while being logically isolated from each other for security and other purposes. Networks can also be logically isolated and physically shared. For cloud, virtual, and shared data storage networks, multitenancy enables resources to be shared while allowing a layer of autonomous access.

Multitenant-enabled solutions also usually include some level of subordinated management in which a subset of commands or capabilities can be delegated without giving up control of the entire environment. Examples of server multitenancy include hypervisors such as Citrix Xen, Microsoft Hyper-V, and VMware vSphere, as well as logical domain or partition managers from others including HP, IBM, and Oracle. Cloud services such as those from Amazon, Rackspace, and most others also provide multitenancy. NetApp MultiStore is among many storage-focused multitenant-enabled solutions.

Orchestration. Orchestration is the process and tools used to combine various IRM activities into a deliverable service. Orchestration facilitates IRM activities involved in service delivery across different technology domains and skill-set disciplines—for example, orchestration of BC or DR along with backup that involves applications, databases, server, storage, networks, and backup or data protection tools and groups. Another orchestration example is virtual server or storage deployment, where various groups in a larger organization coordinate their respective IRM tasks as part of a workflow to make resources available.

PaaS. Platform as a Service provides a means for development and deployment of applications without having to invest in resources (hardware and software). PaaS transforms various resources combined with IRM activities into a solution as a service. SaaS providers may rely on PaaS to run their software.

Policies. Determining what to do when, why, where, and how is the role of policies. Policies can refer to where data is stored, how long it is retained, BC/DR, and data protection, along with performance needs to meet service requirements. Policies can be aligned to service categories in support of SLOs and SLAs managed via manual intervention or automation tools. In addition, policies can determine when to move data to a different tier of storage or a virtual machine to a different server. For cloud and remote data, policies can also be used to implement compliance regulations such as determining what data can reside in various geographic areas or countries.

SaaS. Software as a Service makes applications accessible via the Internet while running on a service or applications provider system. The actual systems supporting the software may in fact be PaaS- and/or IaaS-based. The idea of SaaS is that, instead of investing in your own infrastructure and associated resources requiring management, subscription-based access to software is obtained. Examples of SaaS applications include Salesforce.com, Concur expense reporting as well as various other CRM or ERP, mail, and business analytics tools. (Note that an alternative use of SaaS is Storage as a Service.)

Templates. Similar to how a traditional factory needs instructions and patterns to guide how tools, processes, and procedures will be deployed to produce product, information factories need a template. Templates for information services and IRM activities can have different meanings ranging from document or website or other default item to how service classes or categories are defined and delivered. For example, many blogs or websites are built using a template that is either left as is or modified to expedite development and deployment. Similarly, if starting from scratch, document templates for spreadsheets, word processing, slide presentations, along with applications and databases, can expedite development. IRM service templates are a means of defining and rolling out service classes or categories combined with policies and workflow. An IRM service-oriented template could include types or tiers of storage, RTOs and RPOs, QoS and other SLOs, RAID and data protection requirements, along with BC/DR needs. Ideally, templates should help facilitate rapid manual or automated provisionment of resources when combined with configuration advisors or wizards as user/consumer-oriented ordering of resources.

Workflow. Workflows can apply to various IRM activities across different technology domains (e.g., cross domain), workgroups, departments, and teams as part of ITIL, ITSM, ISO, and other process or project management practices. Workflows can be paper-based or fully automated, leveraging email and other tools for rapid approvals and triggers of downstream tools and technologies. The importance of workflow discussion or cloud and virtual data storage networking is that time is a valuable resource for most organizations.

By streamlining workflows, organizations are able to do more with what they have while reducing per-unit costs of services and at the same time boosting customer satisfaction. Additional benefits include freeing up staff time to focus on higher-value knowledge work and analysis, along with enabling resources to be put into service faster while reducing customer wait time for those services. As a result, staff productivity increases, return on resource investment increases, while enabling customers to innovate with faster time to market.

An example of a workflow is a request to provision storage for a virtual or physical server. The workflow might involve someone determining what tier, type, or category of storage service is needed if not already specified. With the category or class of service determined, assuming that an automated process does not exist to apply the service request to a configuration template, someone or different groups perform the actual IRM tasks. These tasks may involve configuring or assignment of logical units, file systems, and perhaps qtrees for NAS, volume mapping or masking, SAN zoning, snapshots, and replication along with backup/restore setup.

Also, part of the workflow will involve applicable approvals or signoffs, change management tracking, and updates to any applicable BC/DR documents. For some environments, the actual time to implement or provision storage resources can be relatively short, while the time for a request to flow through different workgroups, departments, or teams is much longer. Like many things, actual workflow time will vary with the size and complexity of your environment.

XaaS. While some take on a purist or narrow view that only IaaS, PaaS, and SaaS can be used or refer to clouds, there are many other commonly used variations known generically as XaaS, where "X" is replaced with different letters, for example, AaaS (Application as a Service), HaaS (Hardware as a Service), and DaaS (Disk as a Service), among others. The notion of XaaS is similar to XSP, where X can be ASP (Application Service Provider), ISP (Internet Service Provider), Managed Services Provider (MSP), or SSP (Storage Services Provider), among others. (Exercise caution, however, when using XSP and other XaaS terms besides IaaS, PaaS, and SaaS, as some cloud pundits will give you an ear full if the terms do not fit into their view of service or product capabilities or messaging objectives.)

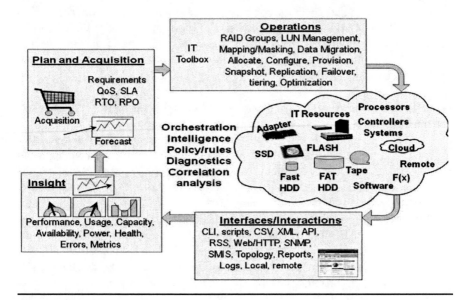

Figure 3.3   IRM continuum.

3.4. Managing IT Resources

Figure 3.3 shows, clockwise, the IRM cycle that starts with the discovery of resources and how they are configured as well as utilized. Part of the planning and acquisition activity is making sure adequate resources exist for support application needs in order to meet SLO and SLA requirements. This process can also involve analysis to determine new service categories or enhancement of existing services and capabilities.

For example, refinement of templates or configuration guides workflows and associated processes. Another activity area is configuration, deployment and provisioning of resources to meet SLO and SLA requirements per service categories and templates.

Part of configuration and operations includes data migration to support retiering for performance tuning or optimization initiatives, consolation, and technology refresh upgrades. Ongoing IRM activities also include remediation or updating of configurations combined with change management. Various interfaces and tools are used to access different metrics to report on the health status, performance, availability, capacity usage, and efficiency of the services being delivered. Having situational awareness proves insight E2E, that is, from applications to storage and all points in between.

3.5. Service Offerings, Categories, and Technology Alignment

Traditional factories may be dedicated to delivery of specific products, but many can be reconfigured to produce other products at various times. What the factory produces is based on templates or work orders, policies, and processes to deliver different products that meet various requirements. Similarly, some information factories are configured to deliver only specific services, while others can adapt to changing workloads or requirements. Information factories should be able to communicate their capabilities and categories of service, including applicable SLAs and costs. Regardless of whether your information factory is a traditional IT environment, virtual, private, and public or hybrid cloud model, knowing your capabilities, and their associated cost and levels of service, are important.

The reason that knowing costs and capabilities is important is to be able to communicate to internal or external customers, as well as to compete for business based on actual versus perceived comparisons. For example, an external service provider of storage resources may appear to be lower-cost than what you can deliver on your own. However, if the service you are delivering provides greater ability in terms of SLOs and SLAs, it is possible your offerings may be lower-cost if that is what the customer is expecting.

Granted, your customer might be expecting that all services have the same SLOs and SLAs and be comparing on a cost basis. Part of service management then becomes confirming with your customers what their service requirements actually are as opposed to what they want or expect. You may be delivering a higher level of service based on a joint belief of what is needed, instead of what is actually required. For example, the managers of a business unit may learn that they do not need the highest tier of your service offerings, making an external service look more attractive if they do not know you have a similar offering. Traditional IT thinking is to provide the highest level of services, but many business units, groups, application stakeholders, or information services consumers can tolerate a lower class of service for some of their functions.

Business functions, applications, and information services have different characteristics in terms of performance, availability, capacity, and economics. These basic characteristics are further broken down into workload or activity, response time, volume or transactions, reliability and accessibility, data protection, security, backup/restore, and BC/DR, along with compliance and other characteristics specific to the organization. Given that different applications or services as well as their consumers of IT services have varying requirements, for most organizations this means avoiding treating everything the same. By not treating everything the same, that is, assigning the applicable resources to meet SLOs and SLAs in a cost-effective manner, the benefit can be economic in addition to stretching resources. What this means is that by creating different categories of services, aligning the applicable technologies, tools, and techniques to meet service requirements, costs can be reduced and resources stretched further.

Service class and category management includes:

- Clarifying business SLOs for various applications
- Establishing IT classes or categories to meet business and application needs
- Alignment of resources (people, hardware, software) to service categories
- Assignment of service categories to meet different business and application needs
- Publication of metrics for performance, availability, capacity, and economics
- Review and realign service categories as needed.

An important point when setting service classes or categories is to make them relevant to the business, application, or information services being delivered. It is necessary to link back to the business and sit with the business liaisons and lay out for them the options you can provide and at what costs to meet their actual needs versus what they think they need.

Figure 3.4 shows an example of four categories (or tiers) of service, ranging from premium to lowest cost. The premium is the highest cost of the service categories, designed to support mission-critical applications or information services. Tier 0 is

Tier 0	Tier1	Tier2	Tier 3
Platinum	Gold	Silver	Bronze
Premium	Standard	Economy	Super Saver
$$$$	$$$	$$	$
Mission	Business	Business	Business
Critical	Essential	Important	Optional
Business cannot	Some impact to	Little impact to	Minimal
Function without	Business	Business	disruption
Time sensitive	Timely access	Some delay ok	Delay tolerable
Highly available	Good availability	Basic availability	Some availability
Low RTO & RPO	Low to medium	Medium RTO/RPO	High RTO/RPO
Must be secure	RTO and RPO	Downtime is	
Time is money	Some downtime	tolerated	
Downtime is a	can be tolerated		
Lost opportunity			

Figure 3.4 IT services classes or categories in business SLO terms.

Tier 0	Tier 1	Tier 2	Tier 3
Platinum	Gold	Silver	Bronze
Premium	Standard	Economy	Super Saver
$$$$	$$$	$$	$
Mission	Business	Business	Business
Critical	Essential	Important	Optional
Function rich	Some functions in	Some functions in	Minimal functions in
VMs, PMs, network	VMs, PMs, network	VM, PMs, network	VM, PMs, network
and storage	and storage	and storage	and storage
Highly available	Good availability	Basic availability	Minimal availability
High performance	Good performance	Basic performance	Minimal performance
No consolidation	Some consolidation	More consolidation	High degree of
Must be secure	Some downtime	More emphasis on	cost savings
Cost of doing	can be tolerated	reducing cost	
business			

Figure 3.5 Service classes, categories, or tiers in IT terms.

designed to provide very high availability with low RTO and RPO to guard against loss of data or loss of access. Also part of Tier 0 is that it is designed for time-sensitive applications. At the other end of service, Tier 3 is designed for applications or services that do not need higher availability or performance.

Note that the examples shown in Figure 3.4 do not mention any technologies or how specific resources are configured; instead they use business or service terms. The idea is to present to information services customers the available services in terms that they understand, so that they can map their business needs to a service template. In other words, learn to speak the language of the business or customers you are supporting, to help guide them to the applicable technology resources they need, rather than making them learn your language.

Figure 3.5 is similar to Figure 3.4, but the bottom half mentions broad or general technology terms such as virtual machines (VMs), consolidation, high performance, and high availability. Figure 3.5 is a middle ground to help convey IRM services capabilities and resource delivery in a manner close to "business speak" while getting closer to the actual underlying technology configuration and deployment templates.

The service classes or categories in Figure 3.6 are further refined into more technically specific language to include the resources, including disk drive speed or capacity along with other techniques, to optimize a given tier of service and its associated cost basis—for example, applicable RAID levels, when and how snapshots or point-in-time copies are made for backup to disk or for BC/DR, along with other data protection tasks.

For some environments, any of the preceding three examples may be adequate for describing services and technology configuration options. However, other environments will need additional detail, leveraging templates to determine configuration details along with SLO and SLAs including specific RTO, RPO, and QoS levels, among other criteria. The three figures have shown technology being aligned to the business or information services application needs. Table 3.2 shows as an example of

Tier 0	Tier 1	Tier 2	Tier 3
Platinum	Gold	Silver	Bronze
Premium	Standard	Economy	Super Saver
$$$$	$$$	$$	$
Mission	Business	Business	Business
Critical	Essential	Important	Optional
Fast resources	Fast resources	Shared resources	Extensive sharing
(servers, storage	(servers, storage	VMs for sharing	slower resources
and networks)	and networks)	and agility	VMs for consolidate
VMs for agility	VMs for agility	Good availability	Basic performance
Tier 0 and 1 storage	Tier 1 storage	Tier 2 and 3 storage	and availability
RAID 10 + Snapshots	RAID 10, 5, 6	Some performance	Lowest cost resources
Local and remote	Snapshots shots	RAID 5, 6, Snapshots	RAID 6, high capacity
replication for HA	replication for HA	some replication	storage at lowest cost
Cost per activity	Cost per activity	Activity and capacity	Cost per capacity

Figure 3.6   Service classes or tiers with technology mappings.

how various storage media or tiers align to different application or usage scenarios from a technology perspective.

By creating multiple service classes, categories, or tiers aligned to different business application or information services needs, the right resources can be allocated to meet service requirements in a cost-effective manner. However, there should be a balance between having too many service categories and the management associated with maintaining them and having too few or doing custom deployments for each service request. The right balance is having enough service categories and associated templates for rapid deployment of resources and then handling exceptions as just that, exceptions as opposed to the norm.

It is important is to understand the challenges, constraints, barriers, and opportunities, and to include them all in an analysis assessment. The more challenging part in addressing those issues is determining what applicable technologies, techniques, and best practices are best suited to address specific business and IT needs in the most effective and efficient manner.

It is necessary to periodically review and clarify service-level objectives. With ongoing SLO review, IT and customers will be able to know what is expected of each other instead of relying on assumptions. The business benefit of clarifying SLOs is to avoid potential higher service delivery costs as a result of assumptions with regard to service expectations.

For some applications or information services, the major requirement may be the lowest cost possible with some or minimal performance and availability. Yet other applications will have an emphasis on performance or availability, while still others may require a balance of all of those attributes and others. Keep in mind that the objective of having service classes or categories for servers (virtual, cloud, and physical) along with storage and networking is to stretch those resources to do more, supporting growth while maintaining or enhancing the quality of service.

Table 3.2 Aligning Higher-Level Service Categories into Tiered Storage Configuration

	Tier 0	Tier 1	Tier 2	Tier 3
	Very high performance	Performance and capacity centric	Capacity and low cost centric	High capacity low cost centric
Usage	Transaction logs and journal files, paging files, lookup and meta data files, very active database tables or indices	Active on-line files, databases, email and file servers, and video serving, needing performance and storage capacity	Home directories, file serving, Web 2.0, data backups and snapshots, and bulk data storage, needing large capacity at low cost	Monthly or yearly full backups, long-term archives or data retention, with accessibility traded for cost or power savings
Comparison	Dollar per IOPS. IOPS or activity per watt of energy and given data protection level	Activity per watt of energy and capacity density and given data protection level	Capacity density per energy used with performance for active data at protection level	Capacity density per energy used with bandwidth when accessed at protection level
Attributes	Low capacity and high performance, very low power consumption. DDR/RAM, FLASH, or some combination	Primary active data requiring availability and performance. 10K or 15K RPM 2.5–in. SAS HDDs	Low cost point, high density. 5 7.2K or 10K RPM SAS or SATA HDDs with capacities in excess of 1TB	Low cost and high capacity or 7.2K RPM SAS or SATA HDDs. Magnetic tape and optical on premise or cloud
Examples	Cache, caching appliances, SSD (FLASH, RAM)	Enterprise and mid-range arrays	Bulk and intelligent power management (IPM)-based storage	Tape libraries, optical storage, removable HDDs

This discussion about service classes is to establish the basis of what to use when, where, why, and how with cloud, virtual, and data storage networking. For example, in Figure 3.7, service categories in business terms are shown at the top, as they were in Figure 3.4, while along the bottom are shown technology-centric terms from Figure 3.6. In the middle is an example from Figure 3.5 that bridges the business and technology aspects.

While it is possible to implement tiered servers, tiered storage, tiered networks, or tiered data protection without service classes or categories, having defined service categories makes tiering easier to deploy. The ease comes from the ability to guide customers to what they actually need and what is best suited for their requirements, rather than what they think they need. You may find that a customer who wants lower cost may not realize that a given level of service ends up costing more in downtime or productivity delays. Likewise, a customer may think that he needs the highest level of service, only to discover when configuring with business stakeholders that there is some tolerance for a lower tier of service.

So, how many tiers or categories of service should you have? That is going to depend on your environment and willingness to manage some number of levels. Too few service categories that treat things the same may mean that you may end up with many custom or exception-based configurations. On the other hand, having too many service categories brings associated management costs for maintaining those services. The best number of categories for you will depend on the service you want to provide and your environment.

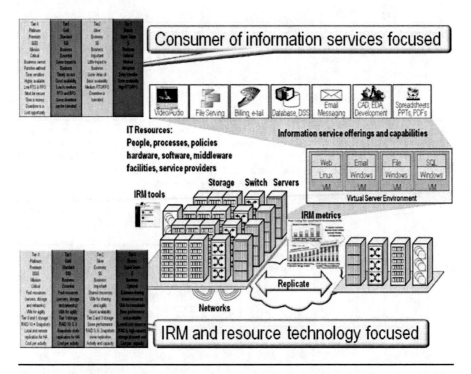

Figure 3.7   Showing service classes and categories and IRM activities together.

3.6. Gaining Situational Awareness and Control

An important need when moving to a cloud or virtualized dynamic environment is to have situational awareness of IT resources. This means having insight into how IT resources are being deployed to support business applications and to meet service objectives in a cost-effective manner. Awareness of IT resource usage provides insight necessary for both tactical and strategic planning as well as decision making. Put another way, effective management requires insight into not only what resources are at hand, but also how they are being used to decide where different applications and data should be placed to meet business requirements effectively.

While virtualization, cloud, and other techniques and tools for enabling dynamic IT environments help to abstract physical resources from applications, the need for E2E management tools providing situational awareness becomes more important. Management tools help identify and track configuration and interdependencies among various server, storage, and networking resources.

While abstraction provides some simplicity, there is also additional complexity that needs to be managed by having a clear and timely view of how resources are being used and allocated. In addition to needing situational awareness via systems resource analysis (SRA) tools, virtualized or abstracted environments also need to have streamlined common workflow management. Speed, agility, and accuracy are important for supporting dynamic IT environments. Consequently, tools that can identity, track, and support automation, along with enabling workflow files for various vendors' technology, become essential for IT organizations moving to abstracted environments.

You cannot effectively manage what you do not know about. Virtual, cloud, and other forms of abstraction help IT organizations enable flexible and scalable services delivery. While abstraction of underlying resources simplifies services delivery from an IT customer's perspective, additional layers of technology and interdependencies still need to be tracked as well as managed. Having E2E situational awareness of available resources and how they are being used (Figure 3.8) is an important part of IRM to enable efficient information services delivery.

By having timely situational awareness via different tools (Figure 3.8) across various technology domains, IT organizations gain insight into how resources can be more effectively deployed in an efficient manner. End-to-end situational awareness removes blind spots from efficient, effective IT services delivery. Other benefits of combining situational awareness with service delivery and IRM activities are to improve cycle times, for example, getting resources into production faster and minimizing the time needed to decommission them when being replaced, and load balancing and elasticity to meet changing workload demands or seasonal surges. All of these have business benefits, including reducing per-unit resource costs.

Figure 3.8 Situational awareness across different resources and IRM focus areas.

The business benefit of virtualization or other forms of abstracting is to provide transparency and agility. However, an additional layer of complexity is introduced that requires E2E cross-technology management. Storage and networks are needed for IT organizations to manage their resources effectively and deliver applications services to business users, SRA tools that support collection and correlation of data from servers. Figure 3.9 shows E2E management and awareness across different technologies and resource domains or IRM activity areas.

The removal of cost and complexity are key enablers for effective service delivery that facilitates agility and flexibility for IT environments. An important capability for virtualized, dynamic, and cloud (public or private) environments is the ability to manage available resources to a given business services level demand in a cost-effective manner. The benefit of SRA in a virtualized environment becomes that of enabling E2E management, thereby providing visibility and tracking of the logical mapping behind abstraction layers.

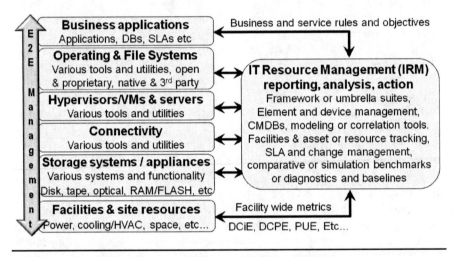

Figure 3.9   Various points of E2E IRM and resource interests.

3.7. From SRM to E2E SRA

Performance and capacity planning can be combined as complementary activities with SRM and utilization or handled as separate tasks. Performance tuning and optimization can initially be seen as reactionary tasks to respond to specific situations. A performance plan and ongoing performance tuning initiative can support a shift from reactionary to tactical and longer-term strategic management approaches. For example, shifting to a performance plan approach, where performance and usage are analyzed and optimized as part of an overall growth plan, can help maximize and optimize spending.

IRM reporting and monitoring tools should allow an IT administrator to see across different technology domains and from virtual server to physical storage for the full IRM picture. In addition, capacity and resource usage tools are adding performance or activity reporting to traditional space or capacity utilization to provide a more holistic view of resource usage for servers, storage, and networks. Performance and utilization should be evaluated in tandem. It's bad policy to scale up utilization only to find that performance suffers.

SRA tools step beyond basic resource reporting tools by providing event correlation and other analysis capabilities across multiple technology domains. Some SRM products have (or will morph into) SRA tools over time, while some SRA products can also function as SRM in addition to providing a configuration management database (CMDB), workflow, automation, and some orchestration tasks.

A flexible storage (or systems) resource analysis tool should:

- Support complex heterogeneous environments with many interdependencies
- Provide project management reporting and interfaces to change management
- Map resources and usage to supported business function service delivery
- Leverage industry standards along with customized run books and workflows
- Enable E2E remediation across different IT resource technology domains
- Execute tasks including hand-off of workflow tasks to third parties

3.8. Search and eDiscovery

There are several functions when it comes to data classification and search tools. These are discovery, classification, and indexing, as well as searching, reporting, and taking action on discovered data, for example, identifying what files to migrate from active on-line storage to off-line storage for archive purposes.

Taking action refers to the ability to interface with various storage systems (on-line, near-line, and off-line), including object-based and archiving systems, to enable management and migration of data. For compliance-related data, taking action includes marking data for litigation hold to prevent tampering of data and deleting data based on policies. Another example of taking action is feeding discovered information to policies' managers or other IRM tools to take data protection action, including replication or making an off-line copy.

SRM and basic data discovery and classification tools include file path and file meta data discovery SRM tools. SRM tools have a vertical focus on storage and file identification for storage management purposes, including allocation, performance, and reporting. Some tools provide basic SRM-like functionality with more advanced capabilities including archiving, document management, email, and data migration capabilities. Deep content discovery, indexing, classification, and analysis tools support features such as word relativity, advanced language support, as well as search and discovery features for vertical markets.

When looking at data discovery and indexing tools, the intended and primary use of the technology should be kept in mind. For example, is the planned use of the tools to perform deep content discovery for compliance, legal litigation, and intellectual property search? Perhaps you are looking to identify what files exist, when they were last accessed, and what might be candidates for moving to different tiers of storage. By keeping primary objectives in focus, you may find that different tools work better for various tasks and that more than one tool is needed.

Architectural considerations include performance, capacity, and depth of coverage, along with discovery, security, and audit trails. Policy management should be considered with policy execution, interfaces with other policy managers, and data migration tools. Some tools also support interfaces to different storage systems such as vendor-specific APIs for archiving and compliance storage. Consider whether the candidate tools have embedded or built-in support for processing different templates, lexicons, syntax, and taxonomies associated with different industries and regulations. For example, when dealing with financial documents, the tool should support processing of data in the context of various financial taxonomies such as banking, trading, benefits, and insurance, among others. If legal documents are being processed, then support for legal taxonomies will be needed.

Classifying data is complex, and for some services providers who merely "house" data, the actual value of the data may not be known. While tools exist, they are limited in their extensiveness and scalability. Interaction with lines of business and those developing the applications is important to understand the value of data. Tiered security is needed, but a methodology also needs to exist and be tied to data value, location, and line of business.

Understanding target applications and needs for discovery tools will help to ensure a positive and successful solution. To understand what files exist on a system to help implement a tiered storage environment, start by looking at traditional SRM-type tools. If, on the other hand, deep data discovery is needed to support litigation, compliance, and other functions, then consider more advanced tools. Some tools can meet multiple objectives, but it is important to know what other aspects of a system may be affected.

3.9. Performance and Capacity Planning

There may not appear to be a link between availability and performance and capacity planning. There is, however, a direct connection: If a resource is not available, performance is impacted; and if a resource has poor performance or limited supply, availability and accessibility are impacted.

Resource usage and capacity planning includes:

- Status and resource monitoring, accounting, event notification, and reporting
- Determining what resources can be consolidated and which ones need scaling
- Performance, availability, capacity, and energy usage reporting and analysis
- Diagnostics, troubleshooting, event analysis, and proactive management
- Interdependency analysis between business functions and various IT resources
- Asset and facilities management

Capacity planning and capacity management are practices used in a variety of businesses. In a manufacturing company, for example, they're used to manage inventory and raw goods. Airlines use capacity planning and capacity management to determine when to buy more aircraft. Electric companies use them to decide when to build power

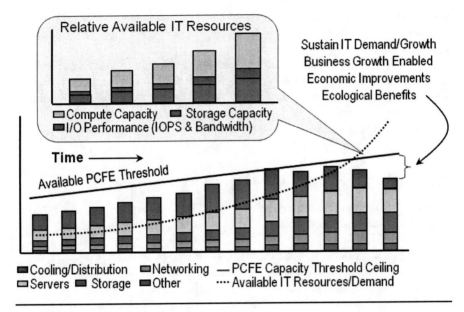

Figure 3.10   IRM capacity forecast example.

plants and transmission networks. By the same token, IT departments use capacity planning and capacity management to derive maximum value and use from servers, storage, networks, and facilities (power, cooling, and floor space) while meeting service-level objectives or requirements. An example of a simple IRM capacity forecast combined with usage tracking is shown in Figure 3.10.

Capacity planning can be a one-time exercise to determine how much and what types of resources are needed to support a given application. A nontactical approach to resource needs assessment and sizing is to simply acquire some amount of resources (hardware, software, networks, and people) and buy more as needed. A strategic approach would evolve from the tactical to make more informed decisions and timed acquisitions. For example, knowing your resource needs ahead of time, you might be able to take advantage of special vendor incentives to acquire equipment that suits your needs on your terms. Similarly, if the terms are not favorable and resource usage is following the plan, you may choose to delay your purchase.

Virtual data centers help to abstract physical resources from applications and users. However, increased complexity needs to be offset with end-to-end diagnostics and assessment tools along with proactive event correlation and analysis tools. Having adequate resources when needed to sustain business growth and meet application service requirements is a balancing act. The balance is having enough servers, storage, and networking resources on hand without having too much, resulting in higher costs—or not enough, resulting in poor service.

Poor metrics and insight can lead to poor decisions and management. Look at servers from more than a percent utilization basis; also consider response time and availability. Think about storage from an IOPS and bandwidth performance perspective, along with response time or latency and in addition to amount of available capacity. Consider networking from a latency standpoint in addition to cost per given bandwidth and percent utilization perspective.

If you are new to capacity planning, check out the Computer Measurement Group (CMG), which is focused on cross-technology, vendor- and platform-neutral performance and capacity planning management. In general, I recommend starting simple, building on existing or available experience and skills while identifying opportunities that will maximize positive results to gain buy-in and evolve to more advanced scenarios.

3.10. Data Movement and Migration

Another IRM activity that has multiple meanings is movement and migrations. Movement or migration can apply to:

- Conversion or upgrades of hardware and software
- Guest operating systems and applications to physical or virtual servers
- Physical to virtual, virtual to virtual, virtual to physical
- Moving data from existing storage to new storage systems
- Data center consolidation or relocation
- Storage and data re-tiering for optimization or relocation to cloud services

Based on the previous examples, migrations can occur in many different ways across various venues and points of interests, for example, across or within data centers, across or within storage systems, in homogenous (all one product) or heterogeneous (across multiple products) solutions.

Common data migration challenges include:

- Project initiation, staffing, and familiarization
- Discovery of existing environment
- Workflow management across groups
- Different groups involved on a global basis
- Introduction of various tools and processes
- Multiple vendors, technologies, and tools
- Intrusive configuration discovery processes
- Cross-site configuration remediation
- Keeping knowledge base up to date

In larger and global environments, data migrations are recurring tasks, thus an opportunity for optimization or cost savings. A common issue is loss of site knowledge when a service delivery is completed. In cases where the site knowledge is retained, it often becomes stale and of little use by not being maintained. The result is that acquired knowledge cannot be effectively leveraged for future migrations or other recurring IT IRM tasks or activities. Mean time to migrate (MTTM) is a metric that can be used to gauge how long from start to finish a data movement or migration process takes. MTTM includes time to actually move or copy data onto a new storage device or off of an old one in support of retiering, consolidation, or technology updates. In addition to copy time, MTTM also includes associated management workflow coordinate task activities. For organizations with recurring data movement and migrations, the lower the MTTM, the better, as resources and personnel can spend more time doing productive work.

Benefits of reduced MTTM include:

- Reduce project start-up/completion time
- Expedite hardware deployments
- Increase storage useful time doing work
- Maximize storage expenditure return on investment (ROI)
- Knowledge retained for future migrations

3.11. Chapter Summary

Infrastructure resource management (IRM) is an important part of delivering information services transforming raw resources (servers, storage, hardware, software) combined with processes and procedures into service categories. Effective IRM for public, private, and hybrid clouds as well as virtual and legacy environments can boost productivity, reduce per-unit costs and stretch resources to support growth.

General action items include:

- Establish key performance indicators to measure resource effectiveness.
- Define and manage service-level objectives and service-level agreements to applicable service expectations.
- Streamline workflows and service alignments to stretch resources further.

There are many vendors with solutions to address various aspects of IRM in a physical or virtual datacenter. Examples include Axios, Aptare, BMC, Bocada, Brocade, CA, Cisco, Commvault, Dell, Egenera, EMC, Emerson/Aperture, HP, IBM, Microsoft, Neptuny, NetApp, Network Instruments, Novell, Opalis, Quest, Racemi, SANpulse, Solarwinds, Storage Fusion, Sun, Symantec, Teamquest, Veeam, Viridity, and VMware.

Chapter 4

Data and Storage Networking Security

It's 3 AM; do you know where your data is and who it is with?

— Greg Schulz

In This Chapter

- Risks and security challenges for cloud, virtual, and data storage networks
- Security should be effective without being a barrier to productivity
- Techniques, technologies, and best practices for securing information resources

This chapter looks at securing data infrastructure resources in cloud, virtual, networked, and storage environments to counter various internal and external threat risks and other security-related challenges. A good defense—having multiple layers, rings, or lines of protection—along with a strong offense of proactive policies combine to enable productivity while protecting resources. Key themes addressed in this chapter include securing data during transit as well as when at rest, authorization, authentication, and physical security. Additional buzzwords include multitenancy, blind spots (dark territories or dark clouds), encryption and key management, data loss prevention (DLP), and self-encrypting disk drives (SEDs), also known as trusted computing group (TCG) OPAL devices.

4.1. Being Secure Without Being Scared

As IT moves farther from the relatively safe and secure confines of data center glass-houses and internal physical networks with interfaces for Wi-Fi mobile and Internet computing, security has become even more important than it was in the past. Cloud, virtual machine (VM), and storage networking with remote access enable flexible access of IT resources by support staff, users, and clients on a local and wide area basis. This flexibility, however, also exposes information resources and data to security threats. This means that any desired increased accessibility must be balanced between data protection and business productivity. As networked storage enables storage and information resources to be accessed over longer distances and outside the safe confines of the data center, more security threats exist and more protection is needed.

Security issues also increase as a result of networking with virtual and physical IT resources and applications or services being delivered. For example, a non-networked, standalone server and dedicated direct attached storage with secured physical and logical access is more secure than a server attached to a network with general access. However, the standalone server will not have the flexible access of a networked server that is necessary for ease of use. It is this flexible access and ease of use that requires additional security measures. As new enabling technologies, including IP-based networks to facilitate distance, are leveraged, they also enable security threats and attacks. These attacks can occur for political, financial, terrorist, industrial, or sheer entertainment reasons.

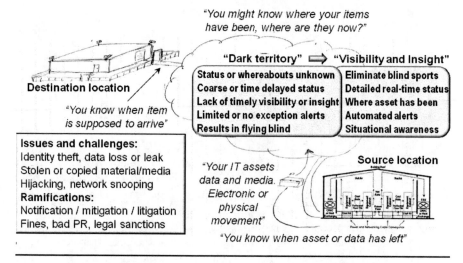

Figure 4.1 Eliminating "dark territory," "dark clouds," and blind spots.

4.2. Eliminating Blind Spots, Gaps in Coverage, or "Dark Territories"

In Chapter 3 we looked at the importance of not treating all applications, their data and associated infrastructure resources, and associated management the same, by using policies and procedures collectively called infrastructure resource management (IRM). Security of information and related assets is an important part of IRM, including data management and different levels of protection to meet various threat risks. Business and threat analysis should be used to determine what to encrypt and the applicable level or granularity of encryption to be used. It is also important to eliminate "dark territories," blind spots, or gaps in coverage (Figure 4.1).

Blind spots or gaps in coverage are not unique to security; enabling an agile, flexible, dynamic, resilient, and converged environment relies on having timely situational awareness of resources and service delivery. Because the focus in this chapter is on logical and physical security of data and information resources on both local and remote bases, the focus of removing dark territories or blind spots is to eliminate gaps in coverage that can result in points of vulnerabilities or threat risks.

When it comes to moving data electronically via a network transfer or by shipping physical media, you may know when and where it left as well as its estimated time of arrival (ETA), but do you know where the data was during transit or while in flight? Do you know who may have had access to it or been able to view its content, particularly if it was not encrypted? Can you provide auditable trails or activity logs of where the data moved or deviated from planned routes or paths?

In the transportation industry, terms such as "dark territory" have historically been used by railroads to indicate areas with minimum to no management or control coverage. Other transportation-related terms include "blind spots" or "flying blind" to indicate lack of situational awareness that can result in loss of management control. What these have to do with cloud and virtual data storage networking is that a "dark cloud" can be considered a resource without adequate insight and awareness of who has access to it and what they may be doing with it.

At the top left of Figure 4.1, various technologies and techniques are shown that are used at the source and destination for managing digital assets and media. Also shown are issues and lack of real-time management insight while assets are being moved in blind spots.

For example, data needs to be moved to public and off-site remote private providers. Once data and applications are in use at public or private providers and on premise, what visibility is there into how secure information and associated resources are being kept safe? When information is being moved, is it via electronic means using networks or bulk movement using removable media (FLASH SSDs, regular hard disk drives (HDDs), removable hard disk drives (RHDDs), optical CDs or DVDs, or via magnetic tape? For example, to move a large amount of data initially to a cloud or managed service provider, a magnetic tape copy of the data may be made to be used for staging at the remote site, where it is then copied to a disk-based solution. What happens to the magnetic tape? Is it stored? Is it destroyed? Who has access to the tape while it is in transit?

Possible areas of "dark territory" or gaps in coverage include:

- Public or private clouds that lack visibility into who is accessing resources
- Shipping containers containing storage systems or media (SSDs, disks, or tapes)
- Lack of leak detection on public and private networking links
- Physical and logical tracking of where data or storage media are during transit
- Who has access to eDiscovery, search or data classification tools, and audit logs
- What physical access and audit logs or trails exist, and how they are preserved

- Tools including radio-frequency identification (RFID) for tracking assets
- Physical security and logical or encryption for data in-flight and at rest
- No video or logs for access to physical resources and facilities

4.3. Security Threat Risks and Challenges

There are many different threat risks (Figure 4.2) for IT cloud, virtual, and traditional data centers and the systems, applications, and data they support. These risks
range from acts of man to acts of nature, and from technology failure to accidental
and intended threats. A common belief is that most threat risks are external, when in
reality most threats except acts of nature are internal. Firewalls and other barriers can
work together to fight attacks from outside, but equally strong protection is necessary
against internal threats. Another common security threat risk within most IT networks
is inadequate security on "core" systems or applications within an environment. For
example, poor password control on enterprise backup/recovery systems, virtualization
systems, and management interfaces may be too common instead of being common
sense to change.

Threats may be physical or logical, such as a data breach or virus. Different threat
risks require multiple rings or layers of defenses for various applications, data, and IT
resources, including physical security. The virtual data center relies on both logical and
physical security. Logical security includes access controls or user permissions for files,
objects, documents, servers, and storage systems along with authentication, authorization, and encryption of data.

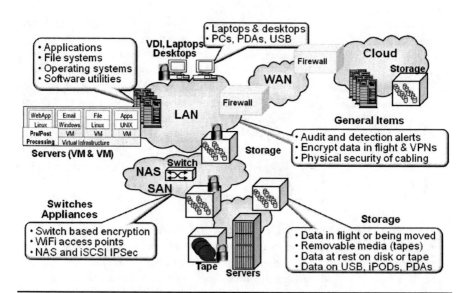

Figure 4.2 Cloud and virtual data storage networking security points of interest.

Additional common threat risks include:

- Logical or physical intrusion from internal and external sources
- Cybercrimes, virus, botnets, spyware, root kits, and denial-of-service (DoS)
- Theft or malicious damage to data, applications, and resources
- Lost, misplaced, or stolen data, or pirated network bandwidth
- Regulatory compliance and information privacy concerns
- Exposure of information or access to IT resources when using public networks
- Internal or external unauthorized eavesdropping or sniffing
- Shift from private physical to virtual and public cloud resources
- Blind spots or dark territory and clouds with loss of visibility or transparency

Another facet of logical security is the virtual or physical destruction of digital information known as digital shredding. For example, when a disk storage system, removable disk or tape cartridge, laptops or workstations are disposed of, digital shredding ensures that all recorded information has been securely removed. Logical security also includes how storage is allocated and mapped or masked to different servers along with network security including zoning, routing, and firewalls.

Another challenge with cloud and virtual environments is how various customers' or business functions' applications and data are kept separate in a shared environment. Depending on the level of the shared or multitenant solution combined with specific customer, client, or information services consumer security and regulatory requirements, different levels of isolation and protection may be required. For example, on a shared storage solution, is having different customers or applications provisioned into separate logical units (LUNs) or file systems sufficient? As another example, for more security-focused applications or data, are separate physical or logical networks, servers, and storage required? In addition to multitenant hardware, software, and networks, either on your own premises under your management or via an on-site managed service provider or external provider, who has access to what, when, where, and for what reasons?

Additional security challenges include:

- Subordinated and converged management of shared resources
- Mobile and portable media, PDAs, tablets, and other devices
- Encryption combined with deduplication, compression, and eDiscovery
- Orphaned data, storage, and other devices
- Classifying applications, data, and alignment of service-level objectives (SLOs)
- Growth of unstructured data, ranging from files to voice and video
- Converged networking, compute and storage hardware, software, and stacks
- Number of and diversity of log files to monitor as well as analyze
- International and multilanguage support via tools and personnel
- Automated policy-based provisioning
- Managing vendors and suppliers along with their access or end points

In addition to the above, other challenges and requirements include compliance requirements such as PCI (Payment Card Industry), SARBOX, HIPPA, HIECH,

BASIL, and others. Security requirements for cloud, virtual, and data storage networks vary and include jurisdiction of specific regulations, fraud and data leak detection notification, data encryption requirements, auditable event, as well as access and activity logs.

4.4. Taking Action to Secure Your Resources

Security of your networks and systems is essential in normal times and crucial during service disruption. Denial-of-service attacks have become the new threat, causing disruptions and chaos. Some security issues to be considered include physical and logical security along with encryption of data, virtual private networks (VPNs), and virtual local area networks (VLANs). Security of the network should extend from the core to the remote access sites, whether home, remote office, or a recovery site. Security must be in place between the client and server (or the Web), and between servers. Securing the home environment includes restricting work computers or PCs, use of VPNs, virus detection, and, of course, system backup. Security becomes more important the farther away you are from a secured physical environment, particularly in shared environments.

Common security-related IRM activities include:

- Authorize and authenticate access.
- Encrypt and protect data in-flight and at rest.
- Monitor and audit activity or event logs.
- Grant or restrict physical and logical access.
- Monitor for data leaks and policy compliance.

As with many IT technologies and services, there will be different applicable threat risks or issues to protect against, requiring various tiers and rings of protection. The notion of multiple rings or layers of defense is to allow for flexibility and enable worker productivity while providing protection and security of applications and data. A common belief is that applications, data, and IT resources are safe and secure behind company firewalls. The reality is that if a firewall or internal network is compromised, without multiple layers of security protection, additional resources will also be compromised. Consequently, to protect against intrusions by external or internal threats, implementation of multiple protection layers, particularly around network access points, is vital.

There are many things that can be done, ranging from protecting physical facilities and equipment to securing logical software and data. Securing coverage should extend in terms of visibility and coverage from physical to virtual, from private to public as well as managed service providers (MSPs). Other things that can be done include preserving segregated administration functions by various technology management groups (servers, operating systems, storage, networking, applications) in a converged, coordinated manner. This means establishing policies and procedures that span technology management domains along with associated visibility or audit tools. Security should also include leveraging encryption, certificates, and tokenization in support of authorization, authentication, and digital rights management.

4.4.1. Physical Security

Physical data protection means securing facilities and equipment and access to management interfaces or workstations.

Physical security items include:

- Physical card and ID if not biometric access card for secure facilities
- Storage media and assets secure and with safe disposition
- Secure digital shredding of deleted data with appropriate audit controls
- Locked doors to equipment rooms and secure cabinets and network ports
- Asset tracking including portable devices and personal or visiting devices
- Limits or restrictions on photo or camera use in and around data centers
- Low-key facilities without large signs advertising that a data center is here
- Protected (hardened) facility against fire, flood, tornado, and other events
- Use of security cameras or guards

Another dimension of physical security includes ensuring that data being moved or transported electronically over a network or physically is logically secured with encryption and physical safeguards including audit trails and tracking technology. For example, solutions are available to retrofit existing magnetic tape and removable hard disk drives with external physical bar-code labels that include an embedded RFID chip. The RFID chips can be used for rapid inventory of media being shipped, to facilitate tracking and eliminate falsely reported lost media. Other enhancements include shipping canisters using Global Positioning System and other technologies to facilitate tracking during shipment.

With the increased density of servers, storage, and networking devices, more cabling is being required to fit into a given footprint. To help enable management and configuration of networking and I/O connectivity, networking devices including switches are often integrated or added to server and storage cabinets. For example, a top-of-rack or bottom-of-rack or embedded network switch aggregates the network and I/O connections within a server cabinet to simplify connectivity to an end-of-row or end-of-area group of switches.

Cable management systems, including patch panels, trunk, and fan-in, fan-out cabling for over-head and under-floor applications, are useful for organizing cabling. Cable management tools include diagnostics to verify signal quality and decibel loss for optical cabling, cleaning and repair for connectors, as well as asset management and tracking systems. A relatively low-tech cable management system includes physically labeling cable endpoints to track what the cable is being used for, along with a cable ledger. A cable ledger, either maintained by hand or using software, keeps track of status, including what is in service or available for maintenance. Software for tracking and managing cabling can be as simple as an Excel spreadsheet or as sophisticated as a configuration management database (CMDB) with intelligent fiber-optic management systems. An intelligent fiber-optic system includes mechanisms attached to the cabling to facilitate with tracking and identify cabling.

Another component for server, storage, and networking I/O virtualization is the virtual patch panel, which masks the complexity by abstracting the adds, drops, moves, and changes associated with traditional physical patch panels. For large and dynamic environments with complex cabling requirements and the need to secure physical access to cabling interconnects, virtual patch panels are a great complement to I/O virtualization (IOV) switching and virtual adapter technologies.

Physical security can be accomplished by addressing the above items, for example, by ensuring that all switch ports and their associated cabling and infrastructure, including patch panels and cable runs, are physical secured with locking doors and cabinets. More complex examples include enabling intrusion detection as well as enabling probes and other tools to monitor critical links such as wide area interswitch links (ISLs). For example, a monitoring device could track and send out alerts for certain conditions on critical or sensitive ISLs for link loss, signal loss, and other low-level events that might appear as errors. This information can be correlated back to other information including maintenance records to see if someone was performing work on those interfaces, or if they have been tampered with in some way.

4.4.2. Logical Security

Logical security complements physical security with a focus on items such as applications or data access. Logical security includes authorization, authentication, and digital rights management along with encryption of data and multitenancy.

Additional areas of logical security on a local or remote basis include:

- Forced regular changes of passwords combined with digital rights management
- Authentication of user credentials and authorization of individual rights
- Logical storage partitions and logical or virtual storage systems
- Tamper-proof audit trails and logs of who accessed what, when, and from where
- Encryption of data at rest (on storage) or in-flight (over a network)
- Secure servers, file systems, storage, network devices, and management tools

4.4.3. Multitenancy

In Figure 4.3, at the top left is an example of a single tenancy with servers and storage dedicated to a given application or function. Moving from left to right across the top of Figure 4.3 are examples of multitenant servers using hypervisors for virtualization hosting multiple applications sharing resources. Also shown are shared storage systems in which various physical machines (PMs) or virtual machines (VMs) share storage or have dedicated LUNs, volumes, partitions, file systems, or virtual storage systems shown at the bottom of Figure 4.3.

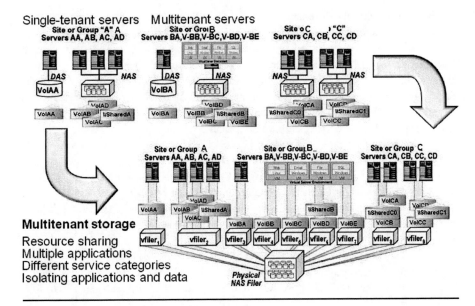

Figure 4.3   Server and storage multitenancy.

The challenge with multitenancy is that underlying resources are shared while keeping applications and their data logically separated. Various solutions provide different options for maintaining multitenant security and protection, with some being able to provide a subset of management capabilities or subordinated management. Subordinated management enables a subset of tasks or functions to be performed (for example, on a virtual machine or virtual file server or file system instance) without exposing other VMs or resource shares. An example of a multitenant storage solution similar to what is shown in Figure 4.3 is NetApp Multi-store; there are also many other offerings from various vendors.

4.4.4. Deciphering Encryption

A common theme among IT professionals is that there is a perception that encryption key management is a complexity barrier to implementation and that multiple levels of data security are needed to counter applicable threats. Another common concern is real or perceived lack of heterogeneous capability and vendor lock-in. Key management is thought to be a barrier for tape, disk (data at rest), and file system based security and, more important, tiered security.

In general, the overwhelming theme is that encryption key management is complex and that this complexity is a barrier to implementation. Not protecting data, particularly data in-flight, with encryption due to fears of losing keys is similar to not locking your car or home for fear of losing your keys. Key management solutions are available from various sources, with some solutions supporting multiple vendors' key formats and technologies.

Encryption should be used to protect data in-flight or during movement over logical (networks) as well as during physical movement. In addition to data in-flight, data at rest both for short- and for long-term preservation or archiving should be encrypted. There are many different approaches as well as locations for performing encryption. Encryption can be done in applications such as Oracle for database or Microsoft Exchange email, for example. Encryption can also be done via operating systems or file systems, or via third-party software, adapters, or drivers.

Encryption can be performed in many places:

- Cloud point of presence (cPOP) or access gateways
- Appliances that sit between servers and storage or networking devices
- IRM tools such as backup/restore, replication, and archiving tools
- I/O adapters, WAN devices, as well as with protocols such as TCP/IP IPSEC
- Storage systems in conjunction with appliances, within the controller
- Tape drives and self-encrypting disks (SEDs)

Additionally, encryption can be accomplished via software running on standard hardware as well as in conjunction with custom hardware (e.g., ASIC or FPGAs) in various combinations.

4.5. Securing Networks

There are several major areas of focus for securing storage and data networks. These include securing the network and its access or endpoints, securing data while in-flight along with where it is stored (locally or remote), and protecting network transports links along with management tools or interfaces. Network security involves physical and logical activities and techniques. Physical activities include firewalls, protecting endpoints and access to cabling and connectors, along with management tools or interfaces. Physical security can also mean having separate networks for different applications or functions.

Logical networking security involves access controls and password-protected tools for virtual private networks (VPNs), virtual LANs (VLANs), and virtual SANs (VSANs) that may be physically connected yet logically isolated for multitenant environments. Traditional network switches have been external physical devices for interconnecting various devices or users. With virtual servers there are also virtual switches implemented in memory as part of a hypervisor, which function similarly to a traditional physical switch. An example is the Cisco Nexus 1000v found in some VMware vSpehere environments.

Concerns for VPNs, VLANs, and VSANs include:

- Encryption of data in transit and while at rest
- Physical and logical media tracking (on/off premise)
- Firewalls and endpoint protection
- Data loss or leak protection along with proactive detection

- Proactive review and analysis of event logs, comparing to known baselines
- Proactive checks, scans, and alerts that leverage automation
- Key management for encryption of data at rest and while in-flight
- Employee, contractor, and supplier screening along with ongoing audit reviews
- For ultra secure applications, leverage dual or multiperson trust model
- For information that is important to retain, having multiple copies

A frequent question is whether the virtual switches are a networking issue or a server management topic, and where the line of demarcation is between the different groups. For some environments the solution is easier when the networking and server teams are part of a larger organization so that activities can be coordinated. For example, the networking team may grant server management personnel subordinate access to the virtual networking switch along with virtual monitoring tools, or vice versa.

Networking and I/O security topics and action items include:

- Secure management consoles, tools, and physical ports on IT technologies.
- Enable intrusion detection and alerts for IT resources.
- Check for network leakage, including lost bandwidth or device access.
- Physically secure networking devices, cabling, and access points.
- Protect against internal threats as well as external threats.
- Implement encryption of data at rest as well as data in-flight over networks.
- Limit access rights to certain IT resources while enabling productivity.
- Utilize VLANs and VSANs along with VPNs and firewall technologies.
- Implement Fibre Channel SAN zoning, authentication, and authorization.
- Enable physical security in addition to logical security.
- Use multiple layers of security for servers, storage, networks, and applications.
- Use private networks combined with applicable security and defense measures.
- Implement key and digital rights management across IT resources.

When looking at controlling access and isolating traffic within a single switch or director as well as in a single fabric of two or more switches, the following techniques can be used. Access control policies are implemented using binding to associate what devices, including servers, can attach to which ports as well as which switches and directors can attach to each other. Access control lists (ACLs) are created to authorize the connection between SAN components to implement security policies. These ACLs implement device to switch access policies (port binding), switch to switch (switch binding), and fabric binding. Binding is used to determine what devices can connect to each other, while zoning is used to determine what devices and ports see and communicate with each other.

Fabric-based World Wide Name (WWN) soft zoning is the commonly used industry standard, particularly in open heterogeneous environments. This provides flexibility to move a device from one port to another in a fabric without having to make a zone change. This implies that the zone follows the device; however, the zone is tied to that device. Should the device be changed, for example, when a tape drive is replaced, the zone must be modified to reflect this new device and its WWN. WWN and zoning have ramifications for virtual servers that are using Fibre Channel when a VM is moved from one PM to another and the hardware address changes. A solution is to use N_Port ID Virtualization (NPIV), where VMs establish their affinity to a virtual N_Port ID that is able to move with the VMs to a different PM without having to change zoning.

With the convergence of traditional networks and storage interfaces via storage networks, there is also a convergence of networking. At a minimum, a basic understanding of relative security mechanisms and their correlations are needed as IP and Ethernet move further into the storage-networking realm beyond NAS file sharing (NFS and CIFS) and for wide area communications. The counterpart of Fibre Channel zoning in the IP networking realm is VLAN (virtual LAN) Tagging, used to segment and isolate LAN traffic.

4.6. Securing Storage

Like securing networks, securing storage involves logical and physical approaches. Given that there are different types of storage devices, systems, and media to support various applications and usage, from high-performance on-line to low-cost removable, multiple approaches are needed. Protecting the endpoints—on one side, the applications and servers (virtual and physical) that access storage and on the other end, the storage itself—is part of the solution. Also involved is protecting the network on a local and a remote basis, as discussed in the previous section.

In general, techniques for protecting data on storage include physical safeguards, protecting access to storage systems, and monitoring fixed or removable media. Removable media include hard disk drives, FLASH solid-state devices, and magnetic tape. Other forms of removable media include CDs, DVDs, and other forms of optical media. Also included in removable media are USB FLASH thumb drives, PDAs, iPhones, Droids, and laptops.

One way of safeguarding data is to make sure that once it is written to a storage medium, it is in the correct format and readable as part of basic data integrity checks. Another form of preserving data is in storage media or systems that support Write Once Read Many (WORM), to ensure that data does not get changed or altered as part of securing it. Since storage can be accessed via block LUNs, devices, partitions, or volumes, a means of protecting access in shared or multitenant environment is LUN or volume mapping and masking.

With LUN or volume masking, only authorized servers are allowed to see the SCSI target when using a shared Fibre Channel or iSCSI SAN. LUN or volume mapping complements the masking or hiding process by enabling the different servers who see only their own storage to view an address as being unique to them. For example, if there are six servers, each accessing its own storage volume or LUN, with masking they would not see each other's storage in a shared environment. Similarly, with mapping, the LUN presented to each server could be numbered 1 to meet operating system requirements, yet each LUN 1 would be unique.

4.6.1. Removable Media Security

Some organizations are exploring virtual desktop solutions as a means of moving away from potential desktop data exposure and vulnerabilities. Many organizations are racing to encrypt laptops as well as desktops. Some organizations limit Universal Serial Bus (USB) ports for printer use only. Some organizations are also beefing up audit trails and logs to track what data was moved and copied where, when, and by whom. USB devices are seen as valuable tools, even given all of their risks, to be able to move and distribute data where networks don't exist or are not practical.

An evolving dimension to protecting data and securing virtual data centers is distributed remote offices and traveling or telecommuting workers who occupy virtual offices. The threat risks can be the same as for a primary traditional data center as well as others including loss or theft of laptops, workstations, PDAs, or USB thumb drives containing sensitive information. When it comes to security, virtual data centers require multiple levels of logical and physical security across different technology domains.

In addition to tape and optical media, another form of removable media includes various forms of FLASH SSDs ranging from thumb drives to PDAs, tablets- or high capacity devices. Removable hard disk drives (RHDDs), more common back in the 1970s and 1980s, have also reappeared. I myself utilize RHDDs for archiving and storing certain backups offsite in a secure safe. I also use cloud-based backup services in addition to local disk-to-disk (D2D) backups.

While lost tapes make the headlines, research indicates that there are, in fact, fewer actual tapes that go missing each year even though there are more reports. What this means is that in the past tapes were not reported missing if they were lost or stolen; however, given current regulations, the increased reporting can make it seem more common. What should be of concern are how many laptops, notebooks, PDAs, cell phones, or USB thumb drives get lost or stolen per month. Are these devices any less of a risk than a lost tape or disk drive? That depends, of course, on what data is stored on the missing device, but it is important to protect the data to be safe as well as to meet applicable compliance regulations.

4.7. Virtual Servers, Physical Servers, and Desktops

Securing storage and storage networking resources starts (or ends) at the server. At the server level, basic security begins with proper security of the individual file systems, directors, files, logical and physical volumes, and access to other storage resources. Access to storage management tools, including volume managers that can be used to provide a layer of abstraction also know as virtualization, should be restricted to those with the appropriate responsibility and capability to make configuration and provisioning changes. Access tools that can be used to affect the availability of storage resources, whether they be path managers for host bus adaptors (HBAs), volume managers, file systems, backup, mirroring, and storage configuration should be secured and safeguarded.

Depending on the environment, access to the servers themselves by system administrators, storage analysts, and database analysts may vary. For example, in some environments, storage resources are presented to a specific server via the storage network, with complete control and access to those resources (LUNs or volumes) at the discretion of the individual system administrator. The system administrator may in turn restrict access and allocation to specific volumes and resources to other administrators who are responsible for their specific pieces of storage. In other environments, a system administrator(s) may have complete end-to-end responsibly and capability to configure the storage network, the storage, and access to it.

Protection of virtual servers or VMs combines aspects of physical servers or PMs, storage, and network hardware and software. What changes with VMs is that another layer of technology is involved in the form of hypervisors or virtualization software. Hypervisors emulate servers, including presenting virtual CPUs, memory, network, and storage adapters, as well as virtual network switches. Security for VMs and virtual desktop infrastructure (VDI) environments includes protecting the guest operating systems and their applications, hypervisors, and underlying physical resources. In addition, when they are not active in memory, VMs are saved on storage as files that also need to be protected.

4.8. Securing Clouds

Many of the same issues, challenges, threats, and, consequently, techniques for networks, storage, and servers also apply to public and private clouds. Given the shared nature of public cloud and MSP resources, additional considerations include managing and monitoring the service provider. Auditing the providers includes reviewing relevant access or event logs along with physical review of facilities and services. This means applying the same management standards as in your own environment to service-provided solutions. Part of reviewing service provider offerings includes understanding who has access to your data and, if applicable, your applications and other resources.

Access to cloud resources is often via a management interface, cloud point of presence (cPOP) or gateway appliance whose management interfaces should be protected as would any other storage and networking device. Given that the value of many cloud providers is to leverage multitenancy, it is important to know how those services isolate your applications, data, and customers. For encrypted data, understand how keys are managed as well as who has access to the keys or other authentication material. Vital themes with clouds, whether public or private, are to be aware of the security, be prepared, and do your due diligence.

Another dimension to cloud or any remote service or destination including your own is how data will move between sites. Networks have gotten faster and bandwidth more plentiful as well as more reliable, accessible, and affordable. However, there is also more data to be moved in the same or less time than in the past. As a result, initial data migration or copy to a cloud service may require a bulk movement using removable media which will need to be secured. Once the initial copy is made, ongoing data access and movement can be done using secure networking techniques.

4.9. Disposing of Digital Assets and Technology

While most technologies and techniques are focused on protecting and preserving data, some of them also add complexity when it comes time to retire storage technologies. Part of data protection and security includes safely destroying digital data. This ranges from ensuring that hard disk drives and FLASH devices on PDAs, laptops, or work-stations are securely erased when discarded to digitally shredding terabytes or petabytes of data on large storage systems or across thousands of tape cartridges.

From a cost standpoint, if you have not already included time and expense to digi-tally destroy or erase disks and storage systems along with FLASH SSD and magnetic tapes when they are retired, now is the time to start doing so. For example, if you about to acquire a 100-TB storage solution, how long will it take to securely erase the data to meet your organization's requirement or application needs? What happens if, instead of 100 TB, the storage medium is 1 PB or 10 PB or larger? Now is the time to start includ-ing into your TCO and ROI models the time and cost to digitally shred or destroy data as part of your data migration activities.

Care should be taken when disposing of storage resources, including disks and tapes, when they are no longer needed. When magnetic tapes are no longer needed, have them properly disposed of, which might entail degaussing or burning. With disk subsystems and storage located in servers, workstations, desktops, and laptops, remove sensitive data and take appropriate steps, including reformatting disks if needed. Sim-ply deleting data can still leave the data recoverable by those interested in doing so. Servers, storage controllers, and switches, if applicable, should also be reset to factory configurations and have their NVRAM cleared.

Historically, digital shredding or secure erasure of data has required use of software or appliances that meet various regulatory or agency certification, for example, U.S. Department of Defense (DoD) secure erase codes using software running on a server or on an appliance that writes successive patterns to ensure the data is safely destroyed. Another means of intentionally destroying data is to degauss devices, which magneti-cally alters the recording medium. In addition, physical destruction techniques include drilling holes through devices such as disk drives and physically shredding disks and tapes. With today's focus on environmental health and safety (EH&S), burning of magnetic media is frowned on if not banned.

A new approach to securely and quickly destroying data involves self-encrypting disks (SEDs), which are being brought to market by various manufacturers including Seagate in conjunction with the Trusted Computing Group (TCG). SEDs are part of the TCG OPAL disk program for enabling disk drives to encrypt themselves in con-junction with servers or storage systems. Instead of relying on software on a server or appliance or within a storage system, the disk drive itself performs the encryption or decryption functions without performance penalties. For organizations that are unsure about using encryption, the side benefit of SEDs is that for most environments, once the SED is removed or its affinity with a given storage controller or server or laptop discontinued, the device is effectively shredded or deactivated. The device can be con-nected to a different controller or server, establishing a new affinity, but all previous data is lost.

Granted, for ultra-secure or sensitive organizations and agencies, additional safeguards should be used, but for most environments, SEDs provide another means to reduce the time required to digitally destroy old data before retiring technology. Consult with your manufacturer on its suggested procedure for safeguarding your information and ensuring that disposal of resources does not compromise your business information. If you have an office of sustainability or someone who handles EH&S, also confer with them along with your security or compliance personnel as to what should be in your specific policies.

4.10. Security Checklist

While far from an exhaustive list, the following provides some basic items pertaining to storage and storage networking security:

- Restrict and limit access to physical components, including networking cables.
- Disable management interfaces and access when not being used.
- Restrict (local and remote) to those who need access to management tools.
- Secure and rationalize access to equipment for vendor support and maintenance.
- Evaluate use of SNMP MIBs and agents.
- Manage maintenance ports, including remote dial-in/dial-out as well as email.
- Utilize storage-based LUN/volume mapping/masking for access control.
- Persistent binding should be combined with some other security mechanism.
- Audit the auditors as well as service providers.

4.11. Common Security-Related Questions

What is the best technology and location at which to do encryption? The best technology and approach is the one that works for you and your environment and that enables encryption without introducing complexity or barriers to productivity. Your environment may require different solutions for various applications or focus areas from a single or multiple vendors. Avoid being scared of encryption for fear of losing keys, performance impacts, or increased complexity. Instead, look at different solutions that complement and enable your environment.

What level of audit trails and logging are needed? Maintain audit trails of who has accessed or made copies of data, with emphasis on more logging and event analysis. As important as what information you collect is how you use and preserve logs for analysis or forensic purposes. Leverage automation tools that can proactively monitor activities and events as well as indentify normal vs. abnormal behaviors.

Who should be responsible for security? Some organizations have dedicated security groups that set policies, do some research, and some forensics while leaving actual work to other groups. Some security organizations are more active, with their own budgets, servers, storage, and software. Security needs to be a part of activity early on in application and architecture decision making as well as across multiple technology domains (servers, storage, networking, hardware, and software) and not just via a policy maker in an ivory tower.

4.12. Chapter Summary

The most secure environment for your data and information resources is also one that inhibits usability. The by-products of having inhibitive security is impacted productivity and the steps people will take to work around the barriers. At the other extreme are completely open environments with little to no security and free access by anyone from anywhere. This results in sensitive information intentionally or accidentally placed there for others to see, share, or exploit. The level of security should be consistent with the risk for your facility or business based on what you do or who you do it for. For example, if at home you are a high-profile figure, you will probably have a high degree of security, including barriers, alarms, cameras, and extra door locks. The same holds true for where you are storing and processing as well as delivering information services, including minimizing calling attention to what your site is doing.

The right approach for your environment will depend on your needs and service requirements. You may find multiple tiers or domains of security that vary by application or information services function or audience focus to be the most workable. The important point is to understand that there are various threat risks, both internal and external, that have different ramifications. Understanding those threat risks along with subsequent exposure combined with knowledge of different techniques, technologies, and best practices results in an effective data security strategy.

Security for storage and storage networking has taken on increased importance, particularly as storage traverses external interfaces. It is easy to look at all the possible threats and fall into a defensive mindset or paradigm. Instead, shift to a strong offense, where security is used as a tool and enabler as opposed to a barrier to productivity. Security solutions need to be easy to acquire, install, set up and configure, and maintain with access to activity logs and notification capabilities. Establishing rings or perimeters of defenses using techniques discussed in this chapter can help safeguard your data. The last line of defense for your storage and storage network is at the storage itself.

General action items include:

- Gain situational awareness to eliminate dark territory or blind spots.
- Establish layers of defense, leveraging physical and logical technologies.
- Don't let security become a barrier to productivity.
- Educate users that awareness of security issues is part of a good defense.
- Many issues are common across physical, virtual, and cloud environments
- Establish a security model that enables while protecting.

Industry trade groups and other relevant organizations or agencies include ANSI T10 (SCSI) and T13 (ATA), CERT, FIPS, IETF, NIST, SNIA, and TCG, to name a few. Vendors with security-related solutions include CA, Cipheroptics, Citrix, Cisco, EMC RSA, Dell, HP, IBM, Intel/McAfee, Kaspersky, Microsoft, NetApp, NetSpi, Oracle, PHP, Seagate, Symantec, Trend, and VMware.

Chapter 5

Data Protection: Backup/Restore and Business Continuance/ Disaster Recovery

Information security: To protect, preserve, and serve.

– Greg Schulz

In This Chapter

- The difference between business continuance (BC) and disaster recovery (DR)
- The importance of an effective data protection plan and strategy
- Why it is time to modernize backup and data protection
- How to reduce costs by using tiered data protection and different technologies

This chapter looks at issues, challenges, and opportunities for protecting data in cloud, virtual, and data storage networks. The focus of data protection in this chapter is on maintaining availability and accessibility of both active and inactive data. In the context of this chapter, data protection builds on the previous chapter's subject of security by expanding our focus to information accessibility and maintenance of data integrity. Key themes, buzzwords, and trends addressed in this chapter include high availability (HA), backup and restore, business continuance (BC) and disaster recovery (DR) along with replication and snapshot-related technologies.

5.1. Getting Started

Mention "DP" to people in IT and, depending on their area of interest and their length of experience, you may get answers such as Dual Platter, Dedupe Performance, Data Processing, Double or Dual Parity, or perhaps even Dance Partner from someone more creatively inclined. For the purposes of this chapter, DP is data protection.

"Data loss" can be a misleading idea: If your data is intact but you cannot get to it when needed, is the data really "lost"? There are many types of data loss, including loss of accessibility or availability and complete loss. Loss of data availability means that somewhere—perhaps off-line on a removable disk, optical drive, tape, or at another site on-line, near-line, or off-line—your data is still intact, but you cannot get to it. There is also real data loss, where both your primary copy and backup as well as archive data are lost, stolen, corrupted, or never actually protected.

Protection of data and information services delivery applies to:

- Workgroups, departments, and remote offices/branch offices (ROBOs)
- Enterprise, small to medium-size business (SMB)
- Small office/home office (SOHO) and consumer environments
- Workstations, laptops, and mobile devices
- Physical and virtual servers, workstations and desktops
- Managed service providers, public and private clouds
- Integrated stacks, converged and unified solutions

5.2. Data Protection Challenges and Opportunities

IT organizations of all sizes are tasked with the basic responsibilities of protecting, preserving, and serving information services when needed. Since new data is continuously created while old data must continuously be handled, there is more data to process, move, and store for longer periods of time than there was even yesterday. Consumers of IT services are dependent on applications and data being readily available and protected by BC and DR activities. A challenge for many organizations is how to balance the cost to protect against various threat risks, regulatory and other compliance requirements, and the demand to protect, preserve, and serve more data for longer periods of time in an economical manner.

Data protection trends and challenges include:

- More data to process, move, protect, preserve, and serve
- Shifting data lifecycle and access patterns while retaining data longer
- Continued focus on cost containment or reductions
- Reliance on information services accessible when and where needed
- Increase in mobile-generated and -accessed information services
- Cloud, virtualized, dynamic, and flexible computing
- Outages resulting from human error or design deficiency

There are other challenges related to protecting data and applications in physical, virtual, and cloud environments. For example, in a nonvirtualized server environment, the loss of a physical server impacts the applications running on that server. In a highly aggregated or consolidated environment, the loss of a physical server supporting many virtual machines (VMs) has a much more significant impact, affecting all the applications supported by the virtual servers. Another challenge is protecting the growing amount of structured and unstructured data in primary data centers along with data in ROBOs, workgroups, field offices, and other locations.

Data protection opportunities include:

- Stretch available budgets further to protect and preserve more data longer.
- Maximize return on investment (ROI) in capital and operating expenditures.
- Improve quality of service (QoS), service-level agreements (SLAs) and service-level objectives (SLOs), including recovery-time objectives (RTOs) and recovery-point objectives (RPOs).
- Modernize data protection including backup/restore and BC/DR.
- Reduce cost of services delivered via improved efficiencies.
- Provide protection of cloud, virtual, and physical resources.
- Leverage cloud and virtualization technologies to mask complexities.
- Reconcile and streamline protection frequencies and retention cycles.

5.3. Protect, Preserve, and Serve Information Services

Disaster recovery (DR) can mean different things to different people; however, for the purposes of this chapter it will mean two things. The first is an overall process, paradigm, or set of best practices that spans across different technology groups and organizational boundaries. The second are the steps taken as a last resort to reconstruct or rebuild, reconfigure, restore, reload, rollback, restart, and resume information and organizational services or functionality in the event of a severe incident or catastrophe. Business continuance (BC) and DR are often used interchangeably to mean the same thing. We will treat them separately, with business continuance focused on disaster prevention, surviving a disaster or incident, and keeping the business running, and disaster recovery as the process of putting all of the pieces back together again if HA, BC, and other steps were either not taken or failed.

Threat risks to information services delivery requiring data protection include:

- More data being generated, stored, and used remotely
- Funding constraints coupled with increased demands
- Accidental or intentional deletion and data corruption
- Operating system, application software, server, or storage failure
- Loss of access to site, servers, storage, or networking resources
- Acts of nature or acts of man, headline and nonheadline incidents
- Local site, campus, metropolitan, regional, or global incidents

- Business or regulatory compliance requirements
- Increased awareness of threat risks and reliance on information services
- Technology failure or inappropriate configuration design
- Planned or scheduled and unscheduled downtime
- Network or communications disruptions including cables being cut
- Problems introduced via configuration changes

Table 5.1 shows various situations or scenarios in which information services have been or could be impacted. The scenarios or situations are categorized into different levels that can be used to help determine what type of data protection to apply to counter applicable threat risks.

Table 5.1 Protecting Against Various Levels of Threats and Impending Risks

Level	Description of Incident or Scenario
1	Systems are running alerts warning of potential threat and disruption received
2	Hardware, software, network, or facilities component has failed
3	Single system or application disruption
4	Single major disruption or multiple lower-level incidents
5	Metropolitan or campus disaster
6	Major local or regional disaster

- *Level 1: Systems are running; alerts or advance warning of potential threat and disruption have been received.* Notification or indications of possible threat or service disruption have been received, ranging from a virus or security issue to a system potentially being compromised or a hardware device logging errors or software indicating that consistency checks should be taken. Weather reports might indicate an approaching storm, or acts of civil unrest or other threats may be anticipated. Left unchecked, or not corrected, Level 1 threats may escalate to a higher threat level or, worse, a rolling disaster.
- *Level 2: A hardware, software, or network/facilities component has failed.* Business functionality has not yet been disrupted. Business functions, information services, and their applications remain operational. The incident might be a failure in a component such as a disk drive, storage controller, server, network path, power supply, or other item that is being protected by redundancy and automatic failover. The threat might also be a virus, software, or data correctable error leveraging a translation log or journal rollback. There is vulnerability of a multiple failure during the repair process escalating into a disaster.
- *Level 3: Single system or application disruption.* Overall business or information services remain available, but some functionally is not currently available. An entire system or application (hardware, software, and network) may have failed or been shut down due to a facilities issue such as circuit breaker or zone cooling issue. Some disruption may occur during failover to a standby site if available

or, if the disruption will be extensive in length, restoration from backup media. Failback occurs when resources are ready, safe, and stable. Databases may be read-only until updates can resume.

- *Level 4: Single major disruption or multiple lower-level incidents.* The data center exists and most systems are functional, but some Level 2 or 3 scenarios may be occurring. Performance may be slow due to rebuild, failover, or loss of primary systems placing heavy demand on standby resources. Disruption may be hardware-, applications-, or data-related. Resolution may require failover to a standby system with good data or restoration from a known good copy or snapshot.
- *Level 5: Metropolitan or campus disaster.* The data center, information, and resources are intact, but access to them has been lost for some period of time due to a localized incident. If a standby or failover site is available in a different location, service may resume; otherwise, recovery occurs elsewhere.
- *Level 6: Major local or regional disaster.* Loss or damage to facilities and related infrastructure, including power, water, communications, or personnel, due to acts of nature (flood, earthquake, hurricane) or acts of man, including terrorism. A determination is made that the primary site will not be available/accessible for an extended period of time, resulting in major disruption to business function for any applications not protected via HA or BC.

Different types or levels (Table 5.1) of disasters or incidents can be localized to a given site, campus, metropolitan, regional, or global basis. Understanding the applicable data protection threat risks or scenarios along with the likelihood of their occurrence and subsequent impact to the business is part of technology or service alignment. The importance of technology and data protection service alignment is to make sure that an appropriate level of protection is applied when and where needed to stretch available budgets as far as possible.

Figure 5.1 shows how distance can be part of enabling business or information services survivability to different threat risks for some environments or applications. If applications or services are focused only on a local or metropolitan audience, then regional or global forms of protection may not be required. Granted, they may be nice to have, and if affordable, then practical.

Distance is important for enabling data protection and survivability. While distance is often thought of in terms of physical space, time can also be a function of distance. This means being able to go back to a particular place or point from which data was copied or protected—known as a recovery-point objective (RPO).

Physical distance can be measured in inches, feet or meters, kilometers or miles. How would distance of inches be enough to enable data protection? By having data on two different storage devices located next to each other in case one fails. However, there would still be a point of failure if the server or storage system in which they were installed failed. The next logical step would be to have data on two different storage devices, which might be feet or meters apart in the same facility, to isolate and protect against device failure. Here the single point of failure would be the site or facility; this can be mitigated by having copies of data on different systems spread across a campus, metropolitan area, and region or on a global basis.

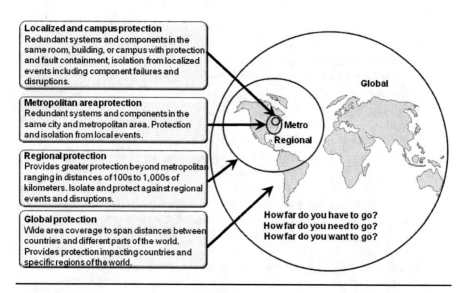

Localized and campus protection
Redundant systems and components in the same room, building, or campus with protection and fault containment, isolation from localized events including component failures and disruptions.

Metropolitan area protection
Redundant systems and components in the same city and metropolitan area. Protection and isolation from local events.

Regional protection
Provides greater protection beyond metropolitan ranging in distances of 100s to 1,000s of kilometers. Isolate and protect against regional events and disruptions.

Global protection
Wide area coverage to span distances between countries and different parts of the world. Provides protection impacting countries and specific regions of the world.

Global

Metro
Regional

How far do you have to go?
How far do you need to go?
How far do you want to go?

Figure 5.1 Protecting against various threat risks to data and information services.

5.3.1. Basic Information Reliability–Availability–Serviceability (RAS)

As the name implies, basic information services availability means limited or no data protection. This could mean that backups occur now and then with no recurring or regular frequency. Availability may be limited to servers or storage that lack failover or redundancy components, for example, storage that lacks RAID (redundant array of independent disks) data availability capabilities or redundant power supplies and cooling fans. Basic availability can be enhanced by increasing the frequency of backups, ensuring that important information is copied to different locations.

In addition to making copies of data that are stored in different locations (a local copy on disk, another copy on a fileserver, another stored at an off-site cloud or managed service provider site), retention is also important. Retention means how long those copies are kept before being deleted or destroyed. For example, if you have multiple copies of data that all expire after 14 days and you are only making copies of data once a week, if something goes wrong with the last backups, you may be facing a disaster situation. On the other hand, having too many copies for too long adds to the cost of protecting data. Managing threat risks needs to be balanced with available budgets as well as business needs.

Other common constraints for data protection include:

- Growing amount of data to protect and preserve
- Time including backup or protection windows
- Budgets (capital and operating)
- Technology interoperability or interdependencies
- Software license restrictions

- Lack of automation, reporting, or analytics for data protection
- False positives when diagnosing problems
- Staffing and in-house expertise
- Cross-technology ownership issues
- Upper management buy-in, support, or sign-off
- Policies or lack there of
- Workflow and paperwork overhead

Items that need to be addressed or included in a data protection plan include:

- Facilities—Floor space, primary and secondary power, cooling, fire suppression
- Networking services—LAN, SAN, MAN, and WAN voice and data services
- Security—Physical and logical security including encryption key management
- Monitoring and management—Infrastructure resource management (IRM)
- Diagnostics tools—End-to-end tools for analysis and troubleshooting
- Software—Applications, middleware, databases, operating systems, hypervisors
- Hardware—Servers, storage, networking, workstations, and desktops
- High availability, backup/restore, snapshots and replication, media maintenance
- Best practices—Documentation, communication, change control
- Testing and audits—Review of plans and processes, random testing of activities

5.3.2. High Availability and Business Continuance

Think of high availability (HA) and business continuance (BC) as disaster prevention. Disaster prevention refers to containing or isolating faults from rolling into a larger event or disaster scenario. Essentially, enabling HA and BC means taking adequate steps within reason as well as budget constraints to eliminate or minimize the impacts of various incidents on information services delivery—in other words, enabling information services to actually service in the face of a disaster. Disaster recovery (DR), on the other hand, involves rebuilding, restoring, recovering, restarting, and resuming business after an incident that could not, within reason or budget, be contained.

Enabling HA and BC involves eliminating single points of failure and containing or isolating faults from spreading by using redundant components and failover software. In addition to hardware, software, and networking redundancy on a local as well as remote basis, another important aspect of both IRM in general and data protection specifically is change control. Change control means testing and validating hardware, software, application, or other configuration changes before they are implemented, updating applicable documents as part of workflow management, and having a plan in case the change does not work.

Having a fallback plan or process to back out of the change quickly can help keep a minor incident from escalating. A simple approach to change management is to have multiple copies of the configurations, applications, or data that is being updated, which can be reapplied if needed. Part of change control management should also be a determination of the interdependences of a change and associated remediation.

Not all incidents or outages are the result of a major disaster. As mentioned above, some can be the result of component failures or faults that were left uncontained and therefore expanded into a disaster. There is also the possibility that an IT environment can be reduced to physical ruins by a fire, flood, hurricane, tornado, or explosion caused by an accident or act of man. In other situations, an IT environment may be completely intact but not usable as a result of loss of access to a facility. For example, an area might be evacuated due to a chemical spill from a truck or railroad car. If the site is automated, with intervention available via remote access, the disruption may be minimal to nonexistent unless utilities were also cut. Having on-site standby electrical power and self-contained cooling would mitigate those risks; however, what about communications for networks along with adequate fuel supplies for backup generators and cooling water?

In other, less drastic, incidents, all hardware, networks, and software may be intact but a data corruption or error occurs, requiring rapid restoration to a previous point in time. If a recent snapshot can be rapidly recalled and restored, log or journal files applied, and integrity and consistency checks completed, the outage can be kept to a minimum. If, instead, you have to wait for data to be brought back on-site, reloaded, and then rollbacks along with consistency checks performed, that will take more time. This is where data protection comes back to a balance of cost versus risk to the business and the value of time. Not all applications will have the same time sensitivity, so not all data and applications should be protected the same way. Aligning the data protection strategy with the sensitivity of the data is one way of maximizing budgets and resources.

5.3.3. Disaster Recovery

As mentioned earlier, disaster recovery can be thought of in two ways, one being the overall process of ensuring business and organizational survivability and the other being the activities involved in reconstructing an environment after an incident. Basic RAS (reliability–availability–serviceability), HA, and BC can all be considered part of enabling an overall DR plan and strategy. The last line of defense to various threat levels (Table 5.1) in DR is the process of reconstructing, restoring, and resuming after a major disaster or incident beyond the abilities of HA and BC to cope (Figure 5.2).

What could cause a disaster and what would create only a minor inconvenience to information services delivery? For example, would a short outage of a few minutes result in any data loss, or simply loss of access to data for a short period of time? What would happen if the short outage turned into a day or longer? Figure 5.2 shows examples of normal running states with various forms of data protection occurring at different frequencies and retention lengths to combat various incidents or disaster scenarios.

Part of supporting growth or increasing business demands while reducing costs and maintaining or enhancing quality of service involves aligning the applicable level of data protection to the likely threat risk scenario. What threats or incidents are most likely to occur, and what would be the impact on your organization if they were not remedied? How much protection do you want, how much do you need, and what can you afford? Put a different way, what can you afford not to do, and what is the sub-sequent impact to specific information services, applications, functions, or the entire business or organization?

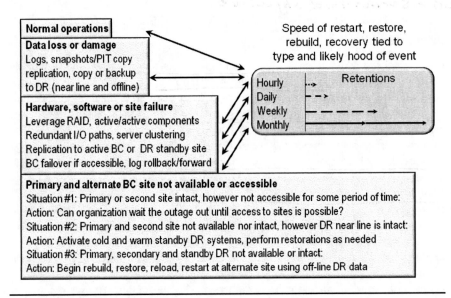

Figure 5.2 RAS, HA, BC, and DR as part of a data protection strategy.

5.3.4. Data Protection vs. Preservation (Backup vs. Archive)

While the two functions are related, backup is focused on protecting data with the intention of it being usable for recovery to a given point in time (the RPO), and archiving is aimed at preserving the state of data or an application for possible future use. They may sound similar, but they differ in retention cycles and in the frequency or interval at which backups are made versus archives.

Archives are usually retained for longer periods of time, such as years, while backups are typically retained for days, weeks, or months. Archives can be established for regulatory compliance purposes as well as to preserve intellectual property (IP) or project data for possible future use. Additionally, archives are used as part of data footprint reduction (DFR) as a means of migrating less frequently used or accessed data off-line or to another medium such as disk, tape, or cloud to reduce online or active storage space needs. The benefit of archiving databases, email, and Microsoft SharePoint or file systems is to free up space while reducing the amount of data that needs to be backed up or protected.

Backups and archives can use the same software and target hardware or service while implementing different policies and business practices. The main difference is that archiving is focused on saving the context of data and applications as of a point in time for long-term retention in case it's needed. Backup, on the other hand, preserves the context of data and applications as of a point in time for routine restoration of a single file or dataset object or database table. Archiving as a tool to optimize storage capacity will be discussed further in Chapter 8.

SLA - Service-level agreement
SLO - Service-level objective

5.4. SLO and SLAs: How Much Availability Do You Need vs. Want

Costs associated with data availability need to be understood to determine availability objectives. Vendors use terms such as "five 9s," "six 9s," or higher to describe their solutions' availability. It is important to understand that availability is the sum of all components combined with design for fault isolation and containment. Seconds of downtime per year are shown in Table 5.2. How much availability you need and can afford will be a function of your environment, application and business requirements, and objectives.

Availability is only as good as the weakest link in a chain. In the case of a data center, that weakest link might be the applications, software, servers, storage, network, facilities, processes, or best practices. This means that, for example, installing a single converged SAN and LAN networking switch with "five 9s" or better availability could create a single point of failure. Keep in mind that the failure may be technology-related, a configuration issue, a software update failure, or something as simple as someone unplugging a physical network connection cable. Virtual data centers rely on physical resources to function; a good design can help eliminate unplanned outages to compensate for failure of an individual component. A good design removes complexity while providing scalability, stability, ease of management and maintenance, as well as fault containment and isolation. Design for both maintenance and to contain or isolate faults from spreading, as well as to balance risk, or the likelihood of something happening to required service levels and cost.

Table 5.2 Availability Expressed as a Number of "9s"

Availability (%)	Number of 9s	Amount of Downtime Per Year
99	Two	3.65 days
99.9	Three	8.77 hours
99.99	Four	52.6 minutes
99.999	Five	6.26 minutes
99.9999	Six	31.56 seconds
99.99999	Seven	3.16 seconds
99.999999	Eight	½ second

RPO - recovery-point objective
RTO - recovery-time objective

5.4.1. RTO and RPO: Balancing Data Availability vs. Time and Budgets

Figure 5.3 shows a timeline example that includes a gap in data coverage between where and when data was last protected and where it can be recovered. Also shown are various component recovery time objectives, such as when hardware becomes available for use for operating systems or hypervisors, data, and applications. While server hardware, hypervisor, and operating system RTOs are important, as are storage and data restoration RTOs, the overall application RTO is what matters to the consumer of the information service or application. Figure 5.3 shows that there are different RTOs that need to be aligned to meet the cumulative service objective for a given class or category of service.

If a given application or information service has, as an example, a 4-hour RTO, it is important to understand what that RTO means. Make sure you know whether the 4-hour RTO is cumulative and when application users or consumers of services can expect to be able to resume work, or whether the RTO is for a given component (Figure 5.3). If the RTO of 4 hours is cumulative, then all other sub-RTOs for data restoration, operating system and hypervisors, database rebuilds or rollbacks, and verification must fit within that 4-hour window.

A common mistake is that multiple groups learn that the RTO is, continuing the example, 4 hours and assume that means they each have 4 hours to complete their required tasks. While some tasks may be done in parallel, some—such as data restoration followed by database verification or rebuild and application verification—are usually done serially; if each team assumes they have 4 hours to complete their task, the 4-hour cumulative RTO cannot be achieved.

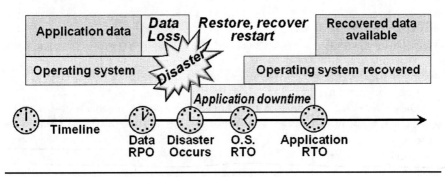

Figure 5.3   End-to-end recovery-time objectives.

5.4.2. Reconciling and Assessing RTO and RPO Requirements

Earlier, we discussed the importance of not treating all applications or data the same so as to do more with what you have while enhancing quality of service. For data protection and availability this is also true, in that an incorrect assumption as to what level of service is desired vs. what is required can increase costs. This means assessing actual availability requirements against what would be nice to have, to be able to align the applicable classes or categories of service and underlying technologies to a given situation.

With a continued industry trend toward using disk-to-disk (D2D) backup for more frequent and timely data protection, tape is finding a renewed role in larger, more infrequent backups for large-scale disaster recovery supporting long-term archiving and data preservation of project data and compliance data. For example, D2D, combined with compression and de-duplication disk-based solutions, is used for local, daily and recurring backups that have shorter retention but that have more granularities (Figure 5.4). Meanwhile, weekly or monthly full backups are sent to disk at a secondary location, cloud server, or to tape, to free disk space as well as address PCFE concerns. These copies occur less often so there are not as many of them, but they are retained for longer periods of time.

By reconciling and tuning data protection frequencies along with retention cycles (Figure 5.4), the overhead of protecting data can be reduced while increasing survivability in a cost-effective manner. The principal idea is that for more commonly occurring incidents, recovery or restart occurs more often, faster, and with more ease than traditional data protection. D2D data protection combined with data footprint reduction (DFR) techniques means more copies of protected data can be kept closer to where it will be needed at a lower cost. Meanwhile, copies of data that are less likely to be accessed occur in longer cycles and are sent to off-line or cloud facilities.

By not aligning the applicable service level along with reviewing service-level objectives (SLOs) and service-level agreements (SLAs), situations where two parties wrongly assume what the other wanted or needed can be avoided. For example, IT or a service provider assumes that a given application requires the highest level of availability and data protection because that is what the business unit, customer liaison, advocate, or consumers indicated that they would like. However, the consumers or customer representatives thought that they would need the highest level of service without considering the cost ramifications or verifying what they actually needed. Upon review of what is actually required, there is sometimes a difference from the level of service being delivered. When questioned about SLOs or SLAs, business or IT services consumers may want to have the higher level of service, but some due diligence may show that they do not actually need it, and this can help stretch their budget.

The previous is an example of a disconnect between customer/consumer and IT services management. If IT understands their services and costs and works with their customers, the applicable level of capabilities can be delivered. In some cases IT services customers may be surprised to find that IT-provided services are cost effective when compared to cloud and MSP solutions on the same SLO and SLA services basis.

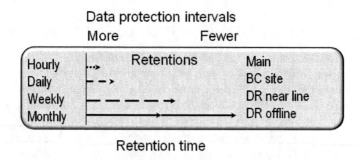

Figure 5.4   Reconciling and tuning data protection intervals and retention cycles.

5.4.3. Tiered Data Protection

Tiered data protection (Figure 5.5) is similar in concept to tiered hypervisors, servers, storage, and networks, in that different types of related technologies exist to meet various needs. The idea of resource tiering is to map the applicable technology or tool in such a way that it meets service requirements in a cost-effective manner. A key theme is to align data protection techniques to meet specific RTOs and RPOs along with other service criteria and cost needs.

Figure 5.5 shows an example of different applications or information services with various service criteria (e.g., RTOs and RPOs). Note that the applications shown along the top of Figure 5.5 do not necessarily correspond one to one with the various data protection techniques shown along the bottom. The important point is that some applications require RTOs and RPOs of zero or close to zero and need technologies such as synchronous replication, data mirroring combined with snapshots, or continuous data protection across multiple sites. Other applications may require clustered servers and highly available storage but can tolerate time delays associated with longer-distance replication or as a means to reduce cost for shorter-distance leveraged asynchronous replication. Applications that need small or zero RPOs will need to have data protection that corresponds to those requirements, while other applications may tolerate longer RTOs and RPOs with longer data protection intervals.

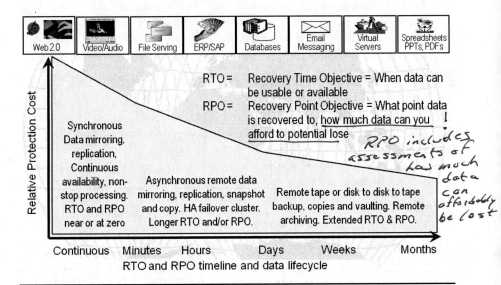

Figure 5.5   Tiered data protection.

5.5. Common-Sense Data Protection

Common-sense data protection (CDP) means complete data protection. Complete data protection means that all data is flushed from applications, databases, file systems, operating systems, and hypervisor buffers to a storage medium before copies (backup, snapshots, and replication) are performed. The importance of quiescence (quieting) applications and capturing all data and information is to establish and preserve the state or transactional integrity of the data as of a given point in time.

Complete and comprehensive data protection architectures should combine multiple techniques and technologies to meet various RTO and RPO requirements. For example, virtual machine (VM) movement or migration tools such as VMware VMotion provide proactive movement for maintenance or other operational functions. These tools can be combined with third-party data movers, including replication solutions, to enable VM crash restart and recovery or basic availability. Such combinations assume that there are no issues with dissimilar physical hardware architectures in the virtualized environment. It is important to be aware of the motivators and drivers for data protection of a virtual server environment when creating the architecture.

Another aspect of common-sense data protection is that if data is important enough to be backed up or replicated, or if it needs to be archived for planned or possible future use, then the data is important enough to make multiple copies. Making multiple copies also means placing copies in different locations on multiple media—for example, a copy on disk locally for rapid recall, a copy at a managed service provider or cloud provider, and a "gold" or master copy on tape or some other medium, "just in case." The idea is that, for critical information, reducing risk for what is most likely to occur and having cost-effective options is a top priority. This means having multiple tiers of data protection aligned to various needs, requirements, and threat risks. If all of your data is copied and protected in the cloud or at a managed service provider, what happens when (not if!) you lose access to that data? On the other hand, if your data is simply copied locally or at an alternate site, what happens if you lose access?

Having options that do not cost more than what the threat risk impact would impose on your organization enables the continued delivery of services. Aligning the right level of service to a given application's or business function's needs is an aspect of business impact analysis. Also keep in mind that loss of access to data is different than loss of data. For example, there have been incidents where customers are not able to get to their data, which at first may appear or be reported as data loss. In reality, the data is intact on some other medium or in a different location that is not yet accessible by the customer. In that type of situation the RPO may be zero or close to zero, meaning no data loss. However, if you cannot get to your data and your RTO requirements require no loss of access, then you cannot wait and need to initiate a recovery or restart. That recovery or restart may involve going to a backup copy of data, perhaps a recent snapshot or D2D copy or, worst case, to an old archive. The difference between the data from the backup and the data at the time of the loss of access may be an actual data loss. If your environment requires very low RTOs, then additional steps, discussed later in this chapter, should also be taken to avoid having to go to a stale backup or deep cold archive.

5.6. Virtual, Physical, and Cloud Data Protection

There are several approaches to achieve server virtualization, including Citrix/Xen, Microsoft Hyper-V, and VMware vSphere, as well as vendor-specific containers or

partitions. Many of the data protection issues are consistent across different environments, with specific terminology or nomenclature. <u>Virtual server environments often</u>
<u>provide tools to facilitate maintenance</u> and basic data protection while <u>lacking tools</u>
<u>for complete data protection or BC/DR</u>. Instead, virtual server vendors provide APIs,
other tools, or solution/software development kits (SDKs) so that their ecosystem partners can develop solutions for virtual and physical environments. For example, solutions from VMware, Citrix, and Microsoft include SDKs and APIs to support pre- and
postprocessing actions for customization and integration with Site Recovery Manager
(SRM), or Microsoft Hyper-V Quick Migration.

Additional cloud, virtual, and physical data protection considerations include:

- RTO and RPO requirements per application, VM guest, or physical server
- How much data changes per day, application-aware data protection
- Performance and application service-level objectives per application
- The distance over which the data and applications need to be protected
- The granularity of recovery needed (file, application, VM/guest, server, site)
- Data retention including short-term and longer-term preservation (archive)
- Data usage and access patterns or requirements to meet business needs
- Hardware, network, or software dependencies or requirements
- Focus on doing more with less or doing more with what you have

Another consideration when comparing data protection techniques, technologies, and implementations is application-aware data protection. Application-aware
data protection approaches ensure that all data associated with an application,
including software, configuration settings, data, and the current state of the data
or transactions, is preserved. To achieve true application-aware and comprehensive
data protection, all data, including memory-resident buffers and caches pertaining
to the current state of the application, needs to be written to disk. At a minimum,
application-aware data protection involves quiescence of file systems and open files
data to be written to disk prior to a snapshot, backup, or replication operation. Most
VM environments provide tools and APIs to integrate with data protection tasks,
including prefreeze (preprocessing) and postthaw (postprocessing) for application
integration and customization.

5.6.1. Tools and Technologies

The basic tool for enabling data protection is common sense or, if you like jargon,
common-sense data protection (CDP), leveraging such ideas as that any technology
can fail if humans are involved. Another tenet is designing for maintenance and fault
isolation or containment, maintaining data protection as a proactive piece of your data
infrastructure strategy rather than just an afterthought. Knowing that technology can
fail due to various reasons, the objective is to align different tools, techniques, techniques, and best practices to mitigate or isolate small incidents from cascading into
larger disasters.

Another aspect of CDP is to make sure that all data is protected, including whatever is still in application, database, file system, or operating system buffers when a snapshot, CDP, or replication operation is performed; everything needs to be flushed to disk to be protected. Common-sense data protection also means balancing threat risks with the likelihood of a given scenario occurring and its impact to your organization or specific application against the cost. This means not treating all data or applications the same, and applying the applicable level of protection to a given threat risk and cost of availability that is needed.

Various tools and techniques can be used for enabling a flexible, scalable, resilient data infrastructure to support cloud, virtual, and physical environments. Tools include data and application migration or conversion, IT management along with asset discovery, tracking, and configuration management databases. Other tools include physical-to-virtual (P2V) migration, virtual-to-virtual (V2V) migration, and virtual-to-physical (V2P) migration, and automation such as using tape libraries that reduce the need for manual intervention. Policy managers, which can be located at different locations, can also help with automation of common tasks when an event occurs, or with manual intervention taking action involving other tools in a prescribed manner. Automated failover of software and redundant hardware including clustering or path managers for applications, operating systems, hypervisors, servers, storage, and networking are also tools for data protection.

Systems or storage resource management (SRM) and systems or storage resource analysis (SRA) tools are needed for insight and situational awareness, providing reporting along with proactive event correlation analysis. The importance of event correlation and analysis is to be able to identify where actual issues are, to avoid chasing false positives. False positives occur when a given diagnosis points to a technology or configuration that is then repaired, after which it is learned that it was not the real problem, but rather a result of the real issue. Change control and configuration management are also important tools and techniques for enabling resilient environments, to make sure things are configured correctly and tested before being put into production and thus to catch potential errors before they occur.

Additional tools and technologies for enabling data protection include:

- Application plug-ins for backup, snapshots, replication, and failover
- Data protection management (DPM) tools for tracking, alerting, and analysis
- Data protection coverage or exposure analysis tools
- Media tracking and management technologies
- Software management media such as tape read verification analyzers
- Archiving, backup/restore, CDP, snapshots, and replication tools
- Data footprint reduction tools including compression and de-duplication
- Test and diagnostic tools for servers, storage, and networks
- Security and encryption tools and key management
- Automatic rebuild along with RAID
- Dual or redundant I/O networking paths and components
- Change control and configuration management

- Testing and auditing of technology, processes, and procedures
- Routine background data, storage, and networking data integrity checks
- Network Data Management Protocol (NDMP) for protecting NAS devices
- API support including VMware vSphere, Microsoft VSS, and Symantec OST

Source-side tools, which are technologies used for collecting or gathering data to be protected while facilitating recovery or restoration, can reside on clients or on servers. Clients may be workstations, laptops, or hand-held devices as well as virtual and physical servers. In the context of data protection, servers' source-side tools include backup or data protection servers on which data is copied or staged before being sent to a local, remote, or cloud virtual or physical device. Servers in this context serve an intermediary role between the items being protected, such as database or application servers, remote client desktops, or mobile laptops.

Intermediary servers may be referred to as a backup or data protection appliances, gateways, or proxies and help off-load the actual source being protected. Both client and servers can implement data footprint reduction technologies including compression, de-duplication along with encryption, and network bandwidth management for optimization and media retention, and for tracking management. In addition, data protection servers can also use policy management functions to determine what is protected when, where, how, and why. For example, based on scheduled or event-based policies, a data protection server can notify another data protection tool to take some action or tell a VM, its guest, and applications that it is time to quiescence to gain a consistent and complete data protection operation.

Examples of source-side data protection include:

- Backup/restore tools, including agent, agentless, and proxy-based servers
- Application, file system, or operating system tools for snapshots and replication
- Database or other application journal and transaction log file shipping
- Archiving tools for databases, email, and file systems
- E2E DPM and SRA tools for situational awareness

Table 5.3 shows several common nomenclatures for data protection, where the source is usually a disk on a client or server to be backed up directly to a target, to an intermediary backup server or other storage system that, in turn, moves data to another location. For example, simply backing up a server, workstation, or laptop to an attached internal or external disk device would be D2D (disk-to-disk) or to a tape drive as D2T or to a cloud MSP as D2C. An example of a client or application server being backed up to a data protection staging device such as a backup server and then to another disk would be D2D2D.

In addition to source-side protection, which also includes intermediary backup or other data protection servers, the other part of data protection is the target to which the data is sent. Targets can be active in that they may be used for read or read and write by other applications at the same or different locations. Targets can also be passive, with data only stored until needed, when it is either restored or accessed as part of a failover

Table 5.3 Various Source and Target Data Protection Schemes

Acronym	Nomenclature	How Data Is Protected
D2T	Disk to tape	Moves data directly from the source disk to a tape device
D2D	Disk to disk	Copies from one disk to another internal or external disk
D2C	Disk to cloud	Data is backed up, copied, or replicated to a cloud or MSP
D2D2D	Disk to disk to disk	Data is copied to an intermediary disk and then copied to a target disk
D2D2T	Disk to disk to tape	Data is copied to an intermediary disk and then copied to tape
D2D2C	Disk to disk to cloud	Data is copied to an intermediary disk and then copied to a cloud
D2D2C2D D2D2C2T	Disk to disk to cloud to disk or tape	Data is copied to an intermediary disk and then copied to a cloud. Once at the cloud, MSP data is also protected on disk or tape

process. Targets can hold data for short-period data protection such as snapshots, replication, and backup or for longer-term protection, including both active and inactive or cold archives for preservation purposes.

Data protection targets may be local, remote, or cloud-based, leveraging fixed (non-removable) or removable media. Fixed media include solid-state devices (SSDs) and hard disk drives (HDDs) installed into a storage solution, removed only for repair and replacement. Removable media include removable hard disk drives (RHDDs), magnetic tape, optical CD/DVDs or portable FLASH SSD devices. Some targets may also be hybrids, with some media that stays fixed while others are exported or sent to a different physical location, where they may be left in cold storage until needed or placed into warm or hot active storage by being imported into a storage system at the remote site.

You might wonder why with modern data networks anyone would still ship data via portable or removable media. While networks are faster, not only is there also more data to move in a given amount of time, high-speed networks may not be available between the source and destination in an affordable manner. Physically moving data may be a one-time process of initially getting large amounts of data to a cloud, MSP, or hosting facility, or an ongoing process when moving it over a network is not a possibility.

Target or destinations for protecting and archiving data include:

- Backup servers in an intermediary role as both a source and a target device
- Data protection gateways, appliances, and cloud point-of-presence devices
- Shared storage, including primary and secondary storage systems
- Disk-based backup, archives, and virtual tape libraries (VTLs)
- Automated tape libraries (TLs) or automated tape systems (ATS)
- Cloud and MSP solutions supporting various protocols or personalities

Reliability–availability–serviceability (RAS) capabilities include redundant power and cooling, dual controllers (active/passive or active/active), and spare disks with automatic rebuild combined with RAID. Just as there are many approaches and technologies to achieve server virtualization, there are many approaches for addressing data protection in a virtualized server environment. Table 5.4 provides an overview of data protection capabilities and characteristics to address various aspects of data protection in a virtualized server environment.

Table 5.4 Data Protection Options For Virtual Server Environments

Capability	Characteristics	Description and Examples
Virtual machine migration	• Move VMs • Facilitate load balancing • Proactive failover or movement vs. recovery	• Vmotion, Quickmigration, and others • May be processor architecture dependent • Moves VM's memory from server to server • Shared-access storage for BC/DR
Failover high availability (HA)	• Proactive VM movement • Automatic HA failover • Fault containment • RAID disk storage	• Proactive move of VM to a different server • May require tools for data movement • Low-latency network for remote HA • Replication of VM and application data
Snapshots and CDP	• Point-in-time copies • Copies of VM state • Application-aware • In multiple locations	• Facilitate rapid restart from crash event • Guest OS, VM, appliance, or storage based • Combine with other tools • For HA and BC/DR or file deletion
Backup and restore	• Application based • VM or guest OS based • Console subsystem based • Proxy server based • Backup server or target resides as guest in a VM	• Full image, incremental, or file level • Operating system and application-specific • Agent or agentless backup • Backup over LAN to backup device • Backup to local or cloud device • Proxy based for LAN- and server-free
Replication	• Application based • VM or guest OS based • Console subsystem based • External appliance based • Storage array based	• Application replication such as Oracle • VM or guest OS or third-party software • Application integration for consistency • Replication software or hardware • Storage system controller based replication
Archiving	• Document management • Application based • File system based • Long-term preservation	• Structured (database), semistructured • Unstructured (files, PDFs, images, video) • Regulatory and noncompliance • Project data preservation for future use
DPM and IRM	• Data protection tools • Analysis and correlation • Backup and replication	• VMware Site Recovery Manager • Data protection advisory and analysis tools • Various aspects of IRM and data protection

5.6.2. Virtual and Physical Machine Movement

Often mistaken, or perhaps even positioned as data protection tools and facilities, virtual machine movement or migratory tools are targeted and designed for maintenance and proactive management. The primary focus of tools such as VMware, vSphere,

VMotion, and Microsoft Hyper-V Quick migration, and others, is to move a running or active VM to a different physical server that has shared access to the storage that supports the VM without disruption.

For example, VMotion can be used to maintain availability during planned server maintenance or upgrades or to shift workload to different servers based on expected activity or other events. The caveat with such migration facilities is that, while a running VM can be moved, those VMs still rely on being able to access their virtual and physical data stores.

This means that data files must also be relocated. It is important to consider how a VM movement or migration facility interacts with other data protection tools including snapshots, backup, and replication, along with other data movers to enable data protection.

In general, considerations pertaining to live movement for VMs include:

- How does the VM support dissimilar hardware (e.g., Intel and AMD)?
- Can the migratory or movement tool work on both a local and wide area basis?
- Will your various software licenses allow testing or production failover?
- How many concurrent moves or migrations can take place at the same time?
- Is the movement limited to virtual file system-based VMs or raw devices?
- What third-party data movers' hardware, software, or network services?

5.6.3. Enabling High Availability

A common approach for high-availability data accessibility is RAID-enabled disk storage to protect against data loss in the event of a disk drive failure. For added data protection, RAID data protection can be complemented with local and remote data mirroring or replication to protect against loss of data access due to a device, storage system, or disk drive failure. RAID and mirroring, however, are not a substitute for backups, snapshots, or other point-in-time discrete copy operations that establish a recovery point.

RAID provides protection in the event of disk drive failures; RAID does not by itself protect data in the event that an entire storage system is damaged. While replication and mirroring can protect data in the event that a storage system is destroyed or lost at one location, if data is deleted or corrupted at one location, that action will be replicated or mirrored to the copy. Consequently, some form of time-interval data protection, such as a snapshot or backup, needs to be combined with RAID and replication for a comprehensive and complete data protection solution.

Techniques and technologies for enabling HA include:

- Hardware and software clustering
- Redundant networking paths and services
- Failover software, pathing drivers, and APIs
- Elimination of single points of failure

- Fault isolation and containment
- Clusters and redundant components
- Active/active and active/passive failover
- Change control and configuration management

Active/passive refers to a standby mode in which one server, storage controller, or process is active and another is in warm standby mode, ready to pick up workload when needed. When failover occurs, the warm standby node, controller, or server and associated software may be able to resume at the point of the disruption or perhaps perform a quick restart, rollback, or roll forward and resume service. Active/active refers to two or more redundant components that are doing work and are capable of handling the workload of a failed partner with little to no disruption. From a performance standpoint, care should be taken to ensure that performance is not impacted if an active/active two-node or dual controller sustains loss and failover of work movers to a surviving member.

For performance-sensitive applications for which service requirements dictate that no degradation in performance occurs during a failover, load-balancing techniques will be needed. If SLOs and SLAs allow short-term performance degradation in exchange for higher availability or accessibility, then a different load-balancing strategy can be used. The key point is that in the course of a storage controller, node, or server failover to a surviving member that provides availability, a subsequent chain of events must not be initiated due to performance bottlenecks, resulting in a larger outage or disruption to service.

Virtual machine environments differ in their specific supported features for HA, ranging from the ability to failover or restart a VM on a different physical server to the ability to move a running VM from one physical server to another physical server (as discussed in the previous section). Another element of HA for physical and virtual environments is the elimination of single points of failure to isolate and contain faults. This can be done, for example, using multiple network adapters (such as NICs), redundant storage I/O host bus adapters, and clustered servers.

Another aspect of HA is when and how new versions of software or configuration changes can be applied. Nondisruptive code load (NDCL) means that new software or configuration can be applied to an application, operation, and hypervisor, networking device, or storage system while in use with no impact. However, the code or configuration changes do not take effect until the next reboot or restart. Nondisruptive code load activation (NDCLA) enables the code to take effect on the fly. If your environment has no planned maintenance windows for scheduled downtime or service interruptions, then NCDLA may be a requirement rather than just a nice-to-have feature. If you do have routine schedule windows when service can be disrupted for a brief period of time for maintenance, then NCDL may be sufficient. Also keep in mind that if you have redundant components and data paths, upgrades can be done on one path or set of components while the others are in use. However, some environments will still schedule updates to one path while the other remains active to occur during scheduled maintenance windows, to avoid the risk of something unforeseen happening.

5.6.3.1. Why RAID Is Not a Replacement for Backup or Time-Interval Protection

RAID provides availability or continued accessibility to data on storage systems, guarding against a device or component—such as a disk drive—failure. Should something happen to the entire RAID storage system, it is a single point of failure if it is not being backed up, snapshots, and replications made to another location, or no other copies of stored data exist.

Another issue is that if the data on the RAID system becomes corrupted, without a point-in-time copy or snapshot, backup copy, or other copy on a different storage system, there is again a single point of failure. Some form of timed recovery-point copy needs to be made and combined with RAID. Likewise, RAID complements time-based copies by maintaining availability in the event a disk drive or component fails, rather than having to go to a backup copy on another disk, tape, or cloud.

Does replication by itself with no time-based copy protect against RAID failure? From the standpoint of maintaining availability and accessibility, the answer can be yes if a complete or comprehensive copy (e.g., all buffers were flushed) maintaining transactional integrity or application state is preserved. However, if data is deleted or corrupted locally, the same operation will occur on the local or remote mirror unless some time-interval copy is introduced. Simply put, combine RAID and replication with some form of time- or interval-based data protection as part of implementing a complete or comprehensive data protection strategy.

5.6.4. Snapshots and Continuous Data Protection

There are a number of reasons why snapshots, also known as point-in-time (PIT) copies, and associated technologies might be utilized. Snapshots are significant in that they create a virtual backup window to enable data protection when a physical backup window is shrinking or no longer exists. Snapshots provide a way of creating virtual time to get essential data protection completed while minimizing impacts to applications and boosting productivity. Different applications have varying data protection requirements, including RTO, RPO, and data retention needs.

Other reasons include making copies of data for test purposes such as software development, regression testing, and DR testing; making copies of data for application processing including data warehouse, data marts, reporting, and data mining; and making copies to faceplate nondisruptive backups and data migration.

Snapshots are a popular approach to reducing downtime or disruptions associated with traditional data protection approaches such as backup. Snapshots vary in their implementation and location, with some being full copies while others are delta (change)-based. For example, an initial full copy is made with deltas or changes recorded, similar to a transaction or redo log, with each snapshot being a new delta or point-in-time view of the data being protected. Another way snapshot implementations can vary is in where and how the snapshot data is stored on the same storage system or the ability to replicate a snapshot to a separate storage system. Space-saving snapshots leverage redirect on writes to allow copies of snapshot volumes to be made and subsequently modified without the overhead of duplicating data. In the absence of a space-saving snapshot, if a 1-TB snapshot were copied three times, for development, for testing or quality assurance, and for decision support or business analytics, the result could be 4 TB of space required (1 TB original + 3 copies). Space-saving snapshots, which vary by vendor implementation, should reduce the storage space needed to a smaller data footprint consisting of the base amount of data, some small amount of overhead, and any changed data for each of the subsequent copies.

Because snapshots can take place very quickly, an application, operating system, or VM can be quiesced (suspended), a quick snapshot taken of the current state at that point in time, and then resume normal processing. Snapshots work well for reducing downtime as well as speeding up backups. Snapshots reduce the performance impact of traditional backups by only copying changed data, similar to an incremental or differential backup but on a much more granular basis. Snapshots can be made available to other servers in a shared storage environment to further off-load data protection. An example is using a proxy or backup server to mount and read the snapshots to construct an off-line backup.

For virtual environments, snapshots can be taken at the VM or operating system layer, with specific features and functionalities varying by vendor implementation. Another location for snapshots is in storage systems that have integration with the guest operating system, applications, or VM. Snapshots can also take place in network or fabric-based appliances that intercept I/O data streams between servers and storage devices. One of the key points is to make sure that when a snapshot is taken, the data that is captured is the data that was expected to be recorded.

For example, if data is still in memory or buffers, that data may not be flushed to disk files and captured. Thus, with fine-grained snapshots, also known as near or coarse continuous data protection (CDP), as well as with real-time fine-grained CDP and replication, 100% of the data on disk may be captured. However, if a key piece of information is still in memory and not yet written to disk, critical data to ensure and maintain application state coherency and transaction integrity is not preserved. While snapshots enable rapid backup of data as of a point in time (RPO), snapshots do not provide protection by themselves in the event of a storage system failure and need to be backed up to another device.

CDP and snapshot considerations include:

- How many concurrent snapshots can take place, and how many can be retained?
- Where is the snapshot performed (application, VM, appliance, or storage)?
- What API or integration tools exist for application-aware snapshots?
- Are there facilities for pre- and postprocessing functions for snapshots?
- Do the snapshots apply to virtual disks or physical disks?
- What is the performance impact when snapshots are running?
- How do the snapshots integrate with third-party tools including replication?
- What are the licensing and maintenance costs for the snapshot software features?
- When a copy of snapshots is made, is a full copy performed?

Initially, CDP entered the market as standalone products and was slow to be adopted. This is shifting, as is often the case when a new technology feature can be imbedded as additional functionality in currently deployed products. While there are still some purpose-built CDP solutions, the functionality has been added as a feature in many software and storage system products.

Keep in mind that with CDP, it is important to capture all information for a complete or comprehensive data protection plan. This means that for complete data protection with CDP, data from applications, databases, operating and file systems, as well as hypervisors' buffers must be flushed to storage as of a known state for transaction and data and data integrity. For example, for interfacing with VMware vSphere, Microsoft Hyper-V, Citrix Xen, SAP, Oracle Database, Microsoft SQLserver, Exchange, Share-Point, and other applications, it is important for data integrity for them to quiese to a known state and flush their buffers to disk. While capturing 100% of data on disk is good, if only 99.999% of the data to maintain application and data integrity is copied, with the other 0.001% still in a buffer, but that small amount of data is crucial for recovery, than that is a weak link in the recovery and data protection chain.

5.6.5. Backup and Recovery

Backups are a time-tested technique for making a point-in-time copy of data that can be used for many different purposes and have been the cornerstone of many data protection and BC/DR strategies for decades.

Some examples of different types of backups include:

- Full, incremental, or differential backup
- Image backup of physical storage or of VM virtual disk
- Bare-metal restore capable to both PM and VMs
- File-level backup or file-level restore from image backups
- File restoration from traditional backups as well as snapshot or CDP copies
- Application integration, for example, with Oracle RMAN or API tools
- Running on a PM, VM, appliance, or as part of a cloud MSP SaaS model
- Server vs. desktop or mobile device backup

Another form of backup is an object base where all systems or servers, applications, and data associated with a function are backed up. For example, an object backup could be made to ensure that everything associated with manufacturing or accounts payable or customer relations management (CRM) or a website are protected. An object backup can span multiple servers running different operating systems such as a database, unstructured files data, and their applications. The idea behind an object backup approach is that everything associated with that function or information service is protected and can be restored in a coordinated manner.

Replacing tape with disk-based solutions can help address tape-based bottlenecks, but it does not address the root issue involved with many backups. That root issue may be how backup software is configured or used along with the age or capability of the data protection tool. Another consideration is the paradigm shift of leveraging disk-based backup instead of generating save sets or other backup copies. It is time to update how backups are done, leveraging different tools and technologies either as a near-term tactical solution or as part of a larger data protection modernization—for example, a shift from doing D2T or D2D backups throughout the day to leveraging snapshots and CDP combined with replication and a copy of log or journal files.

For applications or environments that need to retain tape-based backup processes or procedures, virtual tape libraries (VTLs) that emulate tape as well as combining policy-based management, replication, compression, and deduplication while providing disk-based access using NFS or CIFS are a great way to enable a transition to the future. For example, near-term leverage the VTL interface while processes and procedures and backup configurations are modified to use disk based NFS or CIFS access of the device. Then, when the conversion from a tape-based process is completed, that feature can be disabled or retained for legacy support as needed. In essence, the target data protection solution should leverage virtualization to bridge from what you are currently doing to the future while at the same time changing with you by supporting backup and archiving as well as serving as an ingestion point for snapshot copies or other forms of data movement. A primary tenant of virtualization is "abstraction providing transparency along with emulation," and that has been used for a consolidation focus. This has resulted in a common belief that virtualization equals consolidation and consolidation means virtualization; there is, however, a much larger opportunity for virtualization beyond consolidation. Storage systems that support a VTL interface are examples of leveraging transparency along with emulation by making disks function like tapes to provide a bridge to the current software configuration.

In addition to optimizing the targets where data is sent for protection, another consideration is changing the protection and retention intervals. With disk-based data protection and data footprint reduction techniques, it is possible to keep more frequent backups on-line and readily accessible. The result of having more yet smaller copies of data for fast restoration is the reduction of the number of larger copies retained on other media or in different locations. Data protection and backup modernization then becomes a matter of finding a balance between having better granularity for faster restore of data while having a smaller data footprint without compromising SLOs or SLAs.

Caveats with virtual and physical backups include the fact that backing up many small files can result in lower performance measured in throughput or bandwidth as compared to moving large files. Depending on the type of environment and applications being supported, you could be working with different-sized files. For example, video or photo files can be large, but some applications (energy, seismic, crash test simulation, medical) generate many small time-sliced images (e.g., lots of TIFs, GIFs, or JPGs) that get spliced together for later playback.

Understanding how the size of files impacts data protection is important in order to determine how to configure resources to minimize performance impact or time delays. For example, tape drives work best when data can be streamed to them instead of starting and stopping, which results in "shoe shining" wear and tear. If many small files need to be protected, configure a solution in which those files are staged and able to be streamed directly to tape, disk, or cloud based resources while also using data footprint reduction techniques.

Another dimension to backups involves desktops, workstations, laptops, and mobile devices, including protecting remote office/branch office (ROBO) environments. Some enterprise software provides support for remote or non–data center backups, while other packages are optimized for those functions. Similarly, many cloud and managed service providers have solutions that can be used to protect remote and distributed devices to off-load primary data center solutions. Another approach for protecting remote devices is virtual desktop initiatives (VDIs), centralized applications that are simply presented on workstations or tablets along with terminal services. For some environments, such as call centers or environments with robust networking capabilities, shifting from heavy workstations or desktops to thin or light devices makes sense. For other users, workstations can be protected using tools that back up those systems up to a local or remote server, central location, or a cloud MSP service. The backup can be scheduled, or some solutions can run in a continuous or near-continuous mode, taking routine snapshots and protecting data on an event such as a change or time basis.

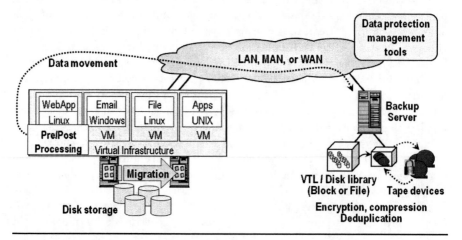

Figure 5.6   Agent-based backup over a LAN.

5.6.5.1. Agent-Based Data Protection

Agent-based backup, also known as LAN-based backup, is a common means of backing up physical servers over a LAN. The term agent-based backup comes from the fact that a backup agent (backup software) is installed on a server, with the backup data being sent over a LAN to a backup server or to a locally attached tape or disk backup device. Given the familiarity and established existing procedures for using LAN and agent-based backup, a first step for data protection in a virtual server environment can be to simply leverage agent-based backup while re-architecting virtual server data protection.

Agent-based backups, shown in Figure 5.6, are relatively easy to deploy, as they may already be in use for backing up the servers being migrated to a virtual environment. The main drawback to agent-based backup is that it consumes physical memory, CPU, and I/O resources, causing contention for LAN traffic and impacting other VMs and guests on the same virtualized server.

Backup client or agent software can also have extensions to support specific applications such as Exchange, Oracle, SQL, or other structured data applications as well as handling open files or synchronizing with snapshots. One of the considerations regarding agent-based backups is what support exists for backup devices or targets. For example, are locally attached devices (including internal or external, SAS, iSCSI, FCoE, Fibre Channel or InfiniBand SAN or NAS disk, tape, and VTL) supported from an agent, and how can data be moved to a backup server over a network in a LAN-friendly and efficient manner?

Physical servers, when running backups, have to stay within prescribed backup windows while avoiding performance contention with other applications on that server and avoiding network LAN traffic contention. In a consolidated virtual server environment, it is likely that multiple competing backup jobs may also vie for the same backup window and server resources, including CPU, memory, and I/O and network bandwidth. Care needs to be exercised when consolidating servers into a virtual environment to avoid performance conflicts and bottlenecks.

5.6.5.2. Proxy-Based Backup

Agent- or client-based backups running on guest operating systems consume physical resources, including CPU, memory, and I/O, resulting in performance challenges for the server and LAN network during backup (assuming a LAN backup). Similarly, an agent-based backup to a locally attached disk, tape, or virtual tape library (VTL) will still consume server resources, resulting in performance contention with other VMs or other concurrently running backups. In a regular backup, the client or agent backup software, when requested, reads data to be backed up and transmits the data to the target backup server or storage device along with performing associated management and record-keeping tasks.

Similarly, on restore operations the backup client or agent software works with the backup server to retrieve data based on the specific request. Consequently, the backup operation places a demand burden on the physical processor (CPU) of the server while consuming memory and I/O bandwidth. These competing demands can and need to be managed if multiple backups are running on the same guest OS and VM or on different VMs.

An approach to addressing consolidated backup contention is to leverage a backup server and configure it as a proxy (see Figure 5.7) to perform the data movement and backup functions. Proxy backups work by integrating with snapshot, application, and guest operating system tools for pre- and postprocessing. As an example, VMware has replaced the VMware Consolidated Backup (VCB) tool with a set of data protection APIs. The APIs enable a VM or guest operating system and applications to be backed up by a proxy process. The proxy process reduces resource consumption (CPU, memory, and I/O) on the PM where the VMs exist, because the work is done via another server. For its part, Microsoft with Hyper-V, being based on Windows technology, leverages Volume Shadow Services (VSS) copy and associated application VSS writers for integration.

Rather, it is an interface to VMware tools and enables third-party backup and data protection products to work. To provide data protection using VMware vSphere APIs, Microsoft Hyper-V VSS and DPM, or other hypervisor-based capabilities, third-party tools are leveraged. These third-party tools provide scheduling, media, and data protection management. Third-party tools also manage the creation of data copies or redirecting data to other storage devices, such as VTLs and disk libraries, equipped with data footprint reduction (DFR) capabilities including compression and data de-duplication. Virtual machine virtual disk images (e.g., VMDK for VMware or HVDs for Hyper-V), depending on allocation and actual usage, may be sparse or hollow. This means that there can be a large amount of empty disk storage space that has been pre-allocated. The drawback is that extra time may be required to back up those files as well as allocate yet-unused disk space being occupied. The good news is that allocated yet unused disk space can lend itself well for thin provisioning and other DFR techniques, including compression and deduplication.

To help speed up backup or data protection operations, VMware has added change block tracking (CBT) into vSphere, which can be leveraged by third-party tool providers. CBT speeds up backup or data protection copy functions by keeping track of which blocks have changed from within the kernel and using a table that maps to the corresponding size of a VM. When a block changes, the vSphere kernel makes an entry in the corresponding table, which is a disk file. Data protection tools can make an initial copy, and then simply look up blocks that have been changed to reduce the amount of time required and the amount of data to copy.

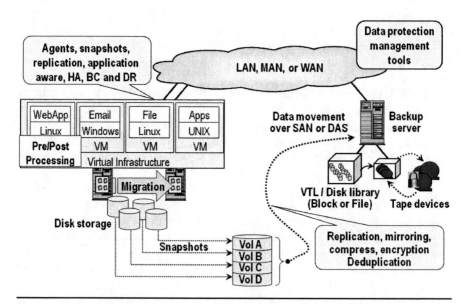

Figure 5.7 Proxy and API-based backup example.

In addition to off-loading the physical server during the proxy backup, LAN traffic is not impacted, as data can be moved or accessed via a shared storage interconnect depending on the specific VM implementation. Third-party backup and data protection software on a proxy server can also perform other tasks, including replicating the data to another location, keeping a local copy of the backup on disk-based media with a copy at the remote site on disk and on a remote off-line tape if needed.

5.6.5.3. Cloud and MSP Backup

For cloud, MSP, and remote backup, there are different options in addition to numerous vendors and service providers. The options are that as an organization you can acquire software from a vendor and deploy your own public, private, or hybrid cloud service, or you can subscribe to a service provider. As a VAR or service provider, you can also acquire software along with hardware resources and provision your own service or work with a larger provider who delivers the capability on your behalf. As a service provider, you can develop your own software running on your or someone else's servers at a hosting, MSP, or cloud site.

Cloud or MSP backups can replace what you are currently doing for backup, or they can complement your existing data protection environment. For example, you could replace your existing backup infrastructure including software and hardware with new tools supplied by the provider and optional on-site staging or caching hardware, if applicable. Some providers allow you to use your existing backup or data protection software, moving the data to the cloud with optional on-site or local copies. Some providers supply software or an appliance that sits at your location to collect information and facilitate transmission to their location or your choice of destinations to be stored.

Some questions and topics to look into regarding cloud and MSP backup providers include how they charge for the service—flat fee for unlimited capacity and bandwidth with no extra fees for access (updates or restores) and views (search, directories, catalogs)? Does the provider charge on a graduated pricing scheme, where there is a base monthly or annual fee plus a fee per gigabyte or terabyte stored? What are the optional or hidden fees in addition to base capacity usage? For example, do they charge for uploading or retrieving files, viewing or generating reports, bulk import and export? Does the provider offer different cloud storage service offerings for parking your data, including the option to select various geographies for regulatory compliance? If there is the option to select different back-end storage service providers, and are the fees the same or do they vary based on SLAs and locations?

Another consideration is how locked in are you to a particular provider. What are your options should you decide or need to switch providers? While your data may reside at a third-party site such as Amazon, is it stored in a format that can be accessible using some other provider's tool? For example, if you start using one service provider to back up your environment and specify Amazon S3 as the target storage pool, what happens if you switch your service to Rack space Jungle disk, which also supports Amazon as a pool?

While Jungle disk gives you the option of storing data at Rack space or Amazon, will it be able to leverage your old backups already stored within the Amazon S3 cloud, or will you have to convert or export and re-import your backups? You may find that to ensure coverage the best option is to maintain access to your old provider until those backups expire and you have sufficient coverage at your new provider. Other considerations include whether you can force your old backups to expire and what is involved in making sure that the provider has taken adequate steps to remove your data and your account profile. During the writing of this book, I switched cloud backup providers and had a period of overlap with additional protection via my normal D2D and D2D2D with a master copy sent off-site to a secure vault.

Additional questions and considerations regarding cloud and MSP backups include:

- In what format are backups stored; can they be accessed without special tools?
- How efficient is the solution in scanning or tracking changes to be backed up?
- What types of data footprint reduction technologies expedite backups?
- How much data can be backed up in a given timeframe with different networks?
- How much data can be restored in a given amount of time with your networks?
- What are your restoration options, including to alternate locations?
- Does the provider offer bulk physical media restoration (e.g., disk or tape)?
- Are there fees for access or bandwidth usage in addition to capacity charges?
- What types of management tools, including automated reporting, are available?
- Can you view your current charges or fees to determine future usage forecasts?
- What is the solution's scaling capabilities, and can it grow to fit your needs?
- Is the solution designed for ROBO or SOHO or mobile or SMB or enterprise?
- What operating system, hypervisors, and application are supported?
- What software requirements are needed; what does the provider supply?
- Do you require any additional hardware at your locations to use the service?
- Can the service support local copies made to existing backup devices?
- What are the security mechanisms, including encryption key management?
- Look beyond the basic cost per gigabyte to understand additional fees and SLAs.

5.6.6. Data Replication (Local, Remote, and Cloud)

There are many approaches to data replication and mirroring, shown generically in Figure 5.8, for local and remote implementations to address different needs, requirements, and preferences. Replication can be done in many locations, including applications, databases, third-party tools, operating systems and hypervisors on host servers (PMs), appliances or networking devices including cloud point-of-presences (cpops) or gateways, as well as primary, secondary, and backup targets such as VTLs or archive systems.

A general caveat is that replication by itself does not provide complete data protection; replication is primarily for data availability and accessibility in the event of a component, device, system, or site loss. Replication should be combined with snapshots and other point-in-time discrete backup data protection to ensure that data can be recovered or restored to a specific RPO. For example, if data is corrupted or deleted on a primary

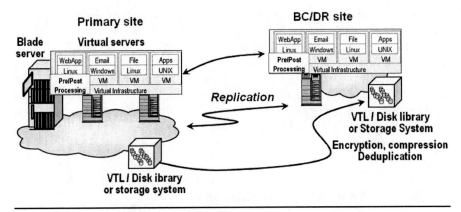

Figure 5.8   Data replication for HA, BC, and DR data protection.

storage device, replication will replicate the corruption or deletion to alternativee sites, thus the importance of being able to recover to specific time intervals for rollback.

Considerations for replication include:

- Application integration with snapshots
- Local, metropolitan, and wide area requirements
- Network bandwidth and data footprint reduction capabilities
- Encryption and data security functionality
- Various topologies including one to one, many to one, one to many
- Homogeneous or different source and destination
- Management reporting and diagnostics
- How many concurrent replication streams or copies

Important factors of data mirroring and replication are distance and latency resulting in data delay and negative performance impacts. Distance is a concern, but the real enemy of synchronous data movement and real-time data replication without performance compromise is latency. The common perception is that distance is the main problem of synchronous data movement as, generally speaking, latency increases over distance. The reality is that even over relatively short distances, latency can negatively impact synchronous real-time data replication and data movement.

Distance and latency have a bearing on replication and data movement by impacting decisions on whether to use synchronous or asynchronous data movement methods. The trade-offs beyond costs are performance and data protection. Synchronous data transfer methods facilitate real-time data protection, enabling an RPO of or near zero. However, the trade-off is that, over distance or high-latency networks, application performance is negatively impacted while waiting for remote I/O operations to be completed. Another approach is to use asynchronous data transfer modes where a time delay is introduced along with buffering. By using a time delay and buffering, application performance is not impacted, as I/O operations appear to applications as having completed. The trade-off with asynchronous data transfer modes is that while performance is not negatively impacted over long distance or high-latency networks, there is a larger RPO exposure window potential for data loss while data is in buffers waiting to be written to remote sites.

Consequently, a combination of synchronous and asynchronous data transfer may be used for a tiered data protection approach, for example, using synchronous data transfer for time-critical data to a reasonably nearby facility over a low-latency network, with less critical data being replicated asynchronously to a primary or alternative location farther away.

5.6.7. Data Protection Management

Data protection management (DPM) has evolved from first-generation backup reporting technology to incorporate mult-vendor and cross technology domain capabilities. In addition, present-generation DPM tools are evolving to manage multiple aspects of data protection beyond basic backup reporting, including replications, snapshot, BC/DR compliance coverage, file system monitoring, and event correlation. Some DPM tools are essentially reporting, status, or event monitoring facilities, providing passive insight into what is happening with one or more data protection IRM focus areas. Other DPM tools can provide passive reporting along with active analysis and event correlation, providing a level of automation for larger environments.

Cross-technology domain event correlation connects reports from various IT resources to transform fragments of event activity into useful information on how, where, why, and by whom resources (servers, storage, networks, facilities) are being used. In virtualized environments, given the many different interdependencies, cross-technology domain event correlation becomes even more valuable for looking at end-to-end IRM activities. The increase of regulatory requirements combined with pressure to meet service levels and 24×7 data availability has resulted in data protection interdependencies across different business, application, and IT entities. Consequently, timely and effective DPM requires business and application awareness to correlate and analyze events that impact service and IT resource usage. Business awareness is the ability to collect and correlate IT assets to application interdependencies and resource usage with specific business owners or functions for reporting and analysis. Application awareness is the ability to relate IT resources to specific applications within the data protection environment to enable analysis and reporting.

Although an environment may have multiple tools and technologies to support IRM activities, DPM tools are evolving to support or coexist with management of multiple data protection techniques including backup (to disk or tape or cloud), local and remote mirroring or replication, snapshots, and file systems. Key to supporting multiple data protection approaches and technologies is the ability to scale and process in a timely manner rapidly increasing large amounts of event and activity log information. At the heart of a new breed of IRM tools, including DPM solutions, are robust cross-technology resource analysis and correlation engines to sift disparate data protection activity and event logs for interrelated information.

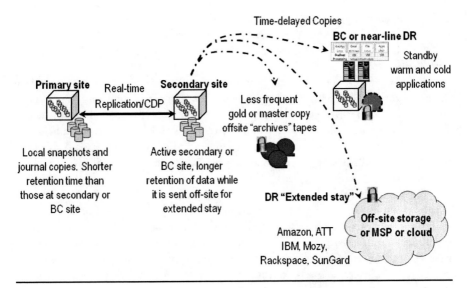

Figure 5.9   HA, BC, and DR solution for virtual and physical servers.

5.7. Modernizing Data Protection and Backup

A good time to rethink data protection and archiving strategies of applications and systems data is when server consolidation is undertaken. Instead of simply moving the operating system and associated applications from a "tin"-wrapped physical server to a "software"-wrapped virtual server, consider how new techniques and technologies can be leveraged to improve performance, availability, and data protection. For example, an existing server with agent-based backup software installed sends data to a backup server over the LAN for data protection. However, when moved to a virtual server, the backup can be transitioned to a LAN-free and server-free backup server. In this case, LAN and other performance bottlenecks can be avoided.

From a historical data protection perspective, magnetic tape has been popular, cost-effective, and the preferred data storage medium for retaining data to meet backup and recovery, BC/DR, and data preservation or archiving requirements. Recently, many organizations are leveraging storage virtualization in the form of transparent access of disk-based backup and recovery solutions. These solutions emulate various tape devices and tape libraries to coexist with existing installed backup software and procedures. From a "green" and economics perspective, magnetic tape remains one of, if not the most, efficient data storage medium for inactive or archived data. Disk-to-disk snapshots; backups, and replication have become popular options for near-term and real-time data protection to meet RTO and RPO requirements.

Figure 5.9 shows how the above scenario works. Starting at the left, normal operations with data are replicated to the secondary or BC site along with routine snapshots, journal, or log file D2D copies made to multiple locations. Should a failure occur at the primary site, such as failure of a disk drive or other component, it can be isolated and contained using HA techniques such as dual adapters, RAID, and active/active failover. Should a more serious incident occur, failover can occur to the secondary or BC site, where access can continue or resume or where recovery can quickly occur to a given point of time.

Should an even more serious incident occur that results in the primary or secondary BC site and their resources not being available, near-line or off-line data at a warm or cold DR site can be leveraged. In Figure 5.9 an additional step is added in which both the primary and secondary or BC site are actively used, with the production load balanced between them. These two sites complement and protect each other. A third site is a warm or cold site where a minimal number of systems are in place and to which critical data is periodically copied.

The idea is that this third or near-line DR site provides a means for recovery at a location some distance away from the primary and secondary sites. Building on this example, there can be a fourth site where off-line data is copied or sent. This site represents where tape or other removable media are shipped and data either remains on the media or is migrated to a cloud accessible storage environment. This site houses data that will be rarely, if ever, accessed—essentially a last-resort source for data restoration.

5.7.1. Expanding from DR to BC, Shifting from Cost Overhead to Profit Center

BC and DR are often seen as cost overhead items for IT and the businesses that they support. This is because capital and operating budget money is spent on hardware, software, services, networking, and facilities for a capability that it is hoped will never be used other than for testing purposes. On the other hand, if those resources can be safely used for production business, those costs can be absorbed as being able to drive workload, thereby reducing per-unit costs. If your BC or secondary site is also your primary or last-resort DR copy, caution needs to be exercised not to contaminate or compromise the integrity of that environment, by keeping DR, master, or gold copies of data physically or logically isolated from on-line production or active data.

5.7.2. Using Virtualization and Clouds to Enhance Data Protection

Most virtualization initiatives undertaken at present are focused on consolidation of heterogeneous operating systems on underutilized servers. Another aspect is to address physical desktops and workstations with virtual desktop infrastructure (VDI), in part for consolidation but also to simplify management, data protection, and associated cost and complexity. The next (or current) wave of server, storage, and desktop virtualization is expanding the focus to include enabling agility and flexibility. This combines the tenets of consolidation with an emphasis on utilizing virtualization to enable dynamic management of servers and dynamic data protection, for example, using virtualization to support redeployment of servers for workload changes and to provide

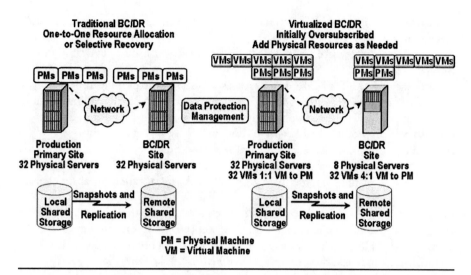

Figure 5.10   Leveraging virtualization to enable HA, BC, and DR.

transparency. In this scenario, consolidation continues to be a driver. However, there is also an emphasis on leveraging virtualization as a tool for applications, servers, and storage that do not lend themselves to being consolidated but can benefit from business and IT IRM-enabled agility, including enhanced performance, HA, DR, and BC.

Virtualization can be used in many ways, including consolidation, abstraction, and emulation, to support load balancing and routine maintenance as well as BC and DR. On the left in Figure 5.10, a traditional BC/DR environment is shown, with dedicated physical resources or selective applications being recovered, or a combination of both.

Challenges include dedicating extra hardware on a one-to-one basis and selecting which servers and applications are recovered to available physical resources. Complexity is involved in maintaining BC/DR plans. This includes testing of configuration changes along with associated costs of hardware, software, and ongoing operational costs of power, cooling, and floor space. Other issues and challenges include difficulties in testing or simulating recovery for training and audit purposes and inefficient use of available network bandwidth, inhibiting the amount of data that can be moved in a timely fashion.

On the right side of Figure 5.10, a solution is shown that leverages virtualization for abstraction and management in which each physical server is converted to a VM. However, the VM is allocated a physical machine, such as a server or server blade, in a one-to-one manner. In the case of a disaster, or for BC or training and testing purposes, multiple VMs can be recovered and restarted on a limited number of PMs, with additional PMs being added as needed to boost or enhance performance to required service-level objectives. To improve data movement and enhance RPO and RTO, reduce the data footprint to boost data movement and data protection effectiveness using a combination of archiving, compression, de-duplication of data being moved or replicated, space-saving snapshots, data replication, and bandwidth optimization. Data protection management tools are used to manage snapshots, replication,

and backup and associated functions across servers, storage, and network and software resources.

Benefits of server virtualization include more efficient use of physical resources;
the ability to dynamically shift workloads or VMs to alternative hardware for routine
maintenance, HA, BC, or DR purposes; support of planned and unplanned outages;
and the enablement of training and testing of procedures and configurations. In addition to supporting HA, BC, and DR, the approach shown on the right of Figure 5.10
can also be used proactively for routine IRM functions, for example, shifting applications and their VMs to different physical severs on-site or off-site during hardware
upgrades or replacement of serves or storage.

A variation of the paradigm in Figure 5.10 uses virtualization for abstraction to
facilitate provisioning, configuration and testing of new server and application deployments. For example, in Figure 5.11, on the left side of the diagram, multiple VMs are
created on a physical machine, each with a guest operating system and some portion of
an application. During development and testing and to support predeployment IRM
maintenance functions, the various applications are checked on what appears to be a
separate server but in reality is a VM.

For deployment, the various applications and their operating system configurations
are deployed to physical servers as shown on the right of Figure 5.11. There are two
options, one being the deployment of the applications and their operating system on a
VM allocated on a one-to-one basis with a physical server as shown. The other option is
to convert the VM, along with the guest operating system and application, to run on a
physical server without a virtualization layer. In the first example, virtualization is used
for abstraction and management purposes as opposed to consolidation. An underlying
VM enables maintenance to be performed as well as giving the ability to tie into a virtualized BC/DR scheme as shown in Figure 5.11.

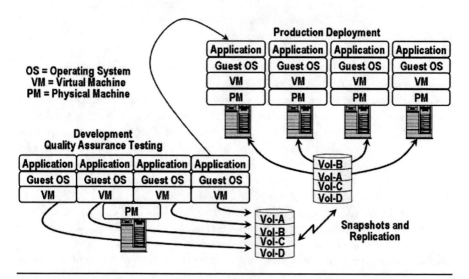

Figure 5.11   Utilizing virtualization for abstraction and server provisioning.

5.8. Data Protection Checklist

There is no time like the present to reassess, re-architect, and reconfigure your data protection environment, particularly if you are planning on or have already initiated a server virtualization initiative. Cloud and virtual server environments require real and physical data protection. After all, you cannot go forward from a disaster or loss of data if you cannot go back to a particular point in time and recover, restore, and restart, regardless of business or organization size.

Some common data protection best practices include the following:

- Some applications, including databases, support automatic log file shipping.
- Most disasters are the result of a chain of events not being contained.
- Leverage common sense and complete or comprehensive data protection.
- Verify support of USB-based crypto for encryption keys with VMs.
- Know what limitations exist for your software license for BC or DR testing.
- RAID is not a replacement for backup; it provides availability.
- Mirroring or replication alone is not a replacement for backup.
- Use point-in-time RPO based data protection such as snapshots with replication.
- Maintain a master backup or gold copy.
- Test restoration of data backed up locally and from cloud services.
- Employ data protection management tools for event correlation and analysis.
- Data stored in clouds needs to be part of a BC/DR and data protection strategy.
- Have a copy of data placed in clouds also in an alternative location for BC/DR.
- Combine multiple layers of protection and assume that what can break will break.
- Determine budget, time frame, tolerance to disruption, and risk aversion.
- Decide which solutions are best for different applications.
- Investigate whether redundant network paths share a common infrastructure.
- Seek out experienced help for assessment, validation, or implementation.

5.9. Common HA-, BC-, and DR-Related Questions

Is tape dead? Tape is alive and continuing to be developed as a technology; however, its role is shifting from routine backup to long-term archiving. D2D backup and data protection combined with data footprint reduction techniques continue to coexist with tape, resulting in more data being stored on tape than in previous history. The key take-away is that the role of tape is shifting to that of long-term or cold data preservation.

What are the barriers to using a cloud or virtualized environment for data protection? There are different constraints associated with the amount of data to be protected, time windows, network bandwidth, RTO and RPO, and budgets. Something else to consider is how your software licenses work or can be transferred to a BC as well as DR site, along with your ability to use those for testing purposes.

Are BC and DR only for large organizations; how can smaller organizations afford them? MSP and cloud-based services along with other technologies that can be installed on servers and workstations are making BC and DR more affordable. As an example, I have a small business and, practicing what I preach, have implemented a multitier data protection strategy including D2D, D2D2C, and D2D2D on a local, remote, as well as with removable technologies. I leverage a cloud backup MSP where encrypted data gets sent even while I am traveling (I have done backups from commercial aircraft using Gogo WiFi), as well as having local copies on disk. Additionally, I have a master copy off-site in a vault that gets routinely updated using removable hard disk drives. There are many different tools, with more on the way, some which will be available by the time you read this. Check my blog and website for news, announcements, and discussions on related topics, trends, and techniques.

What are some key steps or questions to ask when choosing an on-line or cloud MSP for backup or archive services? Balance the cost or fees of the service with the available functionality, SLAs, hidden fees for accessing your data, import or export charges, options for what locations or regions where your data can be stored, and reporting. For example, I get a daily backup report via email from my service provider that I can check manually or set up a script to scan for exceptions. Also look into how your data is reduced using data footprint reduction techniques before transmission, to either move more data in a given amount of time, or with less network bandwidth capability. Also test how long restores take, to avoid surprises when time may be of the essence, and look into options to get larger quantities of data restored in a shorter period of time.

5.10. Chapter Summary

HA, BC, DR, and backup/restore are changing with evolving and maturing techniques and technologies. Clouds and virtualization need to be protected, but, at the same time, they can be used for enhancing protection.

General action items include:

- Avoid treating all data and applications the same.
- Apply the applicable level of data protection to required needs.
- Modernize data protection to reduce overhead, complexity, and cost.
- Combine multiple data protection techniques in a cost-effective manner.
- Don't be afraid of cloud and virtualization, but have a plan.

Vendors include Acronis, Amazon, Aptare, Asigra, BMC, Bocada, CA, Cisco, Citrix, Commvault, Dell, EMC, Falconstor, Fujifilm, Fujitsu, HDS, HP, i365, IBM, Imation, Inmage, Innovation, Iron Mountain, Microsoft, NetApp, Oracle, Overland, Quantum, Quest, Rackspace, Platespin, Rectiphy, Seagate, Sepaton, Solarwinds, Spectralogic, Sungard, Symantec, Veeam, and VMware, among others.

The bottom line: For now, if you are putting data into any cloud, have a backup or a copy elsewhere. Likewise, if you have local or even remote data, consider using a cloud or managed service provider as a means of parking another copy of backups or archives. After all, any information worth keeping should have multiple copies on different media in various venues.

Chapter 6

Metrics and Measurements for Situational Awareness

If you can't measure and monitor something, how can you manage it effectively?
— Greg Schulz

In This Chapter

- Why metrics and measurements are important for managing resources
- Where and how to obtain metrics and measurements
- Chargeback vs. accounting measurements for managing resources
- Ensuring that required resources are available
- Key tenets of metrics and benchmarks for various use scenarios

This chapter looks at measuring, monitoring, and managing information resources for cloud, virtual, and data storage network environments. Situational awareness and timely insight into information services delivery and resources are important for enabling a flexible, scalable, resilient, and cost-effective environment. Key themes discussed in this chapter include end-to-end (E2E) cross-domain measurements and metrics, accounting and chargeback, and performance and capacity of cloud, virtual, and physical IT resources.

6.1. Getting Started

Many different metrics and measurements are applicable to cloud and virtual data storage networking. Metrics show where you are, where you have been, where you are going, and whether you are meeting goals, objectives, and requirements. Metrics show whether your network is improving, staying the same, or deteriorating. Metrics are also used on an ongoing basis to assess the health and status of how a technology is performing to meet service expectations. They relate to availability, reliability, performance, capacity, productivity, and other items. Metrics and measurements range from those used for product selection and acquisition to those used to gauge efficiency and quality of service, known as *key performance indicators* (KPIs). For example, storage efficiency can be measured in terms of capacity utilization or performance. In addition to performance, availability, capacity, energy, and cost, other metrics pertain to quality of service (QoS), service-level objectives (SLOs) and service-level agreements (SLAs) as well as data protection. Metrics are also used for planning, analysis, acquisition comparison, or competitive positioning purposes.

Metrics reflect IT resource usage during active and inactive periods over different time frames. IT resources are described as active when performing useful work and inactive when no work is being performed. In keeping with the idea that IT data centers are information factories, metrics and measurements are similar to those of non-information factories. Factories in general, and highly automated ones in particular, involve resources and technologies used to create goods or services. Efficient and effective factories leverage metrics to know their current inventory or resource status; their near- and long-term requirements, and their expected production or demand schedules. Metrics also help information factories know whether resources and technologies are being used in an effective manner that results in minimum waste or rework, cost-effective use of technologies, and customer satisfaction. In other words, a factory needs to be highly utilized without reaching the point at which rework or waste is a by-product, which leads to higher actual costs. Factories also need to be efficient without hindering the basic need to deliver services to customers in a timely manner while meeting or exceeding SLO and SLA requirements.

Metrics and measurements for cloud and virtual data storage networks include:

- Macro (power usage effectiveness) and micro (device or component level)
- Performance and productivity, showing activity or work being done
- Availability, showing reliability or accessibility of services and resources
- Capacity, the space or amount of resources being consumed or occupied
- Economics and cost of resources and services being delivered
- Energy efficiency and effectiveness, along with environmental health and safety
- Quality of service and customer service satisfaction

Metrics and measurements are used for:

- Troubleshooting and problem remediation
- Planning, analysis, and forecasting
- Tactical and strategic decision making
- Health and status of the environment
- Budgeting and expense management
- Comparison to other environments

- Tuning and optimization initiatives
- Managing suppliers and service providers
- Technology acquisition support
- Managing service delivery
- Resource and service accounting
- Chargeback and billing

Metrics and measurements apply to:

- Applications and information services
- Hardware, software, services, and tools
- Servers (cloud, virtual, and physical)
- I/O and networking
- Storage hardware and software
- Common infrastructure resource management functions
- People and processes

6.2. Making Sense of Metrics and Measurements

Metrics can be focused on activity and productivity, usually reported in terms of performance and availability, and on resource usage and efficiency. Metrics can reflect active work being done to deliver IT services in a given response time or work rate as well as indicate how IT resources are being used. IT equipment can be busy or inactive.

Data storage can be considered when active and responding to read and write requests or I/O operations or by measuring how much data is being stored independent of activity. Consequently, different types of storage, depending on the category and type or tier of storage, need to be compared on different bases. For example, magnetic tape used for off-line archiving and backup data can be measured on an idle or inactive basis in terms of capacity (raw, usable, or effective) per watt for a given footprint, data protection level, and price. While capacity is a concern, on-line active storage for primary and secondary data, including bulk storage, needs to be compared on an activity-per-watt basis as well as according to how much capacity is available at a given data protection level and cost point to meet service-level agreement objectives.

Confusion may arise about the use of megabyte, gigabyte, terabyte, or petabyte per watt when the context of bandwidth or capacity is missing. For example, in the context of bandwidth, 1.5 TB per watt means that 1.5 TB are moved per second at a given workload and service level. On the other hand, in the context of storage space capacity, 1.5 TB per watt means that 1.5 TB are stored in a given footprint and configuration. Be careful not to confuse use of bandwidth or data movement with storage space capacity when looking at terabytes or petabytes and related metrics per watt of energy.

For servers, useful metrics include application response time, I/O queues, number of transactions, Web pages, or email messages processed or other activity indicators and utilization of CPUs, memory, I/O or networking interfaces, and any local disk storage.

Availability can be measured in terms of planned and unplanned outages or for different timeframes such as prime time, nights, and weekends, or on a seasonal basis.

A common focus, particularly for environments looking to use virtualization for server consolidation, is server utilization. Server utilization provides a partial picture, but it is important to look also at performance and availability for additional insight into how a server is running. For example, a server may only operate at a given low utilization rate to meet application service-level response time or performance requirements. For networks, including switches, routers, bridges, gateways, and other specialized appliances, several metrics can be considered, including usage or utilization, performance in terms of number of frames, packets, input/output operations per second (IOPS), or bandwidth per second, as well as latency, errors, or queues indicating network congestion or bottlenecks.

From a storage standpoint, metrics should reflect performance in terms of IOPS, bandwidth, and latency for various types of workloads. Availability metrics reflect how much time or the percentage of time that the storage is available or ready for use. Capacity metrics reflect how much or what percent of a storage system is used. Energy metrics can be combined with performance, availability, and capacity metrics to determine energy efficiency.

Storage system capacity metrics should also reflect various native storage capacities in terms of raw, unconfigured, and configured, including RAID and file systems, and allocated LUNs and file system space for applicable comparisons. Storage granularity can be on a total usable storage system (block, file, and object) disk or tape basis or on a media enclosure basis, for example, a disk shelve enclosure or individual device (spindle) basis. Another dimension is the footprint of the storage solution, such as the floor space, rack space and height, weight, width, depth, and number of floor tiles.

It is important to avoid trying to do too much with a single or limited metric that compares too many different facets of resource usage. For example, simply comparing all IT equipment from an inactive, idle perspective does not reflect productivity and energy affiance for doing useful work. Likewise, not considering low-power modes hides energy-saving opportunities during low-activity periods. Focusing only on storage or server utilization or capacity per given footprint does not reflect how much useful work can be done in that footprint per unit of energy at a given cost and service delivery level.

6.3. Different Metrics for Different Audiences

There are different points of interest for different audiences at varying times during a product or technology lifecycle, as shown in Figure 6.1. For example, a vendor's engineers use comparative or diagnostic measurements at a component and system level during research and development and during manufacturing and quality assurance testing. Performance and availability benchmarks along with environmental, power, cooling, and other metrics are used for comparison and competitive positioning during the sales cycle.

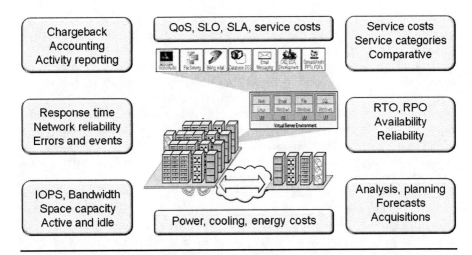

Figure 6.1   Metrics and measurements or metering points of interest.

A server is busy doing work, to some degree, or it is idle. Likewise, a networking device is supporting movement of data in-flight between users and servers, between servers and other servers, between servers and storage, or between storage devices on a local, metropolitan, or wide area basis. Storage devices support active work to satisfy I/O operations such as read and write requests as well as storing data.

Metrics and measurements used will vary depending on usage scenarios and needs. For example, manufacturers or software developers will have different needs and focus areas than sales and marketing departments. Likewise, IT organizations will have different needs and focus areas, including costs, energy usage, number or type of servers, amount of storage capacity vs. how many transactions can be supported. For a given product or solution, metrics will vary at different points of time, including during development, manufacture, and quality assurance, sales and marketing, customer acquisition and installation, integration testing, and ongoing support.

Figure 6.2 shows on the left various points of focus for metrics, ranging from facilities at the bottom to business and application centric at the top of the stack. Various types of metrics and measurements are available in the different categories that feed to the information resource management (IRM) monitoring, notification, logging, reporting, and correlation and analysis tools shown on the right of Figure 6.2.

6.4. Key Performance Indicators

In the context of key performance indicators (KPIs), performance can refer to activity-related metrics and measurements such as how well, or to what level of service, something is being managed and availability. Establishing a baseline set of measurements is important for many reasons, including establishing normal and abnormal behavior, identifying trends in usage or performance patterns, and for forecasting and planning purposes. For example, knowing the typical IOP rates and throughput rates for storage devices, as well as the common error rates, average queue depths, and response times, will allow quick comparisons and decisions when problems or changes occur.

Baselines should be established for resource performance and response time, capacity or space utilization, availability, and energy consumption. Baselines should also be determined for different application work scenarios so as to know, for example, how long certain tasks normally take. Baseline IRM functions, including database maintenance, backups, virus checking, and security scans, can be used to spot when a task is taking too long or finishing too fast, both of which may indicate a problem. Another example is that high or low CPU utilization may indicate an application or device error resulting in excessive activity or preventing work from being done.

From a forecasting and planning perspective, baseline comparisons can be used to determine or predict future resource usage needs while factoring in business and application growth. The benefit is that with a resource usage and performance capacity plan, the right amount and type of resources can be made available in a timely and cost-effective manner when needed. By combining capacity planning across servers, storage, networks, and facilities, different groups from IT and data center facilities organizations can keep each other informed on when and where PCFE resources will be needed to support server, storage, and networking growth.

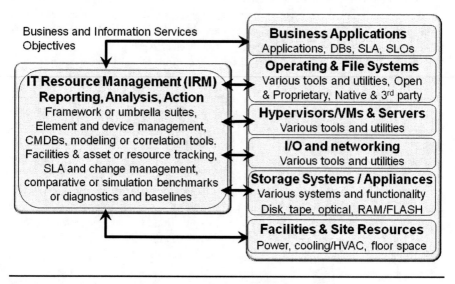

Figure 6.2   Different metrics and measurements for various purposes.

6.4.1. Averages, Rates, and Ratios

Metrics can be point-in-time samples or event-based or cumulative totals or averages. The time sample can vary from instantaneous or real-time to per second, minute, hour, day, week, and month, or on an annual basis. Averages, rates, and ratios can be on a real-time or historical basis spanning different periods of time or durations depending on the intended purpose. Time intervals can also be considered for different focus areas such as prime time, off-hours, evenings, weekends, or holidays as well as for peak seasonal periods. The challenge with averages is to know what the timeframe and the scope or focus are. For example, is "average utilization" for 24 hours a day 365 days a year, or is it for prime time Monday through Friday? Averages provide a quick high-level view, but narrowing the focus to a given context is also important, as is knowing the maximum, minimum, or deviation, to gain more insight and avoid false assumptions or incorrect decisions.

In Figure 6.3, seasonal workload is shown along with seasonal spikes in activity (dotted curve). Figure 6.3 can represent servers processing transactions, file, video, or other activity-based work, networks moving data, or a storage system responding to read and write requests. The resulting impact on response time (dotted line) is shown in relation to a threshold line of acceptable response-time performance. The threshold line is calculated based on experience or expected behavior and is the level of work beyond which corresponding response time will degrade to below acceptable service levels. For example, peaks due to holiday shopping exchanges appear in January and then drop off, increasing again near Mother's Day in May.

Thresholds are also useful from a space capacity standpoint, for example, on servers to determine that particular applications can run at up to 75% utilization before response time and productivity suffer. Another example might be establishing that storage capacity utilization to meet performance needs for active data and storage is 70%, while near-line or off-line storage can be utilized at a higher rate. (Note that the previous threshold examples are just that—examples—and that specific thresholds will vary. Check with application or system software as well as hardware manufacturers for guideline and configuration rules of thumb.)

The importance of rates is to understand activity as well as cause and effect, such as impacts due to loss or limited availability or performance bottlenecks. Rates can apply to many different things such as transactions, IOPS, files or objects being accessed, data movement or access, backup and restore time or data movement and migration

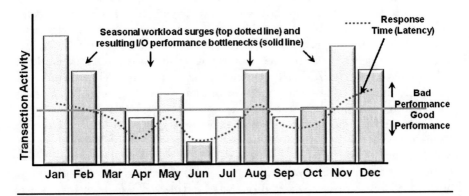

Figure 6.3   I/O bottleneck from peak workload activity.

between locations or devices. Rates are often associated with time, productivity, or activity, while ratios can be used for activity as well as space savings or other improvement measurements. An example of using rates and ratios is for backup and data footprint reduction. Measuring how much data can be moved in a given amount of time, either to backup or to restore, involves rates of activity, while how much the data can be reduced involves ratios. Both rates and ratios are applicable, but, for a given scenario, one may be more important than the other—for example, meeting a backup, restore, or data protection time window will mean more emphasis on rates.

On the other hand, when time is not the primary objective and the focus is on how much space can be saved, ratios, such as compression or dedupe reduction, become more applicable. Another example is caching performance, where, to improve service delivery, one metric is how utilized the resources are vs. how effectively they are being used. A cache or resource may be operating at a high utilization, but what is the hit rate and subsequent reduction in response time? Simply looking at utilization tells that the resource is being used; there is no indication of whether response time or latency has improved or deteriorated, whether activity is being resolved by the cache or the cache is being constantly refreshed due to misses, resulting in lower performance. Thus, it is important to look at multiple metrics and understand where averages, rates, and ratios come into play as well as how they relate to each other and information services delivery.

6.4.2. Compound Metrics

Multiple metrics can and should be considered. It is important, however, to look at them in the context of how and where they are being used. For example, a fast solid-state disk (SSD) will have a high IOPS and low power consumption per physical footprint compared to a traditional disk drive. However, a SSD will usually also have a lower storage capacity and may require different data protection techniques compared to regular disk storage. Another comparison is that while SSD may be more expensive on a capacity basis, on the basis of IOPS per footprint, the SSD may have a lower cost per transaction, IOP, or activity performed than regular disk, albeit with less space capacity.

A metric can consider a single item or can be combined with others to create a compound metric. Examples of single metrics include how many terabytes of storage capacity you have or are using, the total number of virtual machines and physical machines, availability for a given period of time, or measured activity such as IOPs, transactions, files or video accessed, or backup operations in a given time frame. These metrics may be obtained directly using a tool or utility or via some calculation such as determining daily, weekly, monthly, or annual availability.

Compound metrics, made up of multiple metrics, help to put metrics into context. While the amount of terabytes storage capacity may be interesting, it should prompt questions such as whether that is before any RAID or data protection is applied, formatted with file systems or volume managers, on-line primary, secondary, tertiary, or cloud, allocated, free, or unused. Compound metrics add another metric, such as performance or activity, availability or data protection, cost or configuration, energy or facilities or cost, to provide a bigger, clearer picture. A common compound metric is cost per gigabyte or terbyte of storage capacity for a given period of time.

Building on the previous example, a compound metric might be storage capacity per watt of energy or capacity per watt per given physical footprint and data protection. This shows, for a given (or perhaps average) amount of storage, how much energy is used with a specific data protection (availability, RAID, replication, backup/restore) level that occupies a given amount of floor or rack space. Other examples of compound metrics include cost per activity (IOPS, transactions, files or objects accessed, packets or frames moved, bandwidth) or cost per footprint (space, rack space), or cost per data protection and availability, or energy (power and cooling) consumed. In addition to cost, other combinations include IOPS or bandwidth per watt of energy, or combining three or more metrics such as bandwidth per watt of energy that occurs in a given physical floor space and data protection level. Other compound metrics can combine quality of service, service-level objectives, and service-level agreements along with people or staffing—for example, how many terabytes managed per person, time required to provision a physical or virtual machine, and a given amount of storage.

Metrics such as these are important because some vendors will say they will provide a gigabyte of storage for $0.05 per month while another provider, or perhaps your own organization, has a cost of $0.14 per gigabyte per month with a defined SLA and SLO. For $0.14 your storage may have "five 9s" availability, a recovery-time objective (RTO) of an hour or less, and a recovery-point objective (RPO) of under five minutes in addition to no fees for accessing or updating data with a copy also placed at another location. Meanwhile, the gigabyte of storage for $0.05 has a SLA of "three 9s," does not include an extra copy, has a RTO of 48 hours and no RPO plus fees for reading or getting as well as accessing information such as to run a report or check status. If a comparison is based only on the compound metric of cost per gigabyte, you may very well get what you pay for—in other words, the $0.05 per gigabyte may actually cost you more in terms of impact to applications or information services delivery than the $0.14 storage.

Recall the discussion in Chapter 3 about knowing what applications or information services are being delivered as well as SLO and SLA requirements so as to be able to make informed decisions. Knowing that a given use case, application, or information services delivery scenario needs only basic storage may, in fact, make the lower-cost solution the best one. However, that conclusion also suggests that an internal IT or information services delivery provider should establish a lower cost and type of service offering for those applications or consumers that need it. At the same time, knowledge of applicable metrics increases awareness of the importance of education to consumers and the benefit of up-selling to the value of higher-priced service solutions.

6.5. Measuring IT Resources and Services Delivery

Not all storage devices should be compared on the same active or idle workload basis. For example, magnetic tape devices typically store off-line, inactive data and only consume power when data is being read or written. Given that storage is used for some applications that are active and for others with data inactive or dormant for long periods of time, different metrics should be used when analyzing types of storage for different applications. Applications that rely on performance or data access need to be compared on an activity basis, while applications and data that are focused more on data retention should be compared on a cost-per-capacity basis. For example, active, on-line and primary data that needs to provide performance should be looked at in terms of activity per watt per footprint cost, while inactive or idle data should be considered on a capacity per watt per footprint cost basis.

For space capacity–based storage and, in particular, storage for idle data including backup targets or archiving solutions combining data de-duplication, there is a tendency to measure in terms of de-duplication ratios. Ratios are a nice indicator of how, for a given set of data, the data and its footprint can be reduced. Data movement or ingestion and processing rates (the rate at which data can be reduced) is a corollary metric for data reduction ratios. Data reduction rates, including compression rates, give an indication of how much data can be reduced in a given window or time frame.

Another metric variation looks at the amount of storage capacity per watt in a given footprint. This is useful for inactive and idle storage. This type of metric is commonly used by vendors, similar to how dollar per capacity ($/GB) is often used, for comparing different storage technologies. One issue with this metric, however, is whether it is considering the capacity as raw (no RAID, no file system or volume formatting) or as allocated to a file system or as free vs. used. Another issue with this metric by itself is that it does not reflect activity or application performance or effectiveness of energy per unit of capacity to support a given amount of work—for example, watt per tape cartridge when the tape is on a shelf vs. when the tape is being written to or read. Another concern is how to account for hot spare disk drives in storage arrays. Also, the metric should account for data off-line as well as data on-line and in use.

IRM metrics include those for performance and capacity planning of servers, storage, networking, hardware, software, and facilities, along with power and cooling. This means storage space capacity along with performance, availability, and associated software licenses for servers or other software and tools. Other IRM metrics include those for security, such as intrusion alerts or log-in failures, resource access patterns, and errors. Data protection metrics include, in addition to SLO and SLA RTO or RPO, those for speed of restoration, backing up, retention, and recycling as well as error activity. Another IRM metric is how quickly a resource, such as a VM, PM, network, or storage, can be provisioned to fulfill a requirement for service.

6.5.1. Performance, Availability, Capacity, Energy, and Economics (PACE)

Fundamental metrics for IT and information services delivery across all applications include some amount of performance, availability, capacity, energy, and economics, all of which can be broken into more specific subcategories. For example, availability can be subdivided into high availability, access, reliability, data protection, business continuance/disaster recovery, backup/restore, and others.

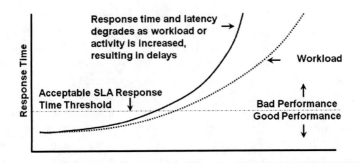

Figure 6.4   I/O response-time performance impact.

6.5.1.1. Performance and Active Resource Usage

Performance- or activity-related metrics measure how much work is done or processed in a given amount of time. Metrics include IOPS, frames or packets or messages, transactions, files or objects accessed, bandwidth or throughput, response time or latency. Metrics can be for reads or writes, large or small random or sequential activity moving, storing, retiering, or checking status of information. Understanding the metric is important in that a large number of small IOPs can create a low throughput value and vice versa. This can be important in determining whether there is a problem if you have a network connection rated at 10 GB per second but are only seeing 3 GB per second, and you have a server supporting many virtual machines. If the aggregate workload of those VMs on the physical machine involves doing many small 4-KB IOPS, a low throughput or bandwidth metric may not be a problem; however, other metrics, including response time or retransmission and errors, should be considered.

If the same 10 GB-per-second network connection were running at 9 GB per second while supporting large sequential data movement and a high number of errors or retransmits are observed, there might be a problem with collisions or the underlying quality of the network connection. Hence the importance of looking at different, related metrics to see the whole picture. This helps avoid false positives when troubleshooting that could result in treating only the symptoms and not the real problem. The reason for using network performance and bandwidth as an example is that I have seen many instances where someone is concerned that they are not getting the rated bandwidth or performance; the advertised rate or speed may be the maximum line rate or speed of the technology, rather than what is effectively available. In some cases it turns out, as in the above example, that what was thought to be a problem was, in fact, normal. Further investigation, however, may uncover other issues or challenges that can lead to opportunities for improvement.

Generally speaking, as additional activity or application workload (including transactions or file accesses) is performed, I/O bottlenecks will cause increased response time. With most performance metrics, such as throughput, you are looking to optimize the highest value or rate. With response time, however, the lower the latency, the better. Figure 6.4 shows that as more work is performed (dotted curve), I/O bottlenecks increase and result in increased response time (solid curve). The specific acceptable response time threshold will vary by applications and SLA requirements. As more workload is added to a system with existing I/O issues, response time will increase correspondingly (as seen in Figure 6.4). The more severe the bottleneck, the faster the response time will deteriorate. The elimination of bottlenecks enables more work to be performed while maintaining response time at acceptable service-level threshold limits.

To compensate for poor I/O performance and to counter the resulting negative impact on IT users, a common approach is to add more hardware to mask or move the problem. But overconfiguring to support peak workloads and prevent loss of business revenue means that excess storage capacity must be managed throughout the nonpeak periods, adding to data center and management costs. The resulting ripple effect is that more storage needs to be managed, including allocating storage network ports, configuring, tuning, and backing up of data. Storage utilization well below 50% of available capacity is common. The solution is to address the problem rather than moving and hiding the bottleneck elsewhere (rather like sweeping dust under the rug).

For activity-based IT data center measurements, that is, where useful work is being done, metrics on activity per unit of energy are applicable. In everyday life, a common example of this type of metric is miles per gallon for automobiles or miles per gallon per passenger for mass transit including commercial aviation. Examples of data center useful work and activity include data being read or written, transactions or files being processed, videos or Web pages served, or data being moved over local or wide area networks.

Activity per watt of energy consumed can also be thought of as the amount of work per energy unit used. A reciprocal is the amount of energy per unit of work performed. Activity per watt can be used to measure transient or flow-through networking and I/O activity between servers and storage devices or between user workstations and an application server. Common examples of work per energy used are megahertz per watt, IOPS, transactions, bandwidth or video streams per watt, storage capacity per watt, or miles per gallon. All indicate how much work is being done and how efficiently energy is being used to accomplish that work. This metric applies to active workloads or actively used and frequently accessed storage and data.

Bandwidth per watt should not be confused with capacity-per-watt metrics such as terabytes of storage capacity space. This metric refers to the amount of data moved per second per energy used. Bandwidth per watt also applies to transient and flow-through networking traffic. It is also used for measuring the amount of data that can be read or written from a storage device or server. Examples include megabytes per second per watt of energy for network (LAN, SAN, MAN, or WAN) traffic or switch. Another example is gigabytes per second per watt of energy for bandwidth or large I/O-intensive storage reads and writes for a server or storage system. IOPS per watt represents the number of I/O operations (read or write, random or sequential, small or large) per unit of energy in a given time frame for a given configuration and response time or latency level.

6.5.1.2. Availability, Accessibility, and Reliability

Availability includes uptime of individual components along with the cumulative availability of everything required for information services delivery to the consumer. Reliability and accessibility are also components of availability, including for data protection activities. Performance equals availability; the inverse, availability equals performance, also holds true. The two are very much intertwined yet seldom discussed. If you do not have availability, you cannot have performance; if you do not have adequate performance to meet quality-of-service or other time-sensitive needs, you do not have availability.

Given current economic conditions and the pressure to do more with less or do more with what you have, IT data center infrastructure and storage optimization are popular topics. In the continued quest to optimize IT infrastructures, including storage, to achieve more efficient use and effective service delivery, a focus has been on space capacity utilization. However, the other aspect of boosting efficiency and productivity is identifying, isolating, and addressing bottlenecks in IT data center infrastructures.

A simple example of how performance and availability are related can be found in RAID (Redundant Array of Inexpensive/Independent Disks). For example, various RAID levels allow different levels of performance and availability and capacity options to be aligned to meet specific needs. Other impacts on performance and availability include failed adapters, controllers, or other components, such as automatic disk drive rebuilds in RAID sets using hot spares. Background tasks including parity scrubbing or data consistency checks, snapshots, replication, deferred or postprocessing for data de-duplication, virus, and other tasks can also manifest as performance or availability impacts.

Availability and performance issues are not limited to storage systems; they also apply to servers and I/O network or data paths including switches and routers. Keep an eye on alternate pathing configurations for I/O adapters as well as error counts. On switches or routers, monitor error counts and retries along with how they compare to normal baseline performance profiles. Availability can be measured and reported on an individual component basis, as a sum of all components, or as a composite of both. Table 6.1 shows various availability- and reliability-related metrics and terms. A balanced view of availability is to look at the big picture in terms of end-to-end or total availability. This is the view that is seen by users of the services supported by the storage network and its applications.

The annual failure rate (AFR) is the association between the mean time between failures (MTBF) and the number of hours a device is run per year. AFR can take into consideration different sample sizes and time in use for a device. For example, a large sample pool of 1,000,000 disk drives that operates 7 × 24 hours a day (8760 hours a year) with 1000 failures has an AFR of 8.76%. If another group of similar devices is used only 10 hours a day, 5 days a week, 52 weeks (2600 hours) a year with the same sample size and number of failures, its AFR is 2.6%. MTBF can be calculated from the AFR by dividing the total annual time a device is in use by the AFR. For the previous example, MTBF = 2600/2.6 = 1000. The AFR is useful for looking at various size samples over time and factoring in duty or time in use for availability comparison or other purposes.

6.5.1.3. Capacity and Storage Space

Capacity can refer to having enough performance or availability. It also is often associated with storage space for cloud, virtual, and physical environments. Storage capacity

Table 6.1 Availability- and Reliability-Related Terms

Term or Acronym	Description
Accessibility	Whether data or services that still exist can be accessed or not
AFR	Annual failure rate, measured or estimated failures per year
Availability	Amount of time a system is able and ready to work
Downtime	Application, service, component, or site not available for use
MTBF	Mean time between failures, measured or estimated reliability
MTTM	Mean time to migrate or move data from one location to another
MTTR	Mean time to repair or replace failed item back into service
MTTR	Mean time to restore a disk, volume, file, file system, or database
Outage	Systems or subsystems are not available for use or to perform work
Rebuild	How long to rebuild a disk or storage system on-line or off-line
Reliability	Systems function as expected, when expected, with confidence
RPO	Recovery-point objective, to which data can be restored
RTO	Recovery-time objective, when recovery data is usable again
Scheduled downtime	Planned downtime for maintenance, replacement, and upgrades
Unscheduled	Unplanned downtime for emergency repair or maintenance

is space being used for various purposes such as primary on-line for active or secondary, tertiary for near-line, and inactive or idle data on a local or remote including cloud-provided. Figure 6.5 shows how storage capacity can be measured at different points

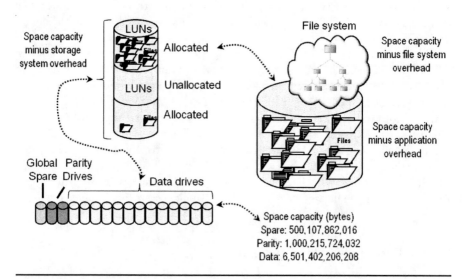

Figure 6.5 Storage space capacity metrics.

with various results. For example, the lower left corner of Figure 6.5 shows 16 500-GB disk drives that are part of a storage system. If you remember from Chapter 2, the 500-GB disk drive has 500,107,862,016 bytes of raw capacity.

Assuming a 13+2 RAID 6, or what NetApp refers to as RAID-DP, two of the disk drives' effective capacity or 1,000,215,724,032 bytes are used for parity information, with 6,501,402,206,208 bytes available for data. Note that while Figure 6.5 shows two disk drives for parity, depending on the actual RAID level and implementation, parity is spread across the actual disk drives. Depending on actual storage system and RAID implementation, the usable storage capacity is 6,501,402,206,208 bytes or less.

In Figure 6.5, the storage capacity is allocated onto three LUNs, which are then allocated to different file systems or operating systems on physical or virtual servers. Once formatted for a file system or operating system, the usable capacity is reduced by applicable overhead plus space for data protection including snapshots. In Figure 6.5, two of the three LUNs are allocated, while the third is inactive and waiting to be provisioned. Another space-related metric for allocated storage is how much of it is free or in use with files or objects. Sparse storage refers to space that is allocated yet only partially used, such as a database table that is 100 GB in size and in which only 20 GB contain data. From a storage capacity standpoint, 100 GB of space is allocated and used even though there are 80 GB free within the database table. This empty or sparse space can also exist in other files or file systems and is sometimes referred to as white or blank space.

The importance of knowing about sparse space is that for physical, virtual, or cloud storage capacity being allocated and then used, while containing sparse or empty space, the total space consumed vs. what is actually used is what may be reported. If you are paying for a service and store a 100-GB file that has only 20 GB of data, you may be charged for the 80 GB of space that you are not actually using. Data footprint reduction (DFR) technologies, including thin provision, space-saving snapshots, compression, and de-duplication can help reduce the overhead or impact of data including sparse storage.

Applicable metrics include storage capacity (raw or formatted); allocated or non-allocated; local, remote, or cloud-based; fast on-line primary, medium-speed near-line secondary, or slower, lower-cost, high-capacity tertiary storage for inactive and idle or dormant data. The importance of understanding different types of storage and capacities is to avoid "apples to oranges" comparisons involving cost, SLOs and SLAs.

6.5.1.4. Energy Efficiency and Economic Effectiveness

For many organizations, there tends to be a focus on both managing power and managing productivity. The two are, or should be, interrelated, but there are some disconnects with some emphasis and metrics. For example, the Green Grid power usage effectiveness (PUE) measurement is a macro facilities-centric metric that does not reflect the productivity, quality, or quantity of services being delivered by a data center or information factory. Instead, the PUE provides a gauge of how efficient the habitat—that is, the building, power distribution, and cooling—is with respect to the total energy consumption of IT equipment.

What's your interest in energy metrics? Is it avoidance as a form of efficiency, or increasing productivity while using the same or less resources for improved effectiveness? Is it macro, such as how well your facility compares to someone else using PUE, or is it how much work you can perform in a cost-effective manner that meets customer SLOs and SLAs? Or are you interested in productivity, such as the amount of work or activity that can be done in a given amount of time, or how much information can be stored in a given footprint (power, cooling, floor space, budget, and management)?

The Green Grid developed the PUE along with other IT facility macro metrics. The PUE metric compares the total amount of energy consumed by the data center to the total amount of energy consumed by the data center's IT equipment. That is, PUE = total data center facility power consumption/IT equipment power consumption. A PUE below 2 is highly effective; above 3, and there are bigger problems than the IT gear. Another Green Grid metric is Data Center infrastructure Efficiency (DCiE), which is the reciprocal of PUE (1/PUE). DCiE is defined as IT equipment power consumption/total data center facility power consumption × 100%.

The Green Grid defines PUE as being greater than or equal to 1.0, and DCiE as being greater than or equal to 100%. IT equipment power consumption includes energy used for servers, storage systems, network equipment, monitors, workstations, printers, copiers, and other associated technologies. Total data center facility power consumption is measured as the energy going into a facility that supports power distribution units (PDUs); uninterruptible power supplies (UPS), generators, standby battery power, cooling, lighting, and IT equipment.

For example, if a data center facility consumes 3000 watts (3 kW) of energy, and IT equipment consumes 2000 watts (2 kW), the PUE is 1.5 and the DCiE is 66.667%. A PUE of 1.5 (considered to be good) means that energy demands are 1.5 times that of the IT equipment deployed in a given data center. On the other hand, a data center consuming 5 kW of energy with IT equipment consuming 1.5 kW would have a PUE of 3.33 or a DCiE of 30%, which is considered less effective.

In the case of EPA Energy Star for Data Centers, which initially focused on the habitat or facility efficiency, the answer is measuring and managing energy use and facility efficiency as opposed to productivity or useful work. The metric for EPA Energy Star for Data Center initially will be Energy Usage Effectiveness (EUE), which will be used to calculate a rating for a data center facility. Note the word "energy" instead of "power," which means that the data center macro metric based on Green Grid PUE rating looks at all sources of energy used by a data center and not just electrical power. What this means is that a macro and holistic facilities energy consumption could be a combination of electrical power, diesel, propane, natural gas, or other fuel sources to generate or create power for IT equipment, HVAC/cooling, and other needs. By using a metric that factors in all energy sources, a facility that uses solar, radiant, heat pumps, economizers, or other techniques to reduce energy demand will achieve a better rating.

What EUE and PUE do not reflect or indicate is how much data is processed, moved, and stored by servers, storage, and networks within a facility. At the other extreme are micro or component metrics that gauge energy usage on an individual device basis. Some of these micro metrics may have activity or productivity indicator measurements associated with them; some don't. This leaves a big gap and opportunity to fill the span between the macro and micro metrics.

Work is being done by various industry groups, including SNIA GSI, SPC, and SPEC, as well as through EPA Energy Star and others to move beyond macro PUE indicators to more granular effectiveness and efficiency metrics that reflect productivity. Ultimately, it is important to gauge productivity, including return on investment and the business value of how much data can be processed by servers, moved via networks, or stored on storage devices in a given energy footprint or cost.

Watch for new metrics looking at productivity and activity for servers, storage, and networks ranging from megahertz or gigahertz per watt to transactions or IOPS per watt, bandwidth, frames or packets processed per watt, or capacity stored per watt in a given footprint. A confusing metric is gigabytes or terabytes per watt, because these can mean storage capacity or bandwidth, so it is important to understand the context of the metric. Likewise, watch for metrics that reflect energy usage for active along with inactive including idle or dormant storage common with archives, backup, or fixed-content data.

What this means is that work continues on developing usable and relevant metrics and measurements not only for macro energy usage but also to gauge the effectiveness of delivering IT services. The business value proposition of driving efficiency and optimization includes increased productivity and storing more information in a given footprint to support density and business sustainability. Remember to keep idle and active modes of operation in perspective when comparing tiered storage.

6.6. Where to Get Metrics

Metrics and measurements can be obtained from many different sources, including tools developed in-house, operating system or application utilities, external probes, sniffers and analyzers, built-in reporting facilities, as well as add-on third-party data collection and reporting tools. Sources for information include event, activity, transaction logs and journals, and operating system and application-based tools. Servers, storage, and networking solutions vendors also provide varying degrees of data collection and reporting capacities.

Performance testing and benchmarks have different meanings and different areas of focus. There is testing for compatibility and interoperability of components. There is performance testing of individual components as well as testing of combined solutions. Testing can be very rigorous and thorough, perhaps beyond real-world conditions, or testing can be relatively simple to verify data movement and integrity. What is the best test for your environment depends on your needs and requirements. The best test is one that adequately reflects your environment and the application's workload and that can be easily reproduced.

Some metrics are measured, whereas others are derived from measured metrics or are developed from a combination of different metrics. For example, a storage system may report the number of I/O operations on a read/write basis along with the amount of data read and written. A derived metric might be created by dividing bandwidth by number of I/O operations to get average I/O size. Similarly, if number of I/O operations and average I/O size are known, bandwidth can be determined by multiplying I/O rate by I/O size. Different solutions will report various metrics at different levels of detail. Third-party measurement and reporting tools, depending on data source and collection capabilities, will vary in the amount of detail that can be reported.

Metrics may be instantaneous burst- or peak-based or sustained over a period of time with maximum, minimum, average, and standard deviation noted along with cumulative totals. These metrics can be recorded and reported according to different time intervals; for example, by hour, work shift, day, week, month, or year.

Other metrics that can be obtained or calculated include those related to recycling, emissions, air flow, and temperature. Different metrics pertain to server CPU, memory, I/O, and network utilization along with capacity usage and performance of local or internal storage. A compound metric is derived from multiple metrics or calculations. For example, IOPS per watt can be determined when base metrics such as IOPS and watts are obtained and calculated together to represent an activity-per-imagery-consumed metric.

Application metrics include transactions, email messages, files, photos, videos, or other documents processed. Metrics for data protection include amount of data transferred in a given time frame, number of successful or failed backup or data protection tasks, how long different jobs or tasks take, as well as other error and activity information. Configuration management information includes how many of different types of servers, storage, and networking components, as well as software and firmware along with how they are configured.

These and other metrics can indicate a rate of usage as a count or percentage of a total, such as server CPU measured from 0 to 100% busy. While percent utilization gives a relative picture of the level of activity of a resource, percent utilization by itself does not provide an indicator of how service is being delivered or of the PCFE impact. Performance of servers, storage, and networks typically degrades as more work is being done, so it is important to look at response time and latency as well as IOPS or bandwidth, percent utilization, and space used.

New and evolving metrics are being developed for storage and energy efficiency, including work being done by EPA Energy Star for data center storage, SNIA Storage Management Initiative Specification (SMIS), SNIA Green Storage Initiative (GSI), SNIA Cloud Storage Initiative and their Cloud Data Management Interface (CDMI), SPEC, SPC, and other industry trade groups. Examples of application– and operating system–based monitoring tools include FC-GS4, dd, df, Iometer, iostat, nfstat, Perfmon, sar, SMF and RMF, timex, SMIS, SNMP MIBS, Vmark, and vmstat, among others from various vendors or service providers.

6.7. Accounting and Chargeback

Do clouds require chargeback? Depending on who you talk to, as well as the context of what is or is not a cloud, the answer, as always, is "It depends." If your perspective of a cloud or service is that of a subscription service where monetary payments are involved, then accounting in the form of chargeback involved and billing is needed along with underlying metering capabilities.

Chargeback and accounting are often intermingled in their use. For cloud or services that do not require billing or actual invoicing and payments, usage and activity reporting or accounting capabilities are needed. If your preference is to refer to the latter as chargeback, then yes, charge is needed. On other hand, if all you need is to meter and track usage of resources, service delivery, and customer satisfaction with SLOs and SLAs, then what you need are accounting, metrics and measurements for management reporting. What is needed is metrics that enable end-to-end management and situational awareness, regardless of whether invoices and bills are being generated as part of a chargeback, budget or planning, or customer information.

What is important is that, for your cloud, virtual, or physical environment, you are able to track for your own use as well as provide awareness and insight to your customers of resource and services costs, with or without formal chargeback. Keeping your customers informed can help them determine if the level of service they think they need or want is what they really need. By generating awareness of the value of enhanced services, SLOs, and SLAs, consumers of services may realize that the cheapest service is not the most cost-effective. Thus it is important to have insight into what it costs to deliver a given level of services, including a bill of materials (BOM) of raw materials, technology resource tools, as well as people and processes, to determine whether you are competitive with other offerings.

In addition, you may discover that external resources or services can be complementary to your own service delivery. However, if you do not know your own costs, you are at a disadvantage to someone trying to sell to you or your customers a competing or alternative service that may in fact have a higher overall cost. As a result, while formal chargeback, invoicing, and billing are not required for non-subscription- or fee-based services or if you are not currently doing chargeback for your existing environment, it is still important to have a metered environment and ability to track services, quality, resources, and costs, just as for a traditional factory.

6.8. Benchmarks and Simulation Comparisons

The best benchmark is your own application, or something closely resembling it, and associated workload levels. This, however, is not always possible to do on your own or even using a testing service or vendor's resources. There are many different workload simulations that can be used for making relative comparisons of how different resources (hardware, software, and network) support a given type or level of service being delivered. Benchmark or workload simulation tools include Netperf, Netbench, Filebench, Iometer, SPECnfs, DVD Store, JEDEC SSD, vMark, TPC, SPC, Microsoft ESRP, Oracle, and Swingbench.

SPC is a collection of benchmark or workload simulations for block-based storage with tests for transactional or IOPs, bandwidth, or throughput, along with system-level and individual components. While SPC is popular with many vendors and provides standard reporting information that includes pricing for a given configuration, applicable discounts, activity, bandwidth including latency numbers and configuration with data protection, it is not applicable for all cases. For example, if your focus is testing or comparing Microsoft Exchange or similar workloads, then look at applicable simulations such as Microsoft Exchange Solutions Reviewed Program (ESRP), or, if NFS and file serving, SPEC for NFS may be more applicable. If you are testing for transactional database, one of the TPC tests may be more appropriate.

The caveats of running standardized workload simulations such as SPC are the opportunities for taking advantage of the results, showing and making apples-to-oranges comparisons on cost per IOP, or other ploys. For example, some vendors can show a highly discounted list price to show a better IOP per cost; however, when processes are normalized, the results may be quite different. However, for those who dig into the SPC results, including looking at the configurations, the latency under workload is also reported.

Where the misleading benchmark or simulation issues can come into play is for those who simply look at what a vendor is claiming, without taking the time to look closely at the results and make the appropriate comparisons for the actual situation. The results are there for those who are really interested in digging in and sifting through the material, even if it seems easier not to do so.

It is important to look at all of the information to make sure, first, that it is applicable or relevant to your environment. If performance and, particularly, response time are important, latency usually does not lie, so use that as an indicator beyond bandwidth or activity per second to get a better idea of how a solution will work for you. If bandwidth or throughput is your focus, look beyond IOPS or transaction activity rates, as they may not be relevant.

What I am saying here is that, generally, latency does not lie. For example, if vendor A doubles the amount of cache, doubles the number of controllers, doubles the number of disk drives, compared to vendor B on a benchmark to get a better value such as IOPs, look at the latency numbers.

Vendor B may be at list price while vendor A is heavily discounted. However, to normalize the pricing and judge fairly, look at how much more equipment vendor A may need to discount the price, offset the increased amount of hardware, and then look at latency.

The latency results may actually be better for a vendor B than for a vendor A. Beyond showing what a controller can actually do in terms of leveraging the number of disks, cache, interface ports, and so forth, the big kicker is for those talking about SSD (RAM or FLASH) in that SSD generally is about latency. To fully and effectively utilize SSD, which is a low-latency device, you want a controller that can do a decent job of handling IOPS; however, you also need a controller that can handle IOPS with low latency under heavy workload conditions.

Keep in mind that the best benchmark is your own application running workloads similar to what you expect to see under normal and abnormal or peak conditions. In the absence of a full simulation or the ability to run your own application, workload simulations that closely resemble your applications or services profile can be used as indicators. Tools such as IOmeter, which can be configured to run subsets of workloads, can be used as long as you have a good understanding and profile of your applications' characteristics. For example, if part of your application does a large number of small read requests while another part does extensive write logging to journals, with yet another piece doing large sequential reads followed by large sequential writes for maintenance or other purposes, a test simulation should accommodate that. Simply running a benchmark using IOmeter or some other tool that does a large number of small 512-byte (½K) I/Os to show a high IOPS rating is not applicable unless that is all your application requires.

The importance of knowing your applications services characteristics is important for planning, analysis, comparison, and other purposes cannot be overstated. Use the applicable metrics that matter for you and your application being tested in a manner as close as possible to how it will be used.

6.9. Common Metrics-Related Questions

What are the best metrics that matter? The answer depends on your needs and requirement. Following are some common questions for cloud and virtual data storage networking environments; if you can answer them for your environment, then you have metrics and management measurements that matter. If you have difficulty or it takes time or a number of people to provide answers, that should give you clues as to where effort is needed to improve your metrics.

- Are all servers, storage, and switches able to support new features?
- Can software licenses be used at stand-by or secondary sites?
- How many seats or software license units are available for use?
- What is the cost per capacity per footprint of a device?
- How long does it take to back up as well as restore data?
- What is the cost to perform a backup or restore operation?
- What is the cost of an IOP, transaction, or message?
- What is the data protection overhead of the capacity installed?
- What hardware technology is due for replacement or upgrading?
- What is the normal baseline performance for applications?
- How much current effective network bandwidth exists?
- What is the network error rate vs. SLA and SLO stated rates?
- Who are the top network traffic users?
- What is your cost to deliver a given level of service?
- Do you know whether your costs are more or less than a third party's?
- Do you know if your data is compressible or de-dupable?
- What are your current data retentions for backup/restore and archives?
- Does your capacity plan cover performance, networking, and software?
- How much of current storage is being used, and by whom?
- What storage is allocated to what servers and applications?
- Where are the performance or applications bottlenecks?
- How much time is spent on reactive tasks vs. proactive?

6.10. Chapter Summary

Cloud, virtual, and physical data centers require physical resources to function efficiently and in a green or environmentally friendly manner. It is vital to understand the value of resource performance, availability, capacity, and energy usage to deliver various IT services. Understanding the relationships between different resources and how they are used is important to gauge improvement and productivity as well as data center efficiency. For example, while the cost per raw terabyte may seem relatively inexpensive, the cost for I/O response time performance also needs to be considered for active data.

Having enough resources to support business and application needs is essential to a resilient storage network. Without adequate storage and storage networking resources, availability and performance can be negatively impacted. Poor metrics and information can lead to poor decisions and management. Establish availability, performance, response time, and other objectives to gauge and measure performance of the end-to-end storage and storage-networking infrastructure. Be practical, as it can be easy to get wrapped up in the details and lose sight of the bigger picture and objectives.

General action items include:

- Establish baseline performance indicators.
- Compare normal baseline performance to problem times.
- Keep availability in perspective.
- Make apples-to-apples, not apples-to-oranges comparisons of resources.
- Look at multiple metrics to get a view of resource usage.
- Look beyond cost per gigabyte and consider the impact on SLOs and SLAs.
- Rates are important for performance, while ratios are useful for space saving.
- Metrics and measurements can be obtained from various sources.
- Use metrics and links to business and application to determine efficiency.
- The most important metrics are those that connect to what you are doing.

Many vendors offer solutions for gathering, processing, or reporting metrics, including Akorri (NetApp), Aptare, BMC, Bocada, Brocade, CA, Citrix, Cisco, Commvault, Crossroads, Dell, Egenera, EMC, Emerson/Aperture, Emulex, Ethereal, Horizon, Hitachi, HP, HyperIO, IBM, Intel, Intellimagic, Jam, Lecroy, LSI, Microsoft, NetApp, Netscout, Network Instruments, nLyte, Novell, Onpath, Opalis, Oracle, P3 (KillAWatt), Qlogic, Quantum, Quest, Racemi, SANpulse, SAS, Scalent, Seagate, Solarwinds, Storage Fusion, Sun, Symantec, Teamquest, Tek-Tools, Treesize Pro, Veeam, Viridity, Virtual instruments, Vizoncore, VKernal, and VMware.

Chapter 7

Data Footprint Reduction: Enabling Cost-Effective Data Demand Growth

Innovation is doing more with what you have or with less while supporting growth without degrading service levels or increasing costs.

— Greg Schulz

In This Chapter

- Issues and challenges of an expanding data footprint impact
- Business and IT benefits of reducing your data footprint impact
- The expanding role and focus of data footprint reduction

This chapter looks at business issues, challenges, and opportunities associated with an expanding data footprint. Key themes, buzzwords, and trends that will be addressed include active and inactive data, archiving, compression, data footprint reduction (DFR), data management, de-duplication, doing more with what you have or with less, primary and secondary storage, RAID and capacity optimization, rates and ratios, space-saving snapshots, storage optimization and efficiency, and storage tiering, along with stretching IT budgets while supporting growth, sustaining business and economic growth in a smaller footprint, and thin provisioning.

While this chapter and its companion (Chapter 8) could very easily comprise an entire book, space limitations require some consolidation of information. Thus, this chapter will concentrate on optimization, doing more with what you have or with less—a common theme for storage and networking—and virtualization as well as cloud or other abstracted environments, enabling more data to be retained in a cost-effective manner without compromising quality of service or increasing associated infrastructure resource management (IRM) complexities.

7.1. Getting Started

If it was not becoming increasingly necessary to process and store more data for longer periods of time in different locations, there would be little need for data storage, networking, IT clouds, or virtualization. Similarly, if there was not n ever-increasing dependence on information being accessible when and where needed—including data that was previously off-line or not even available in a digital format—there would be no need for business continuance (BC), disaster recovery (DR), or backup/restore as well as archiving.

However, as has been discussed in previous chapters, there is no such thing as a data recession and dependence on information continues to grow. Countering data growth and associated infrastructure IRM tasks as well as other data protection costs can be as simple as preventing data from being stored. Perhaps for a very few environments this is possible, along with implementing an aggressive data deletion policy, to counter data growth. However, for most environments, putting up barriers that inhibit business and economic growth are not the answer, although data management should be part of the solution and will be discussed later in this chapter.

Data footprint reduction is also about storing more data in a denser footprint. This includes storing more data managed per person, when the additional data being retained adds value to an organization. Also included is keeping more data readily accessible—not necessarily instantly accessible, but within minutes instead of hours or days—when access to more data adds value to the organization.

Another focus of DFR is to enable IT resources to be used more effectively, by deriving more value per gigabyte, terabyte, etc., of data stored. This also means alleviating or removing constraints and barriers to growth, or at least enabling those constraints to be pushed further before they become barriers. IT resources include people and their skill sets, processes, hardware (servers, storage, networks), software and management tools, licenses, facilities, power and cooling, backup or data protection windows, services from providers including network bandwidth as well as available budgets.

Some aspects of addressing expanding data footprints and DFR include the following:

- Networks are faster and more accessible, but there is more data to move.
- More data can be stored longer in the same or smaller footprint.
- Some DFR can reduce costs while stretching budgets further.
- DFR can reduce the costs of supporting more information without negatively impacting service objectives.
- DFR allows existing resources to be used more extensively and effectively.

- DFR can be used to gain control of data rather than simply moving or masking issues that will pop up later.
- Unless optimized and DFR techniques are applied, data movement to clouds may not be possible in a timely or cost-effective manner.
- Desktop, server, and virtualization create data footprint opportunities.
- Consolidation and aggregation can cause aggravation without DFR.
- Backup/restore, BC, and migration to clouds are enhanced.
- More data can be moved in shorter time, enabling business resiliency.
- If you are going on a journey, what will you be taking with you, and how efficiently and effectively can you pack to move what you will need?

Organizations of all sizes are generating and depending on larger amounts of data that must be readily accessible. This increasing reliance on data results in an ever-expanding data footprint. That is, more data is being generated, copied, and stored for longer periods of time. Consequently, IT organizations have to be able to manage more infrastructure resources, such as servers, software tools, networks, and storage, to ensure that data is protected and secured for access when needed.

It is not only more data being generated and stored that causes an expanding data footprint. Other contributors to expanding data footprints include storage space capacity needed for enabling information availability and data protection along with supporting common IRM tasks. For example, additional storage capacity is consumed by different RAID levels to maintain data accessibility; high availability (HA) and BC to support site or systems failover; backup/restore, snapshots, and replication; database or file system maintenance; scratch or temporary areas for imports and exports; development, testing, and quality assurance; and decision support as well as other forms of analytics.

Debate is ongoing about the actual or average storage space capacity utilization for open systems, with numbers ranging from as low as 15–34% up to 65–85%. Not surprisingly, the lowest utilization numbers tend to come from vendors interested in promoting storage resource management (SRM) and systems resource analysis (SRA) tools, thin provisioning, or virtualization aggregation solutions.

What I have found in my research, as well as in talking and working with IT professionals in various sized organizations around the globe, is that low storage utilization can often be the result of several factors, including limiting storage capacity usage to ensure performance, to isolate particular applications, data, customers or users, to ease of management of a single discrete store system or for financial and budgeting purposes.

A point to keep in mind when consolidating storage is having insight as to where and how storage is being allocated and used (active or idle, updated or read) in order to know what policies can be set for when, where, and for how long to move data. Another important aspect of consolidation is leveraging newer, faster, and more energy-efficient storage technology as well as upgrading storage systems with faster processors, I/O busses, increased memory, faster HDDs, and more efficient power supplies and cooling fans.

Looking at storage utilization from the viewpoint of only space capacity consumption, particularly for active and on-line data, can result in performance bottlenecks and inability to service delivery. A balanced approach to data and storage utilization should include performance, availability, capacity, and energy in relation to the type of application usage and access requirements. When SRM and other storage management vendors talk to me about how much they can save and recoup from a storage budget, I ask them about their performance and activity monitoring and reporting capabilities. The frequent response is that it is not needed or requested by their customers or it will be addressed in a future release.

7.1.1. What Is Driving Expanding Data Footprints

There is no such thing as a data or information recession! Granted, more data can be stored in the same or smaller physical footprint than in the past, thus requiring less power and cooling per gigabyte, terabyte, petabyte, or exabyte. Data growth rates necessary to sustain business activity, enhance IT service delivery, and enable new applications are leading to continuously increasing demands to move, protect, preserve, store, and serve data for longer periods of time.

The popularity of rich media and Internet-based applications has resulted in the explosive growth of unstructured file data, requiring new and more scalable storage solutions. Unstructured data includes spreadsheets, PowerPoint, slide decks, Adobe PDF and Word documents, Web pages, and video and audio JPEG, MP3, and MP4 files.

The trend toward increasing data storage requirements does not appear to be slowing any time soon for organizations of all sizes.

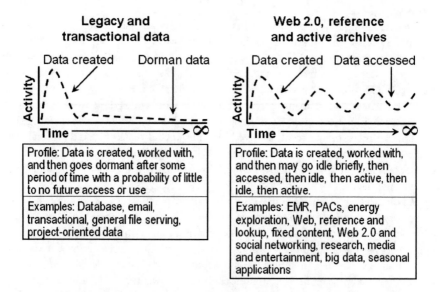

Figure 7.1   Changing access and data lifecycle patterns.

7.1.2. Changing Data Access and Lifecycles

Many marketing strategies are built around the premise that, shortly after it is created, data is seldom, if ever, accessed again. The traditional transactional model lends itself to what has become known as information lifecycle management (ILM), by which data can and should be archived or moved to lower-cost, lower-performing, and high-density storage or even deleted when possible. On the left side of Figure 7.1 is an example of the traditional transactional data lifecycle, with data being created and then going dormant. The amount of dormant data will vary by the type and size of an organization as well as the application mix.

However, unlike the transactional data lifecycle models, under which data can be removed after a period of time, Web 2.0, social media, unstructured digital video and audio, so-called big data, reference, PACS, and related data need to remain on-line and readily accessible. The right side of Figure 7.1 shows data that is created and then accessed on an intermittent basis with variable frequency. The frequency between periods of inactivity could be hours, days, weeks, or months, and, in some cases, there may be sustained periods of activity.

7.1.3. What Is Your Data Footprint Impact?

Your data footprint impact is the total data storage needed to support your various business application and information needs. Your data footprint may be larger than how much actual data storage you have, as in the example shown in Figure 7.2. This example is an organization that has 20 TB of storage space allocated and being used for databases, email, home directories, shared documents, engineering documents, financial, and other data in different formats (structured and unstructured) as well as varying access patterns.

The larger the data footprint, the more data storage capacity and performance bandwidth is needed. How the data is being managed, protected, and housed (powered, cooled, and situated in a rack or cabinet on a floor somewhere) also increases the demand for capacity and associated software licenses. For example, in Figure 7.2, storage capacity is needed for the actual data as well as for data protection using RAID, replication, snapshots, and alternate copies, including disk-to-disk (D2D) backups. In addition, there may also be overhead in terms of storage capacity for applying virtualization or abstraction to gain additional feature functionality from some storage systems, as well as reserve space for snapshots or other background tasks.

On the other hand, even though physical storage capacity is allocated to applications or file systems for use, the actual capacity may not be being fully used. For example a database may show as using 90% of its allocated storage capacity, yet internally there are sparse data (blanks or empty rows or white space) for growth or other purposes. The result is that storage capacity is being held in reserve for some applications, which might otherwise be available for other uses.

As an additional example, assume that you have 2 TB of Oracle database instances and associated data, 1 TB of Microsoft SQL data supporting Microsoft SharePoint,

2 TB of Microsoft Exchange Email data, and 4 TB of general-purpose shared NFS and CIFS Windows-based file sharing, resulting in 9 TB (2 + 1 + 2 + 4) of data. However, your actual data footprint might be much larger. The 9 TB simply represents the known data, or how storage is allocated to different applications and functions. If the databases are sparsely populated at 50%, for example, only 1 TB of Oracle data actually exists, though it is occupying 2 TB of storage capacity.

Assuming for now that in the above example the capacity sizes mentioned are fairly accurate in terms of the actual data size based on how much data is being backed up during a full backup, your data footprint would include the 9 TB of data as well as the on-line (primary), near-line (secondary), and off-line (tertiary) data storage configured to your specific data protection and availability service requirements.

For example, if you are using RAID 1 mirroring for data availability and accessibility, in addition to replacing your data asynchronously to a second site where the data is protected on a RAID 5–based volume with write cache, as well as a weekly full backup, your data footprint would then be at least (9 × 2 RAID 1) + (9+1 RAID 5) + (9 full backup) = 37 TB.

Your data footprint could be even higher than the 37 TB in this example if we also assume that daily incremental or periodic snapshots are performed throughout the day in addition to extra storage to support application software, temporary work space, operating system files including page and swap, not to mention room for growth and whatever free space buffer is used for your environment.

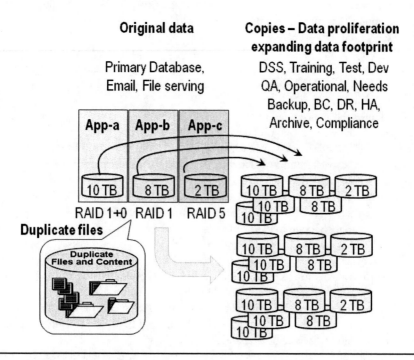

Figure 7.2 Expanding data footprint impact.

In this example, 9 TB of actual or assumed data can rapidly expand into a larger data footprint, which only compounds as your applications grow to support new and changing business needs or requirements. Note that the above scenario is rather simplistic and does not factor in how many copies of duplicate data may be being made, or backup retention, size of snapshots, free space requirements, and other elements that contribute to the expansion of your data footprint.

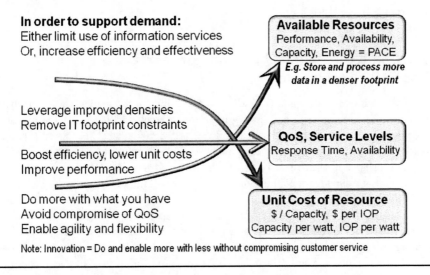

In order to support demand:
Either limit use of information services
Or, increase efficiency and effectiveness

Available Resources
Performance, Availability,
Capacity, Energy = PACE

*E.g. Store and process more
data in a denser footprint*

Leverage improved densities
Remove IT footprint constraints

QoS, Service Levels
Response Time, Availability

Boost efficiency, lower unit costs
Improve performance

Do more with what you have
Avoid compromise of QoS
Enable agility and flexibility

Unit Cost of Resource
$ / Capacity, $ per IOP
Capacity per watt, IOP per watt

Note: Innovation = Do and enable more with less without compromising customer service

Figure 7.3   IT resources, cost balancing, conflicts, and opportunities.

7.1.4. Business Benefits of Data Footprint Reduction

IT organizations of all sizes are faced with a constant demand to store more data, including multiple copies of the same or similar data, for longer periods of time. The result is not only an expanding data footprint but also increased IT expenses, both capital and operational, due to additional IRM activities to sustain given levels of application quality-of-service (QoS) delivery as shown in Figure 7.3.

Common IT costs associated with supporting an increased data footprint include:

- Data storage hardware and management software tools acquisition
- Associated networking or I/O connectivity hardware, software, and services
- Recurring maintenance and software renewal fees
- Facilities fees for floor space, power, and cooling, along with IT staffing
- Physical and logical security for data and IT resources
- Data protection for BC, or DR, including backup, replication, and archiving

As shown in Figure 7.3, all IT organizations are faced with having to do more with what they have—or even with less—while maximizing available resources. Additionally, IT organizations often have to overcome common footprint constraints (available power, cooling, floor space, server, storage and networking resources, management, budgets, and IT staffing) while supporting business growth.

Figure 7.3 also shows that to support demand, more resources are needed (real or virtual) in a denser footprint, while maintaining or enhancing QoS while lowering per-unit resource cost. The trick is improving on available resources while maintaining QoS in a cost-effective manner. By comparison, traditionally, if costs are reduced, one of the other curves (amount of resources or QoS) is often negatively impacted, and vice versa.

7.2. The Expanding Scope and Focus of Data Footprint Reduction

Data footprint reduction is a collection of techniques, technologies, tools, and best practices that are used to address data growth management challenges. De-duplication ("dedupe") is currently the industry darling for DFR, particularly in the scope or context of backup or other repetitive data. However, DFR expands the scope of expanding data footprints and their impact to cover primary and secondary data along with off-line data that ranges from high performance to inactive high capacity.

The expanding scope of DFR is moving beyond backup with dedupe to a broader focus that includes archiving, data protection modernization, compression, as well as other technologies. The scope expansion includes DFR for active as well as inactive, primary along with secondary, on-line and near-line or off-line, physical, virtual, and cloud using various techniques and technologies. Another aspect of the expanding focus of data footprint reduction is that a small percentage change on a large basis can have a big impact, along with the importance of rates in addition to ratios.

The main theme is that there is a bigger and broader opportunity for DFR across organizations to address different performance, availability, capacity, and economic or energy efficiency requirements using various techniques. In other words, avoid missing opportunities becaue you have become tunnel-visioned on just one or a few techniques. This also means you should avoid trying to use just one tool to address all issues or challenges and, instead, align the applicable techniques and tools to the task at hand.

While dedupe is a popular technology from a discussion standpoint and has good deployment traction, it is far from reaching mass customer adoption or even broad coverage in environments where it is being used. StorageIO research shows broadest adoption of dedupe centered around backup in smaller or small/medium business (SMB) environments (dedupe deployment wave one in Figure 7.4), with some deployment in remote office/branch office (ROBO) work groups as well as departmental environments.

There does continue to be early adoption in larger core IT environments, where dedupe complements already-existing data protection and preservation practices. Another current deployment scenario for dedupe has been for supporting core edge deployments in larger environments that provide support for backup and data protection of ROBO, work group, and departmental systems.

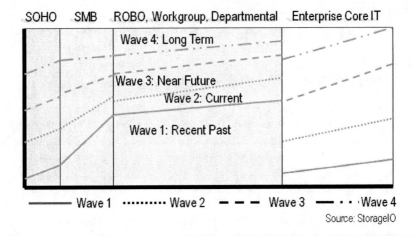

SOHO   SMB   ROBO, Workgroup, Departmental   Enterprise Core IT

Wave 4: Long Term

Wave 3: Near Future
Wave 2: Current

Wave 1: Recent Past

———— Wave 1 ·········· Wave 2 — — — Wave 3 —· · ·Wave 4

Source: StorageIO

Figure 7.4   Dedupe adoption and deployment waves over time.

7.2.1. Reducing Your Data Footprint

Storage has become less expensive per capacity, but as your data footprint expands, more storage capacity and storage management, including software tools and IT staff time, are required to care for and protect your business information. By managing your data footprint more effectively across different applications and tiers of storage, you can enhance application service delivery and responsiveness as well as facilitate more timely data protection to meet compliance and business objectives.

Reducing your data footprint can help reduce costs or defer upgrades to expand server, storage, and network capacity along with associated software license and maintenance fees. Maximizing what you already have using DFR techniques can extend the effectiveness and capabilities of your existing IT resources, including power, cooling, storage capacity, network bandwidth, replication, backup, archiving, and software license resources.

From a network perspective, by reducing your data footprint or its impact, you can also positively impact your SAN, LAN, MAN, and WAN bandwidth for data replication and remote backup or data access as well as move more data using existing available bandwidth.

Additional benefits of maximizing the usage of your existing IT resources include:

- Deferring hardware and software upgrades
- Maximizing usage of existing resources
- Enabling consolidation for energy-effective technologies
- Shortening time required for data protection management
- Reducing your power and cooling requirements
- Expediting data recovery and application restart for DR scenarios

- Reducing exposure during RAID rebuilds as a result of faster copy times
- Enabling more data to be moved to or from cloud and remote sites

7.2.2. Not All Data or Applications Are the Same

Data footprint reduction can be achieved in many ways with different implementations in different places to meet diverse application and IT requirements. For example, DFR can be done when and where data is created and stored, or it can be done after the fact, during routine IRM tasks including backup/restore, archiving, or during periods of application inactivity.

Not all applications and data are the same in terms of access or usage patterns as well as lifecycle patterns (as was seen in Figure 7.1). For example, some data is active—that is, being read or updated—while other data is inactive. In addition, some data and applications have time-sensitive performance requirements, while others have lower demands for performance.

Table 7.1 Different Applications Have Various Data Footprint Reduction Needs

Storage Tier	Tier 0 and Tier 1 Primary On-Line	Tier 2 Secondary On-Line	Tier 3 Tertiary Near-Line or Off-Line
Characteristics focused	Performance focused Some capacity needed	Some performance Emphasis on capacity	Less performance Much more capacity
	Active changing data Databases, active file systems, logs, video editing, or other time-sensitive applications	Less active or changing data, home directories, general file shares, reference data, online backup and BC	Static data with infrequent access, on-line or active archives, off-line backups, archive or master copies for DR purposes
Metric	Cost per activity Activity per watt Time is money	Activity per capacity Protected per watt Mix of time and space	Cost per GB GB per watt Save money
DFR approach	Archive inactive data Space-saving snapshots Various RAID levels Thin provisioning and I/O consolidation, real-time compression, dedupe if possible and practical	Archive inactive data Space-saving snapshots, RAID optimized, modernized data protection, thin provisioning, space and I/O consolidation, compress and dedupe	Data management, target for archived data, tiered storage including disk, tape, and cloud. Dedupe and compress. Storage capacity consolidation

The importance of active vs. inactive data in the context of DFR is to identify the applicable technique to use in order to gain some data reduction benefit without incurring a performance penalty. Some data lends itself to compression, while other data is well suited for dedupe. Likewise, archiving can be applied to structured databases, email, and Microsoft SharePoint and file systems, among others. Table 7.1 shows various applications and data characteristics as they pertain to DFR.

7.3. DFR Techniques

As previously mentioned, there are many different DFR approaches and technologies to address various storage capacity optimization needs. Likewise, there are different metrics to gauge the efficiency and effectiveness of the various approaches, some of which are time (performance) centric whereas others are space (capacity) focused.

In general, common DFR technologies and techniques include:

- Archiving (structured database, semistructured email, unstructured file, NAS, multimedia, and so-called big data)
- Compression including real-time, streaming, and post processing
- Consolidation of storage and data
- Data management including cleanup and deletion of unnecessary data
- Data de-duplication, also known as single instancing or normalization
- Masking or moving issues elsewhere
- Network optimization
- Spacing-saving snapshots
- Thin provisioning and dynamic allocation

7.4. Metrics and Measurements

As mentioned previously, the expanding scope and focus of data footprint reduction also looks at DFR from not just a storage space reduction ratio perspective, but also from a performance basis to support on-line or active applications. There are several different metrics that apply to DFR, involving performance, availability, capacity, energy, and economics tied to various service-level objectives. Common DFR-related metrics are related to storage space capacity savings such as reduction ratios. However, data movement and transfer rates are also important to gauge how much data can be moved or processed in a given amount of time—for example, how much data can be reduced while meeting a backup or data protection window, or how long restoration takes.

Some additional ways of measuring storage capacity and DFR benefits include how much data or storage can be managed to a given service level per person or per management tool. Another way of looking at this is to expand the effectiveness of licensed software functionality on servers or storage systems to derive more value per capacity under management. Also, keep the overhead of managing and protecting storage in perspective. For example, if you have 100 TB of raw storage and are using RAID 10, only 50 TB or 50% of the raw capacity can be used for storing data. However, of that 50 TB, some percentage may also be used for storage virtualization overhead by some tools as well as for snapshots. Thus it is important to keep in mind what the effective usable storage capacity is vs. the raw capacity. The more usable storage compared to raw storage, the better, in that there is less overhead.

7.5. What to Look for in a DFR Technology Solution

There are many different attributes to consider when evaluating DFR technologies. Note that DFR is not a replacement for proper data management, including deletion, but rather a complement to it. In fact, DFR embraces data management as one of many different techniques used to address various needs. While data storage capacity has become less expensive on a relative basis, as data footprints continue to expand to support business requirements, more IT resources will be needed to be made available in a cost-effective, yet QoS-satisfying manner. What this means is that more IT resources, including server, storage, and networking capacity, management tools, and associated software licensing and IT staff time will be required to protect, preserve, and serve information.

An issue to consider is how much delay or resource consumption you can afford to use or lose to achieve a given level of DFR. For example, as you move from coarse (traditional compression) to granular, such as data de-duplication or single instancing, more intelligence, processing power, or off-line postprocessing techniques are needed to look at larger patterns of data to eliminate duplication.

If you are concerned enough to be evaluating other forms of DFR technologies for future use, including archiving with data discovery (indexing, ediscovery) or data de-duplication techniques, leverage appliance-based compression technology for immediate relief to maximize the effectiveness and capacity of existing storage resources for on-line, backup, and archiving while complementing other DFR capabilities.

It is important to understand how other IRM functions, including backup, archiving, DR/BC, virus scans, encryption, and ediscovery, along with indexing for search, interact with DFR technologies. You should maximize the usage of your existing IT infrastructure resources without introducing complexity and costs associated with added management and interoperability woes.

Look for solutions that complement your environment and are transparent across different tiers of storage, business applications, and IRM functions (backup, archive, replication, on-line). Data archiving should be an ongoing process that is integrated into your business and IT resource management functions as opposed to being an intermittent event to free up IT resources.

Also consider your data footprint and its impact on your environment using analysis tools and/or assessment services. Develop a holistic approach to managing your growing data footprint: Look beyond storage hardware costs, and factor in software license and maintenance costs, power, cooling, and IT staff management time. Leverage data compression as part of an overall DFR strategy to optimize and leverage your investment in your existing storage across all types of applications. In short, deploy a comprehensive DFR strategy combining various techniques and technologies to address point solution needs as well as your overall environment, including on-line, near-line for backup, and off-line for archive data.

7.6. Best Practices

While data storage capacity has, in fact, become less expensive, as a data footprint expands, more storage capacity and storage management, including software tools and IT staff time, are required to care for and protect business information. By more effectively managing the data footprint across different applications and tiers of storage, it is possible to enhance application service delivery and responsiveness as well as facilitate more timely data protection to meet compliance and business objectives. To realize the full benefits of DFR, look beyond backup and off-line data improvements to include on-line and active data.

Reducing your data footprint has many benefits, including reducing or maximizing the usage of your IT infrastructure resources such as power and cooling, storage capacity, and network bandwidth while enhancing application service delivery in the form of timely backup, BC/DR, performance, and availability. If you do not already have a DFR strategy, now is the time to develop and begin implementing one across your environment.

There are several methods that can be used to address data footprint proliferation without compromising data protection or negatively impacting application and business service levels. These approaches include archiving of structured (database), semi-structured (email) and unstructured (general files and documents), data compression (real-time and off-line), and data de-duplication.

The benefit of a broader, more holistic DFR strategy is to address your overall environment, including all applications that generate and use data as well as IRM or overhead functions that compound and impact your data footprint. There is, however, the thought that dedupe is only for backup, similar to how archive was hijacked by the compliance marketing folks in the post-Y2K era. There are several techniques that can be used individually to address specific DFR issues or, as seen in Figure 7.5, in combination to implement a more cohesive and effective DFR strategy.

Figure 7.5 shows how multiple DFR techniques and technologies can be combined to address different applications and data from primary and active to inactive and backup as well as archives on a local and remote basis. What this example shows is that archive, dedupe, and other forms of DFR can and should be used beyond where they have been target marketed.

7.7. Common DFR Questions

Why is data footprint reduction important for clouds or virtual environments? There are two main dimensions to why DFR is important: One is being able to move data in a timely and affordable manner to public or cloud resources; the other is that clouds can serve as a target or medium for moving archived or other data to complement and extend use of on-site resources. So, on one hand, it enables data to fit into a cloud, and on the other, it is about using clouds to off-load or enable existing environments to be cleaned up.

What is meant by the statement that a small percentage change has a big benefit on a large basis? This is a basic notion that a 10% change on, say, 10 TB will result in a 1-TB difference, whereas a 50% change will yield a larger, 5-TB improvement. However, if you have, say, 100 TB and only 10% of your data can realize the 50% improvement, this means that still only 5 TB are impacted. However, what if you could realize a 10% improvement across the entire 100 TB? That would yield a 10-TB improvement. Thus the smaller percentage improvement can yield a larger return than a larger percentage on a smaller basis.

Here is another example: Many serial networks use 8-bit/10-bit encoding, where there is a 20% overhead for every 8 bits of data transferred. That may not seem like much, but if you are moving data at 32 GB per second, such as with PCI Gen 3, almost half of the performance improvements from Gen 2 are from switching from 8-bit/10-bit to 128-bit/130-bit encoding, showing how a small change on a large basis has a big benefit.

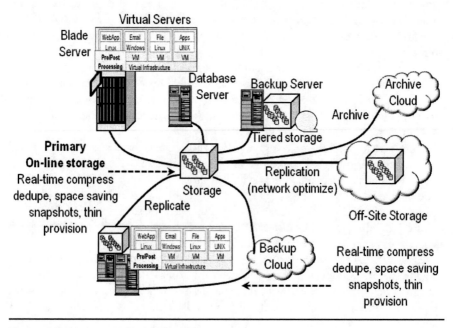

Figure 7.5   How various DFR techniques coexist.

7.8. Chapter Summary

Organizations of all shapes and sizes are encountering some amount of growing data footprint impact that needs to be addressed, either now or in the near future. Given that different applications and types of data along with associated storage mediums or tiers have various performance, availability, capacity, energy, and economic characteristics, multiple data footprint impact reduction tools or techniques are needed. What this means is that the focus of data footprint reduction is expanding beyond that of just de-duplication for backup or other early deployment scenarios.

For some applications, reduction ratios are an important focus, so the need is for tools or modes of operations that achieve the desired results. For other applications, the focus is on performance with some data reduction benefit, so tools are optimized for performance first and reduction secondarily. In response, vendors will expand their current capabilities and techniques to meet changing needs and criteria. Vendors with multiple DFR tools will also do better than those with only a single function or focused tool.

General action items include:

- Develop a DFR strategy for on-line and off-line data.
- Energy avoidance can be accomplished by powering down storage.
- Energy efficiency can be accomplished by using various DFR approaches.
- Measure and compare storage based on idle and active workload conditions.
- Storage efficiency metrics include IOPS or bandwidth per watt for active data.
- Storage capacity per watt per footprint and cost is a measure for inactive data.
- Small percentage reductions on a large scale have big benefits.
- Align the applicable form of DFR for the task at hand.

Chapter 8

Enabling Data Footprint Reduction: Storage Capacity Optimization

The good news is that networks are faster, storage has more space capacity; the bad news is that there is more information to move, process, and store in a given amount of time and within a certain budget.

– Greg Schulz

In This Chapter

- Why to use different technologies for different applications and service needs
- DFR technologies: archive, compression, de-duplication, and thin provisioning
- DFR techniques, including data management

This chapter takes a closer look at different data footprint reduction (DFR) techniques, their characteristics, caveats, and benefits to address various needs. Key themes, buzzwords, and trends that will be addressed include active and inactive data, archiving, compression, data footprint reduction, data management, RAID, thin provisioning, and de-duplication (dedupe).

8.1. DFR Techniques

The importance of data footprint reduction is that it can help drive efficiencies so that more can be done with available resources and technology improvements while supporting demand. By reducing your data footprint, more data can be moved in the same or less time to meet service requirements. Additionally, in order to leverage cloud environments, data needs to be able to be moved effectively in a timely manner. By reducing your data footprint using various technologies, your environment can become more efficient and more effective.

As noted in Chapter 7, there are many different DFR technologies to address various storage capacity optimization needs, some of which are time (performance) centric whereas others are space (capacity) focused. Different approaches use different metrics to gauge efficiency and effectiveness.

In general, common DFR technologies and techniques include:

- Archiving (structured database, semistructured email, unstructured file data)
- Compression and compaction including real time or time deferred
- Consolidation of storage and data
- Data management, including cleanup and deletion of unnecessary data
- Data de-duplication (dedupe), also known as single instancing or normalization
- Masking or moving issues elsewhere
- Network optimization
- Spacing-saving snapshots
- Thin provisioning and dynamic allocation

Table 8.1 shows different DFR technologies and techniques that can be applied across different applications, types of data, and storage.

Which DFR technique is the best? That depends on what you are trying to accomplish in terms of business and IT objectives. For example, are you looking for maximum storage capacity at the lowest cost, with performance not being a concern? Or do you need a mix of performance and capacity optimization? Are you looking to apply DFR to primary on-line active data or applications or for secondary, near-line, inactive, or off-line data? Some forms of storage optimization reduce the amount of data or maximize available storage capacity. Other forms of storage optimization are focused on boosting performance or increasing productivity.

8.2. Archiving

The goal of archiving is to maximize the effective use of on-line or expensive resources by keeping those for active services delivery while preserving information that needs to be retained on lower-cost media. Backup, though similar, focuses on protecting data with a shorter retention period using tools for rapid restoration of a single file, folder, or file system. Archive has longer retention time and a focus on preserving the state of a collection of data as of a point in time for future or possible future access. Archiving can have one of the greatest impacts on reducing data footprint for storage in general, but particularly for on-line and primary storage. For example, if it can be identified in a timely manner what data can be removed after a project is completed, what data can be purged from a primary database, or which older data can be migrated out of active email databases, a net improvement in application performance as well as available storage capacity can be realized.

**Table 8.1 Various DFR Techniques and Technologies
with Different Characteristics**

Technique	Performance	Space or capacity	Comment
Relocation—move problem elsewhere	If off-site, then network issues need to be considered	Keep QoS, SLOs, and SLAs in perspective vs. cost of service	Off-loading to someone else buys time while or until you can optimize
Archive	Maintain or improve general QoS for normal activities in addition to faster data protection or other IRM tasks	Recover space to be used for growth, new applications, or other enhancements. Move archive data to another tier, including cloud or MSP	Applies to regulatory and compliance data or applications, including databases, email, and file shares. Archive, then delete stale or dead data
Backup modernization	Reduce backup/ restore or data protection time	Free up space for more backups/faster restore	Reduce overhead of data protection
Bandwidth optimization	Application or protocol bandwidth vs. latency	More data moved in the same or less time	May boost bandwidth vs. latency
Compression	Minimal to no impact on performance, depending on where and how implemented	Some capacity benefit over broad spectrum of applications with various algorithms	Application, database, operating, file system, network, storage system, or device based
Consolidation	Consolidate IOPS to fast 2.5-in. 15.5K SAS or FC HDDs and SSD devices	Consolidate space to large-capacity SAS and SATA HDDs	Avoid causing bottlenecks as a result of aggregation
Data dedupe	Some impact possible on performance in exchange for data reduction benefit	Good data reduction benefit over some types of data or applications	Verify ingest or dedupe rate in addition to restore or re-inflate rate
RAID	May be better option for some data mirroring	Parity-based has less overhead vs. mirroring	Look at number of HDDs per RAID group
Space-saving snapshots	Make copies faster to enhance service delivery	Reduce overhead or space needed for copies	Data distribution, development/ testing, analytics
Storage tiering	SSD, 15.5K SAS/FC	2-TB HDDs and tape	Storage may be in cloud
Thin provisioning	Improve SSD utilization	Improve capacity usage	Avoid overbooking

Applying archiving as a form of DFR for cloud or virtualized environments enables more data to be retained in a denser, more cost-effective footprint and reduces the amount of data and associated resources. Archiving can be used to clean up and either discard data that is no longer needed or move it to another medium or resource where the associated management costs are lower. Dedupe and/or compression simply reduce the data's impact; while they may be applicable for some data, they are also similar to treating the symptom instead of the disease.

Archive applies to:

- Transactional structured and unstructured data
- Medical and healthcare environments, including Picture Archiving and Communication System (PACS), as well other Digital Imaging and Communications in Medicine (DICOM) accessible data
- Email, instant messaging (IM), and messaging including voice mails
- Energy and mineral exploration, along with simulation modeling
- Databases such as IBM DB2, Oracle, SAP, MySQL, and SQLserver
- Collaboration and document management, including Microsoft SharePoint
- Engineering drawings, diagrams, and other records retention
- Home directories and file shares or project repositories
- Digital Asset or Archive Management (DAMs) for video and audio
- Security and gaming video surveillance

Data archiving is often perceived as a solution for compliance, but archiving can also be used for many noncompliance purposes, including general DFR, performance boosting, and enhancing routine data maintenance and data protection. The reality is that while regulatory compliance data, including HIPPA, Hitech, PCI, SarBox, and CFR financial or HIPAA medical, require long-term retention, other common application data for almost every business, including those that do not fall under regulatory requirements, can benefit from—if not require—long-term data retention. There are opportunities and DFR benefits of leveraging archive as a storage optimization and green IT enabling technology across all types of data or applications.

Archiving can be applied to structured databases data, semistructured email data and attachments, and unstructured file data. Archiving is evolving and important for preserving information, with clouds as a synergistic opportunity for parking or preserving data. For example, data archived from an on-line database, email, SharePoint, or file system can be migrated to lower-cost, high-capacity disk or tape, or to a cloud MSP service. Key to deploying an archiving solution is having insight into what data exists along with applicable rules and policies to determine what can be archived, for how long, in how many copies, and how data may ultimately be retired or deleted. Archiving requires a combination of hardware, software, and people to implement business rules.

A challenge with archiving is having the time and tools available to identify what data should be archived and what data can be securely destroyed. Also complicating matters is that knowledge of the data value is needed, which may well involve legal issues about who is responsible for making decisions on what data to keep or discard. If a business can invest in the time and software tools, as well as identify which data to archive, the return on investment can be very positive toward reducing the data foot-print without limiting the amount of information available for use.

8.2.1. Tools and Targets

While I was writing this chapter, I had a conversation with someone in the storage industry who commented that he thought clouds were going to be the magic bullet for enabling archive and that archiving was the application to drive mass cloud adoption. After further discussion, we came to the conclusion that clouds will be another target medium or virtual medium for archiving. In that role, assuming that cloud and MSP services are cost-effective, trusted, and safe and secure, they can help stimulate archiving deployment where targets or devices are the barriers. However, where the storage medium or target is not the primary barrier to archive adoption, discussion about clouds and optimization may stimulate management interest to get a project underway.

Some common discussion points concerning archiving include what applications and functions you need to support. For example, healthcare may involve Picture Archiving and Communication System (PACS) for medical images as well as Electronic Medical Records (EMR) such as those from Caché-based databases or lab and radiology systems using DICOM-based access protocols. Will you be archiving an entire project, including all files in folders or a file system, or indicial items? Do you also need to archive applications necessary for using the data? If you are archiving a database, are you simply removing rows of data after they have been copied to another table or destination, or do you also have to preserve the context of the data, including business rules with XML wrappers? From a regulation or compliance perspective, what are the requirements of where data can be placed, and how many copies are needed? For example, if your objective is to move archive data to a cloud or MSP service, first verify that there are no regulations stipulating in what geographic are your particular applications data can reside. Some local or national governments regulate what types of data can leave or cross borders into other states or countries.

Indexing or data classification can occur at the application layer via native or optional plug-in capability, via archiving software, or, in some solutions, in the target device, or even all of the above. For legal management systems support, redaction (blanking or marking out of certain data) may be needed along with litigation hold of data to prevent accidental deletion or digital shredding. Other archiving features include encryption for security, write once/read many (WORM), and access audit trails along with reporting.

Archive target devices include disk-based systems that support various interfaces and protocols including NAS, DICOM, or VTL, or object-based access using various APIs including XAM. Various types of media can be found in archive targets ranging from SSD to high-capacity HDDs and tape. Some storage targets support path to tape as well as gateway or bridge functions to remote storage systems or cloud service providers. There are various approaches to energy efficiency, including intelligent power management (IPM), ranging from disk drive spindown to varying performance and power consumption to the amount of work being done along with removable media. Other features often include replication, compression, and dedupe.

An effective archiving strategy or deployment includes:

- Policies such as what to archive where and for how long, how to dispose of data
- Management buy-in and support for implementing policies and procedures
- Organizational involvement from different interests across the business
- Server, storage, or system resource management and discovery tools to determine what you have and its usage profiles
- Application plug-ins to interface with data movers and policy managers
- Archiving tools to interface with applications and target devices or cloud services
- Compliance and security (physical as well as logical) of data and processes
- Storage target devices or cloud and MSP services

Leveraging the right technology, tool, and best practice techniques is important for an optimized data storage environment. To obtain maximum reliability, routine maintenance should be performed on all magnetic media including disk and tape. Routine maintenance includes regular proactive data or media integrity checks to detect potential errors before they become a problem. For disk-based on-line primary as well as secondary and disk-to-disk solutions, media maintenance involves drive integrity checks or powering up spun-down disks along with background RAID parity checks. Media verification can be accomplished using software, appliances, as well as functionality found in some tape libraries.

In addition to media management, another import best practice is securing data during transmission and transportation as well as at rest. This means leveraging encryption to provide data security and information protection compliance, which for some geographic locations is a regulatory requirement. As part of a long-term data retention strategy and data protection, verify that encryption keys are also safely secured as well as available when needed.

General tips and comments:

- Factor in total cost of ownership (TCO) and return on investment (ROI).
- Include time and cost for safe, secure digital destruction of data (tape and disk).
- Archiving is useful for managing compliance and noncompliance data.
- Long-term data retention applies to all types of data that has business value.
- Implement tape and media tracking along with data protection management.
- Adhere to vendor-recommended media management and handling techniques.
- Align the applicable technology, for example, storage tier, to the task at hand.

Keep in mind that you cannot go forward if you cannot go back: As a business, to provide sustainably, being able to go back in time and access preserved and protected data insures business sustainability.

8.3. Compression and Compaction

Compression is a proven technology that provides immediate and transparent relief to move or store more data effectively, not only for backup and archiving, but also for primary storage. Data compression is widely used in IT and in consumer electronic environments. It is implemented in hardware and software to reduce the size of data to create a corresponding reduction in network bandwidth or storage capacity.

If you have used a traditional or TCP/IP-based telephone or cell phone, watched a DVD or HDTV, listened to an MP3, transferred data over the Internet or used email, you have likely relied on some form of compression technology that is transparent to you. Some forms of compression are time-delayed, such as using PKZIP to zip files, while others are real-time or on the fly, such as when using a network, cell phone, or listening to an MP3.

Compression technology is very complementary to archive, backup, and other functions, including supporting on-line primary storage and data applications. Compression is commonly implemented in several locations, including databases, email, operating systems, tape drives, network routers, and compression appliances, to help reduce your data footprint.

8.3.1. Compression Implementation

Approaches to data compression vary in time delay or impact on application performance as well as in the amount of compression and loss of data. Two approaches that focus on data loss are lossless (no data loss) and lossy (some data loss for higher compression ratio). Additionally, some implementations make performance a main consideration, including real-time for no performance impact to applications and time-delayed where there is a performance impact.

Data compression or compaction can be timed to occur:

- On-the-fly, for sequential or random data, where applications are not delayed
- Time-delayed, where access is paused while data is compressed or uncompressed
- Postprocessing, time-deferred, or batch-based compression

Data compression or compaction occurs in the following locations:

- Add-on compression or compaction software on servers or in storage systems
- Applications including databases and email as well as file systems
- Data protection tools such as backup/restore, archive, and replication
- Networking components including routers and bandwidth optimization
- Cloud point of presences (cPOPs), gateways, and appliances
- Storage systems, including primary storage, tape drives, disk libraries, or VTLs

8.3.2. Real-Time and On-the-Fly Compression

With active data, including databases, unstructured files, and other documents, caution needs to be exercised not to cause performance bottlenecks and to maintain data integrity when introducing data footprint reduction techniques. In contrast to traditional ZIP or off-line, time-delayed compression approaches that require complete decompression of data prior to modification, on-line compression allows for reading from or writing to any location in a compressed file without full file decompression and the resulting application or time delay. Real-time appliance or target-based compression capabilities are well suited for supporting on-line applications including databases, On Line Transaction Processing (OLTP), email, home directories, websites, and video streaming without consuming host server CPU or memory resources, or degrading storage system performance.

With lossless compression, compressed data is preserved and uncompressed exactly as it was originally saved, with no loss of data. Generally, lossless data compression is needed for digital data requiring an exact match or 100% data integrity of stored data. Some audio and video data can tolerate distortion in order to reduce the data footprint of the stored information, but digital data, particularly, documents, files, and databases, have zero tolerance for lost or missing data.

Real-time compression techniques using time-proven algorithms, such as Lempel-Ziv (LZ) as opposed to MD5 or other compute, "heavy-thinking" hashing techniques, provide a scalable balance of uncompromised performance and effective data footprint reduction. This means that changed data is compressed on the fly with no performance penalty while maintaining data integrity and equally for read operations. Note that with the increase of CPU server processing performance along with multiple cores, server-based compression running in applications such as database, email, file systems, or operating systems can be a viable option for some environments.

LZ is of variable length for a wide range of uses and thus is a popular lossless compression algorithm. LZ for compression generally involves a dictionary or map of how a file is compressed, which is used for restoring a file to its original form. The size of the dictionary can vary depending on the specific LZ-based algorithm implementation. The larger the file or data stream, combined with the amount of recurring data, including white spaces or blanks, results in a larger effective compression ratio and subsequent reduced data footprint benefit.

Real-time data compression allows the benefits associated with reducing footprints for backup data to be realized across a broader range of applications and storage scenarios. As an example, real-time compression of active and changing data for file serving as well as other high-performance applications allows more data to be read from or written to a storage system in a given amount of time. The net result is that storage systems combined with real-time compression can maximize the amount of data stored and processed (read or write) without performance penalties.

Another example of using real-time compression is to combine a NAS file server configured with high-performance 15.5K SAS and Fibre Channel HDDs with FLASH-based SSDs to boost the effective storage capacity of active data without introducing the performance bottleneck associated with using larger-capacity HDDs. Of course, compression will vary with the type of solution being deployed and the type of data being stored.

Benefits of real-time compression for on-line active and high-performance DFR include:

- Single solution for different applications
- Improved effective storage performance
- Increased capacity for fast disk drives
- Enhanced data protection capabilities
- Extended useful life of existing resources

In some DFR implementations, a performance boost can occur as a result of the compression, because less data is being transferred or processed by the storage system and offsetting any latency in the compression solution. The storage system is able to react faster during both operations and take up less CPU utilization without causing the host application server to incur any performance penalties associated with host software-based compression.

Another scenario for using real-time data compression is for time-sensitive applications that require large amounts of data, including on-line databases, video and audio media servers, Web and analytic tools. For example, some databases such as Oracle support NFS3 direct I/O (DIO) and concurrent I/O (CIO) capabilities to enable random and direct addressing of data within a Network File System (NFS)–based file. This differs from traditional NFS operations, where a file is sequentially read or written. To boost storage system performance while increasing capacity utilizations, real-time data compression that supports NFS DIO and CIO operations expedites retrieval of data by accessing and uncompressing only the requested data. Additionally, applications do not see any degradation in performance, because CPU overhead off-loaded from host or client servers to act as storage systems does not have to move as much data.

One of the many approaches to addressing storage power, cooling, and floor space challenges is to consolidate the contents of multiple disk drives onto a single larger-capacity but slower disk drive—for example, moving the contents of three 600-GB 15,000-RPM SAS or Fibre Channel disks drives to a single 7200-RPM 2-TB SAS or SATA disk drive to avoid power consumption, at the expense of performance and cost for data movement.

An alternative approach is to use real-time compression to boost the effective capacity of each of the fast 600-GB 15.5K-RPM disk drives to approximately the same as the single 7200-RPM 1-TB to 2-TB SAS or SATA disk drive. The benefit is that real-time compression boosts the effective storage capacity by several times that of a single 1-TB or 2-TB HDD without the corresponding 3–4× drop in performance to achieve energy efficiency. This approach is well suited to environments and applications that require processing large amounts of unstructured data, improving their energy efficiency without sacrificing performance access to data. Some applicable usage examples include seismic and energy exploration, medical PACS images, simulation, entertainment and video processing of MP3 or MP4 as well as JPEG and WAV files, collection and processing of telemetry or surveillance data, data mining, and targeted marketing.

Examples of real-time-enabled compression DFR solutions are VTLs for backup and primary enabled on-line storage; EMC CLARiiON is an early adopter, with IBM real-time compression technology acquired in 2010 via their acquisition of Storwize and NetApp, which supports both real-time compression and dedupe in its FAS storage systems and V-series gateways. Other examples include databases such as Oracle, Microsoft Exchange Email, and various file systems as well as storage system–based compression.

8.3.3. Postprocessing and Deferred Compression

Postprocessing and deferred compression are often misunderstood as real-time data compression. These processes dynamically decompress data when read, with modified data being recompressed at a later time. The benefit to this method is that static data that seldom changes can be reduced, freeing storage space, while allowing applications to read more data in a given timeframe.

The downside to this approach is that changing data, including fileservers, email, office documents, design, and development, as well as database files, is written without the benefit of compression. The impact is that more space on disk is required to write the data, with no performance improvement benefit during write operations plus the overhead of a subsequent read and rewrite operation when data is eventually recompressed. An example of this is the Ocarina technology that was acquired by Dell in 2010.

8.4. Consolidation and Storage Tiering

Another form of DFR is consolidating underutilized storage capacity onto fewer larger-capacity devices for lower-performance or inactive data. For higher-performance applications and data, underutilized data can be consolidated onto fewer yet faster devices such as SSD and 15K-RPM SAS or Fibre Channel devices. Consolidating and retiering data onto different storage tiers may seem a little like rearranging the deck chairs on a sinking ship, particularly if that is the only thing being done or if it does not line up with the preferences of some other DFR technique. However, if you have a limited (or no) budget and need some quick relief, combining consolidation along with with techniques such as data management, data deletion, or other DFR techniques mentioned in this chapter can provide near-term relief and serve as a foundation for additional DFR tools.

A caveat for consolidating and retiering is the potential to cause bottlenecks or aggravation as a result of aggregation. Reduce this possibility by consolidating active data onto fewer slower high-capacity disk drives instead of smaller, faster devices. Remember that the objective is to reduce costs and maximize resources to support growth without introducing barriers to business productivity and efficiency.

Retiering means realigning data to the right class or category of technology while balancing needs for performance, availability, capacity, energy, and economics to a given service level objective (SLO). For example, using fewer yet faster devices, combined with some larger-capacity 2-TB 3.5–in. SAS or SATA devices for inactive or less frequently accessed data, to consolidate activity, or IOPS, onto SSD enables fast 15.5K SAS or FC drives to be more effective in terms of space utilization. Similarly, combining consolidation and retiering with archiving enables less frequently accessed data to move off primary storage—including out of structured databases, email, SharePoint or file systems—onto lower-cost media and helps stretch resources further.

8.5. Data De-duplication

Data de-duplication (dedupe) is a technique or technology for eliminating duplicate or recurring data. It is a more intelligent form of data compression.

Some common alternate names or references to dedupe include:

- Intelligent compression
- Normalization by database professionals
- Differencing or elimination of recurring data
- Commonalty factoring to reduce duplicate data
- Single-instance storage (SIS)

Dedupe facilitates:

- Multiple versions of documents without the overhead
- Improving economics of disk- and tape-based backup
- Facilitating faster local backups, and restores
- Boosting storage capacity and utilization
- Improved network bandwidth utilization
- Supporting ROBO or satellite office data protection

Dedupe has become a function found in various products from hardware to software. For example, dedupe can be found or implemented in:

- Operating systems or file systems
- Layered software utilities
- Backup or other data protection software
- WAFS/WAAS/WADM and other bandwidth optimizers
- Agents, appliances, and gateways
- VTL or VxLs and storage systems, including NAS

Deduplication normalizes the data being processed by eliminating recurring or duplicate data that has already been seen and stored. Implementations vary, with some working on a file basis while others work in a fixed block, chunk, or byte boundary; still others are able to adjust to variable-size byte streams. For example, in a backup usage scenario, data that is being backed up is analyzed to see if it has already been seen and stored. If the data has been previously stored, then an entry is made indicating where the data is stored and the new copy is discarded (deduped).

If new data is seen, it is stored and a reference pointer is made along with an entry in the dedupe database (otherwise known as a dictionary, index, repository, or knowledge base). How the incoming data stream is analyzed and what size or amount of data is compared varies by implementations, but most use some form of computed hash value of data being analyzed to enable rapid lookup of known data. This is where the intelligence comes in with regard to dedupe vs. traditional algorithms such as LZ, because the more data that can be seen over time and in different contexts, the more reduction can occur, as is the case with global dedupe (discussed a bit later in this chapter).

While data compression essentially performs a coarse elimination of recurring data patterns, data de-duplication works on a more granular level and requires more processing power and intelligence. Data dedupe builds on traditional coarse compression by adding intelligence, leveraging processing power and awareness of what data has been seen in the past to reduce the data footprint. Essentially, dedupe, regardless of where it is implemented, trades time (thinking and looking at data access patterns or history) for space (capacity) reduction. For example, by being application-aware, data dedupe can look at backup save sets (also known as "tarballs") to identify recurring or redundant files and save a single copy with a pointer to reduce data storage capacity needs. Some dedupe-enabled solutions, such as virtual tape libraries, also combine basic data compression with dedupe to further reduce data footprint requirements.

Current industry and market focus on dedupe is targeted on backup, given its predominance of redundant data. This is not to say that there are not other opportunities; some vendors are finding success with VMs or VDIs, where there are additional duplicates. Focus is also on ratios, where the need is to expand to rates to enable transition to larger, more performance-sensitive environments that are still dominated by tape.

8.5.1. Dedupe Fundamentals

A common technique to check for duplicate data is to use a hash key lookup based on a checksum or chunks of data being seen. Hash keys, computed based on some amount of data being viewed, are compared to stored keys in a database, dictionary, knowledge base, or index of previously stored or known data. When there is a match of a hash of incoming data to known existing data, there is duplicate data. If there is a miss, then there is new data to be stored and a new hash to be added to the index or knowledge base. SHA-1 (Secure Hash Algorithm-1) has been used as an algorithm for creating a comparison or lookup hash in many dedupe solutions.

Other hashing algorithms include SHA-2, with SHA-3 in development, along with MD5. The importance of algorithms being enhanced with more bits is to produce a unique hash key to span larger amounts of data without collisions to maintain data integrity while boosting performance. For example, SHA-1 produces a 160-bit (20-byte) hash, which is adequate for many deployments; however, with larger amounts of storage and expanding data footprints, larger hash keys are needed to avoid collisions.

Where dedupe has more intelligence than traditional compression is in the extensiveness of the dictionary, index, or knowledge base of what has been seen combined with the algorithms for computing hash values. The challenge with dedupe, and why it trades time for space capacity savings, is that time is needed to compute the hash key and look it up to determine whether it is unique.

The ingestion rate for dedupe, or how fast a given amount of data can be processed, depends on the specific algorithms, the size of the available dictionary, and the pool of reduced data, along with available processing performance. As such, dedupe is typically not well suited for low-latency, time-sensitive applications, including databases or other active changing storage use scenarios.

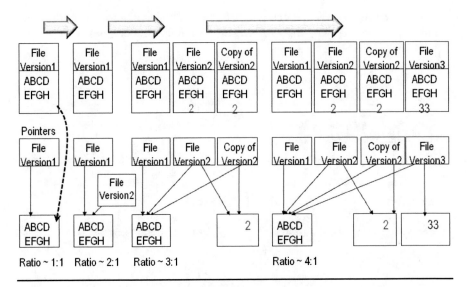

Figure 8.1   Example of dedupe benefit on files with similar data.

Some data dedupe solutions boast spectacular ratios for data reduction given specific scenarios, such as backup of repetitive and similar files, while providing little value over a broader range of applications. This is in contrast with traditional data compression approaches, which provide lower yet more predictable and consistent data reduction ratios over more types of data and applications, including on-line and primary storage scenarios. For example, in environments where there are few or no common or repetitive data files, data de-duplication will have little to no impact, while data compression generally will yield some amount of DFR across almost all types of data.

In Figure 8.1, on the left is an example of a file that is initially processed (ingested) by a generic dedupe engine (actual reduction and compaction will vary with specfic vendor product). Depending on the specfic implementation, the initial savings may be minimal, but after a copy of the first file is made, then some changes made to it and saved, there begin to be reduction benefits. Moving from left to right in Figure 8.2, as additional copies and changes are made, resulting in more duplicate data being seen, additional reduction benefits occur, resulting in a higher reduction ratio.

Figure 8.2 builds on Figure 8.1 in that the data reduction or dedupe ratio continues to rise over time as additional copies or duplicate data are seen by the dedupe engine. As more copies of the data are seen, such as with daily backups, the potential for recurring data increases and, thus, the opportunity for a higher dedupe reduction ratio appears. This capabiltity has contributed to why dedupe has been intially targeted for backup/restore, given the potential for a high degree of duplicate data occuring over time and the resulting space-saving benefit.

Figure 8.3 extends the same example by showing how the DFR benefit continues to improve as more copies of the same or similar data are seen. Depending on the specific dedupe implementation, the reduction benefit may be higher or lower, depending on a number of factors including the specfic algorithms used, local or global view of data, type of data, file or block based, and others.

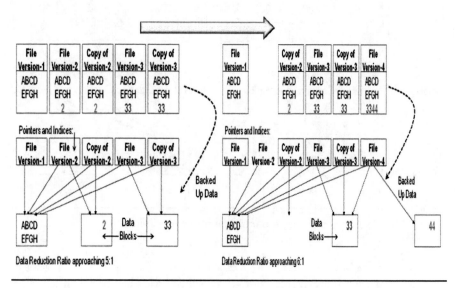

Figure 8.2 Example of dedupe benefit on files with similar data.

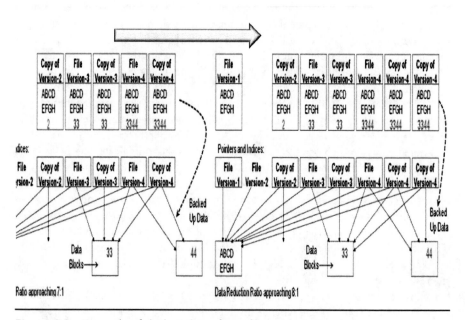

Figure 8.3 Example of dedupe benefit on files with similar data.

8.5.2. How and Where Dedupe Is Implemented

Where is the best place for doing dedupe, and what is the best method? Unless you have a preference or requirement for a particular approach or product, the answer is "It depends."

Some solutions have been optimized for single streams of data, others for dual or multiple streams; some for parallel, others for multithreading to support high concurrency; some are good at ingesting data and others at re-inflating it, while still others do immediate or post or a mix. Some are optimized for scaling, with multiple nodes sharing a global memory, while others have multiple nodes yet are independent. Some are a single-target, others support complex topologies. Dedupe can be implemented in many different ways (Figure 8.4) and locations, even in nonstorage devices such as networking applications or protocol optimizers.

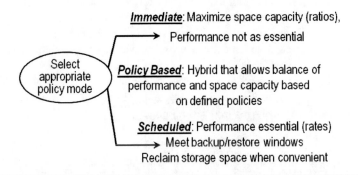

Figure 8.4   Dedupe modes to meet different service-level objectives.

8.5.2.1. Immediate Mode

One mode of operation is to dedupe data immediately as it is processed, either via source-side software or using a target device or appliance. The principle of immediate mode, also known as inline, inband, and real-time or synchronous, is to process (dedupe) the data as it is moved. The benefit of immediate mode is the reduction of the amount of storage space needed at the target and, in the case of source, the reduction of the amount of data being moved across networks.

A drawback of immediate mode is that the time required to process data on the fly can impact data movement. This is very implementation-specific, and vendors have been making great strides in both real-time ingestion (deduping) and real-time restoration (re-inflation) of data to boost performance. This aligns with a growing trend of awareness that data transfer rates (performance), or the amount of data that can be deduped as well as restored in a given time frame, are as important for some environments as reduction ratios or capacity space savings.

8.5.2.2. Deffered or Postprocessing

Whereas immediate-mode dedupe enables DFR to occur during or before data lands on the target device or at the destination, deferred or postprocessing trades space savings for performance. By using additional capacity at the target destination, deferred dedupe enables data to be streamed to meet backup windows and reduced at a later time in the background. This is similar to how some compression solutions work by ingesting the data in its normal format so as not to impact application performance, then transparently reducing the footprint in the background.

As with immediate mode, implementations vary by different vendors' products, so "your mileage may vary" based on type of data and usage. Another thing to keep in mind with postprocessing mode is the restoration rate or performance for a single file as well as for larger amounts of data, including an entire volume or file system. The amount of time delay before reduction occurs also varies by implementation. Some solutions wait until all data has been placed on the target destination, others start the postprocessing almost immediately, after a short time interval or after a certain amount of data is captured.

Some solutions that were initially focused on immediate or deferred techniques are now adding hybrid support for both. These solutions can be configured to process in either immediate or deferred mode, based on specific service-level objective requirements. Essentially, hybrid (Figure 8.4) or policy-based dedupe provides the best of both worlds, by adapting to customers' different application needs. With policy-based enabled solutions, it is possible to, for example, have one stream support immediate mode while another is operating in deferred mode.

Table 8.2 Where to Perform Dedupe

	Source	Target
Drawback	Disruptive to existing BC/DR and backup/restore tools. New software or software upgrades may be required. CPU and memory are consumed on server where dedupe is done.	Extra functionality added to VTL or VxL or storage system or via an appliance or gateway. Does not address reducing data footprint for data that must be moved over networks on a local or remote basis.
Benefit	Performs reduction closer to data source, enabling less data to be moved, making more efficient use of networking resources for local as well as for sending from ROBO or sending to cloud-based target destinations.	Plug and play with existing BC/DR as well as backup/restore software and skill sets. When combined with global capabilities, a larger knowledge base can be leveraged for additional DFR benefits.

8.5.3. Dedupe Locations (Hardware, Software, Appliance, Source, and Target)

In addition to when dedupe is done (immediate or deferred), other variations include where it is implemented, such as in hardware storage systems or appliances as a target destination (Table 8.2), or in software as part of a source backup or data protection tool.

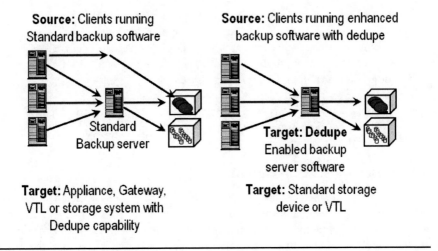

Figure 8.5   Source- and target-based dedupe.

General characteristics of dedupe include:

- Solutions tend to be software-based (or positioned that way).
- Most solutions are "tin wrapped" software (e.g., appliance/gateway).
- Data reduction occurs at or near data target/destination.
- Flexibility with existing backup/data protection software.
- Enables robust scaling options for larger environments.
- Multiple "ingest" streams from sources enable high reduction ratios.
- Examples include dedupe enabled VTLs, gateways, or appliances.
- A knowledge base, dictionary, index, map of what data has already been seen.

Basic aspects of source- and target-based dedupe (Figure 8.5):

- Source can be standard backup/recovery software without dedupe.
- Source can be enhanced backup/recovery software with dedupe.
- Target can be a backup server that in turn dedupes to storage target.
- Target can be a backup device, storage system, or cloud service with dedupe.

Common characteristics of source dedupe include:

- Data reduction occurs via software, at or near the data source.
- Network (LAN, MAN, WAN) activity is reduced.
- Some backup software dedupes at the client, some at the backup server.
- Dedupe is independent of target devices.
- Source dedupe may not achieve the same reduction ratios as target dedupe.

Common characteristics of target or destination-based dedupe include:

- Supports immediate, deferred, or policy mode to adapt to different needs
- Can be a backup server or a storage server, appliance, or gateway
- Optimized for backup/restore, archiving, or general storage needs
- Access via block tape emulation (VTLs)
- File access using an NFS or CIFS interface
- Some support replication to other devices, including VTLs
- Optional support for path to tape, including support for the Open Storage Technology (OST) backup API

8.5.4. Global vs. Local Dedupe

Local dedupe is so named because the dictionary has a scope of only what has been seen by a given dedupe engine instance. A dedupe engine instance might be either source- or target-based, functioning in either immediate or deferred mode. Since the dedupe engine (the algorithm or software functionality) sees only what it processes, the view is localized to that instance. For example, on the left in Figure 8.6, three sources are backing up to a dedupe-enabled device, a target storage system, a VTL, or a backup node. This means that data can be reduced based only on the three streams or backup sources that are seen. As another example, if an environment has six servers being backed up, following the Figure 8.6 example, the dedupe engine on the left does not know about the servers and their data on the right, and vice versa. If dedupe is local, then for a dedupe engine that has multiple nodes, each with a separate instance to boost scaling of performance, availability, and capacity, each instance or engine has its own knowledge base and is limited to only what it has seen.

Consequently, since dedupe reduction ratios or benefits are a product of what data has been seen previously, a localized dictionary or knowledge base can limit the full DFR capabilities for a given environment, and the DFR is limited to the localized environment. This is not all that different from basic compression algorithms, whose DFR benefit or ratio is limited to what they see. What this means is that multiple instances of the dedupe engine cannot benefit from the economics of scale and knowledge of having seen a broader scope of data. It should also be mentioned that local dedupe does not mean that data cannot be sent to a removed destination. For example, a backup solution on a server enabled with source-side dedupe could have a local knowledge base that reduces the amount of data being sent across a network to a remote device target or cloud service.

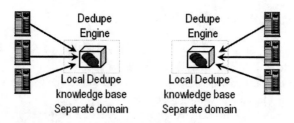

Figure 8.6   Local (nonglobal)-based dedupe.

It is possible that the target destination or cloud or managed service provider also leverages some form of DFR, including target dedupe, to further reduce data by examining multiple input streams. Likewise, a devise enabled as target-based dedupe could be physically at the same local site as the source of the backup or data movement, or it could be remote, however, any data sent over a network with target-based dedupe does not realize the benefits of DFR.

Many dedupe-enabled solutions initially appeared with localized scope–based knowledge bases, because these are easier to engineer and deploy. An emerging trend with dedupe solutions, for source-based as well as target-based solutions, is the ability for multiple dedupe engine instances to communicate with each other or some other entirety, enabling a shared knowledge base. While it is more complex to engineer and coordinate multiple dedupe instances while maintaining performance and data integrity, the benefit is increased DFR capabilities. By having a shared or global database, knowledge base, or index where the results of what has been seen by different dedupe engine instances can be compared, additional redundancies can be eliminated. For example, if six different servers, as shown in Figure 8.6, are configured and load-balanced across a pair of dedupe engines (applications, nodes, backup nodes, or other targets), and they are backing up similar files or data that has duplicate occurrences across the nodes, de-duplication can be enhanced.

Global dedupe is not limited to targets; source-based dedupe implementations also have the ability or potential, depending on where specific vendors are with their technology deployments, to share information. An example would be six different servers backing up or copying or storing data on a common target, which might be a destination storage system, a VTL, an appliance, or even a cloud provider server. The different sources or clients can communicate with the target to get maps or fingerprints of information for comparison, to further reduce data before sending to the destination.

How much information is shared with the source nodes is a vendor- and product-specific implementation, so check with your solution provider as to its specific capabilities. Note that while a common knowledge base or dictionary is used to help enable DFR on a broader basis, a side benefit can be increased resiliency or redundancy. The knowledge base should not be a single point of failure, as it is very important to protect that information in order to be able to re-inflate or undedupe data that has been reduced.

Also note that global dedupe does not have to be limited to a shared or common storage pool where data is actually placed. Another note is that the mere presence of multiple nodes, for example, in a grid or clustered dedupe solution, does not necessarily mean that global dedupe is in use. For some scenarios, multiple nodes may look on paper as if they have global dedupe capabilities (Figure 8.7), yet they may actually have only local dedupe capability.

In addition to where (source or target), how (hardware or software, local or global), and when (immediate or deferred), other dedupe considerations include how the solution works with other DFR techniques, including compression, granularity, or flexibility in data comparison size, support for replication, as well as retiering of data, including path to tape. Another consideration is the different topologies that various solutions can support. One variation is many sources sending data to a single target destination (many to one). Another has one target destination that replicates to one or many other targets in the same or different locations, including those from managed service or cloud providers.

When looking at deduplication solutions, determine whether the solution is designed to scale in terms of performance, capacity, and availability, along with how restoration of data will be impacted by scaling for growth. Other items to consider include how data is re-duplicated, such as in real time using in-line or some form of time-delayed postprocessing, and the ability to select the mode of operation. For example, a dedupe solution may be able to process data at a specific ingest rate in-line until a certain threshold is hit, and then processing reverts to postprocessing so as not to cause performance degradation to the application writing data to the dedupe solution. The downside of postprocessing is that more storage is needed as a buffer. It can, however, also enable solutions to scale without becoming a bottleneck during data ingestion.

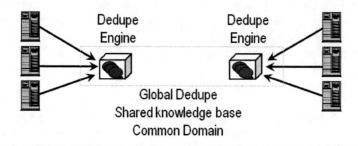

Figure 8.7   Global dedupe.

8.6. DFR and RAID Configurations

Redundant Arrays of Independent Disks (RAID) is an approach to addressing data and storage availability and performance. As a technique and technology, RAID is about 20 years old, with many different types of implementations in hardware and software. There are several different RAID levels to align with various performances, availability, capacity, and energy consumption levels, as well as cost points.

When your budget is restricted, you may have to make do by reconfiguring to get more usefulness out of what you already have. RAID may seem like a very low-tech approach, but ou should reassess your service-level agreements, including RPO/RTO expectations, to verify that they are in fact what is expected rather than what is assumed, and then align the technology. Granted, changing RAID levels may not be easy for some systems; take some time to reassess what RAID levels are tied to your SLA commitments.

Different RAID levels (Figure 8.8) will have a partial impact on storage energy effectiveness similar to various HDD performance capacity characteristics; however, a balance among performance, availability, capacity, and energy (PACE) needs to occur to meet application service needs. For example, RAID 1 mirroring or RAID 10 mirroring and striping use more HDDs, and thus more power, but yield better performance than RAID 5. RAID 5 yields good read performance and uses fewer HDDs, reducing energy footprint at the expense of write or update performance. An effective energy strategy for primary external storage includes selecting the applicable RAID level and drive type combined with a robust storage controller to deliver the highest available IOPs per watt of energy consumed to meet specific application service and performance needs.

In addition to the RAID level, the number of HDDs supported in a RAID group set can have a performance and energy efficiency impact. For example, in Figure 8.8, N is the number of disks in a RAID group or RAID set; more disks in a RAID 1 or RAID 10 group will provide more performance with a larger power, cooling, floor space, and energy (PCFE) footprint. On the other hand, more HDDs in a RAID 5 group spreads parity overhead across more HDDs, improving energy efficiency and reducing the physical number of HDDs; however, this should be balanced with the potential exposure of a second HDD failure during a prolonged rebuild operation. A compromise might be RAID 6, or even emerging triple parity, along with distributed protection schemes, particularly with solutions that accelerate parity calculations and rebuild operations.

General notes and comments regarding RAID include the following:

- Larger RAID sets can enable more performance and reduce overhead.
- Some solutions force RAID sets to a particular shelf or drive enclosure rack.
- Match performance and availability to type of data, active or inactive.
- Boost performance with faster drivers; boost capacity with large-capacity drives.
- Rebuild time will be impacted by drive size for large-capacity SAS and SATA.
- Balance exposure risk during drive rebuild with appropriate RAID level.
- Design for fault containment, balancing best practices and technology.

	Performance	Availability	Performance Overhead	Availability Overhead
RAID 0	Very Good	None	None	N + 0 = 0%
RAID 1	Good	Very Good	Minimum	50%
RAID 5	Poor Writes	Good	High on Write	(1P / N) 6%
RAID 6	Poor Writes	Better	High on Write	(2P / N) 12.5%

Figure 8.8   Summary of RAID levels balancing PACE for application service levels.

8.7. Space-Saving Snapshots

Part of backup or data protection modernization that supports data footprint reduction includes space-saving snapshots. Space-saving or space-efficient snapshots can be used for more than data protection. They also support making copies of production data that can be used for quality assurance or testing, development, decision support, and other uses. The importance of a space-saving snapshot is to reduce the overhead of extra space needed every time a copy or snapshot of a snapshot is made. First-generation snapshots which have been deployed in various systems for many years, if not decades, have continued to improve in terms of performance and space efficiency.

The next wave has been to enable copies of copies using change tracking and redirection on write techniques to reduce the amount of storage required while enabling fast copies to be made. The importance of space-saving as well as traditional snapshots is that as part of a data protection modernization, changing the way information is copied can reduce the overhead of storage needed, enabling a leaner data footprint. The object is to be able to store and retain more data in a smaller, more economical footprint.

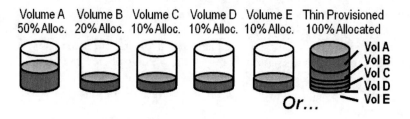

Figure 8.9   Example of thin provisioning.

8.8. Thin Provisioning

Thin provisioning is a storage allocation and management technique that presents an abstracted or virtualized view to servers and applications of how much storage has been allocated yet is actually physically available. In essence, thin provisioning, as seen in Figure 8.9, allows the space from multiple servers that have storage allocated but not actually used to be shared and used more effectively to minimize disruptions associated with expanding and adding new storage.

In Figure 8.9, each server thinks that it has, perhaps, 10 TB allocated, yet many of the servers are using only 10% or about 1 TB of storage. Instead of having to have 5 × 10 or 50 TB underutilized, a smaller amount of physical storage can be deployed yet thinly provisioned with more physical storage allocated as needed. The result is that less unused storage needs to be installed—and consuming power, cooling, and floor space—until it is actually needed. The downside, however, is that thin provisioning works best in stable or predictable environments where growth and activity patterns are well understood or good management insight tools on usage patterns are available.

Thin provisioning can be thought of as similar to airlines overbooking a flight based on history and traffic patterns. However, like airlines' associated disruptions and costs when overbooking a flight, thin provisioning can result in a sudden demand for more real physical storage than is available. Thin provisioning can be part of an overall storage management solution but needs to be combined with management tools that provide history and insight on usage patterns.

8.9. Common DFR Questions

Storage is getting cheaper; why not buy more? It is true that the cost per gigabyte or tera-byte continues to decline and that energy efficiencies are also improving. However, there are other costs involved in managing, protecting, and securing data. In addition to those costs, there is the complexity of how many gigabytes or terabytes can be effec-tively managed per person. A data footprint reduction strategy enables more gigabytes, terabytes, or petabytes to be effectively managed per person.

Why not use dedupe for everything? Perhaps in the future, as processors become even faster, algorithms more robust, and other optimizations occur, dedupe may become more widespread. However, in the near term, dedupe will continue to evolve and find new deployment opportunities where it can be used with data that can be reduced. Other types of data, including graphic or video images, lend themselves better to com-pression or other forms of reduction, so having multiple tools in your DFR toolbox enables more opportunities.

8.10. Chapter Summary

Organizations of all shapes and sizes are encountering some amount of growing data footprint impact that needs to be addressed, either now or in the near future. Given that different applications and types of data along with associated storage mediums or tiers have various performance, availability, capacity, energy, and economic characteristics, multiple data footprint impact reduction tools or techniques are needed (Table 8.3).

Table 8.3 Data Footprint Reduction Approaches and Techniques

	Archiving	Compression	De-duplication
When to use	Database, email, and unstructured data	Email, file sharing, backup or archiving	Backup or archiving or recurring and similar data
Characteristics	Software to identify and remove unused data from active storage devices	Reduced amount of data to be moved (transmitted) or stored on disk or tape	Eliminate duplicate files or file content observed over a period of time to reduce data footprint
Examples	Database, email, unstructured file solutions	Host software, disk or tape (network routers), appliances	Backup and archiving target devices and VTLs, specialized appliances
Caveats	Time and knowledge to know what and when to archive and delete, data and application aware	Software-based solutions require host CPU cycles, impacting application performance	Works well in background mode for backup data to avoid performance impact during data ingestion

What this means is that the focus of data footprint reduction is expanding beyond that of just de-duplication for backup or other early deployment scenarios. For some applications, reduction ratios are an important focus, so the need is for tools or techniques that achieve those results. For other applications, the focus is on performance with some data reduction benefit, so tools are optimized for performance first and reduction second. In response, vendors will expand their current capabilities and techniques to meet changing needs and criteria. Vendors with multiple DFR tools will also do better than those with only a single function or focused tool.

General action items include:

- Look at data footprint reduction in the scope of your entire environment.
- Different applications and data will need various tools and techniques.
- Some data reduction focuses on space; other techniques trade space for time.
- Have multiple tools in your DFR toolbox.

Vendors with DFR solutions, targets, or enabling capabilities include Amazon, AT&T, CA, Cisco, Commvault, Dell, EMC, Exagrid, Falconstor, Fujitsu, Hitachi, HP, IBM, Index Engines, Iron Mountain, Microsoft, NEC, NetApp, Overland, Oracle, Permabit, Prostor, Quantum, Quest, Rackspace, Riverbed, Seagate, Sepaton, Solix, Spectra, StoredIQ, Sungard, Symantec, Toshiba, Veeam, Verizon/Terremark, WD, and many others. The bottom line is to use the most applicable technologies or combination of technologies along with best practices for the task and activity at hand.

Chapter 9

Storage Services and Systems

Storage can be like a box of chocolates: You never know what you might get.

— Greg Schulz

In This Chapter

- Storage functionalities can support information services.
- Cloud and virtualization can leverage storage and networking functionalities.
- Cloud and virtualization technologies can complement storage.
- Storage solutions should be considered and compared beyond price per gigabyte.

This chapter looks at issues, challenges, and opportunities involved with data storage systems and solutions that support cloud, virtual, and physical environments. Key themes, buzzwords, and trends addressed in this chapter include tiered storage, performance, availability, capacity, energy, and economic efficiencies. Additional buzzwords include archive, backup, block and file, cluster and cloud storage, primary and secondary storage, solid-state devices (SSDs), and RAID and beyond.

9.1. Getting Started

Data storage technologies are used to store and access data, applications, and virtual machines on an internal or external, local or remote (including cloud and managed service provider) basis. There are many different types of storage and points of interest

(Figure 9.1) to meet various usage needs and requirements. Figure 9.1 shows how storage can be found in SAN, NAS, or cloud systems, servers, workstations, laptops, and other portable devices. These various types of storage have different features and functionalities, purposes, architectures, and costs or price bands. Some storage solutions are purpose-built, while others leverage commercial off-the-shelf technology; others are open software–based, while some are proprietary, perhaps using open-source kernels. Some storage is targeted for high-performance on-line data, while others are for inactive idle archive or backup/restore and data protection.

General storage characteristics include:

- Internal or external to a server, or dedicated or shared with others
- Performance in bandwidth, activity, or IOPS and response time or latency
- Availability and reliability, including data protection and redundant components
- Capacity or space for saving data on a storage medium
- Energy and economic attributes for a given configuration
- Functionality and additional capabilities beyond read/write or storing data

Different types of storage to support various application or usage scenarios include on-line or primary with a focus on providing performance and availability for active environments. Another type of storage is near-line or secondary, with a focus on more capacity at a lower cost, for less frequently used data. A third type of storage is off-line or tertiary, with a focus on very low cost, for inactive, idle, or dormant data. These three categories can be subdivided further in terms of specific usage needs or alignments in addition to meeting specific vendor product classifications.

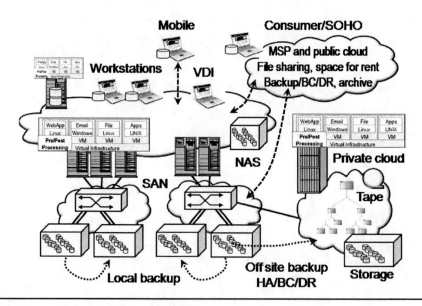

Figure 9.1   Storage points of interest.

Why can't there be just one type of data storage? Could a cloud provide that capability? For some applications or environments, storage needs beyond what is kept locally on PDAs, tablets, notebooks, workstations, servers, shared SAN or NAS, or thin clients can be supported by using a public or private cloud or managed service provider (MSP). The underlying technology that supports the MSP, public, or private cloud environment may actually leverage different types or tiers of storage to meet various performance, availability, capacity, and economic objectives. This is similar to how different types and categories of physical servers and networks have various attributes to meet usage needs.

9.2. Tiered Storage

Tiered storage is often referred to according to the type of disk drive or medium, by price band, by the architecture, or by its target use (on-line for files, emails, and databases; near-line for reference or backup; off-line for archives). The purpose of tiered storage is to configure various types of storage systems and media for different levels of performance, availability, capacity, and energy or economics (PACE) capabilities to meet a given set of application service requirements. Other storage media, such as SSDs, magnetic tape, optical, and holographic storage devices are also used in tiered storage.

Storage tiering means different things to different people. For some it means describing storage or storage systems tied to business, application, or information services delivery functional need. Others classify storage tiers by price band or how much the solution costs. For others it's the size or capacity or functionality. Another way to think of tiering is by where it will be used, such as on-line, near-line, or off-line (primary, secondary, or tertiary). Price bands are a way of categorizing disk storage systems based on price to align with various markets and usage scenarios—for example, consumer, small office/home office (SOHO), and low-end small to medium-size business (SMB) in a price band of less than $5000, mid- to high-end SMB in middle price bands from $50,000 to $100,000, and small to large enterprise systems ranging from a few hundred thousand dollars to millions of dollars.

Another method of classification is as high-performance active or high-capacity inactive or idle. Storage tiering is also used in the context of different media, such as high-performance solid- SSDs or 15.5K-RPM SAS or Fibre Channel hard disk drives (HDDs), or slower 7.2K and 10K high-capacity SAS and SATA drives or magnetic tape. Yet another categorization is internal dedicated, external shared, networked, and cloud-accessible using different protocols and interfaces. Adding to the confusion are marketing approaches that emphasize functionality as defining a tier, in an attempt to stand out and differentiate one solution from the competition. In other words, if you can't beat someone in a given category or classification, then just create a new one.

Another dimension of tiered storage is tiered access, meaning the type of storage I/O interface and protocol or access method used for storing and retrieving data. For example, high-speed 8-GB Fibre Channel (FC) and 10-GB Fibre Channel over Ethernet (FCoE) vs. older and slower 4-GB FC or low-cost 1-GB Ethernet and high-performance 10-GB Ethernet-based iSCSI for shared storage access or serial attached SCSI (SAS) for direct attached storage (DAS) and shared storage between a pair of clustered servers. Additional examples of tiered access include file- or NAS-based access of storage using network file system (NFS) or Windows-based Common Internet File system (CIFS) file sharing, among others.

Different categories of storage systems, also referred to as tiered storage systems, combine various tiered storage media with tiered access and tiered data protection. For example, tiered data protection includes local and remote mirroring, in different RAID levels, point-in-time (pit) copies or snapshots, and other forms of securing and maintaining data integrity to meet various service-level, response-time objective (RTO) and response-point objective (RPO) requirements. Regardless of the approach or taxonomy, ultimately, tiered servers, tiered hypervisors, tiered networks, tiered storage, and tiered data protection are about and need to map back to the business and applications functionality.

9.3. Storage Reliability, Availability, and Serviceability (RAS)

Data storage, regardless of its tier, type, location, or packaging, has the fundamental purpose of retaining information for a given amount of time, level of performance, and reliability at a given cost. All technology, including storage, will fail at some point, on its own due to hardware or software problems, because of human intervention or configuration errors, or due to loss of power and cooling capabilities or other facility issues. What is controllable is how technology is deployed, configured, and managed in a manner that meets performance, availability, capacity, energy, and economic service-level objectives (SLOs) and quality-of-service (QoS) requirements. Given budget constraints and service delivery demands, a balancing act is necessary to acquire and deploy technologies to meet needs while staying within constraints. Part of the balancing act is weighing applicable and likely threat risk scenarios, discussed in Chapters 5 and 6, against different service requirements, covered in Chapter 3.

Storage reliability, availability, and serviceability combines:

- Redundant components: power, cooling, controllers, spare disks
- Fault containment: automatic leveraging of redundant components
- Self-healing: error correction, data integrity checks, rebuild and repair
- High availability: redundant components, replication with snapshots
- Business continuance: failover or restart at alternate site
- Disaster recovery: rebuild, restore, restart, and resume at alternative site
- Management tools: Notification, diagnostics, remediation and repair

The reliability, availability, and serviceability of a storage product or service is the sum of all parts or components that make up a solution (Table 9.1). For example, an individual HDD's reliability and availability are based on a collection of components internal to the package of the individual device, including the medium, recording read/write heads, motors and electronic circuitry, firmware or microcode, bad block replacement and revectoring, error-correction schemes and other mechanical items including bearings. To make an individual HDD useful, a power source is needed, either as part of an enclosure or supplied via a cable from another source. The power supply or source is then added to the sum of the components. Building on the sum of the pieces' reliability and availability along with serviceability, combine the enclosures where the storage devices are installed, their power and cooling sources, I/O and networking connectivity, controllers or adapters, and associated management tools.

Table 9.1 Reliability, Availability, and Serviceability Components

Area of Focus	How Reliability, Availability, and Serviceability Are Enabled
Application and data	Local and remote mirroring combined with snapshots or other forms of time-based copies, including backups, logs, and journal files to facilitate restart or restore to a RPO within an RTO.
Operating system and virtual machine or hypervisor	Automated local and remote failover or, with advance warning, manual or proactive failover. Replication and snapshots.
Server or physical machine	Cluster with other servers used for load balancing during normal processing, along with redundant I/O networking paths.
Networking or I/O connectivity	Alternate paths not interconnected nor converging on or through common facilities or carriers. Failover software and path manager to use redundant components automatically.
Individual component	Fault containment and isolation using redundant components to replace or repair failed components or device before impact of subsequent failure.
Storage system	Local replication copy or surviving members in a cluster. Failover to HA or BC site if available. Recover from snapshot backup if needed.
Power and cooling	Stand-by uninterruptable power source such as battery and flywheel for controlled shutdown or carryover until backup generators come on-line and stabilize. Failover to alternative HA and BC site if available.
Site or facility	Failover to stand-by or active site, restart or restore at stand-by or cold site, depending on HA, BC, and DR strategy being used.

9.4. Aligning Storage Technology and Media to Application Needs

Given that data storage spans categories from active on-line and primary data to off-line, infrequently accessed archive data, different types of storage media addressing different value propositions can be found in a single storage solution. For example, to address high-performance active data, the emphasis is on work per unit of energy at a given cost, physical, and capacity footprint. For off-line or secondary data not requiring performance, the focus shifts from energy efficiency to capacity density per cost, unit of energy, and physical footprint.

Tiered storage media or devices include magnetic disks such as fast high-performance Fibre Channel and SAS and lower-performing, high-capacity SAS and SATA HDDs. Other types of tiered storage media include FLASH or DRAM-based SSD, optical (CD, DVD, BluRay) and magnetic tape. Table 9.2 shows different tiers of storage independent of specific architectures (for example, cache-centric or monolithic frame–based; modular, distributed, or clustered) or tiered access methods (DAS, SAN, NAS, or CAS), comparing performance, availability, capacity, and energy consumption as well as relative cost positioning.

Building from Table 9.2, SSD and cache (tier 0) provide very good IOPS per watt or bandwidth per watt of energy used and capacity per watt. There is, however, a trade-off between cost and capacity. As an example, 1 TB or more of usable FLASH-based SSD can fit into 2 rack units' height (2U) in a standard 19-in. rack, consuming 125 watts or 0.125 kWh of power, capable of delivering hundreds of MB/second bandwidth performance, enabling I/O consolidation when there is a smaller amount of active data.

Table 9.2 Different Tiers of Storage and Service Characteristics in the Same Footprint

	Tier 0	Tier 1	Tier 2	Tier 3
	Very-high-performance or low-latency, small data footprint; very available	Mix of high-performance with a larger data footprint and also very available	Emphasis shifts from performance to low cost per capacity in a given usable footprint	Emphasis on lowest cost for highest capacity for inactive or dormant data
Usage	Log, journal, paging meta data or index files, performance consolidation	Active files, email, databases, video, VM and VDI hosting, audio, Web serving	Home directories, file serving, data warehouse, mining, analytics, backups, BC/DR	Archive, master backup copy, long-term, high-capacity data retention at low cost or energy usage
Metrics	Time is money Cost per IOPS Activity per watt Doing more work per watt of energy	Time is money Cost per IOPS Activity per watt Doing more work per watt of energy	Low cost per high-density capacity, avoiding energy consumption when not in use	Space is premium Cost per terabyte in a given footprint or configuration Energy savings
Examples	Cache, caching appliances, SSDs (FLASH, RAM)	Enterprise and mid-range storage: 15K, 2.5-in. SAS, 15K, 3.5-in. FC HDDs	10K and 7.2K SAS and SATA HDDs supporting 2 TB or more space	High-capacity SAS, SATA HDDs and tape storage systems and VTLs

For active storage scenarios (tier 1 in Table 9.2) that do not require the ultralow-latency of SSDs but need high performance and large amounts of affordable capacity, energy-efficient 15.5K-RPM 2.5- and 3.5-in. SAS HDDs provide a good balance between activity per watt, such as IOPS per watt and bandwidth per watt, and capacity—as long as the entire capacity of the drive is used to house active data. For dormant data (tiers 2 and 3 in Table 9.2) and ultralarge storage capacity environments with a tolerance for low performance, larger-capacity 2-TB and larger 2.5-in. as well as 3.5-in. SAS or SATA HDDs that trade I/O performance for higher storage capacity provide a good capacity per watt of energy.

Another variable to consider is how the storage system is configured in terms of RAID level for performance, availability, and capacity. RAID levels affect energy consumption based on the number of HDDs or SSD (FLASH or DDR/RAM) modules being used. Ultimately, the right balance of PACE should be weighed with other decision and design criteria, including vendor and technology preferences, to address various PCFE issues.

9.4.1. Hard Disk Drives

The roles of hard disk drives are changing; in fact, SSD is going to help keep HDDs around. Just as disk is helping to keep magnetic tape around, SSD (both DRAM and FLASH) will help take some performance pressure off HDDs so that they can be leveraged in more efficient and economical ways. While magnetic HDDs continue to decline in price per capacity, FLASH price per gigabyte is declining at a faster rate, which makes storage using SSDs a very complementary technology pairing to balance performance, availability, capacity, and energy across different application tiers. HDDs can be found in consumer products ranging from digital video recorders (DVRs) to media servers, laptop and desktop computers, servers and other computers, as well as storage systems that span from consumer scale to large-scale enterprise. The use of HDDs ranges from primary storage internal to a laptop, workstation, or server to dedicated or shared external storage accessible via USB, SAS, SATA, FC, FCoE, iSCSI, NAS, NFS, or CIFS file serving. HDDs are increasingly being used in archive, backup/restore, and other storage systems that support data protection, either replacing or complementing and coexisting with magnetic tape.

As a technology, magnetic HDDs are over 50 years old and have evolved significantly over that time. They continue to evolve, with improved usable capacity, performance, and availability along with reductions in physical footprint, power consumption, and cost. The mainstays of data center storage solutions until recently, the 3.5-in. high-performance enterprise and high-capacity desktop HDDs, are now giving way to small-form-factor 2.5-in. high-performance enterprise and high-capacity SAS HDDs.

With a growing focus on "green" storage while addressing power, cooling, and floor space issues, a popular trend is to consolidate data from multiple smaller HDDs onto a larger-capacity HDD to boost the ratio of storage capacity to energy usage in a given density. For idle or inactive data, consolidating storage is an approach to addressing PCFE issues, but for active data, using a high-performance drive to get more work done using fewer HDDs is also a form of energy efficiency. Some 3.5-in. HDDs will continue to be used for ultrahigh-capacity storage, similar to how some 5.25-in. HDDs remained after the introduction of 3.5-in. HDDs some years ago.

Large-capacity drives store more data at less power per gigabyte. This comes, however, at the cost of reduced performance, which can aggregate due to density. While it is easy to compare drives on a power-per-gigabyte basis, it is also important to consider the drive in the context of how it is intended to be used. Look at efficiency and how power is used with respect to how the storage is being used. That is, for storage of active data, consider how much work can be done per watt of energy, such as IOPS per watt, bandwidth per watt for sequential, or video streams per watt of energy. If the data is inactive or idle, then consider the energy required to support a given capacity density while keeping in mind that, unless it is for deep or time-delayed access, some amount of performance will be needed.

A technique that should allow HDDs to keep evolving with increased capacity for several more years is heat-assisted magnetic recording (HAMR) technology. HAMR technology enables more bits of information to be recorded per square inch, increasing the aerial density or usable capacity per device. With HAMR, higher densities can be obtained in a given footprint by more precisely placing data bits closer together with stability. HAMR builds on other techniques, such as perpendicular recording, that have continued to break through recording and storage barriers.

Another functional improvement to HDDs is the ability for a drive to use read/write heads that are not currently being used to accelerate RAID rebuild or other data protection copy operations. Since most HDDs have multiple platters for storing data, there are read/write heads for both sides of a platter. For example, if a HDD has two platters, there can be up to four surfaces for writing and reading data, each of which would has a read/write head attached to the actuator arm.

9.4.2. Hybrid Hard Disk Drives

Hybrid hard disk drives (HHDDs) are, as their name implies, a combination of large- to medium-capacity HDDs with FLASH SSDs. The result is a mix of performance and capacity in a cost-effective footprint. HHDDs have not seen much penetration in the enterprise space and may not see much more, given how many vendors are investing in the firmware and associated software technology to achieve hybrid results using a mix of SSDs and high-capacity disk drives. Where HHDDs could have some traction is in secondary or near-line solutions that need some performance enhancements while having a large amount of capacity in a cost-effective footprint. For now, HHDDs are appearing mainly in desktops, laptops, and workstations that need lots of capacity with some performance but without the high price of SSDs.

An example of a HHDD is the Seagate Momentus XT 500-GB 7.2K-RPM 2.5-in. SATA device with 4 GB of FLASH and 32 MB of DRAM that I used in my laptops while writing this book. The benefit I found was that large or frequently accessed files and applications loaded faster compared to traditional 7.2K-RPM HDDs while not being restrictive to the capacity of my smaller 64-GB SSDs. Before I installed the

HHDDs in my laptops, I initially used one as a backup and data movement device, and I found that large, gigabyte-sized files could be transferred as fast as with SSDs and much faster than via my WiFi-based network and NAS. The easiest way to characterize where HHDDs fit is where you want an SSD for performance, but your applications do not always need speed and you need a large amount of storage capacity at an affordable price.

9.4.3. Removable Hard Disk Drives

Removable media have taken many different forms over the decades, ranging from large and bulky low-capacity disks in the 1970s and 1980s to 1-MB rigid floppy and optical media and ZIP drives. As their name implies, removable hard disk drives (RHDDs) are HDDs that have enhanced packaging and connectors to facilitate portability. The packaging varies by vendor implementation or product, as do the connectors, which may require a docking station or conversion cable for connectivity to servers or storage systems.

HDDs are designed to be installed and, if needed, occasionally disconnected from the server or storage system to which they are attached. RHDDs may be frequently connected and disconnected, so part of the packaging is connectors with longer life or duty cycles. Also part of the package for RHDDs is skins or casings that are more durable for when a device is dropped and for antishock or static protection, similar to what is found on magnetic tape cartridges. The primary use of RHDDs is for portability or physical transport of data where sufficient network bandwidth is not available or to move and place a copy of data in a long-term backup or archive facility. Another use for RHDDs, or portable media in general, is for moving large amounts of data to a MSP, cloud, or other service provider as part of a staging or bulk data movement. Once the bulk data is moved via portable media, subsequent updates can be handled via network connectivity, including replication, snapshots, or traditional backup.

The advantage of RHDDs over other portable media is that they are based on HDDs, so any data is randomly accessible. As a result, for quick recovery, software or tools can tell the RHDD to go directly to the location where the specific files or data are located, rather than streaming to a given location on sequential media such as tape. The downside to RHDDs vs. other portable media such as tape is the higher cost of HDDs plus packaging, and the potential need for docking stations or devices able to connect and access the devices.

I have been using RHDDs for several years, initially as a removable backup medium (before leveraging MSP or cloud-based backup a few years ago) to complement local disk-to-disk backups. I still use RHDDs for archive and as a gold or master backup copy that is encrypted and sent offsite to a secure facility, complementing both local and cloud-based backup. I also use them to archive data that does not routinely get backed up. Essentially, I'm using tiered data protection with different types of media along with data footprint reduction to reduce the time and cost associated with increasing the resiliency of my applications and data. I'm "practicing what I preach," albeit on a smaller scale than some.

9.4.4. Solid-State Devices

Solid-state devices (SSDs) are storage media that utilize dynamic RAM (DRAM), NAND FLASH, or other semiconductor-based memories. DRAM-based memories are commonly found in servers or workstations as main memory and in storage systems or on controllers as nonpersistent cache. SSDs can be found in cameras (as SD cards), cell phones, iPods, and PDAs, as well as in notebooks, netbooks, laptops, tablets, and workstations. SSDs are also appearing in larger servers, appliances, and storage systems from consumer to enterprise level.

When compared strictly on a cost per gigabyte or terabyte basis, HDDs are cheaper. However, if compared on the ability to process I/Os and the number of HDDs, interfaces, controllers, and enclosures necessary to achieve the same level of IOPS or bandwidth or transaction or useful work, then SSDs should be more cost-effective. The downside to DRAM compared to HDDs on a capacity basis is that electrical power is needed to preserve data. Some early-generation SSDs were based on DRAM combined HDDs for persistency with battery-backed power supplies to enable memory to be written to disk when powered off. Today the most common form of SSD is based on NAND FLASH in a variety of different packaging and solutions.

FLASH-based memories have risen in popularity given their low cost per capacity point and that no power is required to preserve the data on the medium. FLASH memories have gained ground at the low end, ranging from SD cards or chips for cameras or smart phones to USB thumb drives and MP3 players, given their lower power, low cost, and good capacity points while preserving data when powered off. There are two common types of FLASH memories, single-level cell (SLC) and multilevel cell (MLC). SLC FLASH stores a single data bit per memory cell, whereas MLC stacks multiple data bits per cell, enabling higher capacities at a lower cost. SLC-based FLASH memories are typically found in or associated with premium products including enterprise storage systems. Typically, MLC-based FLASH is found in solutions that have a higher capacity per price point. Another emerging type of persistent SSD is the emerging phase change memory (PCM) technology.

A point to consider with FLASH-based memories is that their performance, particularly on writes, while faster than HDDs, is not as good as DRAM-based memories. Another concern with FLASH-based SSDs has been that of duty cycle, or cells wearing out over time. With current generations of enterprise-class FLASH, these duty cycles are much higher than consumer or "throwaway-class" FLASH-based products. In addition to newer generations of FLASH having longer duty cycles, storage system and controller vendors have also been optimizing their solutions to reduce wear or decreased lifespan. The Joint Electron Devices Engineering Council (JEDEC), an American National Standards Institute (ANSI)-accredited organization subcommittee (JC-64.8) for solid state drives has established endurance metrics and test methods. These tests and metrics have been developed to provide meaningful, representative insight into endurance or duty cycle and reliability for selecting SSD solutions or components. Two standards include JESD218 SSD requirements and endurance test method along with JESD219 SSD endurance workloads, which can be found at www.jedec.org.

Beyond the benefits of using FLASH-based storage for consumer products, SSDs are gaining popularity in cloud, virtual, and traditional data centers to address I/O

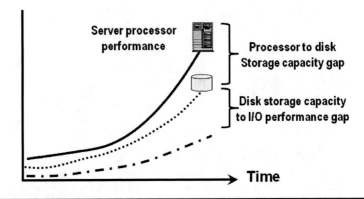

Figure 9.2   Server–storage I/O performance gap.

performance bottlenecks and improve storage effectiveness. A challenge for many environments is the decades-old issue of addressing the server–storage I/O performance gap (Figure 9.2). The cost of hardware continues to decrease, while servers are becoming faster and smaller. Storage capacity and availability also continue to increase, while physical footprint and price decrease, but there is still a gap between storage capacity and server and storage performance. The result is that, for some applications, to achieve a given level of performance, more resources (disks, controllers, adapters, and processors) are needed, resulting in a surplus of storage capacity.

In an attempt to reduce the excess storage capacity, consolidation is sometimes done without an eye on performance, looking only at the floor space, power, and cooling benefits of highly utilized storage. Then, to address storage performance bottlenecks, the storage is reallocated across more storage systems, and the cycle starts again.

The left side of Figure 9.3 shows 16 HDDs attached to a storage system or controller configured to meet an application's performance requirement of at least 3600 IOPS. In this example, the available performance may not be enough if controller optimization or caching is not providing an additional benefit. A by-product of the configuration shown in Figure 9.3 is underutilized storage capacity and missing quality-of-service SLOs. As a solution, I/O consolidation is shown on the right side of Figure 9.3. I/O consolidation involves using a high-performance storage device, such as an SSD, capable of exceeding current IOPS and QoS requirements. The benefits, in addition to meeting QoS or performance requirements, are less wasted space (capacity as well as power, cooling, and physical footprint) as well as reduced complexity and cost.

Figure 9.4, while similar to Figure 9.3, is focused on consolidating storage space capacity instead of performance. In Figure 9.3 the focus is on consolidating I/O or performance where there is a relatively small amount of data onto lower-capacity, high-performance devices while considering cost per IOP or IOP per watt of energy. In Figure 9.4 the goal is consolidating storage devices, such as many smaller-capacity HDDs, where there is unused capacity and low performance requirements, onto fewer, larger-capacity 2-TB (or larger) SAS and SATA HDDs.

A challenge with SSDs has been where to locate them and how to use them in a transparent manner as well as identifying data or applications that can benefit from

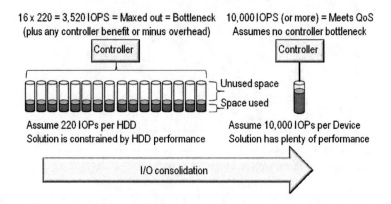

Figure 9.3   Storage I/O consolidation.

the technology. Another challenge may be the disruption to applications while moving data from its existing location to a SSD. There are various approaches for using SSDs, including as cards or modules for installation into a server, for example, using a PCIe expansion slot.

The benefit of a SSD or a cache card in a server is that I/O and storage performance can be localized close to the application. Storage is an extension of main memory and,

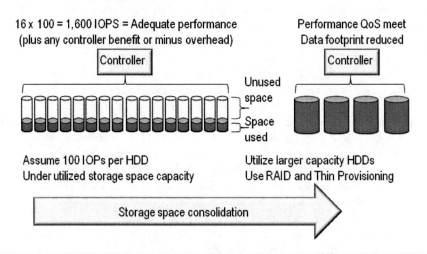

Figure 9.4   Storage space capacity consolidation.

as for real estate, location matters but comes at a price. With server-based SSD cards, applications with localized and relatively small amounts of data can benefit from the improved effective performance. SSD cards are also appearing in storage systems as an enhancement to controllers, complementing their existing DRAM-based caches.

A challenge with card or server-based SSDs, however, particularly PCIe-based solutions that do not exist in shared or I/O virtualization (IOV) solutions, is that they are local to that server only unless clustering or server-to-server communications are added for data sharing. Other approaches for deploying SSDs include devices with the same form factor and SAS or SATA interfaces to plug and play with existing server adapters, RAID controller cards, or storage systems. SSDs can also be found in caching appliances using cards, disk format–sized devices or a combination, DRAM, or tiering or caching software. Storage systems have for many years supported mirrored and battery-backed DRAM read and write caches, including some systems with the ability to partition some memory as SSD devices. Recently, storage systems are being optimized to utilize FLASH-based SSDs more effectively, including increasing duty cycles, write performance optimization, and automated tiering. Storage system-—based solutions enable transparent access of SSDs via caching, virtualization, and tiering functionalities.

Table 9.3 Technology Coexistence: What Storage Techniques and Technology to Use

	Short-Term Data Protection	Long-Term Data Retention
Retention	Hours, days, weeks	Weeks, months, years
Storage media	Disk-to-disk, tape, local and remote snapshots and replication	Local and off-site tape, cloud including tape services
Data footprint reduction, green IT, storage optimization	Archive inactive data, backup modernize, compression, de-duplication, snapshots, tiered storage (disk, tape, cloud)	Disk-to-disk-to-tape (D2D2T), copies of tape sent off-site, compress, verify and encrypt tape media

9.4.5. Magnetic Tape

For some organizations, tape may be dead, but for many organizations, tape is very much alive and taking on new roles (for example, as bulk storage for long-term data preservation, including archiving). For others, the thinking is that public or even private clouds will finally eliminate tape and, again, this may end up being true for some. Overall, however, tape is not dead, though its role and usage are changing while as a technology it continues to be enhanced. Disk is keeping tape alive by changing its role. By using a combination of disk and tape (Table 9.3), backup data can be staged to disk-based technologies and more effectively streamed to tape to boost tape drive and media utilization, leveraging built-in compression and encryption capabilities.

While disk-to-disk (D2D) backups continue to gain popularly, tape usage, particularly in mid- to larger-sized environments, continues to be relied on, though in changing roles. For example, to boost utilization of tape drives while reducing the number of devices required to accomplish backup, archive, or other data protection functions in a given amount of time, D2D solutions are functioning as a buffer or cache for tape. By performing a D2D backup, perhaps from a snapshot or replication copy, data is buffered such that when it is ready to be written to tape, a drive with adequate configuration can actually stream the data in more effectively. The net result is that the tape drives themselves can be used at closer to 100% utilization, besides while changing media or during routine maintenance.

With the recently released LTO (Linear Tape Open) and other tape product roadmaps, it is safe to say that there is plenty of life left in this data storage medium. These roadmaps show a continuing trend toward enabling more data to be safely protected and stored on an individual tape cartridge, helping to support continued data growth. Tape continues to evolve in terms of its usage and deployment scenarios as well as a technology. Table 9.4 shows how tape, specifically LTO, continues to evolve with its planned roadmap. Table 9.4 shows improvement in terms of native as well as compressed data storage space capacity in the same form factor and performance enhancements.

For applications and environments that need the lowest-energy-consuming storage and where response time or application performance are not required, for example, off-line storage, magnetic tape remains a good option and companion to HDD-based on-line and near-line storage systems. For others, tape may continue to exist, although its location may shift to the cloud. Some cloud and MSPs are figuring out that the way to convince some enterprises or ultraconservative organizations that clouds are safe is by actually offering back-end tape capabilities.

Table 9.4 LTO (Linear Tape Open) Roadmap Showing Tape's Evolving Future

LTO	Year	Capacity, Native	Performance, Native	Capacity, Compressed	Performance, Compressed	Functionality*
1	2001	100 GB	20 MB/sec	200 GB	40 MB/sec	2:1 Compress
2	2003	200 GB	40 MB/sec	400 GB	80 MB/sec	2:1 Compress
3	2005	400 GB	80 MB/sec	800 GB	160 MB/sec	2:1 Compress, W
4	2007	800 GB	MB/sec	1.6 TB	240 MB/sec	2:1 Compress, W, E
5	2010	1.5 TB	140 MB/sec	3 TB	280 MB/sec	2:1 Compress, W, E, P
6	TBA	3.2 TB	210 MB/sec	8 TB	525 MB/sec	2.5:1 Compress, W, E, P
7	TBA	6.4 TB	315 MB/sec	16 TB	788 MB/sec	2.5:1 Compress, W, E, P
8	TBA	12.8 TB	472 MB/sec	32 TB	1180 MB/sec	2.5:1 Compress, W, E, P

*W = WORM, E = Encryption, and P = Partition.

9.4.6. Different Storage Media Are Better Together

Technology alignment, that is, aligning the applicable type of storage medium and devices to the task at hand in order to meet application service requirements, is essential to achieving an optimized and efficient IT environment. For very I/O-intensive active data, Figure 9.5 shows a balance of high-performance SSD (FLASH or RAM) tier 0 for high-I/O active data and fast 15.5K SAS or Fibre Channel tier 1media as examples of aligning the right technology to the task at hand. For low-activity applications or inactive data, such as disk-based backup, where storing as much data as possible at the lowest cost is the objective, slower, high-capacity SATA storage systems are a good fit. For long-term bulk storage to meet archiving or other retention needs while storing large weekly or monthly full backups, tape provides a good combination of performance, availability capacity, and energy efficiency per footprint.

Leveraging the right technology, tool, and best-practice techniques is important for an optimized data storage environment. To obtain maximum reliability, routine maintenance should be performed on all magnetic media, including disk and tape. Routine maintenance includes regular proactive data or media integrity checks to detect potential errors before they become a problem. For disk-based on-line primary as well as secondary and D2D solutions, media maintenance involves proactive drive integrity checks or powering up spun-down disks along with background RAID parity checks.

General tips and comments:

- Factor in the total cost of ownership (TCO) and return on investment (ROI).
- Audit and periodically test all data protection media, processes, and procedures.
- Adhere to vendor-recommended media handling techniques.
- Incorporate a media and data migration plan as part of a data retention strategy.
- Align the applicable technology to the task at hand.

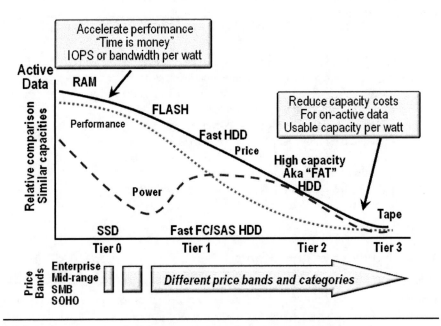

Figure 9.5 Balancing storage PACE to service and cost requirements.

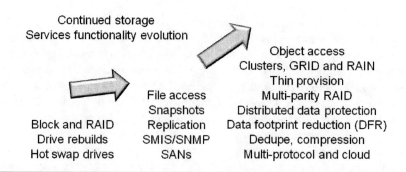

Figure 9.6 Storage system functionality evolution.

9.5. Storage Services and Functionalities

Storage and data management functionalities (Figure 9.6) exist in many different places and are packaged in various ways, depending on the vendor or product solution. Storage functionalities can be implemented natively within a storage system, appliance, gateway, or virtualization device as well as via network switches, cloud point-of-presence gateways, and software running on servers. Storage functionality is also offered by cloud services that are deployed using a variety of technologies and basic building blocks discussed in this, and other, chapters. Functionalities can be embedded in a combination of hardware, firmware, and software, while other features can be found in software running on a server or appliance that is integrated or packaged as part of a solution.

Storage services and functionalities include:

- Block-, file- and object-based access
- Thin and dynamic provisioning or allocation
- Multitenancy, partion, LUN, or volume mapping and masking
- Security, authentication, and encryption
- Self-healing, high availability, RAID, snapshots, and replication
- Automated data movement and storage tiering
- Intelligent power management (IPM) or disk spin-down
- Application integration and API support
- Data footprint reduction (compression and de-duplication)
- Virtualization and cloud access

9.5.1. Redundant Components

Redundant components include power supplies, cooling fans, controllers or storage processor nodes, cache memories, and storage devices. These components may be hot-swappable while a solution is running or during downtime for repair or maintenance. Keep in mind that availability and reliability are the sum of all parts, meaning that an individual compliment may have five or six "9s" of availability but the total solution is only as resilient as all of the parts working and configured properly together.

Storage controllers or processor nodes can be active/active or active/passive. With active/active, both controllers and storage nodes are functioning, doing useful work, with one being able to handle the other's activity in the event of a failure. Depending on the specific product or vendor implementation, both controllers may be active; however, a LUN, volume, or file system may only be active via a single controller at a time. For example, if there are two file systems or two LUNs, one could be active on each of the controllers but not on both at the same time. In the event of a failure, both LUNs and file systems would failover to the surviving member. Some storage solutions have the ability for a file system or LUN to be accessible via both members in either a read/write or read-only mode.

Active/passive means that one controller is busy doing work while the other is in a stand-by mode, able to failover work or activity to the surviving member. People frequently ask why their performance is not better with dual controllers. They are surprised to learn that their single LUN or volume or file system is only running on a single controller, with the other node or controller either sitting in stand-by mode, idle, or supporting some other file system.

Another redundant component is mirrored and battery-backed DRAM write cache memory. Given that DRAM is volatile, some form of battery-backed mechanism, such as a battery on the controller or cache board, or a large-capacity or external UPS, is needed to store data until it is written to HDDs. Some cache designs use an on-board battery sized to hold data for several hours or days until the drives can be powered up. Other designs rely on UPS to keep drives powered up long enough for the cache to be written to destaged. Why not use FLASH memory instead of DRAM and eliminate the issues of nonpersistent memory? DRAM can be written to and modified with no concern over duty lifecycles and is also faster on writes than FLASH. FLASH is being used is as a destaging device for cache so that data can be written, destaged, or flushed faster than to a traditional spinning drive that requires more power. What cache has to do with availability is that without performance, an application or information service may appear as being down or unavailable. Similarly, without availability, performance is of no use.

In addition to supporting hot-swappable disk drives that enable a failed HDD or SSD to be replaced while the rest of the system is in use, many storage systems also support a dynamic or hot-spare device. Depending on the size of the storage system and user configuration, there may be a dedicated spare or multiple global spare devices. How many spare devices are needed is a decision to be made while balancing threat risk against the expense of having spares and the cost of downtime if they do not exist. The host spare drives are used by storage systems to rebuild or reconstruct using surviving data from RAID or other means.

Having more drives means being able to protect against multiple device failures. Of course, more drives mean a higher cost, so you need to determine the risk reward of this "insurance policy." Consider whether the hot-spare devices are global or dedicated to a particular shelf or cabinet for larger systems. If they are global, then they can be used to protect any RAID volume on a first-come basis during a failure or, in the event of an alert, a proactive copy initiated. In addition to global or dedicated hot spares, some solutions require a failback or recopy back to the original drive that was replaced once it is repaired. The decision on whether to do a second copy back to the replaced drive and return to a normal running configuration will depend on your preferences. For those who are not concerned with where your spare drive exists, allowing the system to manage itself will take a different path than that for those who want to revert to a known good condition with a more hands-on management approach.

9.5.2. RAID and Data Availability

RAID (Redundant Arrays of Independent Disks) is an approach to addressing data and storage availability and performance. RAID as a technique and technology is about 20 years old and has many different types of implementations in hardware and software. There are several different RAID levels to align with various performance, availability, capacity, and energy-consumption levels, along with cost points.

RAID is commonly deployed in and using:

- Workstations, servers, and other computers
- Storage systems, gateways, and appliances
- RAID adapter cards that install into servers or appliances
- Application, file, or volume managers as well as operating systems
- Software using standards processors to reduce cost
- Hardware using custom ASICs to boost performance

RAID functionalities and differences between solutions include:

- Support for two or more drives in mirror set
- Mirroring or replicating to dissimilar or different target devices
- Ability to combine various-sized HDDs into a RAID group
- Transparent migration or conversion between RAID levels
- Variable chunk size, or how much data is written per drive at a time
- Number of drives or drive shelves supported in a RAID set
- Wide stripe size across drives in the same or different shelves
- Background parity scrub and data integrity checks
- Number of concurrent drive rebuilds
- Hardware acceleration using custom ASIC or off-load processors
- Support for Data Integrity Format (DIF) and device-independent RAID
- On-line and while-in-use RAID volume expansion

Different RAID levels (Table 9.5) will affect storage energy effectiveness similar to various HDD performance capacity characteristics; however, a balance of performance, availability, capacity, and energy needs to occur to meet application service needs. For example, RAID 1 mirroring or RAID 10 mirroring and striping use more HDDs and, thus, power, will yield better performance than RAID 5.

Table 9.5 RAID Levels and Their Characteristics

Level	Characteristics	Applications
0	No availability, data stripped across disks for performance	Data that can tolerate loss of access to data until restored
1	Mirroring data across two or more disks gives good performance and availability at the expense of capacity	I/O-intensive, OLTP, email, database, write-intensive, needing HA
0 + 1 1 + 0	Data Stripe plus mirroring or mirroring with stripe provides mix of availability and performance (n + n)	I/O-intensive applications requiring performance and availability
3	Stripes with single dedicated parity disk, n + 1 (n = number of data disks)	Good performance for large sequential single-stream applications
4	Similar to RAID 3 with block-level parity protection (n + 1)	Using read and write cache is well suited to file-serving environments
5	Striping with rotating parity protection using n + 1 disks	Good for reads including Web or files, write performance affected if no write cache
6	Disk striping with dual parity using n + 2. Reduces data exposure during a rebuild with larger-capacity HDDs	Large-data-capacity–intensive applications that need better availability than RAID 5 provides

RAID 5 yields good read performance and uses fewer HDDs, reducing the energy footprint at the expense of write or update performance. An effective energy strategy for primary external storage includes selecting the applicable RAID level and drive type combined with a robust storage controller to deliver the highest available IOPs per watt of energy consumed to meet specific application service and performance needs.

In addition to the RAID level, the number of HDDs supported in a RAID group set can have a performance and energy efficiency impact. For any RAID level, n is the number of disks in a RAID group. For example, a RAID 1 $n + n$, where n is 5, would be a 5 + 5 (basic mirror) or 5 + 5 + 5 (triple mirror) or 5 + 5 + 5 + 5 (for a quad mirror). A RAID 5 and $n = 5$ would be 5 + 1 for a total of six drives, one being for parity. RAID 1 has a higher protection overhead in terms of nonusable capacity compared to RAID 5. However, RAID 1 also has more drives available for protection and, depending on configuration and vendor implementation, the ability to incur multiple drive failures without losing access to data. Of course, there is also a cost in that those extra drives with RAID 1 are not usable for capacity, and they are not free (someone has to buy and power them). However, with RAID 1, if downtime is not an option for some applications or subsets, the price of providing that level of availability offsets the cost of downtime or disruption.

At the other extreme from RAID 1 is RAID 0, where no data availability or protection is provided. The objective, instead, is to use all of the available drives' performance. I am sometimes asked if anyone actually uses RAID 0, and why would they do so. There are organizations that use RAID 0 for the purpose of performance of mainly read data with changes or updates logged or written to other storage using various protection schemes. The idea is to balance performance and the risk of downtime to the given application or data function. In the case of those using RAID 0, they have configured their environments so that should there be a disruption or drive failure, data access would occur, while data loss would not happen. Of course, for those relying on data that was on RAID 0, it would appear the data was lost until it was restored from some other storage. Do not use RAID 0 if you cannot afford the risk of downtime or data loss by not having current copies elsewhere.

Between RAID 0 and RAID 1 is the commonly deploy RAID 5, providing low protection overhead, good capacity and performance for many applications in a cost-effective manner. RAID 5 spreads parity overhead across more HDDs, improving energy efficiency and reducing the physical number of HDDs; however, this should be balanced against the potential exposure of a second HDD failure during a prolonged rebuild operation. To improve survivability and reduce the impact of a double drive failure, RAID 6, or what NetApp refers to as RAID-DP (RAID Double Parity), can be used. If more protection is needed, then try one of the solutions that provide triple parity. Note that for larger RAID sets (e.g., number of drives grouped together), the parity overhead decreases while the risk of a drive failing goes up.

At some point, performance, availability, capacity, and energy efficiency tied to economics need to be reevaluated. The "perfect" balance is part design, part RAID level, and part the products themselves. RAID trade-offs are read and write perfor-mance, protection overhead, and risk. Adding to the complexity is how the RAID is implemented and what sort of hardware assist is proved. The reward of using RAID 5 is a lower protection overheard in exchange for taking the risk of only one drive failing until a previous rebuild is complete. RAID 6 can extend the risk/reward equation by adding an extra parity drive that on the same number of disks adds some capacity over-head but improves survivability. Or you could have a double, triple, or quad mirroring, which trades higher protection overhead for lower risk.

RAID remains relevant and continues to evolve and be deployed into new market segments and usage scenarios while it, and data protection in general, continues to evolve. One of the more common challenges discussed is how long it takes to rebuild a disk drive when it fails, particularly with the advent of 2-TB and larger disk drives on the horizon. It should not be a surprise that a disk with more capacity will take longer to rebuild or copy; and with more disk drives, the likelihood of one failing sta-tistically increases. In the late 1990s and early 2000s there was a similar concern with the then large 9-GB, 18-GB, and emerging 36-GB and 72-GB drives. There have been improvements in RAID (Figure 9.7) and rebuild algorithms along with other storage system software or firmware enhancements, including a boost in processor or IO bus performance.

What is not discussed by most vendors, particularly those who have had products on the market for a decade or more, is what improvements they have made during that time. Not all storage systems are equal, even if they use the same underlying processors, IO busses, adapters, or disk drives. Some vendors have made significant improvements in their rebuild times, with each generation of software or firmware able to recon-struct a failed drive faster. Yet for others, each iteration of larger-capacity disk drives brings increased rebuild times. For example, some vendors' products have the ability to rebuild a 1-TB (or larger) disk drive in the same or less time than it took a decade ago to rebuild a 9-GB drive. While that progress is good, if it took a day a decade ago to rebuild a 9-GB drive and it takes a day today to rebuild a 1-TB or 2-TB or larger drive, while more data can be processed in the same amount of time, there is still room for improvement. If disk drive rebuild times are a concern, ask your vendor or solution provider what they are doing as well as what they have done over the past several years to boost their performance. Look for signs of continued improvement in rebuild and reconstruction performance and a decrease in error rates or false drive rebuilds.

In addition to the traditional RAID levels and their variations, additional data availability protection schemes are being implemented (see the bottom of Figure 9.7). For example, instead of striping data across drives with common or rotating parity, a variation of $N + N$ protection is used, where $1/N$ of a drive's data is copied to another drive. For example, if there seven 2-TB drives, the total capacity, assuming no hot spares, is $(7 \times 2)/2 = 7$ TB minus any system overhead for tracking or mapping tables. An example is IBM XIV, with 180 2-TB drives with 12 drives in 15 different modules and one hot spare per module. The usable capacity is $\{[(180 - 15) \times 2 \text{ TB}] \times 0.96\}/2 = 79.2$ TB. For the previous example, if the 15 spare drives are subtracted, the system's 4% overhead is also removed from the usable configuration. In comparison, a 180-drive RAID 1 $N + N$ or $90 + 90$ will yield about 90 TB usable, depending on the specific vendor implementation. The value proposition of distributed data protection modes is to spread data over more drives to reduce the impact of a failed drive while expediting rebuild of large-capacity disk drives compared to RAID 5 or other parity schemes.

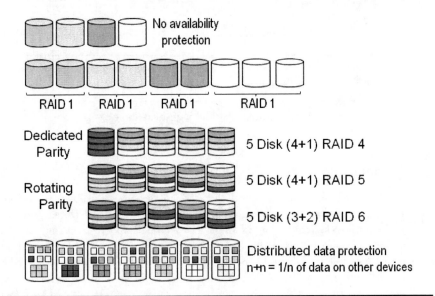

Figure 9.7 Synopsis: RAID and data protection.

Traditionally, most vendors' controllers, storage systems, or software write data to disk in 512-byte blocks; however, a few have used 520- or 528-byte blocks. The extra 8 to 16 bytes do not contain data and are only seen by RAID or storage controllers supporting additional data integrity information or meta data. Depending on the implementation, meta data might include information to help with rebuilding a RAID set if the Contents on Disk (COD) mapping tables are lost or destroyed. Recently, many vendors are beginning to rally around the Data Integrity Format (DIF), which wraps data written to disk with extra bytes of integrity information. To be clear, applications, operating systems, servers, and SAN or networking equipment do not see or notice the change unless they are also DIF-enabled. Instead, those resources continue to work with 512-byte blocks or pages of memory, with the extra wrapper bytes added once written to disk. The benefit of DIF is to add an additional data integrity layer beyond basic bad block replacement or CRC checks at the drive and storage system levels. Over time, vendors may implement DIF further along the I/O path from applications through servers to storage.

Another change that is occurring to data blocks is moving from 512-byte blocks to 4096-byte or 2-kbyte blocks. This is a slow change that will eventually extend from operating systems to storage devices, with the objective of improving utilization of larger-capacity storage and file system as files become larger.

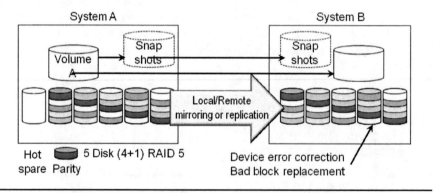

Figure 9.8 Multiple data protection and high-availability techniques working better together.

9.5.3. Enhancing Data Availability and Protection

Figure 9.8 shows basic or fundamental data and storage system availability capabilities and how they complement each other. In Figure 9.8, the two storage systems, called system A and system B, could both be local, or one could be local and the other remote. Multiple layers of protection and availability are used to guard against various threats such as those in Table 9.1. For example, disk drives (SSDs, HDDs, HHDDs, or RHDDs) leverage built-in CRC, bad-block replacement, and other availability and integrity features combined with notification capabilities such as SMART (Self Monitoring Analysis and Reporting Technology). In addition to the data integrity and self-healing repair capabilities in the drives themselves, multiple drives are configured using different RAID levels to meet performance, availability, capacity, and energy price-point requirements. In this example, RAID 5 is shown in a 5 + 1 for both system A and system B. System A also has a hot spare disk drive, while system B does not. The RAID protection enables the storage system and applications using it to continue to operate, maintaining data accessibility in the event of a drive failure.

For added protection, system A is mirrored or replicated to system B, so that changes are copied in real time. To guard against a data corruption or accidental file deletion occurring in system A being replicated to system B, point-in-time or time-interval-based data protection using snapshots are also shown. For additional protection, the snapshots are also replicated from system A to system B. What is not shown is that a redundant network or I/O connectivity between system A and system B should also exist. The snapshots can occur at the storage system level or via an external appliance or from host server software. In addition, snapshots can be integrated with hypervisors, operating systems, and applications to ensure that a complete or comprehensive data protection model is achieved.

The importance of complete or comprehensive data protection is to ensure that all data in an application's buffers or memory is flushed or destaged to disk and copied for transactional integrity. For anyone who is nostalgic, you may recall that system configurations similar to Figure 9.8 were classified by the RAID Advisory Board (RAB) as DTDS+ (Disaster Tolerant Disk Subsystem Plus) in the mid-1990s as part of evolving beyond basic RAID. (If DTDS+ is not familiar, simply Google "DTDS+ disk storage.")

Something that is not shown in Figure 9.8 is how many controllers, storage processors, or nodes exist in system A and system B. For example both system A and B could have a single controller, with the combined solution running as a distributed active/active system. In the event of a failure of system A, system B takes up the workload, similar to how a traditional or localized active/active storage system functions. Another variation of Figure 9.8 might be storage systems that have dual or multiple controllers in both system A and system B, so a local controller failure would not require failing over to the remote or secondary system. This would be an example of fault containment to isolate, remediate, or repair with self healing or via intervention unless a decision were made to proactively fail system A over to system B. Also not shown and tied to controllers or storage nodes is cache coherency, which for reads is a lot simpler than with distributed write caches. Cache coherency, as its name implies, makes sure that any updates to cache in system A are replicated over to system B to maintain data integrity consistency.

Other variations of Figure 9.8 include having multiple sites to which system A mirrors data or replicates. The mirroring or replication might be in real time or synchronous with applications waiting for confirmation that data has been safely written at the target destination. Asynchronous is another option; where an application receives confirmation before data is actually written. However, this may cause performance bottlenecks when using either slow or long-distance, high-latency networks. The trade-off is that synchronous provides confirmation that data has been written but is time latency dependent, while asynchronous can be used for longer distances or on lower-cost networks with a time delay. Still another variation on Figure 9.8 would have system B as the same or a different type of storage solution than system A at either a customer or MSP cloud site.

Keep in mind that it's not whether technology will fail, but rather when, why, and where. What you can do from a best-practices and IRM standpoint is to reduce that risk. Also remember that many disasters are tied to human intervention or errors that were not contained or isolated. The right amount of data protection and availability will be determined by your specific application and business needs.

9.5.4. Automated Storage Tiering and Data Movement

The terms data migration, movement, and automated storage tiering are sometimes used interchangeably, yet they can also refer to different things. For example, data migration can involve moving information from one storage system to another (inter system) at the same or a different location to support technology upgrades, product replacement or refresh, retiring, as well as site or system consolidation. Intersystem data movement would also be used for establishing a BC site as part of an initial synchronizing effort and for moving data to cloud and MSP services. Data movement can occur at an entire storage system, file system, file, volume, or sub-LUN (also known as block-level) basis. It's not as advanced as enterprise-class solutions, but if you have ever installed a new hard drive or storage system that came with a tool or software for moving your files, you have used a form of intersystem data movement.

Another type of data migration, also referred to as storage tiering, involves moving data within a storage system for tuning or load balancing and capacity optimization (intrasystem). Depending on specific implementation, some inter- and intra-system data migration may require that applications be paused from updates and be in a read-only mode while information is moved, while other solutions enable data to be read and written during the move. The granularity of the data movement varies from vendor to vendor, based on their different design philosophies and customer pain points, or challenges looking to be addressed. The data movement functionality can be done via host-based volume managers and file systems, or by vendor or third-party software running on a server or appliance, including via virtualization platforms, in addition to within storage systems.

Storage systems that support intrasystem data migration do so with different objectives, including completely automated, manual, or automated with manual override and approvals. Some storage systems with intrasystem tiering promote data from slow storage to faster cache basis when active on an entire LUN, volume, file, or block basis. For example, NetApp, with its Virtual Storage Tier approach, promotes data from slower storage media to faster cache in 4-KB chunks of data and then, as it cools or activity slows, data access is moved back to disk where the data resides. This approach leverages the notion of "park the data and change the access," using cache with persistent FLASH memory to expedite performance and store data on disk on a larger, more complex scale compared to the HHDD mentioned earlier. Another approach used by Hitachi in its dynamic tiering approach is to move down using automated page tiering with 42-MB chunks of data. With the Hitachi intrasystem approach, data starts in

DRAM cache and works its way down through FLASH SSD to 15.5K SAS to slower 10-K or 7.2-K larger-capacity SAS or SATA HDDs. As data heats up or becomes active, it works its way back up through the storage pools transparently to the applications. Hitachi also supports intersystem migration between their different products or using third-party virtualization appliance or software that is able to move between different vendors' products. EMC has both intra- and intersystem movement and migration capabilities as part of their Fully Automated Storage Tiering (FAST) initiative, as do most other storage vendors to varying degrees.

Items to look for and consider with regard to data movement and migration include:

- Where does the data migration or movement software tool run?
- What is the granularity of data movement, storage system, file, or block?
- Can the data being moved be both read and written to during the migration?
- What is the performance impact to other applications during migrations?
- For intrasystem migration, what is the size of storage moved (file or blocks)?
- For intrasystem migration and tiering, what is the management?
- Is the solution designed for supporting upgrades and refresh or for retiering?
- For sub-file or block migration, what is the size of data chunks moved?
- What tools are provided to help visualize hot and cold spots for tiering?

Something to keep in mind with storage systems that do a lot of data movement on an intrasystem basis is that extra processing performance is needed as well as internal bandwidth to support those operations. Automated tiering may help reduce storage cost per capacity, but with the potential risk of impacting quality of service or scalability.

9.5.5. Performance Optimization

Performance is synonymous with activity or getting work done and can range from low or infrequent activity to high performance. For storage, performance is about how much or how fast data can be read or written to a storage system.

Key performance metrics for storage include:

- Response time or latency, to gauge how fast work is done or data accessed
- Queue depths or backlog of work to be done
- Activity per unit of time, such as IOPS, transactions, packets, or frames
- I/O size in bytes or blocks of data being transferred
- Throughput or bandwidth amount of data moved per time (e.g., second)
- Random or sequential, reads and writes
- Errors and retransmissions or time-outs
- Cache hits and effectiveness vs. cache utilization

For some applications or information services, performance is measured in bandwidth or throughput—how many bytes, kilobytes, megabytes, or gigabytes are moved in a given amount of time (usually 1 second). Other applications or services measure performance by how much activity is done in a given amount of time—for example, IOPS, transactions, frames, packets, messages, or files read or written per second. Typically, for applications or IRM functions that rely on a large amount of data being moved at a given rate, such as large video files or backup/restore, operations will see a higher throughput and lower IOP or activity value.

Conversely, applications that make small read or write requests, such as database, email messaging, small image files, VDI object access, or Web page items, typically see higher activity in the form of IOPS, pages, messages, or files processed per second but with a lower throughput. What this means is that as the size of an I/O request goes up, so should the throughput or transfer rate, while the activity rate decreases. As smaller requests are made, the activity rate should go up and throughput decline. The reason I bring this up is that I hear from people who comment that they are not getting the advertised bandwidth, or that they don't need a faster storage system becomes their throughput is not that high. When I ask them what their activity rate is in terms of IOPS, reads and writes, or I/O size, they often respond with either a high value or are surprised when they check what it is. For example, if you have 10 servers that are each doing 10 MB per second, that may not seem like a lot for a 1 GbE capable of about 100 MB (line rate specification); however, that same server may be doing over 600 16K I/Os per second, shifting the performance characteristic focus from throughput to activity and response time or latency.

Techniques and technology for boosting storage I/O performance include:

- Application and database tuning or optimization
- Archiving to reduce the amount of inactive data taking up space
- Tools for monitoring performance and I/O activity
- Fast networks and servers for fast storage
- Controllers optimized to support fast interfaces and storage
- Cache using DRAM or FLASH in a server, as an appliance or as a storage system
- Cache effectiveness optimization algorithms (boost usefulness vs. utilization)
- SSD and fast 15.5K SAS HDDs in servers, appliances, or storage systems
- RAID level to meet performance, availability, and capacity requirements

9.5.6. Unified, Multiprotocol, and Function Storage

Over the past couple of years, multifunction systems that can do both block- and file-based storage have become more popular. These systems simplify the acquisition process by removing the need to choose while enabling flexibility to use something else later. NAS solutions have evolved to support both NFS and CIFS and other TCP-based protocols, including HTTP and FTP, concurrently. NAS or file sharing–based storage continues to gain popularity because of its ease of use and built-in data management capabilities. However, some applications, including Microsoft Exchange or databases, either require block-based storage using SAS, iSCSI, or Fibre Channel, or have manufacture configuration guidelines for block-based storage.

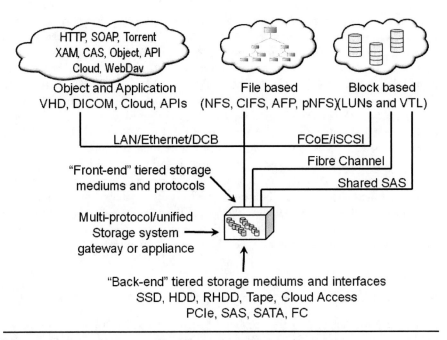

Figure 9.9   Multiprotocol and function unified storage examples.

Multiprotocol storage products enable the following:

- Acquisition and installation without need for a specialist
- Use by professionals with varied skills
- Reprovisioning for different applications requirements
- Expansion and upgrades to boost future capacity needs

Figure 9.9 shows variations of how storage systems, gateways, or appliances can provide multiple functionality support with various interfaces and protocols. The exact protocols, interfaces, and functionalities supported by a given system, software stack, gateway, or appliance will vary by specific vendor implementation. Most solutions provide some combination of block and file storage, with increasing support for various object-based access as well. Some solutions provide multiple block protocols concurrently, while others support block, file, and object over Ethernet interfaces. In addition to various front-end or server and application-facing support, solutions also commonly utilize multiple back-end interfaces, protocols, and tiered storage media.

For low-end SMB, ROBO, workgroup, SOHO, and consumers, the benefit of multiprotocol and unified storage solutions is similar to that of a multifunction printer, copier, fax, and scanner—that is, many features and functionalities in a common footprint that is easy to acquire, install, and use in an affordable manner.

For larger environments, the value proposition of multiprotocol and multifunctionality is the flexibility and ability to adapt to different usage scenarios that enable a storage system to take on more personalities. What this means is that by being able to support multiple interfaces and protocols along with different types of media and functionalities, a storage system becomes multifunctional. A multifunction storage system may be configured for on-line primary storage with good availability and performance and for lower-cost, high-capacity storage in addition to being used as backup target. In other scenarios, a multifunction device may be configured to perform a single function with the idea of later redeploying it to use a different personality or mode of functionality.

An easy way to determine whether you need multiprotocol storage is to look at your environment and requirements. If all you need is FC, FCoE, SAS, iSCSI, or NAS, and a multiprotocol device is going to cost you more, it may not be a good fit.

If you think you may ever need multiprotocol capability, and there's no extra charge for it, go ahead. If you're not being penalized in performance, extra management software fees, functionality or availability, and you have the capability, why wouldn't you implement a unified storage system? Look for products that have the ability to scale to meet your current and future storage capacity, performance, and availability needs or that can coexist under common management with additional storage systems.

9.5.7. Intelligent Power Management and "Green" Storage

I am continually amazed at the number of people in the IT industry—customers, vendors, media personnel, and even some analysts—who associate "green" IT only with reducing carbon footprints. The reality is that green IT, while addressing carbon footprint, is really about efficiency and optimization for business economic benefits that also help the environment. From a near-term tactical perspective, green IT is about boosting productivity and enabling business sustainability during tough economic times by doing more with less or doing more with what you have. In strategic terms, green IT is about continued sustainability while also improving top- and bottom-line economics and repositioning IT as a competitive advantage resource.

It is a common misconception that to be green and optimized ,you must practice energy avoidance while boosting storage capacity. It is also a myth that optimized green storage is not appropriate for environments that want to boost productivity, enhance quality of service, reduce response time, or improve performance. The reality is that there are optimization models that yield production, environmental, and economic benefits.

There are four basic approaches (in addition to doing nothing) to energy efficiency. One approach is to avoid energy usage, similar to following a rationing model, but this approach will affect the amount of work that can be accomplished. Another approach is to do more work using the same amount of energy, boosting energy efficiency, or its complement—do the same work using less energy. The energy efficiency gap is the difference between the amount of work accomplished or information stored in a given footprint and the energy consumed. In other words, the bigger the energy efficiency gap, the better, as seen in the fourth scenario, doing more work or storing more information in a smaller footprint using less energy.

Some forms of storage devices can be powered off when they are not in use, such as off-line storage devices or media for backups and archiving. Technologies such as magnetic tape or removable hard disk drives that do not need power when they are not in use can be used to store inactive and dormant data. Not all applications, data, or workloads can be consolidated or powered down, of course, because of performance, availability, capacity, security, compatibility, politics, financial, and many other reasons. For those applications that cannot be consolidated, the trick is to support them in a more efficient and effective way, leveraging faster, higher-performing resources (servers, storage, and networks) to improve productivity and efficiency.

Green, efficient, and effective storage techniques and technologies include:

- Data footprint reduction, including archiving, compression, and de-duplication
- I/O consolidation using fewer, faster storage devices
- Space consolidation using fewer, larger-capacity storage devices
- Modernization of backup and data protection
- Storage tiering using applicable media for the type or class of data activity
- Intelligent power management (IPM)

9.5.8. Management Tools

Storage management is a part of information resource management that focuses on how resources are acquired, configured, provisioned, monitored, and kept secure for effective use. Tools for managing storage can be based on operating system or hypervisor applications, or focused on a storage system from a solution's vendor or third party. Some tools are tied tightly to a storage system solution, while others work with technologies from multiple vendors and have various acquisition and licensing or maintenance costs. Storage management tools may run off a dedicated management appliance or console device, using a general-purpose application server, or may be accessed via a Web-based browser interface. Interfaces include GUI, CLI, and Web browsers as well as APIs including SNMP, SNIA SMIS, and CDMI, among others.

Storage management tools include:

- Product-specific device and element managers
- System and storage resource management (SRM)
- System and storage resource analysis (SRA)
- Data protection management (DPM)
- End-to-end (E2E) and federated frameworks

Storage management functionalities include:

- Application integration such as VMware vSphere API support
- Security, backup/restore, and data protection
- Automation and policy management
- Search and discovery
- File system and volume management
- Troubleshooting and diagnostics
- Change tracking and configuration management

- Configuration and provisioning
- Identification of hot and cold (active or idle) files and storage
- Tuning and storage tiering
- Data movement and migration
- Performance and capacity planning
- Notification, reporting, and accounting
- Path management and failover

9.6. Storage System Architectures

Storage solutions focus on the architecture or packaging of the storage system. Solutions range from small, entry-level multifunction systems to large-scale, enterprise-class systems, with many different variations between. System differences include high-end cache-centric or monolithic frame-based systems typically found in upper-price-band systems, mid-range modular, and clustered storage systems. These differences have become interface- , protocol-, and host application-independent, whereas in the past there were clear lines of delineation between different storage system architectures, similar to traditional lines of demarcation for various types of servers.

In addition to supporting both open systems and mainframe servers natively, high-end cache-centric storage systems, as their name implies, have very large amounts of cache to boost performance and support advanced feature functionality. Some systems support over 1000 HDDs, including ultrafast FLASH-based SSD devices, fast SAS HDDs (replacing Fibre Channel drives), and lower-cost, high-capacity SAS as well as SATA HDDs. While smaller mid-range storage systems can, in some cases, rival the performance of cache-centric systems while consuming less power, an advantage of the larger storage systems can be to reduce the number of storage systems to manage for large-scale environments.

Mid-range and modular storage systems span from the upper end of price bands 6 and 7 for enterprise solutions to price band 1 for low-end storage solutions geared toward small and medium-sized businesses. Price bands, as their name implies, refer to how technology, including storage, can be characterized or grouped based on cost. The characteristics of mid-range and modular storage systems are the presence of one or two storage controllers (also known as nodes), storage processors or heads, and some amount of cache that can be mirrored to the partner controller (when two controllers exist). Dual controllers may be active/passive, with one controller doing useful work and the other in stand-by mode in the event of a controller failure.

Mid-range and modular controllers attach to some amount of storage, usually with the ability to support a mix of high-performance, fast HDDs and slow, large-capacity HDDs, to implement tiered storage in a box. The controllers rely on less cache than cache-centric solutions, but some scenarios leveraging fast processors and RAID algorithms can rival the performance of larger, more expensive cache-centric systems.

As with most storage systems, it is not the total number of HDDs, the quantity and speed of tiered-access I/O connectivity, such as iSCSI, SAS, 4GFC, 8GFC, 16GFC, or 10GbE and FCoE ports, the type and speed of the processors, or even the amount of cache memory that determines the performance. The performance differentiator is how a manufacturer combines the various components to create a solution that delivers a given level of performance with lower power consumption. To avoid performance surprises, be leery of performance claims based solely on the speed and quantity of HDDs or the speed and number of ports, processors, and memory. How the resources are deployed and how the storage management software enables those resources to avoid bottlenecks are more important. For some clustered NAS and storage systems, more nodes are required to compensate for overhead or performance congestion in processing diverse application workloads and performance characteristics. Other items and features to consider include support for industry-standard interfaces, protocols, and technologies.

Table 9.6 Examples of Storage Solutions Using Open Technology

Type of Storage	Examples
Primary block storage	Dell (Compellent), HP (Lefthand), IBM DS8000 (pSeries servers) and XIV, Oracle 7000, Exadata II
Data warehouse, business analytics, and "big data"	EMC Greenplum, HP Vertica, IBM Netezza, Oracle Exalogic, Teradata
Multiprotocol block and file sharing	Dell NX (Microsoft), HP Xseries (HP IBRIX or Polyserve or Microsoft), Oracle 7000 (ZFS), Quantum Stornext
Scale-out NAS, bulk, and cloud storage	Dell (Exanet), EMC ATMOS, HP Xseries (HP IBRIX or Polyserve, IBM SONAS, Oracle 7000 (ZFS), Symantec
Backup/restore, virtual tape libraries, and data protection appliances	EMC Datadomain and Avamar, Fujitsu, IBM ProtecTier, NEC, Quantum DXI, Falconstor, Sepaton, Symantec
Archive and object retention appliances	Dell, EMC Centera, Hitachi HCP, HP, IBM IAS, NetApp (StorageGrid aka Bycast), NEC, Quantum

9.6.1. Servers as Storage, Storage as Servers

"Open storage" can mean either storage for open systems or a storage system using open technologies. The value propositions of storage systems that leverage open technologies or techniques include the flexibility of choosing your storage software stack and running it on the hardware platform of your choice, as opposed to using a turnkey solution. Another benefit is that you can buy turnkey solutions that appear to be proprietary yet leverage open technology internally. For example, a common approach is to use a general-purpose server and deploy either open-source software or a vendor's proprietary software on the hardware. One of the most common scenarios includes ZFS or Microsoft Windows Storage Server software packaged as part of a turnkey solution.

Storage systems (Table 9.6), gateways, and appliances using open technologies include proprietary software or storage management tools that run on open or industry-standard hardware such as an x86-based PC server or, in the case of IBM, the pSeries used by the DS8000 enterprise system. Another variation of open storage is solutions that leverage open-source software running on open hardware instead of proprietary software running on proprietary hardware. In some cases these storage systems or appliances leverage "white box," open system, commercially available servers, such as those from Supermicro or Intel, instead of using name-brand Dell, HP, or IBM boxes. For some of the solutions, internal dedicated SAS, SATA, and/or SSD disk drives are used. Other solutions may use a mix of internal and external or all external storage, either JBOD (Just a Bunch Of Disks) enclosure shelves or complete storage systems. JBOD disk shelf enclosures are available from several vendors, including DotHill, JMR, Newisys, Xiotech, and Xyratex, some of whom also develop RAID and storage controllers, and adapters as well as complete solutions that are original equipment manufactured (OEM) and then sourced and resold by other vendors.

In addition to the storage systems shown in Table 9.6, other common storage-related users of open technology, particularly hardware platforms, are cloud gateway and other specialized appliances. In the case of cloud access gateways or appliances [cloud point of presence (cPOP) to those in the datacom world], local storage may be included for use as a cache, buffer, or temporary work area, receiving snapshots, backups, or other data before it is moved to the cloud. Cloud-based storage systems (public and private) often leverage open platform approaches combining a mix of proprietary and open software. Many cloud solutions, services, or service providers leverage technologies, including some of those shown in Table 9.6. Another use of open platforms is stacks or solution bundles leveraging different vendors' x86-based server platforms combined with pre-integrated Citrix, Microsoft, or VMware virtualization hypervisors.

9.6.2. Clustered and Grid Storage

Clustered and grid storage, also known as bulk or scale-out systems, can be block-, file-, or object-based, providing different functionalities for on-line primary, secondary, backup, and archiving. Organizations of all sizes can benefit from ultrascalable, flexible, clustered storage that supports variable performance, availability, capacity, and functionality. From a performance standpoint, some systems may be optimized for many concurrent small random or sequential operations to files such as JPEGs or Web pages and meta data look-up. Other systems may be optimized for large sequential parallel access of videos, images, or other complex data, while some solutions can support mixed workloads. Some solutions scale performance with minimal capacity, while others are optimized for large amounts of dense storage space. What this means is that presence of a cluster or grid storage solution should not automatically infer that there will be equal scaling of performance or availability with capacity.

The term *cluster* means different things to different people, particularly when clustered storage is combined with NAS or file-based storage. For example, clustered NAS may infer a clustered file system when, in reality, a solution may only be multiple NAS filers, NAS heads, controllers, or storage processors configured for availability or failover. What this means is that a NFS or CIFS file system may only be active on one node at a time, and in the event of a failover, the file system shifts from one NAS hardware device (e.g., NAS head or filer) to another. On the other hand, a clustered file system enables a NFS, CIFS, or other file system to be active on multiple nodes (NAS heads, controllers, etc.) concurrently. The concurrent access may be for small random reads and writes, for example, supporting a popular website or file-serving application, or it may be for parallel reads or writes to a large sequential file.

Clustered storage solutions may be accessed via block (iSCSI, FC, or FCoE), file (NFS, pNFS, or CIFS), object, HTTP, APIs, or proprietary approaches. For backup and archive compatibility with existing software tools, some clustered storage solutions provide virtual tape emulation (VTL) in addition to NFS for file-based access, while others support object or content-addressable storage (CAS) modes. Clustered storage in general is similar to using clustered servers, providing scale beyond the limits of a single traditional system—scale for performance, scale for availability, and scale for capacity and to enable growth in a modular fashion—adding performance and intelligence capabilities along with capacity. For smaller environments, clustered storage enables modular pay-as-you-grow capabilities to address specific performance or capacity needs. For larger environments, clustered storage enables growth beyond the limits of a single storage system to meet performance, capacity, or availability needs.

Applications that lend themselves to clustered, bulk, grid, and "big data" storage solutions include:

- Unstructured data files
- Data warehouse, data mining, business analytics
- Collaboration including email, SharePoint, and messaging systems
- Home directories and file shares
- Web-based and cloud or managed service providers
- Backup/restore and archive
- Rich media, hosting, and social networking Internet sites
- Media and entertainment creation, animation rendering and postprocessing
- Financial services and telecommunications, call detail billing
- Project-oriented development, simulation, and energy exploration
- Look-up or reference data
- Fraud detection and electronic surveillance
- Life sciences, chemical research, and computer-aided design

Clustered storage solutions go beyond meeting the basic requirements of supporting large sequential parallel or concurrent file access. Clustered storage systems can also support random access of small files for highly concurrent on-line and other applications. Scalable and flexible clustered file servers that leverage commonly deployed servers, networking, and storage technologies are well suited for new and emerging

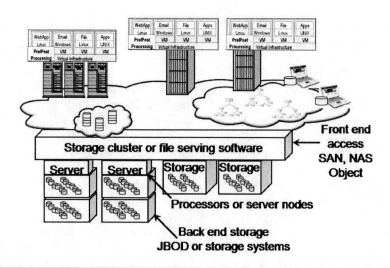

Figure 9.10　Cluster and grid storage.

applications, including bulk storage of on-line unstructured data, cloud services, and multimedia, where extreme scaling of performance (IOPS or bandwidth), low latency, storage capacity, and flexibility at a low cost are needed.

The bandwidth-intensive and parallel-access performance characteristics associated with clustered storage are generally known; what is not so commonly known is the breakthrough to support small and random IOPS associated with database, email, general-purpose file serving, home directories, and meta-data look-up (Figure 9.10). Note that a clustered storage system, and in particular, a clustered NAS, may or may not include a clustered file system.

Scalable and flexible clustered file server and storage systems provide the potential to leverage the inherent processing capabilities of constantly improving underlying hardware platforms. For example, software-based clustered storage systems that do not rely on proprietary hardware can be deployed on industry-standard high-density servers and blades centers and utilize third-party internal or external storage.

Considerations for grid, clustered, big data, and scale-out storage include the following:

- Can memory, processors, and I/O devices be varied?
- Is there support for large file systems with many small or large files?
- What is the performance for small, random, concurrent IOPS?
- What is the performance for single-threaded and parallel or sequential I/O?
- How is performance enabled across the same cluster instance?
- Can a file system and file be read and written to from all nodes concurrently?
- Are I/O requests, including meta-data look-up, sent to a single node?
- How does performance scale as nodes and storage are increased?
- How disruptive is adding new or replacing existing storage?

- Is proprietary hardware needed, or can industry-standard components be used?
- What data management features, including load balancing, exist?
- What interface and protocol options are supported?

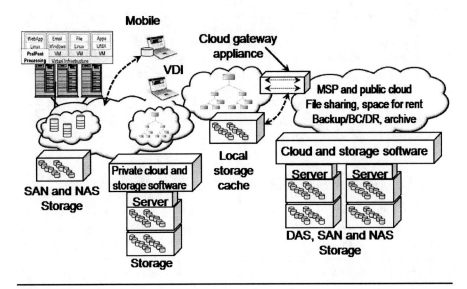

Figure 9.11   Cloud storage examples.

9.6.3. Cloud Storage

Cloud storage (Figure 9.11) can be public or private, an architecture, point product, or solution comprised of hardware, software, networking, and services. Some cloud storage services or solutions are targeted for specific use cases such as file sharing, backup/restore, archiving, BC/DR, or parking multimedia such as photos, video, and audio. Other cloud service products are optimized for video surveillance and security, database or email and Web hosting, healthcare electronic medical records (EMR), or digital asset management (DAM), including Picture Archiving Communication Systems (PACS).

How you access cloud storage will vary depending on the type of service or product. Some services and solutions present a NAS file-based interface natively or via an access gateway, appliance, or software driver module. In addition to NAS, cloud services also present different protocols and personalities (Figure 9.11) accessible via cloud appliances or gateways. Cloud access gateways, appliances, or software tools, in addition to providing access, also include functionalities such as replication, snapshots, bandwidth optimization, security, metering, reporting, and other capabilities. Cloud services leverage different approaches for supporting their solution, with some using traditional server, storage, and networking products combined with their own or vendor-supplied file systems and associated management tools. Some cloud providers, such as Google, make extensive use of custom software and hardware, whereas others use a more hybrid approach. Read more about public and private cloud storage solutions, products, services, architectures, and packaging in Chapter 12.

9.7. Storage Virtualization and Virtual Storage

There are many different forms of storage virtualization, including aggregation or pooling, emulation, and abstraction of different tiers of physical storage providing transparency of physical resources. Storage virtualization can be found in different locations such as server software bases, network, or fabric, using appliances, routers, or blades, with software in switches or switching directors. Storage virtualization functionality can also be found running as software on application servers or operating systems, in network-based appliances, switchers, or routers, as well as in storage systems.

9.7.1. Volume Mangers and Global Name Spaces

A common form of storage virtualization is volume managers that abstract physical storage from applications and file systems. In addition to providing abstraction of different types, categories, and vendors' storage technologies, volume managers can also be used to support aggregation, performance optimization, and infrastructure resource management (IRM) functions. For example, volume managers can aggregate multiple types of storage into a single large logical volume group that is subdivided into smaller logical volumes for file systems.

In addition to aggregating physical storage, volume managers can perform RAID mirroring or striping for availability and performance. Volume managers also provide a layer of abstraction to allow different types of physical storage to be added and removed for maintenance and upgrades without impacting applications or file systems. IRM functions that are supported by volume managers include storage allocation and provisioning and data protection operations, such as snapshots and replication; all of which vary by specific vendor implementation. File systems, including clustered and distributed systems, can be built on top of or in conjunction with volume managers to support scaling of performance, availability, and capacity.

Global name spaces provide another form of virtualization by presenting an aggregated and abstracted view of various file systems. A global name space can span multiple different file systems, providing an easy-to-use interface or access view for managing unstructured file data. Microsoft Domain Name System (DNS) for Windows CIFS or Network Information Services (NIS) for NFS support global name spaces.

9.7.2. Virtualization and Storage Services

Virtual storage and storage virtualization are about enabling agility, resiliency, flexibility, and data and resource mobility to simplify IRM. Some storage virtualization solutions are focused on consolidation or pooling, similar to first-wave server and desktop virtualization. The next broad wave of virtualization will be to move beyond consolidation. That means expanding the focus of virtualization from consolidation, pooling, or LUN aggregation to include enabling transparency for agility, flexibility, data or system movement, technology refresh, and other common time-consuming IRM tasks.

Various storage virtualization services are implemented in different locations to support various tasks. Storage virtualization functionality includes pooling or aggregation for both block- and file-based storage, virtual tape libraries for coexistence and interoperability with existing IT hardware and software resources, global or virtual file systems, transparent data migration of data for technology upgrades, maintenance, and support for high availability, business continuance, and disaster recovery.

Storage virtualization functionalities include:

- Pooling or aggregation of storage capacity
- Transparency or abstraction of underlying technologies
- Agility or flexibility for load balancing and storage tiering
- Automated data movement or migration for upgrades or consolidation
- Heterogeneous snapshots and replication on a local or wide area basis
- Thin and dynamic provisioning across storage tiers

Aggregation and pooling for consolidation of LUNs, file systems, and volume pooling and associated management are intended to increase capacity utilization and investment protection, including supporting heterogeneous data management across different tiers, categories, and price bands of storage from various vendors. Given the focus on consolidation of storage and other IT resources along with continued technology maturity, more aggregation and pooling solutions can be expected to be deployed as storage virtualization matures.

While aggregation and pooling are growing in popularity in terms of deployment, most current storage virtualization solutions are forms of abstraction. Abstraction and technology transparency include device emulation, interoperability, coexistence, backward compatibility, transitioning to new technology with transparent data movement, and migration and supporting HA, BC, and DR. Some other types of virtualization in the form of abstraction and transparency include heterogeneous data replication or mirroring (local and remote), snapshots, backup, data archiving, security, compliance, and application awareness.

Virtual tape libraries provide abstraction of underlying physical disk drives while emulating tape drives, tape-handling robotics, and tape cartridges. The benefit is that VTLs provide compatibility with existing backup, archive, or data protection software and procedures to improve performance using disk-based technologies. VTLs are available in stand-alone as well as clustered configurations for availability and failover as well as scaling for performance and capacity. Interfaces include block-based for tape emulation and NAS for file-based backups. VTLs also support functions including compression, de-duplication, encryption, replication, and tiered storage.

Storage virtualization considerations include:

- What are the various application requirements and needs?
- Will it be used for consolidation or facilitating IT resource management?

- What other technologies are currently in place or planned for the future?
- What are the scaling (performance, capacity, availability) needs?
- Will the point of vendor lock-in be shifting or costs increasing?
- What are some alternative and applicable approaches?
- How will a solution scale with stability?

Building a business case for VTLs or disk libraries to support technology transition and coexistence with existing software and procedures can be a straightforward process. Similarly, cases for enabling transparent data migration to facilitate technology upgrades, replacements, or reconfigurations along with ongoing maintenance and support can be mapped to sustaining business growth. For example, if a reduction can be made in the amount of time it takes to migrate data off older storage systems and onto newer technology while maintaining data availability and application access, the result is that the storage resource technology can be used for longer periods of time, thus decreasing the amount of time the technology is not fully utilized due to conversion and migration time. Another benefit is that newer, energy-efficient technologies can be migrated in and older, less energy-efficient technologies can be migrated out more quickly.

This is not to say that there are not business cases for pooling or aggregating storage, rather that there are other areas where storage virtualization techniques and solutions can be applied. This is not that different from server virtualization shifting from a consolidation role, which is the current market and industry phase, to one of enablement to support migration, maintenance, and scaling, particularly for applications and workloads that are not conducive to consolidation, such as those where more performance, capacity, or availability is needed or those that need to isolate data or customers.

Yet another scenario is to enable data to be moved or migrated to lower-cost tiers of storage for on-line active and reference data. Data migration can also be used to enable archiving to move data from on-line storage to near-line or off-line storage. Lower-cost storage can also be used as a target for replicating data for HA, BC, and DR or as a target for regular data backups. Data replication and movement can be accomplished using host-based software, including volume managers or migration tools, network- or fabric-based data movers and appliances, as well as via storage systems.

Another form of storage virtualization is virtual storage servers (see Figure 9.12) or storage partitions that enable a single consolidated storage system to appear to applications and servers as multiple individual storage systems or file servers. The primary focus of virtual storage servers or partitions is to be able to isolate, emulate, and abstract the LUNs, volumes, or file systems on a shared storage server. An example is enabling a common or consolidated storage server to be shared by different applications while preventing data from being seen or accessed across applications, customers, or users.

Some storage virtualization solutions based on software running on an appliance or network switch or on a hardware system have focused on emulating or providing competing capabilities to those of mid- to high-end storage systems. The premise has been to use lower-cost, less feature-enabled storage systems aggregated behind the appliance, and switch or hardware-based systems, to provide advanced data and storage management capabilities found in traditional higher-end storage products.

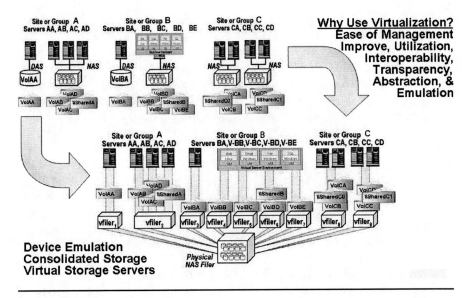

Figure 9.12 Storage virtualization and partitions.

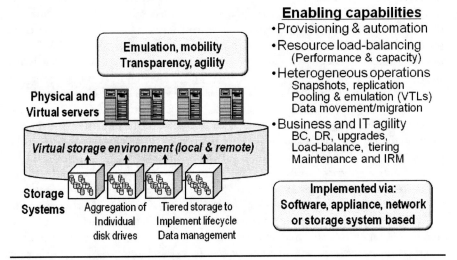

Figure 9.13 The many faces of storage virtualization.

9.7.3. Storage Virtualization Locations

Storage virtualization can be implemented in several different locations (Figure 9.13), including within servers, on appliances or in networking devices, and in storage systems. There are varying thoughts as to what determines that a solution is virtual. One school of thought is that storage virtualization must support different vendors' products, while another approach looks at the functionality across a single vendor's product or products. Which is the correct approach will depend on your preferences toward technology or vendor thinking and may, in fact, lead to a place for both.

The best type of storage virtualization and the best place to have the functionality will depend on your preferences. The best solution and approach are the ones that enable flexibility, agility, and resiliency to coexist with or complement your environment and adapt to your needs. Your answer might be one that combines multiple approaches, as long as the solution that works for you and not the other way around.

9.8. Common Storage Questions

What is the best storage? The one that works best for your specific application or information services needs, meeting SLOs and SLAs while enabling productivity or allowing the ability to store more data in the same or less space economically. Generally speaking, there is not bad storage, just some poor implementations, deployments, or usage of technology.

Why are more servers, memory, ports, or storage not always better? Ideally, a storage solution that is free of internal architecture, hardware, or software bottlenecks should be able to leverage more servers, memory, ports, and controller nodes. However, not all solutions are implemented similarly; some have more refined algorithms, software, firmware, microcode, acceleration, off-load chips, or ASICs. Some rely on the off-the-shelf capacity of commodity hardware to keep costs low and are not able to leverage the benefits of additional resources. As a result, the mere presence of more disks, ports, memory, cache, or processors should not be assumed to provide better availability. Instead, it is the sum of all of the pieces working together and their ability to support your application under applicable workloads or activity levels that should matter.

Do cloud and virtual servers need cloud and virtual storage? If your cloud or virtual server is running at or on a public cloud, such as Amazon or rack space, you may want to access the available cloud and virtual storage. If your virtual server is running on one of your servers, you may be fine using traditional shared storage.

Do virtual servers need networked storage? Virtual servers need shared storage; the type of shared storage, whether block or file, NAS, iSCSI, SAS, FC or FCoE, is up to you.

Does cloud storage eliminate the need for physical storage? The first cloud storage solution that can be safely and economically deployed without using underlying physical storage will be an industry first and truly revolutionary. Until then, physical storage will remain in some shape or form, local or remote, in the cloud base. What will change is how and where storage is used and how cloud complements your on-site environment and vice versa.

9.9. Chapter Summary

There are many different types of storage devices, systems, and solutions for addressing various needs, with varying performance, availability, capacity, energy, and economic characteristics.

General action items include:

- SSD attached to slow or high-latency controllers can introduce bottlenecks.
- Fast servers need fast I/O paths, networks, and storage systems.
- Review RAID configuration for low-cost near-term opportunities.
- Align tiered storage to performance, availability, capacity, and energy needs.
- Look beyond IOPS and bandwidth, keeping response time or latency in focus.
- Cloud and virtual servers need physical storage.
- Develop a data footprint reduction strategy for on-line and off-line data.
- Energy efficiency can be accomplished with tiered storage for different needs.
- Compare storage based on both idle and active workload conditions.
- Storage efficiency metrics include IOPS or bandwidth per watt for active data.
- Storage capacity per watt per footprint and cost is a measure for inactive data.

Storage systems, appliances, and cloud services solution providers include Apple, Cisco, Dell, Datadirect, Dothill, EMC, Falconstor, Fujitsu, HP, IBM, Infotrend, Intel, Iomega, Kaminaro, Kingston, Micron, NEC, NetApp, Netgear, Nimble, Nexsan, Oracle, Overland, Panasas, Pivot3, PMC, Promise, Quantum, Rackspace, Samsung, SANdisk, Sandforce, Seagate, STEC, Storsimple, Solidfire, Supermicro, Symantec, Synology, TMS, Toshiba, Western Digital, Xiotech, Xyratex, and Zetta.

Chapter 10

Server Virtualization

Software that truly does not require hardware will be revolutionary.

— Greg Schulz

In This Chapter

- Differences between physical and virtual servers
- The many faces of server, storage, and networking virtualization
- Opportunities to leverage virtualization that go beyond consolidation

This chapter looks at issues, challenges, and opportunities involved with virtual servers for cloud and storage networking environments. Key themes, buzzwords, and trends addressed in this chapter include tiered servers, virtual machines (VMs), physical machines (PMs), and virtual desktop infrastructures (VDIs).

10.1. Getting Started

Physical machines (PMs) or servers form the foundation on which virtual machines (VMs) are enabled and delivered. Some applications and information services will continue to utilize standard servers or PMs, while others migrate to VMs hosted either onsite or via cloud or managed service provider (MSP). Given the importance of underlying servers, let's take a few moments to look at some trends with PMs. With each successive generation of new servers and processing chip technology, more processing capability or compute power is available in a smaller footprint, as shown in Figure 10.1.

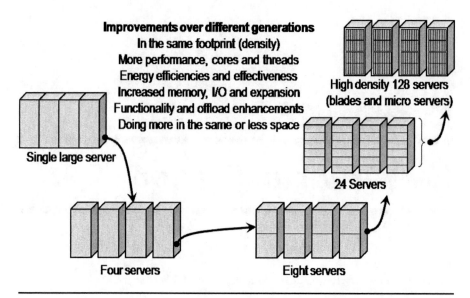

Figure 10.1 PM and server evolution: doing more in the same footprint.

The smaller footprint includes less power per cycle or compute operation packaged in a physically smaller footprint. However, the compounding effect is that while more processing power exists in a given physical footprint, the aggregate power and cooling demands continue to rise on a floor space, cabinet, or rack and shelf or rack unit (U) basis to meet the demand for more compute capability.

For some environments, the result of reducing size while increasing performance and lowering costs for servers can be more available floor space or energy savings. For environments that are growing and adding more demanding applications and supporting larger amounts of data to be processed, any savings in power, cooling, or floor space are used for expansion to support and sustain business growth. For example, in Figure 10.1, a reduction in physical size and increase in processing performance capabilities will result in lower operating costs and recovered floor space for some organizations. For growing businesses, the resulting floor space is consumed by expansion of denser technologies that place a burden on facilities by requiring more electrical power and cooling per footprint. Moving forward, as servers become faster, there will be an emphasis on further reducing the amount of electrical power consumed and necessary cooling while enabling more work to be done.

10.2. Virtual Servers

The primary purpose for enabling virtualization and cloud technologies across different IT resources is to boost overall effectiveness while improving application service delivery (performance, availability, responsiveness, and security) to sustain business growth in an economic and environmentally friendly manner. In other words, most organizations do not have the luxury of time or budget to deploy virtualization or other green-related technologies and techniques simply for environmental reasons: There has to be a business case or justification. Using virtualization to consolidate servers and storage resources is a popular approach being used in many environments to boost resource utilization and contain costs—for example, using VMware to combine the applications and operating systems images from underutilized physical servers to virtual machines on a single server or, for redundancy and high availability (HA), onto multiple servers.

Scaling with stability means that as performance is increased, application availability or capacity is not decreased or additional management complexity or cost introduced. That is, scaling with stability means that as capacity is increased, performance and availability do not suffer and performance is not negatively impacted by growth, increased workload, or application functionality. This includes eliminating single points of failure and supporting fault isolation and containment, self-healing, supporting mixed performance of small and large I/Os, and additional functionality or intelligence in technology solutions without adding cost or complexity.

10.3. Inside Virtual Servers and Virtual Machines

Virtualization is not new technology for servers. Virtualization has been around for decades on a proprietary basis, with PC emulation, logical partitions (LPARs) and hypervisors, virtual memory, and virtual devices. What is new is the maturity and robustness of virtualization as a technology, including broad support for x86-based hypervisors and other proprietary hardware solutions. The x86 systems are not the only ones that support hypervisors and virtualization; other solutions are the IBM pSeries (e.g., AIX and RS/6000) and the IBM zSeries mainframe. I mention server virtualization outside the context of x86-based because now and then I'm told by vendors and others that the mainframe and other environments do not support virtualization. Not surprisingly, those people are usually new to the industry and, thus, were not aware that other platforms, particularly proprietary ones, have had virtualization for years.

Virtualization in general and server functionality in particular include:

- Agility—flexibility to adapt dynamically for common IRM tasks and BC/DR
- Emulation—coexistence with existing technologies and procedures
- Abstraction—management transparency of physical resources
- Multitenancy—segmentation, isolation of applications, users, or other entities
- Aggregation—consolidation of applications, operating systems, or servers
- Provisioning—rapid deployment of new servers using predefined templates

Server virtualization can be implemented in hardware or assisted by hardware, implemented as a standalone software running bare metal with no underlying software system required, as a component of an operating system, or as an application running on an existing operating system. Figure 10.2 shows on the left a pair of PMs with shared storage supporting multiple VMs with Windows- and Linux-based

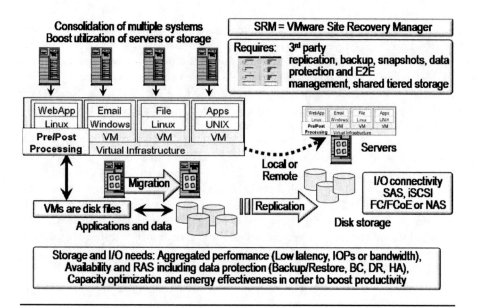

Figure 10.2   Virtual and physical servers.

guests. This system replicates some or all VMs to a HA, BC, or DR PM on the right side of Figure 10.2.

For servers and applications that lend themselves to being aggregated, there are different approaches to consolidation. For example, a server's operating system and applications can be migrated as a guest to a VM existing in a virtualization infrastructure such as Citrix, Microsoft, Oracle, or VMware. The VMs can exist and run on a virtualization infrastructure, such as a hypervisor, that runs bare metal or natively on a given hardware architecture or as a guest application on top of another operating system. Depending on the implementation, different types of operating systems can exist as guests on the VMs—for example, Linux, UNIX, and Microsoft Windows all coexisting on the same server at the same time, each in its own guest VM. For x86 server virtualization environments, the most popular guests are Microsoft Windows variants. On IBM zSeries mainframe system hypervisors, except for traditional zOS or zVM legacy operating system environments, the most common guests are Linux-based VMs.

VMs are virtual entities represented by a series of data structures or objects in memory and stored on disk storage in the form of a file (Figure 10.3). Server virtualization infrastructure vendors use different formats for storing the virtual machines, including information about the VM itself, configuration, guest operating system, application, and associated data. When a VM is created, in the case of VMware, a VMware virtual disk (VMDK) file, Microsoft Virtual Hard Disk (VHD), or DMTF Open Virtual Format (OVF) is created that contains information about the VM, an image of the guest operating system, associated applications, and data. A VMDK or VHD can be created by converting a physical server to a VM in a process known as physical-to-virtual (P2V). P2V involves taking a source image of the physical server's operating system installation, and configuration, boot files, drivers, and other information along with installed applications are created and mapped into a VMDK or VHD. There are a number of commercial as well as free tools available to assist with P2V, as well as with virtual-to-virtual (V2V) migration between different hypervisors and virtual to physical (V2P) migration.

The hypervisor essentially creates multiple virtual servers, each with what appears to be a virtual CPU or processor, complete with registers, program counters, processor status words, and other items found in the hardware instruction set architecture being emulated. The theory is that with a full implementation and emulation of the underlying hardware resources being shared, guest operating systems and their applications should be able to run transparently. The reality is that, like many things in IT, the devil may be in the details of the specific version of the hypervisor and virtualization infrastructure, hardware firmware versions, operating system type and version, as well as application-specific dependencies on the underlying operating system or server features. It is important to check with virtualization, server, operating system, and application vendors for specific supported configurations and compatibility charts and for recommended best practices.

With a hypervisor-based VM, the VM presents to the guest operating system what appears to be a CPU, memory, I/O capabilities including LAN networking and storage, and keyboard, video, and mouse devices. Hypervisors include virtual NICs, HBAs, and virtual LAN switches, all implemented in memory. The virtual LAN switch is used by the virtual NICs to enable the VMs to communicate using IP via memory, instead of via a traditional physical NIC and LAN, when operating on the same physical server. A different form of hypervisor-based virtualization, known as para virtualization, has guest operating systems and, perhaps, applications modified to take advantage of features in the hypervisor for improved performance. While performance is a benefit of

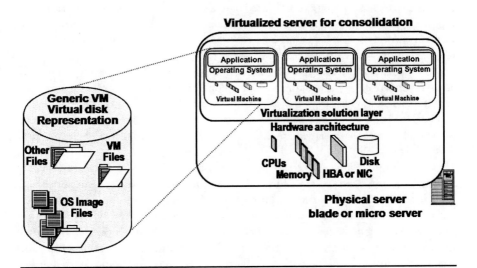

Figure 10.3 Virtual servers and virtual disk representation.

para virtualization, the downside is that not all operating systems and applications customize their software to support different hypervisor features.

Popular hypervisors, including those from Microsoft, VMware, and Citrix/Xen, provide emulation and abstraction of x86-based hardware instruction sets. Other vendors, depending on specific products, support other hardware instruction sets and environments. For example, the IBM zSeries mainframe supports logical partitions and virtual machines for existing legacy mainframe operating systems and applications and for Linux. In the case of an IBM zSeries mainframe, Linux can be supported as a guest on a VM using zVM or as a native Linux, depending on the Linux implementation. Conversely, ports or emulations of IBM mainframe operating systems exist on x86-based systems for development, research, marketing, training, and other purposes.

For underutilized servers, the value proposition of consolidation is sharing a server's CPU processor, memory, and I/O capabilities across many different VMs, each functioning as if it were a unique server, to reduce electrical power, cooling, and physical footprint and associated hardware costs of dedicated servers. The impact is that utilization of a server hosting many VMs via a virtualization infrastructure is increased, while other servers are surplus or redeployed for other uses, including growth. A technique that can be used for servers that are busy during the daytime and idle during evening periods is to migrate those servers to a VM. During the daytime the VM and guest operating system and application are migrated to a dedicated server or blade in a blade center to meet performance and QoS requirements. In the evening or during off-hours or during seasonal periods of inactivity, the VM can be migrated to another physical server where other VMs have been consolidated, enabling some servers or blades to be powered off or to be put into a low-power mode.

The downside to overconsolidating, or putting too many VMs on a given server, is resource contention, performance bottlenecks, instability that negatively impacts availability, and creation of a single point of failure. A single point of failure results when, for example, eight servers are consolidated onto a single server; if that single server fails, it now impacts eight VMs and their guest operating systems, applications, and users. Consequently, there is a balancing act among performance, availability, capacity, and energy consumption with server consolation.

Another example (Figure 10.4) is moving applications that run on the same operating system to different containers, zones, domains, or partitions of a larger server running the same operating system. In this scenario, the operating system enables applications and users to be isolated from each other while running the same instance or, depending on the implementation, a different version or instance of the same operating system.

Depending on hardware and software configuration, underlying hardware resources such as CPU processors, memory, disk or networking, and I/O adapters may be shared or dedicated to different partitions. In Figure 10.4, a single operating system instance is shown with three separate zones, partitions, or containers, where different applications are running and isolated from each other. For performance and QoS purposes, memory is allocated and shared across the different partitions. In this example, the server is a four-way processor with four discrete CPU cores, with two allocated to the leftmost partition or container and one each to the middle and rightmost containers.

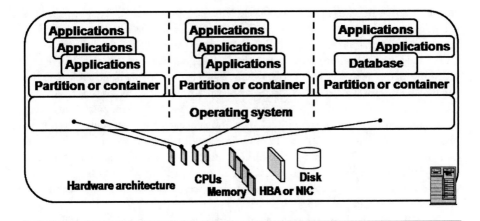

Figure 10.4   Server and operating system containers and partition example.

Depending on implementation, a hypervisor can support different guest operating systems that run on the emulated hardware instruction set. Operating system, or hardware processor–based, partitions, containers, zones, and domains usually only support the same operating system. Operating system container-based approaches, particularly when the same instance of an operating system is being used, can be vulnerable to operating system exploits and errors, thereby impacting the entire operating system and all applications. Another consideration with container-based approaches is having the same operating system versions, including service packs and patches, installed.

Another server virtualization technology (Figure 10.5) is an application virtual machine that runs as a guest application on an operating system. An application virtual machine provides an abstraction or instance of a virtual machine to support a given application or environment such as Java. Applications written in Java or other languages or environments capable of being run on a Java Runtime Environment (JRE) and Java

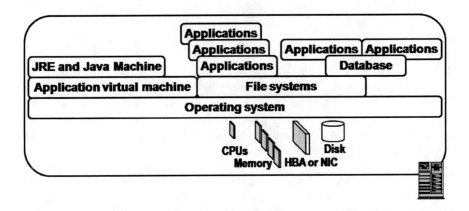

Figure 10.5   Application virtual machine examples.

virtual machine are portable across different hardware and server environments as long as there are a JRE and JVM present. For example, a JRE and JVM can exist on a laptop PC running Windows, on a UNIX or Linux server, on an IBM mainframe, or on a PDA device or cell phone. Another example of an application virtual machine and runtime environment is Adobe Flash, where FLASH-based applications are written to run on a FLASH-based server (not to be confused with FLASH SSD storage).

In general, more memory is better; however, the speed of the memory is also very important. Different versions and implementations of virtualization solutions support various memory configurations and limits. Check with specific vendors for their current compatibility lists for supported configurations and memory requirements. Also check with vendors for supported configurations for 32-bit and 64-bit processors, single-core, dual-core, quad-core, or eight-way processors, along with I/O cards and drivers for networking and storage devices.

Note that while server consolidation can reduce hardware operating and associated costs along with power and cooling, software licensing and maintenance costs for applications and operating systems may not change unless those are also consolidated. Near-term physical consolidation addresses power, cooling, and associated hardware costs, however, longer term, additional cost savings can be obtained by addressing underutilized operating system images and application software footprints. Another potential cost savings or resource maximization benefit can come from addressing underutilized operating system images and other licensed software. Hardware savings are often discussed as a benefit of virtualization and consolidation, but given the cost and management complexity of maintaining licensed software images, it makes sense to maximize those resource footprints as well.

Other VM considerations include specific hardware support such as Intel VT assist, 32-bit or 64-bit capabilities, and management tools. Management tools include metrics and measurements for accounting, tracking, capacity planning, service management, and chargeback. Hypervisors also support APIs and management plug-in tools such as Hyper-V working with VSS writers with application or guest integration. VMware vSphere has APIs for data protection (VADP) and vStorage API for Array Integration (VAAI), which offloads functionality to compatible storage systems. For VMware vSphere APIs, VADP provides a framework for third-party or independent software vendors (ISVs) to more easily develop solutions to protect virtual server environments. An example is change block tracking (CBT), where vSphere maintains an internal table or map of data blocks that is updated for an active VM. Using CBT, instead of reading through a file system to determine which data blocks, objects, or files have been modified, an application or software tool can access the CBT table to quickly determine what needs to be copied. The result is a faster backup. Microsoft Hyper-V leverages underlying Windows VSS capabilities with application integration to enhance data protection including backup.

Another vSphere API is VAAI, which enables offloading some functions from the VM to a compatible storage system that supports specific features. VAAI functionality includes granular SCSI lock management on shared storage volumes or LUNs, hardware-assisted VM cloning or copy, and data migration for VM movement.

For storage systems that do not support VAAI, those functionalities (zero copy move, SCSI enhanced locking, etc.) are performed by the hypervisor running on the physical server. Another vSphere functionality to help address scaling of multiple busy VMs on a common PM is Storage I/O Control (SIOC), which enables a proprietary scheme for load balancing. With SIOC, those VMs that need I/O performance can be tuned accordingly to prevent bottlenecks from occurring.

A VM consideration is the use of raw device mapping (RDM) or VM file system (VMFS) storage, which can be block shared SAS, iSCSI, FC or FCoE, or NAS NFS. RDM device file contains meta data, along with other information about the raw LUN or device, and optional information for support of VMotion or live migration, snapshots, and other applications. RDM can be used to minimize overhead associated with VMFS, similar to legacy applications such as databases bypassing files to perform raw and direct I/O. Much like traditional file systems on different operating systems, with each generation or iteration, performance improvements enable file systems performance to be on par with direct or non–file system–based I/Os while leveraging file system features including snapshots and enhanced backup.

RDM devices may be required for certain application software or IRM-related tools. Check with your specific hypervisor provider as to which functions work with raw vs. VM file systems as well as storage interfaces (block or file).

10.4. Virtual Desktop Infrastructure

A virtual desktop infrastructure (VDI) complements virtual and physical servers, providing similar value propositions as VMs. These value propositions include simplified management and a reduction in hardware, software, and support services at the desktop or workstation, shifting them to a central or consolidated server. Benefits include simplified software management (installation, upgrades, repairs), data protection (backup/restore, HA, BC, DR) and security. Another benefit of VDI similar to VMs is the ability to run various versions of a specific guest operating system at the same time, similar to server virtualization. In addition to different versions of Windows, other guests, such as Linux, may also coexist. For example, to streamline software distribution, instead of rolling images out to physical desktops, applications are installed into a VM that is cloned, individually configured if necessary, and made accessible to the VDI client. From a cloud perspective, VDIs are also referred to as Desktop as a Service (DaaS) (not to be confused with Disk as a Service or Data as a Service). VDI vendors include Citrix, Microsoft, and VMware, and various platform or client suppliers ranging from Dell to Fujitsu, HP, IBM, and Wyse.

The VDI client can be a zero device that essentially functions as a display, such as an iPad, Droid, or other smart phone or tablet. Another type of VDI client is a thin device that has less compute and expansion capabilities, with or without a HDD, requiring less maintenance as there are no moving parts or dedicated installed software images that result in a lower cost. Normal workstations, desktops, and laptops can also be used as thick clients where more capabilities are needed or for mobile workers who can benefit from the enhanced capabilities of such devices. By moving the applications and their associated data files to a central server, local storage demands are reduced or eliminated, depending on the specific configuration. However, this means that, with applications running in part or in whole on a server, there is a trade-off of local storage and I/O on a workstation or desktop with increased network traffic. Instead of the desktop doing I/O to a local HDD, HHDD, or SSD, I/Os are redirected over the network to a server.

Figure 10.6 shows a resilient VDI environment that also supports nondesktop VMs. In addition to supporting thin and zero VDI clients, mobile desktops are also shown, along with E2E management tools. The shared storage contains the VM images stored as VHD, VMDK, or OVF on shared storage that is also replicated to another location. In addition, some VMs and VDIs are protected as well as accessible via a cloud.

Depending on how the VDI is being deployed—for example, in display mode—less I/O traffic will go over the network, with activity other than during workstation boot mainly being display images. On the other hand, if the client is running applications in its local memory and making data requests to a server, then those I/Os will be placed on the network. Generally speaking, and this will vary with different types of applications, most workstations do not generate a large number of IOPS once they are running. During boot or start-up, there is a brief flurry of activity that should not be too noticeable, depending on your specific configuration and network.

If many clients boot up at the same time, such as after a power failure, maintenance, upgrade, or other event, a boot storm could occur and cause server storage I/O

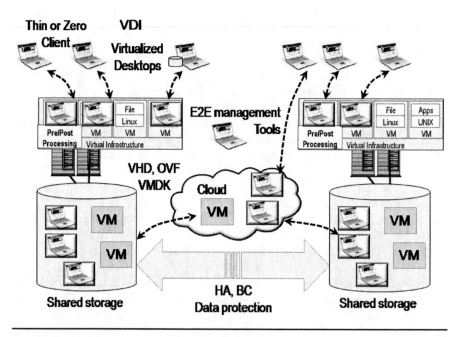

Figure 10.6 Virtual desktop infrastructures (VDIs).

and network bottlenecks. For example, if a single client needs 30 IOPS either in a normal running state when it is busy or during boot, most servers and networks should support that activity. If the number of clients jumps from 1 to 100, the IOPS increases from 30 to 3000, well in excess of a single server HDD capability and requiring a faster storage system. Going further to 1000 clients needing 30 IOPS, the result is 30,000 IOPS of storage I/O performance. IOPS can be read or write and will vary at different times, such as more reads during boot or writes during updates. While this simple example does not factor in caching and other optimization techniques, it does point to the importance of maintaining performance during abnormal situations as well as normal running periods Part of a VDI assessment and planning should be to understand the typical storage I/O and networking characteristics for normal, boot, and peak processing periods to size the infrastructure appropriately.

VDI can also help streamline backup/restore and data protection along with antivirus capabilities, by centralizing those functions instead of performing them on an individual desktop basis. VDI considerations in addition to server, storage, I/O and networking resource performance, availabity, and capacity should include looking at application availability requirements, as well as verification of which versions of guest operations systems work with various hypervisor or virtualization solutions. This includes verifying support for 32-bit and 64-bit modes, USB device support for encryption or authorization key, biometric security access control, video graphic driver capabilities, and management tools. Management tools include the ability to capture video screens for playing to support training or troubleshooting purposes, pausing or suspending running VDIs, and resource monitoring or accounting tools. Licensing is another consideration for VDIs, for the hypervisor and associated server side software and any updates to guest applications.

10.5. Cloud and Virtual Servers

Virtual servers and clouds (public and private) are complementary and can rely on each other or be independent. For example, VMs can exist without accessing public or private cloud resources, and clouds can be accessed and used by nonvirtualized servers. While clouds and virtualization can be independent of each other, like many technologies they work very well together. VMs and VDIs can exit on local PMs or on remote HA and BC or DR systems. VMs and VDIs can also be hosted for BC and DR purposes or accessible for daily use via public and private clouds. Many public services, including Amazon, Eucalyptus, GoGrid, Microsoft, and Rackspace, host VMs. Types of VMs and formats (VMDK, VHD, OVF) will vary by service, as will functionality, performance, availability, memory, I/O, and storage capacity per hour of use. The benefit of using a cloud service for supporting VMs is to utilize capacity on demand for elasticity or flexibility to meet specific project activities such as development, testing, research, or surge seasonal activity. Some environments may move all of their VMs to a service provider, while others may leverage them to complement their own resources.

For example, at the time of this writing, Microsoft Azure compute instance pricing for an extra-small VM with 1.0-GHz CPU, 768 MB of memory, 20 GB of storage, and low I/O capabilities is about $0.05 per hour. For a medium-size VM with 2 × 1.6-GHz CPU, 3.5 GB memory, 490 GB storage, high I/O performance, cost is about $0.24 per hour. A large VM with 8 × 1.6-GHz CPU, 14 GB memory, 2 TB of storage with high performance costs about $0.96 per hour. These are examples, and specific pricing and configuration will vary over time and by service provider in addition to SLAs and other fees for software use or rental.

10.6. Can and Should All Servers or Desktops Be Virtualized?

The primary question should not be whether all servers, workstations, or desktops can or should be virtualized. Rather, should everything be consolidated? While often assumed to mean the same thing, and virtualization does enable consolidation, there are other aspects to virtualization. Aggregation has become well known and a popular approach to consolidate underutilized IT resources including servers, storage, and networks. The benefits of consolidation include improved efficiency by eliminating underutilized servers or storage to reduce electrical power, cooling requirements, floor space, and management activity, or to reuse and repurpose servers that have been made surplus to enable growth or support new application service capabilities.

For a variety of reasons, including performance, politics, finances, and service-level or security issues, not all servers or other IT resources, including storage and networking, lend themselves to consolidation. For example, an application may need to run on a server at a low CPU utilization to meet performance and response-time objectives or to support seasonal workload changes. Another example is that certain applications, data, or even users of servers may need to be isolated from each other for security and privacy concerns.

Political, financial, legal, or regulatory requirements also need to be considered with regard to consolidation. For example, a server and application may be owned by different departments or groups and, thus, managed and maintained separately. Similarly, regulatory or legal requirements may dictate, for compliance or other purposes, that certain systems are kept away from other general-purpose or mainstream applications, servers, and storage. Another reason for separation of applications may be to isolate development, test, quality assurance, back-office, and other functions from production or online applications and systems and to support business continuance, disaster recovery, and security.

For applications and data that do not lend themselves to consolidation, a different use of virtualization is to enable transparency of physical resources to support interoperability and coexistence between new and existing software tools, servers, storage, and networking technologies—for example, enabling new, more energy-efficient servers or storage with improved performance to coexist with existing resources and applications.

Another form of virtualization is emulation or transparency providing abstraction to support integration and interoperability with new technologies while preserving existing technology investments and not disrupting software procedures and policies. Virtual tape libraries are a commonly deployed example of storage technology that combines emulation of existing tape drives and tape libraries with disk-based technologies. The value proposition of virtual tape and disk libraries is to coexist with existing backup software and procedures while enabling new technology to be introduced.

10.7. Virtualization Beyond Consolidation: Enabling IT Agility

Another facet of virtualization transparency is to enable new technologies to be moved into and out of running or active production environments to facilitate technology upgrades and replacements. Another use of virtualization is to adjust physical resources to changing application demands such as seasonal planned or unplanned workload increases. Transparency via virtualization also enables routine planned and unplanned maintenance functions to be performed on IT resources without disrupting applications and users of IT services.

Virtualization in the form of transparency, or abstraction, of physical resources to applications can also be used to help achieve energy savings and address other green issues by enabling newer, more efficient technologies to be adopted faster. Transparency can also be used for implementing tiered servers and storage to leverage the right technology and resource for the task at hand as of a particular point in time.

Business continuance and disaster recovery are other areas where transparency via virtualization can be applied to in a timely and cost-efficient manner in-house, via a managed service provider, or in some combination. For example, traditionally speaking, a BC or DR plan requires the availability of similar server hardware at a secondary site. A challenge with this model is that the service and servers be available when needed. For planned testing, this may not be a problem; in the event of a disaster,however, a first-come, first-served situation could be encountered due to contention of too many subscribers to the same finite set of physical servers, storage, and networking resources.

Figure 10.7 shows the expanding scope and focus of virtualization beyond consolidation. An important note is that Figure 10.7 is not showing a decrease or deemphasis of consolidation or aggregation with virtualization, but rather an overall expanding scope. In other words, there will continue to be more virtualization across servers, storage, workstations, and desktops for consolidation or aggregation purposes. However, there will also be an expanding focus to include those applications that do not lend themselves to consolidation or that are not in high-density aggregation scenarios.

A high-density consolidation virtualization scenario might be dozens of VMs per PM, where, in the next wave, some systems will be deployed with a single or a couple of VMs to meet different SLO, SLA, and QoS requirements—for example, a SQLserver database supporting a time-sensitive customer facing applications needs to meet specific performance QoS SLOs from 7 a.m. to 7 p.m. While it is possible to have other VMs as guests on the same PM, for QoS and SLA requirements, instead of consolidating the SQLserver database and its applications, it will be deployed on a faster server with plenty of memory to get more work done faster with a by-product of improved productivity. The reason for placing the SQLserver database in a VM with a dedicated

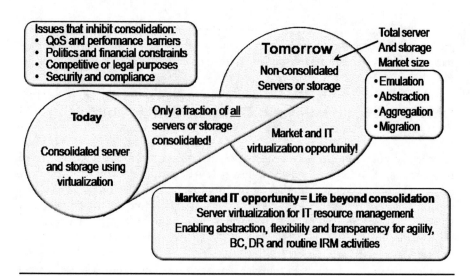

Figure 10.7   Expanding focus and scope of virtualization.

PM is to gain agility and flexibility, including the ability to proactively move for HA or BC purposes and to facilitate easier DR.

Another reason for placing the SQLserver database in a VM is that during the 7 a.m.–7 p.m. prime-time period, the PM is dedicated to that application, but during off-hours, other VMs can be moved onto the PM. For example, the fast PM can be used for running nightly batch or other applications in addition to using the PM for IRM tasks such as backup or database maintenance. The net result is that the PM itself is used more effectively around the clock, while making a faster resource available to a time-sensitive application and thereby achieving efficiency and effectiveness. In other words, leverage the x86 servers in a manner similar to how larger proprietary and mainframe systems have been managed to higher efficiency and effectiveness levels in the past. It's not always about how many VMs you can put on a PM, but rather how that PM can be used more effectively to support information services.

If you are a vendor, a value-added reseller (VAR), or a service provider and ask a prospective customer if he is looking to virtualize his servers, desktops, or storage, and he replies that he is not, or only on a limited basis, ask him why not. Listen for terms or comments about performance, quality of service, security, consolidation, or third-party software support. Use those same keywords to address his needs and provide more solution options. For example if the customer is concerned about performance, talk about how to consolidate where possible while deploying a faster server with more memory to address the needs of the application. Then talk about how that fast server needs fast memory, fast storage, and fast networks to be more productive and how, for HA and BC, virtualization can be combined. The net result is that instead of simply trying to sell consolidation, you may up-sell a solution to address different needs for your customer, helping him be more effective as well as differentiating from your competitors who are delivering the same consolidation pitch.

Similar to servers, the same scenarios for virtual desktops apply in that some workstations or laptops can be replaced with thin or stripped-down devices for some usage or application scenarios. However, where the focus is enabling agility, flexibility, and reducing IRM costs, workstation or desktop virtualization can be used for nonthin clients. For example, a workstation or laptop for a user who needs portability, performance, and access to localized data may not be an ideal candidate for a thin device and a virtual desktop. Instead, consider a hypervisor or VM existing on the PM to facilitate IRM activities, including software install or refresh, HA, and BC. For example, when something goes wrong on the workstation it is usually tied to a software issue as opposed to hardware.

A common solution is to reload or rebuild the software image (e.g., re-image) on the workstation. Instead of sending the workstation in to be re-imaged or dispatching someone to repair and re-image it, virtually repair the device and software. This is possible via a hypervisor installed on the PM or workstation with a primary guest VM for the user and maintenance VMs that can be used for rapid refresh or re-image. Instead of reloading or re-imaging, use a VM clone followed by restoration of unique settings and recent changes.

10.8. Common Virtualization Questions

What is the difference between SRM for virtualization and SRM for systems or storage? In the context of server virtualization, and in particular VMware vSphere, SRM stands for Site Recovery Manager, a framework and tools for managing HA, BC, and DR. SRM in the context of storage, servers, and systems in general stands for Systems or Storage or Server Resource Management, with a focus on collecting information, monitoring, and managing resources (performance, availability, capacity, energy efficiency, QoS).

Does virtualization eliminate vendor lock-in? Yes and no. On one hand, virtualization provides transparency and the flexibility of using different hardware or supporting various guest operating systems. On the other hand, vendor lock-in can shift to that of the virtualization technology or its associated management tools.

Why virtualize something if you cannot eliminate hardware? To provide agility, flexibility, and transparency for routine IRM tasks, including load balancing and upgrades in addition to HA, BC, and DR.

Do virtual servers need virtual storage? No, virtual servers need shared storage; however, they can benefit from virtual storage capabilities.

What is meant by "aggregation can cause aggravation"? Consolidating all of your eggs into a single basket can introduce single points of failure or contention. Put another way, put too many VMs into a PM and you can introduce performance bottlenecks that result in aggregation.

I have a third-party software provider who does not or will not support us running their applications on a virtual server; what can we do? You can work with the application provider to understand its concerns or limitations about VMs. For example, the provider may have a concern about performance or QoS being impacted by other VMs on the same PM. In that case, do a test, simulation, or proof of concept showing how the application can run on a VM with either no other or a limited number of VMs, with no impact on the solution.

Another scenario could be that they require access to a special USB or PCI adapter device that may not be supported or shared. In the case of PCI adapters, work with the solution provider and explore some of the shared PCIe Multi-Root (MR) I/O Virtualization (IOV) topics discussed in Chapter 11. Another possibility is to work with your hypervisor provider, such as Citrix, Microsoft, or VMware, who may already have experience working with the third-party application provider and/or the server vendor and VAR you may be using. Bottom line: Find out what the concern is, whether and how it can be addressed, work through the solution, and help the third party enable its solution for a virtual environment.

10.9. Chapter Summary

There are many different uses for virtualization, from consolidation of underutilized systems to enabling agility and flexibility for performance- oriented applications. Not all applications or systems can be consolidated, but most can be virtualized. Virtual and cloud servers require physical CPUs, memory, I/O, and storage, in addition to software licensing and tools.

General action items include the following.

- Not all applications can be consolidated.
- Many applications can be virtualized, paying attention to QoS.
- Balance the number of VMs running on a PM and meeting SLOs.
- Use caution when consolidating, to avoid introducing bottlenecks.
- Look into how virtualization can be used to boost productivity.
- Explore technologies that support energy efficiency and effectiveness.
- Understand data protection issues pertaining to virtualization.
- Consider virtualization to enable HA, BC, and DR for nonconsolidated servers.

Server and workstation hardware and software, along with related services vendors, include Amazon, AMD, Cisco, Citrix/Xen, Dell, Desktone, Fujitsu, HP, IBM, Intel, Microsoft, NEC, Oracle, Racemi, Rackspace, Redhat, Sea Micro, Supermicro, Solarwinds, Wyse, and VMware.

Chapter 11

Connectivity: Networking with Your Servers and Storage

Are your servers and storage well connected?

– Greg Schulz

In This Chapter

- What type of network is best for cloud and server virtualization
- What topologies to use when, where, and why
- The importance of I/O and networking
- How tiered access can be used to address various challenges
- The basics of I/O, converged data, and storage networking

This chapter looks at issues, challenges, and opportunities involved with I/O and networking in support of cloud, virtual, and physical environments. Key themes, buzzwords, and trends addressed in this chapter include LAN, SAN, MAN, and WAN, along with associated network protocols, interfaces, tools, and management techniques.

11.1. Getting Started

Perhaps you have heard the expression that someone is "well connected." Are your servers, storage, applications, data, and public (or private) cloud services well connected?

Are they well connected to you? Are the connections flexible, scalable, and resilient while being robust and productive, or are they marginal, with single points of failures or other challenges that can become barriers?

The amount of data being generated, copied, and retained for longer periods of time is elevating the importance of data storage and infrastructure resource management (IRM). Networking and I/O connectivity technologies enable access to or between various resources, including cloud, virtual, and physical servers and storage, and the information services they support on a local or wide area basis. There are many different types of networks supporting different applications and functionality along with protocols ranging from voice or datacom (data communications) to video, compute, and unified communications solutions.

Networks use a use a variety of communication technology, from cabled (copper or optical) to wireless (WiFi, WiMax, Microwave, free space optics, satellite or terrestrial, and others). Examples of networks and I/O connectivity include internal server-based, such as processor area networks (PANs), including Peripheral Component Interconnect (PCI), and external, including local area networks (LANs), storage area networks (SANs), metropolitan area networks (MANs), wide area networks (WANs), and plain old telephone systems (POTs).

Traditional I/O and storage connectivity, along with LAN or datacom, are converging and becoming highly interdependent in support of cloud, virtual, and physical data storage networks, so it is worthwhile to discuss them in a converged manner.

In general, I/O and networking are characterized by supporting some amount of distance, performance, interoperability, availability, connectivity, and functionality capabilities.

- Distance—from meters with PCI to thousands of kilometers with WANs
- Performance—bandwidth or throughput, activity (IOPS or frames), latency
- Interoperability—media, types of transports, and devices working together
- Availability—reliability and resiliency of the networking technology
- Connectivity—how many devices can be supported
- Functionality—types of applications, upper-level protocols (ULPs), quality of service (QoS), and features

Cloud, virtual, and traditional information services delivery relies on physical resources including servers, storage, and networks along with software and services. Figure 11.1 shows traits that clouds have in common with networks, servers, and storage. (Networks and other aspects of IT systems have, over the past several decades, been shown pictorially as a cloud, to abstract their underlying complexities.)

On the left side of Figure 11.1, users or consumers of information-related services access them via a cloud. The cloud provides abstraction and masks the underlying technologies as well as complexities which begin to appear through the clearing of the clouds in the middle. On the right of Figure 11.1 are shown the underlying technologies, including networks, tiering, various locations, and resources ranging from physical to virtual and cloud.

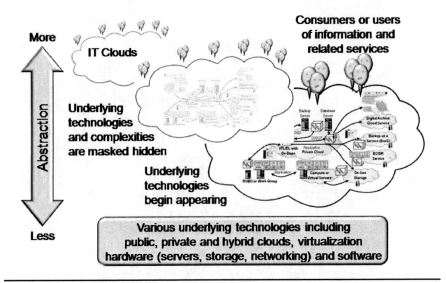

Figure 11.1 Clouds as a means of abstracting underlying complexities.

11.2. Networking Challenges

In general, the faster a processor or server is, the more prone it is to a performance impact when it has to wait for slower I/O operations. Consequently, faster servers need better-performing I/O connectivity and networks. "Better-performing" means lower latency, more IOPS, and improved bandwidth to meet various application profiles and types of operations.

Physical and virtual computers of all types rely on I/O for interaction with users directly via keyboards, video monitors and pointing devices such as mice (KVM), along with network access to other computers and Web-based services (Figure 11.2). Another use of I/O and networking capabilities is storing and retrieving continually growing amounts of data both locally and remotely. I/O is also important for computers to interface with storage devices for saving and retrieving stored information.

To say that I/O and networking demands and requirements are increasing is an understatement. The good news is that I/O and networking are becoming faster, more reliable, and able to support more data movement over longer distances in a shorter timeframe at a lower cost. However, as with server and storage technology improvements, the increase in networking and I/O capabilities is being challenged by continued demand to move or access more data over longer distances in even less time and at an even lower cost. Another challenge is last-mile access distance between your location and the nearest high-speed, low-latency networks.

Dependency on public cloud, managed service providers (MSPs), or other remote services places a demand on networks being available and accessible, similar to demands being placed on servers and storage. Another challenge, around for decades and a concern with every emerging technology, is how to overcome internal organizational barriers

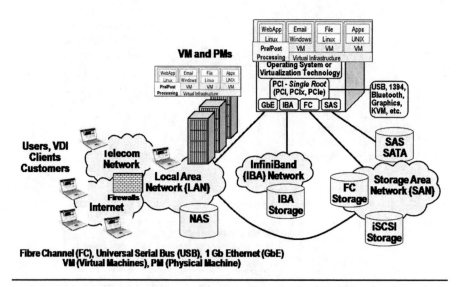

Figure 11.2   Data center I/O and networking—the big picture.

to convergence. Organizational barriers include who owns the network and associated switches, routers, gateways, and adapters and whether it is a storage or a data infrastructure. Later in the chapter we will talk more about the people and organizational challenges, along with what can be done to remove those barriers to enable true converged networking.

Demand drivers for I/O and networking capabilities also include increased use of WebEx for on-line conferences, with the corresponding increase in use of animation, multimedia graphics, video and audio boosting the size of the content, and corresponding impacts on networks. Time-sensitive IP-based telephone services, Web TV, instant messaging (IM), as well as text messaging and email usage, also continue to put more pressure on existing networks. An additional demand driver is the growth of on-line service providers such as MSPs for Internet access, email, Web hosting, file sharing, storing on-line digital photos, data backup, business continuance (BC), disaster recovery (DR), archiving, and general-purpose on-line Web or cloud-based storage services.

The popularity of Internet, MSP, and cloud-based services also places increasing demands on local, wide area, and global networking capabilities. Services range from on-line email and website hosting to portals for storing vacation videos and photos. Software, or Storage as a Service (SaaS), is becoming a popular means of accessing various applications in lieu of buying or leasing the software and supporting it on your own or on an Infrastructure as a Service (IaaS) or Platform as a Service (PaaS) delivery model.

11.3. I/O and Networking Bits and Bytes, Decoding Encoding

In Chapter 2 we discussed how different number schemes using base 2 (binary) and base 10 (decimal) are used for counting data. In an example a 500-GB disk drive was used to show how the number of blocks and bytes differed when counted in decimal or binary; this also applies to networking. With networking, care should be taken to understand whether a given speed or performance capacity is being expressed in bits or bytes. Other considerations (and potential points of confusion) are line rates (GBaud) and link speed. These can vary based on encoding and low-level frame or packet size. For example, 1-GbE along with 1-, 2-, 4-, and 8-Gb Fibre Channel and Serial Attached SCSI (SAS) use an 8b/10b encoding scheme. This means that at the lowest physical layer, 8 bits of data are placed into 10 bits for transmission, with 2 bits for data integrity.

With an 8-Gb link using 8b/10b encoding, 2 out of every 10 bits are overhead. To determine the actual data throughput for bandwidth or number of IOPS, frames or packets per second is a function of the link speed, encoding, and baud rate. For example, 1-Gb FC has a 1.0625-Gb/s speed. Multiply that by the current generation, so 8-Gb FC or 8-GFC is 8 × 1.0625 = 8.5 Gb/s. However, remembering to factor in that encoding overhead (e.g., 8 of 10 bits are for data with 8b/10b), usable bandwidth on the 8-GFC link is 6.8 Gb/s or 850 MB (6.8 Gb/8 bits) per second. 10 GbE and 16 GFC use 64b/66b encoding, which means that for every 64 bits of data, only 2 bits are used for data integrity checks, meaning there is less overhead.

What this means is that, for fast networks to be effective, they also have to have lower overhead to avoid moving extra data—using that capacity instead for productive work and data. This relates to the discussion in Chapters 8 and 9, where the focus was at a higher level around data footprint reduction (DFR). To support cloud and virtual computing environments, data networks need to become faster as well as more efficient, to avoid paying for more overhead per second rather than productive work. For example, with 64b/66b encoding on a 10-GbE or FCoE link, 96.96% of the overall bandwidth, about 9.7 Gb/s, is available for useful work. By comparison, if 8b/10b encoding is used, the result is only 80% of available bandwidth for useful data movement. For environments or applications, this means better throughput, while for applications that require shorter response time or latency, it means more IOPS, frames, or packets per second. This is an example of a small change such as the encoding scheme having a large benefit when applied to high-volume environments.

11.4. I/O and Networking Fundamentals

To address challenges and demands, networks and I/O need to support good performance, flexibility, and reliability in an affordable manner. Given the diversity of applications and usage needs as well as types of servers and storage devices, there are many different protocols and network transports. Networks and I/O interfaces vary in price, performance, and best uses for local and wide area needs.

I/O and networking components include:

- Host bus adapters (HBA) and host channel adapters (HCA)
- Network interface cards/chips [NICS, Converged Network Adapters (CAN)]
- Switches (embedded, blade, edge, or access) and switching directors
- Routers and gateways for protocol conversion, distance, and segmentation

- Distance and bandwidth optimization for remote data access and movement
- Managed service providers and bandwidth service providers
- Diagnostic and monitoring tools, including analyzers and sniffers
- Cabinets, racks, cabling and cable management, and optical transceivers
- Management software tools and drivers

Block-based storage access involves a server requesting or writing data to a storage device and specifying a start and stop or range of bytes to be processed, usually in increments of blocks of storage. Storage is organized into blocks of 512, 1024, 2048 byte, or larger blocks. Another form of data access is file-based, where data is accessed by requesting and accessing a file. Ultimately, all data written to storage is handled via block-based access, because it is the foundation for all data movement and storage.

Most applications and users interact with a file system or volume manager of some type that operates on a file basis. The file requests are resolved and processed as blocks by a file system and volume manger or by a file server or with block attached storage. Common file-based access protocols include Network File System (NFS), Parallel NFS (pNFS), and Windows Common Internet Format (CIFS), also known as SAMBA. Object- and message-based access of information or services are also commonly used for accessing websites, email, and other applications.

Figure 11.3 shows a comparison of various networking and storage I/O interfaces and protocols to support different application needs. Transmission Control Protocol (TCP) and Internet Protocol (IP) are core protocols for supporting local and wide area application access and data movement. If there were such a thing as a virtual network, it would be TCP/IP, at least from a nonphysical network transport perspective. TCP/IP can be considered a virtual network due to the frequency with which it is deployed and its transparency over various local and wide area networks to meet various price and performance requirements.

OSI Layer	x Description	Fibre Channel (FC) SAN Layer	Gigabit Ethernet Network	IP Network
7	Application	Filesystem	FTP, Telnet	FTP, Telnet
6	Presentation	SCSI Commands	HTTP, NFS	HTTP, NFS
5	Session	FCP, IP, FICON	CIFS, iSCSI	CIFS, iSCSI
4	Transport			TCP, UDP
		FC-4 ULP		
3	Network		TCP/IP, UDP	IP
		FC-3 Services		
		FC-2 Framing	MAC client	LAN/WAN
2	Datalink	Flow control		MAN
		FC-1 Encoding, Link		
1	Physical	FC-0 Physical	Physical	Physical

Figure 11.3 OSI stack and network positioning.

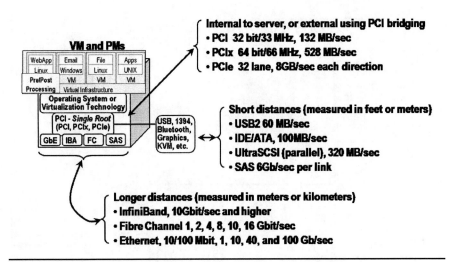

Figure 11.4   Tiered I/O and networking access.

11.5. Server (Physical, Virtual and Cloud) Topics

There is a saying in IT that the best I/O, regardless of whether it is local or remote, is an I/O that does not have to occur. I/O is an essential activity for computers of all shapes and sizes to be able to read and write data to memory, including external storage, and to communicate with other computers, networking devices, and Internet-based services. The challenge with I/O is that some form of connectivity, with associated software and time delays while waiting for reads and writes to occur, is required. I/O operations (Figure 11.4) closest to the CPU or main processor should be the fastest and occur most frequently for access to main memory, including random access memory (RAM), with internal local CPU-to-memory interconnects.

I/O and networking connectivity have similar characteristics to memory and storage: The closest operation to the main processor has the fastest I/O connectivity; however, it will also be the most expensive, distance-limited, and require special components. Moving farther away from the main processor, I/O remains fast, with distance measured in feet or meters instead of inches but more flexible and cost-effective. An example is the PCIe bus and I/O interconnect, which is slower than processor-to-memory interconnects but able to support attachment of various device adapters with very good performance in a cost-effective manner.

Farther from the main CPU or processor, various networking and I/O adapters can attach to PCIe, PCIx, or PCI interconnects for backward compatibility supporting various distances, speeds, types of devices, and cost.

11.5.1. Peripheral Component Interconnect (PCI)

The importance of a faster and more efficient PCI express (PCIe) bus is to support more data moving in and out of servers while accessing fast external networks and

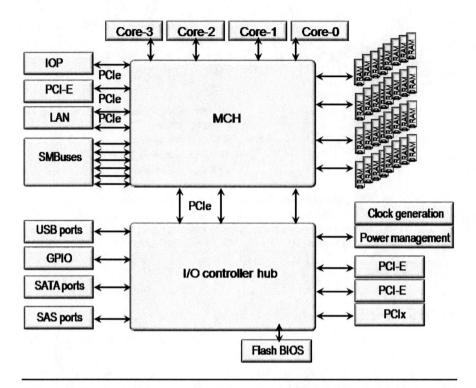

Figure 11.5   The importance of PCI for server internal and access to external networks

storage. PCIe is a standard that specifies the chipsets used to communicate between CPUs and memory and to the outside world of I/O and networking device peripherals (Figure 11.5). For example, a server with a 40-GbE NIC or adapter needs a PCIe port capable of 5 GB/s. Many servers are still in the process of moving from 1 GbE to 10 GbE; I mention 40 GbE because, as more VMs are consolidated onto PMs and as applications place more performance demands, in terms of either bandwidth or activity (IOPS, frames, or packets) per second, more 10-GbE adapters will be needed until the price of 40 GbE becomes more affordable. It's not if but when you will grow into the performance needs on either a bandwidth/throughput basis or to support more activity and lower latency per interface.

Figure 11.5 shows an example of a PCI implementation including various components such as bridges, adapter slots, and adapter types. The most current version of PCI, as defined by the PCI Special Interest Group (PCISIG), is PCIe. Backward compatibility exists by bridging previous generations, including PCIx and PCI, off a native PCIe bus or, in the past, bridging a PCIe bus to a PCIx native implementation. Beyond speed and bus width differences for the various generations and implementations, PCI adapters also are available in several form factors and applications. Some examples of PCI include PCIx- and PCIe-based implementations such as Ethernet, Fibre Channel, Fibre Channel over Ethernet, InfiniBand, SAS, SATA, SCSI, Universal Serial Bus, and 1394 Firewire, as well as many specialized devices such as analog-to-digital data acquisition, video surveillance, and other data collection and import devices.

PCIe leverages multiple serial unidirectional point-to-point links, known as lanes, compared to traditional PCI, which used a parallel bus–based design. With traditional PCI, the bus width varied from 32 to 64 bits, while with PCIe, the number of lanes combined with PCIe version and signaling rate determines performance. PCIe interfaces can have 1, 2, 4, 8, 16, or 32 lanes for data movement, depending on card or adapter format and form factor. For example, PCI and PCIx performance can be up to 528 MB/s with a 64-bit 66-MHz signaling rate.

Table 11.1 shows performance characteristics of various PCIe generations. With PCIe Generation 3, the effective performance essentially doubles; however, the actual underlying transfer speed does not double as it has in the past. Instead, the improved performance is a combination of about 60% link speed and 40% efficiency improvements by switching from an 8b/10b to 128b/130b encoding scheme, among other optimizations.

Table 11.1 PCIe Generations

	PCIe Generation 1	PCIe Generation 2	PCIe Generation 3
Gigatransfers per second	2.5	5	8
Encoding scheme	8b/10b	8b/10b	128b/130b
Data rate per lane per second	250 MB	500 MB	1 GB
× 32 lanes	8 GB	16 GBs	32 GB

11.5.2. Adapters, NICs, and CNAs

Network interface cards (or chips), also known as NICs, host bus adapters (HBAs), host channel adapters (HCAs), storage NICs (SNICs), converged networking adapters (CNAs), mezzanine and daughter cards, are technologies that enable access to external I/O and networking resources, as shown in Figure 11.4. Physical servers or physical machines (PMs) utilize physical adapters for performing I/O and networking functions, including access to other devices on a local or remote basis. Virtual servers or VMs typically access a virtual adapter that in turn uses a physical adapter or NIC via a hypervisor or abstraction layer. Adapters provide connectivity from an internal bus, typically PCIe, to an external interface such as those shown in Figure 11.4, including USB, SAS, Fibre Channel, InfiniBand, Ethernet, and FCoE.

Some host adapter characteristics include:

- Type of storage interface (Fibre Channel, GbE, InfiniBand, SSA, ATA/SATA)
- Type of protocol (FCP, FICON, SCSI, iSCSI, RDMA)
- Port speeds (1 Gb, 2 Gb, 4 Gb, 8Gb, 10 Gb, 16Gb)
- Interface media (XAUI, GBIC, SFP, copper, electrical)
- Number of ports per adapter (single, dual, quad)
- Buffer credits for supporting distance with different optics or transceivers
- Variable buffer and frame sizes (jumbo frames for IP) for performance
- Remote boot support for VMs and PMs
- Hot-swap support for physical adapters and devices
- TCP off-load engines (TOEs) to off-load servers from processing TCP traffic
- Hypervisors and operating system driver support

The physical packaging of adapters varies as much as the functionality provided. For example, PCIe adapters vary in physical size, number of ports, protocols or interfaces supported, buffers, and off-load capabilities. Some adapters, such as mezzanine cards, are designed for the small, dense footprint of blade servers, while others support multiple ports to maximize PCIe expansion port capabilities. Historically, adapters have been single-purposed, such that an InfiniBand HCA could not be a Fibre Channel HBA, a Fibre Channel HBA could not be an Ethernet NIC, and an Ethernet NIC could not be a SAS adapter, though they all plugged into a PCIe bus.

What is changing with CNAs is the ability to have a single adapter with multiple ports that can support traditional Ethernet LAN traffic including TCP/IP on the same physical port as FCoE using DCB as peers. Some CNA adapters also support the ability to change a Fibre Channel port to an Ethernet and FCoE port for redeployment purposes. This flexibility enables an adapter to be purchased and then repurposed or provisioned as needed, hopefully increasing its useful life and providing a better return on investment (ROI). Some adapters are removable from PCIe expansion slots or as mezzanine cards in blade servers while others are fixed on to mother or main circuit boards on servers or storage system controllers. A marketing term used by some vendors is a cLOM, or converged LAN On Motherboard.

Servers are not the only resources that use HBAs in some shape or form. Some storage systems simply use off-the-shelf adapters with drivers interfaced to their storage operating systems, while others have mezzanine or flex connections to change out interfaces as needed. Other storage systems have dedicated fabric attachment (FA) or host side ports on director or controller cards, which are used for attaching to servers or SANs, and back-end ports for attaching to storage devices.

Unless there is no need for resiliency, dual or multiple HBAs should always be used and attached to redundant fabrics. In addition to providing redundancy and resiliency, multiple adapters and I/O paths can improve availability by supporting failover during maintenance of different components. Path manager software, available as part of operating systems, volume managers, and file systems or via third parties including storage vendors, enables automatic failover for high availability (HA) on adapters. In addition to failover for HA, path managers can provide load balancing across the ports and metrics for management purposes. Additional functionalities can be added to path managers, including encryption, compression, or cloud access.

11.6. I/O and Networking Devices

In addition to adapters or NICs for servers and access ports on storage systems or other access points or targets, other networking devices include switches, directors, bridges, routers, gateways, and appliances as well as test, diagnostic, and management tools. These are connected via cabling (copper or optical) or wireless components.

A switch (or director) is a device that performs layer 2 switching functions between storage networking devices. Unlike a hub concentrator with shared bandwidth between ports, a switch provides dedicated bandwidth between ports. Switches and directors can be used as stand-alone or single-device fabrics, in pairs to create multiple single-device SAN islands, or connected together to create a fabric. Fabrics or networks are used to increase the number of ports beyond what is physically available on fabric devices and to support different topologies for various applications and environments. Switches and director ports can also isolate local traffic to particular segments, much as traditional network switches isolate LAN traffic. Storage networking switching devices can range from simple 4-ports to large multiprotocol devices with hundreds of ports. A Fibre Channel switch provides the same function as a standard network switch in that it provides scalable bandwidth among various subnets, segments, or loops. Converged switches combine traditional Fibre Channel SAN with LAN support including FCoE as a single platform.

A networking director is a highly scalable, fully redundant switch supporting blades with multiple interfaces and protocols, including Fibre Channel, Ethernet, and Fibre Channel over Ethernet, FICON and wide area, bridging or other access functionality. Directors vary in port size and can replace or supplement fabrics of smaller switches. Fabric devices, including directors and switches, can be networked into various topologies to create very large resilient storage networks of hundreds to thousands of ports. Inter-Switch Links (ISLs) are used to connect switches and directors to create a fabric or SAN. An ISL has a port on each switch or director to which the ISL is attached. For redundancy, ISLs should be configured in pairs.

A core switch sits at the core of a network as a single device or with other switches attached in various topologies. Often a core switch is a physically large device with many network connections, trunks, or ISLs attached between it and edge or access switches along with storage or other target devices. In some scenarios, a core switch may be a physically smaller device functioning as a convergence point between large edge or access switches and directors and other switches that provide access to storage or other targets.

Edge or access switches, also known as top of rack (TOR), middle of row (MOR), or end of row (EOR), vary in size, providing an aggregation point for many servers to fan-in to storage systems or other devices connected at the core of a network. Historically, edge or access switches have been physically smaller, as a means to reduce cost and aggregate multiple slower servers onto a higher-speed ISL or trunk attached to a larger core switch or director. For example, 10 stand-alone servers may each need only about 1 GbE of bandwidth or equivalent IOPS, packets, or frames per second performance.

In the previous scenario a 1-GbE port per each server (two for redundancy) might make sense from a cost perspective. If those 10 servers are consolidated using a hypervisor such as Citrix/Xen, Microsoft Hyper-V or VMware vSphere, the combined or aggregated performance needs would saturate a single 10-GbE port. With blade systems and TOR configurations, those switches can attach to larger core devices in a flat network where storage and other devices are connected. Consequently, when consolidating or aggregating servers, applications, or other workloads, be aware of the possibility of causing aggravation or introducing performance bottlenecks.

Another type of networking device includes gateways, bridges, routers, and appliances. These devices enable bridging between different types of networks handling interface, protocol, data translation, and other functionalities on a local and wide area basis.Some gateways, bridges, routers, and appliances include:

- SAN and LAN over MAN and WAN distance devices
- Bandwidth and protocol or application optimization
- Protocol conversion and routing, including FC to FCoE
- Security, including firewalls and encryption devices
- File systems and other content caching devices
- Cloud point-of-presence appliances, gateways, and software
- Storage services and virtualization platforms

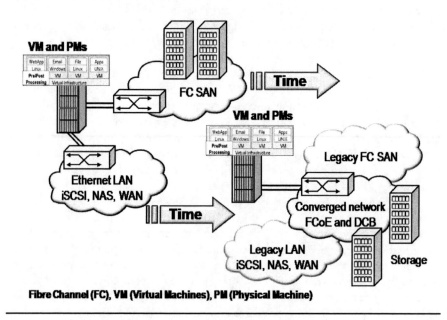

Figure 11.6   Example of unified or converged networking.

11.7. Converged and Unified Networking

Figure 11.6 shows an example using virtual HBAs and NICs attached to a switch or I/O director that connects to Ethernet-based LANs and Fibre Channel SANs for network and storage access. Examples of converged networks include Fibre Channel over Ethernet using an enhanced Ethernet, Fibre Channel and Ethernet virtual HBAs and NICs using InfiniBand as a transport, and inside servers using PCIe IOV.

The importance of Figure 11.6 is to show how convergence with I/O and networking is occurring from physical product, product, and interface standpoints. From a product standpoint, adapters and switches (including directors) can support both LAN and SAN traffic with their respective traditional interfaces (Ethernet and Fibre Channel) as well as protocols (TCP/IP for LAN and Fibre Channel along with FICON for SAN). Protocol and interface convergence examples include supporting the SCSI command set on TCP/IP (e.g., iSCSI), Fibre Channel-over-IP (FCIP) to enable distance, and Fibre Channel-over-Ethernet (FCoE). Table 11.2 shows characteristics of traditional storage and data networking environments.

Table 11.2 shows the values and characteristics of storage and networking, which are converging, to help in understanding why things are done or done differently. Understanding from a LAN perspective why things are done with storage a certain way or from a storage perspective why networking professionals do things differently can help identify areas beyond technology that can be converged.

Table 11.2 Storage and Networking Characteristics

	Server and Storage I/O Channels	Data and Voice Networks
Configuration	DAS and SAN Flat or point to point Copper or optical	LAN, MAN, and WAN Multilevel, flat, or point to point Copper, optical, or wireless
Media	Block (SCSI for open systems) using serial interfaces such as SAS and FC	Ethernet/802.x, SONET/SDH, MPLS, WDM/DWDM
Upper-level protocols	SCSI command set for open systems, Count Key Data for IBM mainframe	TCP/IP, TCP/UDP, among others
Characteristics	Deterministic, lossless, low latency, server off-load, data center storage	Consumer to data center, low cost, broad adoption, interoperability
Standards	ANSI T10 and T11	IEEE
Trade groups	SCSITA, FCIA, SNIA	Ethernet alliance
Adapters and NICs	PMC, LSI, Emulex, Qlogic, Mellanox	Broadcom, Intel, Qlogic, Emulex, Brocade
Switches	Cisco, Brocade, Qlogic, Mellanox	Cisco, Brocade, Qlogic, HP 3COM, Huawai, IBM/Blade, Juniper, Alcatel

11.7.1. PCI-SIG I/O Virtualization

Traditional PCI has been limited to a main processor or internal to a computer, but current generations of PCI Express (PCIe) include support for PCI Special Interest Group (PCI) I/O virtualization (IOV), enabling the PCI bus to be extended to distances of a

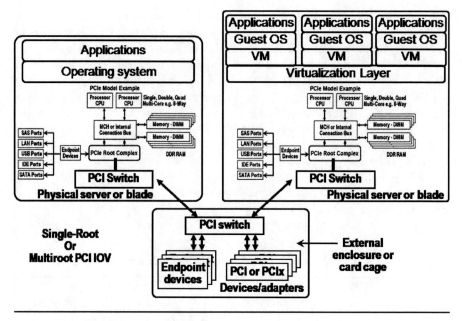

Figure 11.7   PCI SIG I/O virtualization.

few meters. Compared to local area networking, storage interconnects, and other I/O connectivity technologies, a few meters is a very short distance, but when compared to previous limits of a few inches, extended PCIe enables the ability for improved sharing of I/O and networking interconnects.

At the heart of servers' ability to perform I/O functions with external devices is the PCIe bus root complex along with connections or bridges to older PCI ports or other interfaces. PCI SIG IOV (Figure 11.7) consists of a PCIe bridge attached to a PCI root complex and an attachment to a separate PCI enclosure. Other components and facilities include address translation service (ATS), single-root IOV (SR-IOV), and multiroot IOV (MR-IOV). ATS enables performance to be optimized between an I/O device and a server's I/O memory management. Initially, SR-IOV enables multiple guest operating systems to access a single I/O device simultaneously, without having to rely on a hypervisor for a virtual HBA or NIC. The benefit is that physical adapter cards, located in a physically separate enclosure, can be shared within a single physical server without having to incur any potential I/O overhead via virtualization software infrastructure. MR-IOV is the next step, enabling a PCIe or SR-IOV device to be accessed through a shared PCIe fabric across different physically separated servers and PCIe adapter enclosures. The benefit is increased sharing of physical adapters across multiple servers and operating systems.

Figure 11.7 shows an example of a PCIe switched environment, where two physically separate servers or blade servers attach to an external PCIe enclosure or card cage for attachment to PCIe, PCIx, or PCI devices. Instead of the adapter cards physically plugging into each server, a high-performance short-distance cable connects the servers

PCI root complex via a PCIe bridge port to a PCIe bridge port in the enclosure device. In the example, either SR-IOV or MR-IOV can take place, depending on the specific PCI firmware, server hardware, operating system, devices, and associated drivers and management software.

An SR-IOV example is one in which each server has access to some number of dedicated adapters in the external card cage, for example, InfiniBand, Fibre Channel, Ethernet, or FCoE HBAs. SR-IOV implementations do not allow different physical servers to share adapter cards. MR-IOV builds on SR-IOV by enabling multiple physical servers to access and share PCI devices such as HBAs and NICs safely and with transparency. The primary benefit of PCI IOV is to improve utilization of PCI devices, including adapters or mezzanine cards, as well as to enable performance and availability for slot-constrained and physical footprint– or form factor–challenged servers.

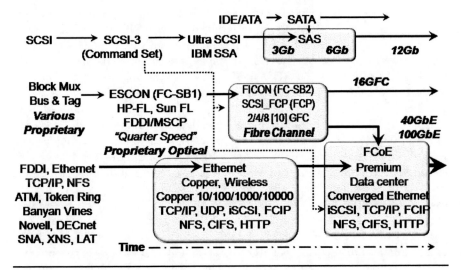

Figure 11.8   Network and I/O convergence paths and trends.

11.7.2. Converged Networks

I/O and general-purpose data networks continue to converge to enable simplified management, reduce complexity, and provide increased flexibility of IT resource usage. Converged networks and virtualized I/O are taking place at both the server level internally with PCIe enhancements as well as externally with Ethernet, Fibre Channel, and InfiniBand. Even SAS and SATA, discussed earlier in this chapter, are a form of convergence, in that SATA devices can attach to a SAS controller and coexist with SAS devices to reduce complexity, cabling, and management costs. Figure 11.8 shows how various network and I/O transports and protocols have been on a course of convergence for several decades. The evolution has been from vendor proprietary interfaces and protocols to open industry standards. For example, SCSI is both a parallel cabling scheme and a protocol command set.

The SCSI command set has been implemented on SAS, Fibre Channel, and InfiniBand (SRP), and on IP in the form of iSCSI. LAN networking has evolved from various vendor-specific network protocols and interfaces to standardize around TCP/IP and Ethernet. Even propriety interfaces and protocols such as IBM mainframe FICON, which evolved from ESCON, on propriety fiber optic cabling, now coexist in protocol intermix mode on Fibre Channel with open systems SCSI_FCP.

Ethernet supports multiple concurrent upper-level protocols (ULPs) (See Figure 11.8), for example, TCP/IP and TCP/UDP, along with legacy LAT, XNS, and others, similar to how Fibre Channel supports multiple ULPs such as FICON for IBM mainframes and FCP for open systems. Over the past decade, networking and storage I/O interfaces have been refined to an industry standard providing flexibility, interoperability, and variable cost to functionality options.

Propriety mainframe interconnects, such as bus & tag (block mux), gave way to ESCON and early and propriety derivative implementations of quarter-speed Fibre Channel (less than 25 MB/s). Later, ESCON gave way to FICON, which leverages common underlying open Fibre Channel components to enable FICON to coexist with open systems Fibre Channel FCP traffic in protocol intermix mode. Similarly, parallel SCSI evolved to UltraSCSI and separation of the SCSI command set from physical parallel electrical copper cables, enabling SCSI on IP (iSCSI), SCSI on Fibre Channel (FCP), SCSI on InfiniBand (SRP), serial attached SCSI (SAS), and other technologies. Traditional networks, including FDDI and Token Ring, have given way to the many different 802.x Ethernet derivatives. The continuing evolution of convergence is to leverage the lower-level MAC (Media Access Control) capabilities of an enhanced Ethernet. Enhancements around quality of service to improve latency and enable lossless communications allow Fibre Channel and its ULPs to coexist on a peer basis with other Ethernet ULPs including TCP/IP.

Moving forward, one of the premises of a convergence-enhanced Ethernet supporting FCoE is the ability to carry Fibre Channel traffic, including both FCP and FICON, on an Ethernet that can also transport TCP/IP based traffic concurrently. This differs from current approaches, where Fibre Channel traffic can be mapped onto IP using FCIP for long-distance remote replication. With FCoE, the TCP/IP layer is removed along with any associated latency or overhead, but only for local usage. A common question is why not use iSCSI, why the need for FCoE, why not just use TCP/IP as the converged network? For some environments, where low cost, ease of use, and good performance are the main requirements, iSCSI or NAS access for storage is a good approach. However, for environments that need very low latency, good or very good performance, and additional resiliency, Fibre Channel remains a viable option. For environments that need FICON for mainframes, iSCSI is not an option because iSCSI is only an SCSI implementation on IP and not a mapping of all traffic.

Given the broad market adoption of Ethernet for general-purpose networking, including application access, data movement, and other functions, it makes sense for further convergence to occur to Ethernet. The latest enhancements to Ethernet beyond 10-Gb, 40-Gb, and 100-Gb performance improvements include improved quality of service and priority groups along with port pause, lossless data transmission, and low-latency data movement. Initially, FCoE and enhanced Ethernets will be premium solutions, however, over time, as adoption picks up, reduced pricing should occur, as has been the case with previous generations of Ethernet.

These and other improvements by the Internet Engineering Task Force (IETF), the organization that oversees internet and Ethernet standards, as well as improvements by ANSI T11, the group that oversees Fibre Channel standards, have resulted in a converged enhanced Ethernet. Fibre Channel over Ethernet (FCoE) combines the best of storage networking with low latency, and deterministic performance with lossless data transmission with Ethernet's broad adoption and knowledge base. By mapping Fibre Channel to Ethernet, essentially encapsulating Fibre Channel traffic into Ethernet frames, upper-level protocols of Fibre Channel, including SCSI_FCP and IBM mainframe FICON (FC-SB2), should be able to coexist on the enhanced Ethernet with other Ethernet based traffic, including TCP/IP.

InfiniBand IOV solutions exist as an alternative to Ethernet solutions. Essentially, InfiniBand approaches are similar, if not identical, to converged Ethernet approaches including FCoE, with the difference being InfiniBand as the network transport. InfiniBand HCAs with special firmware are installed into servers that then see a Fibre Channel HBA and Ethernet NIC from a single physical adapter. The InfiniBand HCA also attaches to a switch or director that in turn attaches to a Fibre Channel SAN or Ethernet LAN network.

11.8. Local Networking (DAS, SANs, and LANs)

Data storage systems, like computer servers, continues to evolve in terms of functionality, flexibility, performance, available capacity, energy efficiency, and configuration options. With the advent of open systems computing there has been a continued move toward standardized and converged I/O and storage interface protocols. Various block storage options for servers include shared external DAS, networked SAN [iSCSI, Fibre Channel, Fibre Channel over Ethernet (FCoE), InfiniBand (SRP or iSCSI), and SAS] or NAS, such as NFS and Windows CIFS file sharing. In some cases, storage is moving off-site, utilizing public or private clouds and MSPs.

11.8.1. The Role of Networking with Storage

Over the past decade, networked storage, both SAN and NAS (file sharing), has become more common, but there still remains a large installed base of direct attached external and dedicated internal storage. With the diversity of environments and application needs, it is important to have options for resilient, flexible, and scalable server, storage, and I/O infrastructures. Also, it is important to keep in mind that DAS does not have to mean dedicated internal storage; it can also mean external shared direct accessible storage using SAS, iSCSI, InfiniBand, or Fibre Channel in a point-to-point topology configuration. Tiered access enables the most applicable tool to be used for the given task, factoring in cost, performance, availability, coexistence, functionality, and applicable application service needs. This includes Fibre Channel at different speeds, iSCSI,

InfiniBand, NAS, SAS, and others to align the access to the level of service needed. Figure 11.9 shows an example of how different storage and I/O networking protocols and interfaces can coexist to meet various application requirements and need.

Looking at Figure 11.9, a common question is why so many different networks and transports are needed: Why not just move everything to Ethernet and TCP/IP? Later in this chapter, converged network architecture will be discussed, showing how, in fact, the number and type of protocols and interfaces continue to converge. For now, the simple answer is that the different interfaces and transports are used to meet different needs, enabling the most applicable tool or technology to be used for the task at hand.

TCP/IP is in a state of transition, evolving from IPv4 to IPv6 and shifting from a 32-bit address to 128 bits, to boost the number of addresses available in a network. To boost performance and off-load servers from having to perform TCP/IP operations, TCP off-load engine (TOE) adapters or NICs are available. The idea with TOEs is to off-load the processing of TCP networking operations to a specialized card instead of using server CPU resources. While TOEs are valuable for off-loading compute overhead from servers to support fast networks, the added cost of specialized TOE adapters, relative performance improvements by servers, and faster Ethernet networks have stymied TOE adoption for all but high-performance servers or storage devices.

TCP/IP is commonly deployed on network transports ranging from WiFi/WiMax, Ethernet, and InfiniBand to wide area optical networks. TCP/IP is used today for both general access of applications and for server-to-server communication including cluster heartbeat and data movement. TCP/IP is also being used increasingly for data storage access and movement, including iSCSI block-based access, NAS for file access and data sharing, as well as for remote mirroring and replication using FCIP. Refer to the Glossary at the back of this book for additional applications, services, and protocols that leverage TCP/IP.

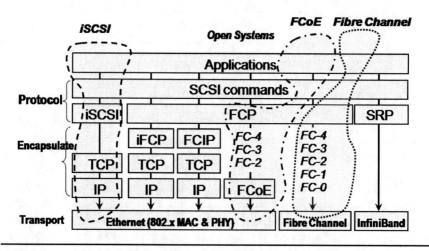

Figure 11.9 Positioning of I/O protocols, interfaces, and transports.

11.8.2. Ethernet (802.1)

Ethernet is a popular industry-standard networking interface and transport used in consumer as well as enterprise environments for a variety of different applications. The popularity of Ethernet can be traced to its interoperability and affordability, which have helped make it a ubiquitous networking standard that continues to evolve. Ethernet has emerged and replaced various proprietary networking schemes over the past several decades while boosting speeds from 10 Mbits to 10 Gbits per second, with 40 Gbits and 100 Gbits per second in development. Ethernet is deployed on different physical media including fiber optic and copper electrical cabling. Versions of Ethernet include 10 Mb/s, 100 Mb/s (fast), 1000 Mb (1 GbE), and 10,000 Mb/s (10 GbE) and emerging 40 GbE and 100 GbE. Ethernet at 10 Gb, 40 Gb, and 100Gb can be utilized as an alternative to SONET/SDH for metropolitan area networking environments leveraging dedicated dark fiber and optional DWDM technology.

In addition to various speeds and cabling media and topologies, Ethernet has several other advantages, including link aggregation, flow control, quality of service, virtual LAN (VLAN), and security. Other capabilities include the support for power over Ethernet to provide electrical power to low-powered devices, simplifying cabling and management. No longer associated with just LAN access of computers and applications, Ethernet is also being used for metropolitan and wide area services and for supporting storage applications.

As a convergence technology enabler, there remains some decades-old FUD (fear, uncertainty, and doubt) about Ethernet that is, however, fading away. For example, some storage-centric understanding of Ethernet may be from a decade or more ago, when Networking 101 educations covered 10/100 carrier-sense multiple-access collusion detection (CSMA/CD) and 1 GbE on copper networks. The reality is that Ethernet has come a long way and now runs on both copper and optical networks at speeds up to 40 GbE or 100 GbE for trunks and is also being used for WiFi networks. With IEER 802.1 Data Center Bridging (DCB) enhancements, including P802.1Qbb (Priority Flow Control-PFC), P802.1Qaz Enhanced Transmission Selection-ETS), DCB Capabilities Exchange Protocol (DCBX), and others, the platform for enabling additional storage and LAN consolidation is developing.

Another past concern with Ethernet was preventing loops from occurring over redundant and bridged links. The Spanning Tree Protocol (STP), IEE 802.1D, enables a loop-free logical topology when physical paths for redundancy exist. STP has enabled Ethernet to have redundant links that are not used for active data movement until a failover, when they are automatically enabled. A challenge with STP is, that unlike Fibre Channel, which can leverage redundant links to improve performance using Fabric Shortest Path First (FSPF), standby links are nonutilized resources. To improve on the resource usage or maximize ROI on networking expenditures as part of a converged networking environment, IETF RFC 5556, Transparent Interconnect of Lots of Links (TRILL), is being developed to leverage multiple Ethernet switch links, particularly for non-FCoE traffic.

In the past, a common concern about Ethernet for some storage professionals was dropped packet and performance as well as misperceptions about TCP/IP. With DCB and enhanced Ethernet, marketed as Data Center Ethernet (DCE) or Converged Enhanced Ethernet (CEE), Ethernet adds traditional storage interface characteristics to address concerns about deterministic performance and lossless data transmission. Today's Ethernet is a far cry from what was used or available a decade or more ago. In fact, what some networking and storage professionals may not realize is that at the lowest levels (e.g., encoding and physical transport), Ethernet and Fibre Channel have several attributes in common, including use of common cabling and transceivers (not at the same time without Wave Division Multi pathing or FCoE) and encoding schemes.

11.8.3. Fibre Channel (FC)

Connectivity technology supports multiple concurrent upper-level protocols (ULPs) for open systems and mainframe server-to-storage, storage-to-storage, and, in some cases, server-to-server I/O operations. FC ULPs include FC-SB2, more commonly known as FICON, along with SCSI Fibre Channel Protocol (aka FCP), which is commonly referred to simply as Fibre Channel. FC has evolved from propriety implementations operating at under 1 Gbit/s to shared-loop 1 Gb (1 GFC) to 1 GFC, 2 GFC, and 4 GFC switched, and, more recently, 8 GFC. 10 GFC has mainly been used for trunks and interswitch links (ISLs) to support scaling and building of backbone networks between switches. 16 GFC and 32 GFC are on the Fibre Channel Industry Association (FCIA) roadmap, along with other enhancements.

Topologies supported include point to point (no switches involved), core edge with access switches at the edge attached to larger switches, or direct at the core. Core edge can also be thought of as fan-in or fan-out, where multiple servers converge and fan-in to a shared storage system or, if viewed from the storage system, fan-out. Fan-out from a server perspective involves a group of servers with attachment to many storage devices. Various other topologies are possible, including switch to switch on a local or remote basis.

The value proposition, or benefit, of Fibre Channel is the ability to scale performance, availability, capacity, or connectivity over longer distances (up to 10 km natively with long-range optics) with speeds currently at 8 Gb/s, with 16 Gb/s on the radar. A challenge of Fibre Channel has been its cost and complexity. Larger environments can absorb the cost and complexity as part of scaling, but it remains a challenge for smaller environments. Most FC deployments utilize fiber optics with electrical connections, used mainly in the backplanes of servers, storage, and networking devices. Fibre Channel distances can range from a few meters to over 100 km, depending on distance enablement capabilities including optics and flow control buffers, adapters, switches, and cabling.

With the emergence of Fibre Channel over Ethernet (FCoE), utilizing a new and enhanced Ethernet, much of the existing Fibre Channel installed base can be expected to migrate to FCoE, with some switching to iSCSI, NAS, InfiniBand, or staying on dedicated Fibre Channel. If you are currently using FC for open systems or FICON for mainframe or protocol intermix mode (PIM) (FCP and FICON concurrently) and have no near-term plans for migrating open systems storage to IP-based storage using iSCSI or NAS, then FCoE is a technology that you should consider moving forward in addition to near-term 8-Gb Fibre Channel (8 GFC). I/O and networking infrastructures take time to deploy in larger environments and thus take time to switch out, not to mention investment protection of hardware, people skill set, and tools. Some organizations will move faster to FCoE, some will take longer; some won't go for some long time, instead sticking with FC using 16 GFC and perhaps 32 GFC. Others may jump to iSCSI. Some may consolidate and further downsize, some may continue to use NAS, while others will have mixed environments.

11.8.4. Fibre over Ethernet (FCoE)

Ethernet is a popular option for general-purpose networking. Moving forward, with extensions to support FCoE with enhanced low latency and lossless data transmission, Ethernet will eliminate the need to stack storage I/O activity onto IP. IP will remain as a good solution for spanning distance, for NAS, or for a low-cost iSCSI block-based access option coexisting on the same Ethernet. Getting Fibre Channel mapped onto a common Ethernet converged or unified network is a compromise among different storage and networking interfaces, commodity networks, experience, skill sets, and performance or deterministic behavior.

For the foreseeable future, FCoE is for local environments and not for long-distance use. Unlike iSCSI, which maps the SCSI command set onto TCP/IP, or FCIP, which maps Fibre Channel and its ULPs onto TCP/IP for long-distance data transmission to enable remote replication or remote backup, FCoE runs native on Ethernet without the need to run on top of TCP/IP for lower latency in a data center environment. For long-distance scenarios such as enabling Fibre Channel or FICON remote mirroring, replication, or backups to support BC, DR, HA, or clustering requiring low-latency communications, use FCIP, DWDM, SONET/SDH, or time-division multiplexing (TDM) MAN and WAN networking solutions and services. For IP networks, DWDM, SONET/SDH, Metro Ethernet, and IPoDWDM can be used.

With FCoE, the option of a converged network exists. The degree of convergence and the path to get there will depend on timing, preferences, budget, and other criteria as well as vendor storage offerings and support. As with other techniques and technologies, the applicable solution should be aligned to meet particular needs and address specific pain points while not introducing additional complexity.

Given that FCoE will require a different, more expensive, converged enhanced Ethernet (CEE), iSCSI can continue to leverage the low-cost economic value proposition that has enabled it to expand its footprint. For existing open systems and IBM mainframe environments that are using Fibre Channel and FICON, the next upgrade option is to go from 4 GFC to 8 GFC and reasses in 3 years or so the possibility of 16 GFC and the status of an FCoE ecosystem. For open systems environments that are heavily invested in Fibre Channel, the natural progression will be from 4 GFC to 8 GFC, with some attrition due to shifting over to iSCSI and NAS for some applications.

For environments that are not as heavily invested or committed to Fibre Channel, the opportunity to jump to 10-GbE iSCSI will be appealing. For those who do make the commitment for at least one more round of Fibre Channel at 8 GB, in 3 to 4 years time, there will be a need to decide whether to stay with legacy Fibre Channel, assuming 16 GFC is ready, jump to FCoE at 10 Gb or the emerging 40 Gb, jump to iSCSI, or some combination. Table 11.3 explains various FCoE, virtual, and converged networking terms.

Table 11.3 Virtual and Converged Storage Networking Terms

Term	Description
CNA	Converged Network Adapter
E_Port	Expansion or switch-to-switch port for interconnect or ISLs
F_Port	Fabric port on an FC switch
FCF	FC Forward
FIP	FCoE initialization Protocol
FSPF	Fabric Shortest Path First
ISL	Interswitch link
N_Port	Server or storage FC port
N_PVID	N_Port virtual ID
Trill	Transparent Interconnect of Lots of Links
ULP	Upper-level protocol
VE_Port	Virtual E_Port
VF_Port	Virtual F_Port
VLAN	Virtual LAN
VN_Port	Virtual N_Port
VPORT	Virtual port
VSAN	Virtual SAN

Figure 11.10 shows a traditionally separate fiber optic cable being dedicated (bottom of figure) in the absence of wave division multiplexing technology. With FCoE, Fibre Channel is mapped onto an enhanced low-latency, lossless with quality-of-service (QoS) Ethernet to coexist with other traffic and protocols including TCP/IP.

Note that FCoE is targeted for the data center, as opposed to long distance, which would continue to rely on FCIP (Fibre Channel mapped to IP) or WDM-based MAN for shorter distances. For example, in Figure 11.10, the traditional model for cabling a LAN and SAN has separate physical copper or optical cables for each network, unless DWDM (dense wave division multiplexing) multiplexed optical network is being used. With FCoE, the next step in the converged network evolution takes place with enhanced Ethernet being the common denominator that supports both FCoE and other Ethernet-based networks concurrently on a single Ethernet network.

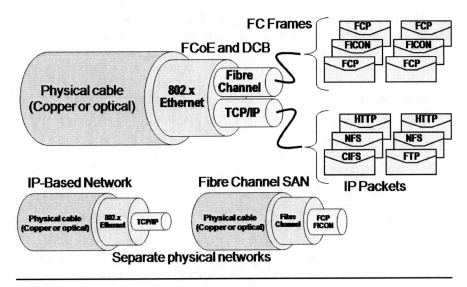

Figure 11.10 Converged network (top) and separate networks (bottom).

11.8.5. InfiniBand (IBA)

InfiniBand is a unified interconnect that can be used for storage and networking I/O as well as interprocess communications. IBA can be used to connect servers to storage devices, storage to LANs, and servers to servers, primarily for applications within the data center. InfiniBand is also used in some storage systems as a back-end or internal interconnect running TCP/IP and RDMA or some other protocol. As a unified interconnect, IBA can be used as a single adapter capable of functioning as multiple logical adapters. IBA enables a channel to extend outside a single server up to about 100 m (greater distances may be possible with future iterations), while current bus distances are measured in inches. IBA enables memory-to-memory (DMA) transfers to occur with fewer overheads to improve storage, networking, and other activity.

Some Intel server core chipsets support a native integrated PCIe InfiniBand port that is physically extended to an external connection, but most deployments rely on external PCIe adapter cards. A host adapter for IBA, called a host channel adapter (HCA), connects a server to a switch for attachment to storage devices or other servers. Protocols that are supported on IBA include TCP/IP for NAS, iSCSI, as well as support for server-to-server communications including clusters. SCSI Remote Protocol (SRP) maps the SCSI command set for block storage access onto IBA. Gateways and other devices enable IBA networks to communicate with Ethernet and Fibre Channel networks and devices. IBA has found success in high-performance compute or extreme compute scaling environments where large numbers of servers require high-performance, low-latency communication, including for cluster and grid applications.

Another use for IBA has been to combine the physical networking and HCAs with a gateway or router attached to Fibre Channel and Ethernet networks with software to create virtual and converged network adapters. For example, an InfiniBand HCA is installed into a server and, with software and firmware, the operating system or virtual machine infrastructure sees what appear to be a Fibre Channel adapter and Ethernet NIC. The benefit is that for nonredundant configurations, a single physical HCA replaces two separate adapters, one for Fibre Channel and one for Ethernet. This consolidation is useful where servers are being virtualized to reduce power, cooling, and floor space, as well as for environments where redundancy is needed yet adapter slots are constrained.

11.8.6. iSCSI (Internet SCSI)

iSCSI, which is the SCSI command set mapped onto IP, is a means of supporting block-based storage access over Ethernet LANs and WANs using existing hardware. While iSCSI adapters with TCP off-load engines that improve performance by off-loading host servers of TCP/IP and iSCSI protocol processing overhead exist, most deployments leverage software-based initiators and drivers with standard onboard 1-GbE NICs. The number of 10-GbE iSCSI deployments has increased, but the market "sweet spot" for adoption has been low-cost leveraging of existing technology that tends to be 1 GbE, which does not incur the costs of more expensive 10-GbE adapters and networking switches.

The benefit of iSCSI (SCSI mapped onto TCP/IP) has been the low cost of using built-in 1-GbE network interface cards/chips (NICs) and standard Ethernet switches combined with iSCSI initiator software. In addition to low cost for 1-GbE iSCSI, other benefits include ease of use and scalability. A challenge of iSCSI is lower performance compared to faster dedicated I/O connectivity, so that when a shared Ethernet network is used, increased traffic can affect the performance of other applications. iSCSI can operate over 10-GbE networks, this approach requires expensive adapter cards, new cabling, and optic transceivers and switch ports that increase the cost of shared storage solutions that require high performance.

11.8.7. Serial Attached SCSI (SAS)

Serial attached SCSI (SAS) is known as an interface for connecting hard disk drives to servers and storage systems; it is also widely used for attaching storage systems to servers. SAS based on the SCSI command set continues to evolve, with support for faster, 6-Gbs speed, 10+ m cable lengths (up to 25 m using active cables), and a very good price-to-performance ratio. The combination of price, performance, shared connectivity, and distances is well suited for clustered and high-density blade server environments. SAS is being used as a means of attaching storage devices to servers as well as a means of attaching hard disk drives to storage systems and their controllers.

The SAS ecosystem is broad, ranging from protocol interface chips to interposers and multiplexers to enable dual port of SATA disks to SAS interfaces, SAS expanders, SAS host-based PCI-X and PCIe, as well as external RAID controllers and 3.5-in. and 2.5-SAS HDDs and other components. SAS HDDs are being deployed inside storage systems across different price bands and market segments for both block-based and NAS file storage solutions. SAS product offerings vary based on their target market or specific solution target price band for deployment, with components first, followed by adapters and entry-level block and NAS storage systems, followed by enterprise-class solutions.

For high-density scale-up and scale-out environments, storage is moving closer to servers in the form of shared and switched SAS. While the cloud service and the servers providing the functionality may be located some distance from the servers accessing them, a good cost-effective back-end storage solution being used increasingly is shared or switched SAS. In the past there was a gap in terms of connectivity or the number of servers that could be attached to a typical shared SAS or DAS storage system. This has changed with the use of native 6-Gb/s ports and using the SAS switch to increase the fan-out (from storage to server) or fan-in (servers to storage) number of attached servers. Another example of storage getting closer to servers is virtualization, which leverages industry-standard processes with external storage. Last but not least, consolidation results in servers and storage coming closer together.

Applications or environments that are well suited for shared and switched 6-Gb/s SAS include:

- Storage for high-density servers and blade systems
- Disk-to-disk backup/restore and data protection appliances
- Video and multimedia, security or gaming surveillance, and seismic analysis
- Database, data warehouse, and business analytics
- Scale-out NAS, object and cloud storage solutions
- Application and server clustering (MSCS and Oracle RAC)
- Email, messaging, and collaboration (Microsoft Exchange and SharePoint)
- Server and desktop virtualization

Figure 11.11 shows configurations of shared and switched 6-Gb/s SAS storage supporting different application or environment needs. On the left side of Figure 11.11

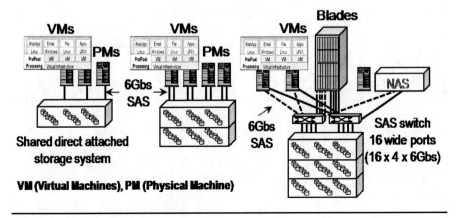

Figure 11.11   Shared and switched SAS.

are six single attached servers with a dual attached NAS gateway or storage appliance. A growing industry trend is the use of NAS file serving appliances that can attach to shared or switched storage, such as SAS, for hosting unstructured data including virtual servers. The six servers are configured for non-high availability (non-HA) while the NAS storage is configured for HA.

In the middle of Figure 11.11 are three servers dual attached in a HA configuration with a NAS gateway. The NAS devices that are shown in Figure 11.11 leverage the shared direct attached or switched SAS storage, supporting traditional and virtual servers. Two of the servers, for example, the PMs in the middle of Figure 11.11, are configured as a cluster hosting VMs for hypervisors such as Citrx/Xen, Microsoft Hyper-V, or VMware vSphere. On the right of Figure 11.11 the configuration is enhanced by adding a pair of 6-Gb/s 16-port SAS switches and a high-density blade system. Server blades in the blade system can be configured for a mix of different applications that access the shared SAS storage system via SAS wide ports for performance and availability provided by the HA configuration. Various applications can be deployed on the blade system, for example, Microsoft Exchange, SQLserver, and SharePoint, or a single scale-out application requiring multiple servers and high-performance storage.

Table 11.4 Server and Storage I/O SAN Technologies

Attribute	1-GbE iSCSI	6-Gb/s SAS	8-Gb/s FC	10-GbE iSCSI/ FCoE
Point-to-point Switched	Yes Yes	Yes Yes	Yes Yes	Yes Yes
Cost	Low	Low	Higher	Higher
Performance	Good	Very good	Very good	Very good
Distance	Data center and wide area	Up to 25 m	Data center or campus	Data center or campus
Strength	Cost, simplicity, distance	Cost, performance, simplicity	Performance, scalability, distance	Performance, scalability, distance, common technology
Limitation	Performance	Distance	Cost, complexity	Cost, FCoE emerging
Servers	10s to 100s	10s	100s to 1000s	100s to 1000s

11.8.8. The Best Protocol for Block Storage

The decision about what type of server and storage I/O interface and topology is often based on cost, familiarity with available technologies, their capabilities, and, in some cases, personal or organizational preferences.

Table 11.4 compares and positions different SAN or storage sharing approaches to help determine which applicable technique, technology, or tool to use for a given task.

Each of the different SAN connectivity approaches can be used to do many different things, but doing so can also extend it beyond its design or economic and quality of service (QoS) comfort zone.

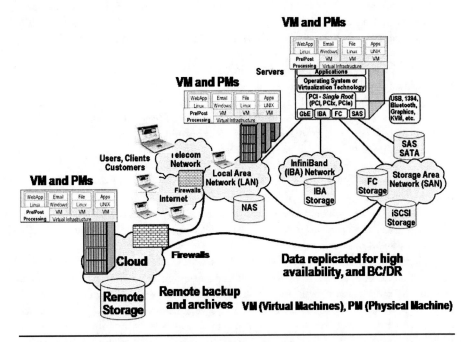

Figure 11.12   Wide area and Internet networking.

11.9. Enabling Distance (MANs and WANs)

Distance-enabling networking and I/O technology is important for virtual data centers to allow data to be moved among locations, remote users, and clients to access data and support traveling workers or home-based workers. Wide area networks need to be safe and secure for access by users of IT resources, including use of virtual private network (VPN) and physical private networks. With the growing popularity of cloud, SaaS, and managed service provider solutions, wide area networks take on an additional role in addition to supporting HA, BC, DR, email and other applications (Figure 11.12).

Virtual and physical data centers rely on various wide area networking technologies to enable access to applications and data movement over distance. Technologies and bandwidth services to support wide area data and application access include DSL, DWDM, Metro Ethernet Microwave, MPLS, Satellite, SONET/SDH, IPoverDWDM, 3G/4G, WiFi and WiMax, T1, T3, optical carrier (OC) networking using OC3 (3 × 51.84 Mbps), OC12 (622.08 Mbps), OC48 (2.488 Gbps), OC96 (4.976 Gbps), OC192 (9.953 Gbps), or even OC768 (39.813 Gbps), as well as other wavelength and bandwidth services.

Distance is a friend and a foe for distance-based networking. From a positive standpoint, distance enables survivability and continued access to data. The downside for data protection is the cost penalty in terms of expense, performance (bandwidth and latency), and increased complexity. When looking at networks to span distances, bandwidth is important and latency is critical for timely data movement, to ensure data consistency and coherency.

Some examples of how MAN and WAN networking are used include:

- Remote and hosted backup and restore
- Data archiving to managed or hosted remote locations
- Data snapshots and replication for HA, BC, and DR
- Data movement and migration along with distribution services
- Remote access of centralized or distributed resources and applications
- Access to cloud and MSP servers

High-speed wide area networks are becoming indispensable for critical applications. Business continuance, remote mirroring and replication, cloud computing, SaaS, access to MSPs, and connecting regional data centers are all tasks that require optical WANs. With many optical options and prices, picking the best technologies and techniques to transport data is challenging.

When comparing network and bandwidth services, it is important to look beyond stated line rate or spec sheet numbers and determine what the effective performance and corresponding latency will be. For example, a network service provider may offer a lower rate for a shared high-speed bandwidth service; however, that rate may be based on upload or download speeds and be independent of latency. Another example is a higher-cost bandwidth service that may appear to have the same amount of bandwidth, but on closer investigation there is a better effective (usable) bandwidth with lower latency and higher availability service.

Understanding what layers are involved in the network is important, because each layer adds complexity, cost, and latency. Latency is important to understand and to minimize for storage and data movement where consistency and transaction integrity are important for real-time data movement. The specific amount of latency will vary from negligible, almost nonexistent, to noticeable, depending on the types of technologies involved and their implementation. Depending on how the IP traffic is moved over a network, additional layers and technologies may be involved, for example, IP mapped to SONET, MPLS, IPoDWDM, or other services. The trade-off in performance and latency is the ability to span greater distances using variable-cost networking and bandwidth services to meet specific business requirement or application service-level objectives. Distance is often assumed to be the enemy of synchronous or real-time data movement, particularly because latency increases with distance. However, latency is the real enemy, because even over short distances, if high latency or congestion exists, synchronous data transmissions can be negatively impacted.

Optical networks are assumed to be and can be faster than electrical or copper wire networks, but they are not necessarily so. While data has the ability to travel at the speed of light on an optical network, actual performance is determined by how the optical network is configured and used—for example, dense wave division multiplexing (DWDM) where 32 or 64 different networks interface, each at 40 Gbit/s, is multiplexed onto a single fiber optic cable.

General considerations pertaining to wide area networking include:

- Distance—How far away do applications and data need to be located?
- Bandwidth—How much data can be moved and in what timeframe?
- Latency—What are application performance and response-time requirements?
- Security—Level of protection is required for data in-flight or remote access?
- Availability—What are the uptime commitments for the given level of service?
- Cost—What will the service or capability cost initially and over time?
- Management—Who and how will the network service be managed?
- Type of service—Dedicated or shared optic or other form of bandwidth service?

Wide area networking options and technologies include:

- Dedicated and dark fiber optic cabling and wavelength services
- Wave division multiplexing (WDM) and dense WDM (DWDM)
- SONET/SDH optical carrier (OC) networking and packet-over-SONET (POS)
- TCP/IP services, networks, and protocols, including FCIP and iSCSI
- Multiprotocol label switching (MPLS) services
- Wireless WiFi, fixed WiFi, WiMax, and 4G cell phone services
- Satellite and microwave wireless transmission
- Data replication optimization (DRO) and bandwidth optimization solutions
- Firewalls and security applications

11.9.1. Bandwidth and Protocol Optimization

WAFS, also known by vendor marketing names including wide area data management (WADM) and wide area application services (WAAS), is generically a collection of services and functions to help accelerate and improve access to centralized data. WAFS and other bandwidth, data footprint reduction (DFR), and data reduction optimization (DRO) techniques either accelerate performance or reduce the amount of bandwidth needed to move a given amount of data. In other words, these techniques and technologies can maximize what you currently have to do more or to support the same amount of activity with fewer resources.

Bandwidth optimization techniques have evolved from general-purpose compression to application-specific optimization. Application-specific functionalities range from protocol-specific ones such as CIFS, NFS, and TCP/IP to remote replication or data mirroring, remote tape copy, and cloud access. Some solutions are focused on maximizing bandwidth, while others are optimized to reduce latency, leverage caching, or enhance other techniques. For example, for environments that are looking to consolidate servers and storage resources away from ROBO locations, WAFS can be an enabling technology coexisting in hybrid environments to enhance backup of distributed data. Another example is for moving data to or from cloud or remote backup services, bandwidth optimization can occur in the form of data footprint reduction at the source as well as protocol and network technologies.

11.10. Cloud, Virtualization, and Management Topics

What networking, I/O interfaces, and protocols to use for a virtual data center, including virtual server and storage scenarios, will depend on specific needs and QoS requirements. Other factors include the type of I/O profile—large or small, random or sequential reads or writes—and the number of VMs and type of device adapters. Depending on the version of a virtual infrastructure, such as VMware or Microsoft, some advanced features are supported only with certain protocols. For example, a VM may be able to boot off of any network interface or protocol, while the virtualization hypervisor may have restrictions or specific configuration requirements.

Another consideration is virtual desktop infrastructure (VDI) boot requirements that result in a spike in network activity that would have otherwise been handled by a local disk device. On one hand, VDIs shift their disk I/Os to a server that in turn sends the data over a network to be used or accessed on the thin client or desktop. On the other hand, placing the applications and data on disks attached to a server shifts the focus or burden of backing up desktops and subsequent networking demands. However, trading network resources to support backup rather than enabling a VDI is not an even trade, because backups tend to be large sequential streams focused on bandwidth, while VDI traffic may be smaller, burstier IOP, frame, or packet per second with a focus on low latency. Exercise caution with VDIs to avoid simply moving a problem or causing a new one elsewhere instead of indentifying and eliminating bottlenecks to improve QoS and customer service experience.

While some VMs can use and leverage local dedicated and nonshared storage, most features for scaling and resiliency, including HA, BC, and DR, require some form of shared storage. Shared storage includes dual or multiported SAS storage arrays attached to two or more servers, iSCSI and Fibre Channel block storage, and NFS NAS storage. Other features, including clustering, dynamic VM movement or relocation, and server-free backup, will vary depending on version and type of I/O interface and protocol being used.

Performance will vary depending on specific VM configuration, underlying hardware architecture, guest operating system and drivers, and storage system configuration. Virtualization vendors have configuration guides and on-line forums covering various configurations and supported options, as do server and storage vendors. There is debate in the storage community among iSCSI, Fibre Channel, and NFS NAS vendors as to which protocol is the most efficient and best to use. Not surprisingly, some vendors claim their protocol and interface is the best. Others take a more neutral and consultative approach by considering what is the best tool and technique for the task at hand, along with individual preferences and existing or planned technology decisions.

Other applications, such as Microsoft Exchange, can also have a requirement of running on block-based storage or on a Microsoft file system. Traditional databases such as Oracle, Microsoft SQL, or IBM DB2/UDB have had a preference and a recommendation, if not a requirement, to run on block-based storage. Databases such as Oracle can and do run on NFS storage and, by leveraging a feature in NFS V3 or later called direct I/O (DIO), can perform blocklike access of NAS-based storage without having to read or write an entire file. These rules and requirements are changing, and it is important to consult with vendors or product specialists as to specific guidelines and recommendations.

Networks and I/O connectivity are important and, with continuing convergence, the lines between storage interfaces and networks are becoming blurred. Networks and I/O involve networking, server, storage, and data professionals to coordinate the various interdependencies across the different technology domains. For example, if a virtual server is moved from a VM on one physical server to another VM on a different physical server, unless NPIV is being used, SAN personnel have to make zoning and configuration changes, as do server and storage personnel. Various tasks and activities are required to keep I/O and network capabilities in good order to support virtual data centers.

Metrics for networking include:

- Bandwidth of data moved
- Latency and response time
- Frames or packets per second
- Availability and quality of service
- Top talkers between source and destinations
- Error counts, including retransmissions

Not to be forgotten or diminished in their importance are test and diagnostic devices. These include protocol analyzers, performance probes, network sniffers, and fault and error detection equipment. Some other examples include network and physical cable monitoring and diagnostic devices and workload generators. Some of these devices are protocol-based, while others work at the networking interface layer and still others at the physical cable level. These tools can be integrated and complemented by additional management software tools as part of an overall storage and storage networking management solution set.

Testing and diagnostic equipment can be utilized for design and development of components as well as testing of components individually and as part of an overall storage network. For example, a component may work fine by itself and with other devices under certain conditions, but when additional devices and workload are added, things may change. Unit and component testing for verification and validation and stress testing of an entire system under various workloads may uncover issues not seen in normal testing, such as impacts on memory or memory and network leaks. The combination of various equipment, operating systems, patches, and device drivers can add to the complexity of testing and diagnostics.

11.10.1. Accessing Cloud Storage and Services

Both public and private cloud services rely on some form of network access. The network resources required depend on the function or role of the cloud service being accessed and its location—for example (see Figure 11.13), if using a cloud or MSP backup service, that network bandwidth is available to support the amount of data to be protected in a given amount of time. Building on the cloud backup example, in addition to having enough network bandwidth to support data protection requirements, what other optimization capabilities exist in either the network or cloud access tools?

The cloud access tools (Figure 11.13) may be software installed on servers, workstations, or laptops, or access to the service may be via a gateway, router, bridge, or appliance. Cloud access tools either running on your workstations, laptops, or servers or via appliances include some form of optimization, security, and other functionalities specific to the service being accessed. TCP/IP is a common denominator for accessing cloud services on a local or wide area basis. Depending on the service or cloud access tool, other protocols may be used, for example, NFS or CIFS for NAS file serving/sharing, HTTP, REST, and industry- or vendor-specific APIs.

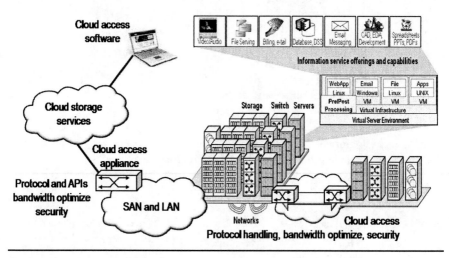

Figure 11.13   Cloud and MSP service access.

11.10.2. Virtual I/O and I/O Virtualization (IOV)

On a traditional physical server, the operating system sees one or more instances of Fibre Channel and Ethernet adapters even if only a single physical adapter, such as an InfiniBand-based HCA, is installed in a PCI or PCIe slot. In the case of a virtualized server, for example, VMware vSphere, the hypervisor can see and share a single physical adapter or multiple adapters for redundancy and performance to guest operating systems. The guest systems see what appears to be a standard Fibre Channel and Ethernet adapter or NIC using standard plug-and-play drivers.

Virtual HBA or virtual network interface card (NIC) and switches are, as their names imply, virtual representations of a physical HBA or NIC, similar to how a virtual machine emulates a physical machine with a virtual server. With a virtual HBA or NIC, physical NIC resources are carved up and allocated as virtual machines, but instead of hosting a guest operating system such as Windows, UNIX, or Linux, a Fibre Channel HBA or Ethernet NIC is presented. Are IOV or VOI a server topic, a network topic, or a storage topic? Like server virtualization, IOV involves servers, storage, network, operating system, and other infrastructure resource management technology domain areas and disciplines. The business and technology value proposition or benefits of converged I/O networks and virtual I/O are similar to those for server and storage virtualization.

Benefits of IOV include being able to reduce the number of physical interconnects, enabling higher densities, improved air flow, and energy efficiency that can have cost advantages. Other benefits include the ability to support rapid reprovisioning or configuration changes that would in the past have required physical hardware changes such as from one adapter type to support SAN to a different one for LAN. Another advantage is maximizing available PCIe expansion slots to do more with what's available, including boosting performance and availability.

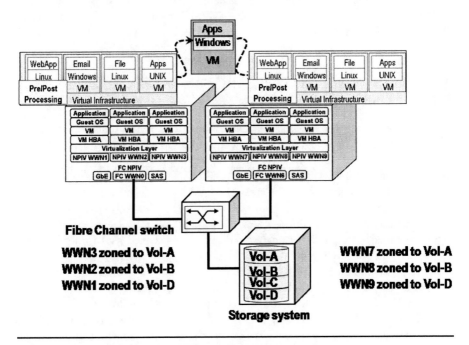

Figure 11.14   Fibre Channel NPIV examples.

11.10.3. N_Port ID Virtualization (NPIV)

N_Port_ID Virtualization (NPIV), shown in Figure 11.14, uses an ANSI T11 Fibre Channel standard to enable a physical HBA and switch to support multiple logical World Wide Node Names (WWNN) and World Wide Port Names (WWPN) per adapter for shared access purposes. Fibre Channel adapters can be shared in virtual server environments across the various VMs, but the VMs share a common worldwide node name (WWNN) and worldwide port name (WWPN) address of the physical HBA. The issue with a shared WWNN and WWPN across multiple VMs is that, from a data security and integrity perspective, volume or LUN mapping and masking have to be performed on a coarse basis.

By using NPIV supported by a target operating system or virtual server environment and associated HBAs and switches, fine-grained allocation and addressing can be performed. With NPIV, each VM is assigned a unique WWNN and WWPN, independent of the underlying physical HBA. By having a unique WWNN and WWPN, VMs can be moved to different physical servers without having to make changes for addressing of different physical HBAs or changes to Fibre Channel zoning on switches. In addition, NPIV enables fine-grained LUN mapping and masking to enable a specific VM or group of VMs to have exclusive access to a particular LUN when using a shared physical HBA. A by-product of the fine-grained and unique WWPN is that a LUN can be moved and accessed via proxy backup servers, such as VMware VCB, when properly mapped and zoned. The benefit is that time-consuming changes to SAN security and zoning for new or changed devices do not have to be made when a VM moves from one physical server and HBA to another (Figure 11.14).

11.11. Configuring for Reliability, Availability, and Serviceability (RAS)

Most storage applications are time-sensitive and require high throughput (bandwidth) and low latency with zero data loss. Bandwidth is the measure of how much data can be transferred over a network or I/O interface in a particular time, for example, per second. Latency, also known as response time, is the length of time it takes for an I/O activity or event to take place or the measure of how much delay occurs when sending or receiving data.

Effective bandwidth is a measure of how much of the available bandwidth can actually be used, taking into consideration dropped packets and retransmission due to congestion and protocol inefficiency. A common mistake is to look at bandwidth simply in terms of dollars per Gb/s. The effective or actual usage amount is important, and with bandwidth that includes what level of utilization at a given response time (latency level) can be maintained without congestion and packet delay or loss.

Another mistake to be avoided is prototyping a storage application at a reduced workload and assuming that heavier workloads will scale linearly with regard to bandwidth and latency. Rather than scaling linearly, effective bandwidth can drop significantly as workload is added. This, together with additional latency, results in poor performance, particularly for synchronous storage applications. First and foremost, an understanding of an organization's particular needs and goals along with the capabilities of the different technologies is necessary.

One of the keys to building a resilient storage network is to have dual or redundant SANs or fabrics, each providing a separate and isolated path between the host server and the storage devices or other host systems. Avoid overconnection or the temptation to have everything connected to everything. There is a trade-off in that in order to prevent blockage or congestion, various switches in a fabric may have to be interconnected to provide adequate bandwidth using the interswitch Links (ISLs). The preferred method is to create two fabrics or SANs, each with its devices interconnected, but not the SANs themselves.

Diverse network paths are important for resilient data and information networks. Bandwidth service providers can provide information as to how a diverse network path exists, including through partner or subcontractor networks. Also determine how the service provider will manage and guarantee network performance (low latency and effective bandwidth). Generally speaking, the more technology layers there are, including networking protocols, interfaces, devices, and software stacks for performing I/O and networking functions, the lower will be the performance and the higher will be the latency.

Be aware of where the fiber goes and where it is on shared bandwidth and infrastructure. Make sure that you have unique paths and that your alternate vendors are not converging on the same fiber optic cable and connection points. Another precaution is to physically isolate and separate where external fiber connections come into your premises so that they are better isolated from cable cuts. There have been numerous outages around the world, some that were publicized and many that were not, where a backhoe or some other digging device cuts a fiber optic cable and the stand-by circuit that happened to be in the same trench.

11.11.1. Flat Networks

Moving toward a flatter network topology is part of leveraging converged SAN and LAN networking technologies. As its name implies, a flat network has fewer layers than a traditional LAN topology and may also look more like SANs are designed. The trend is for LAN Ethernet networks to move toward flatter designs (right side of Figure 11.15) to reduce complexity and costs while improving QoS by removing a layer to become more of a core-edge topology.

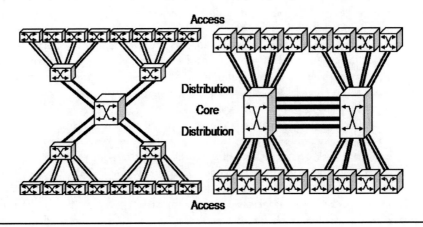

Figure 11.15 Hierarchy and flat networks.

Ethernet LAN environments have evolved to multiple layers to balance cost with performance and connectivity needs, resulting in tiered networks (left side of Figure 11.15). One of the design premises of a tiered or hierarchy network topology is to leverage lower-cost aggregation switches to support connectivity of multiple ports that have low performance requirements to better utilize faster trunk, uplink ,or ISL connections to core switches. With servers either on their own with single applications or via consolidation with VMs using hypervisors that result in aggregated performance, the need for more performance means that LAN design is evolving closer to traditional SAN approaches. SANs have also benefited from traditional LAN approaches with the introduction several years ago of host optimized or shared bandwidth ports.

Traditional SAN and storage design philosophy has been to give each server or storage port its own full or deterministic performance as opposed to sharing, which could result in oversubscription. Oversubscription occurs when many ports or users try to use the same available resource or performance, resulting in busy signals or delays. A common example is when you are at a busy event and many people try to use their cell phones at the same time. Calls do not get dropped, you just have to wait in line to get a circuit; if you are using network or data service in such an environment, you have a connection but it may be slow. With host optimized or shared bandwidth ports, system designers are able to engineer their SANs to allocate full-performance ports to those servers or storage systems that need low latency or high performance while reducing costs by sharing performance resources across lower-performing or less demanding ports.

11.11.2. Configuration and Topologies

There are many different topologies for LAN and SAN networks that can be used to scale beyond the limits of the physical devices or to combine various devices to meet different application needs. In addition to scaling for larger storage, flexible topologies and interconnects are also being used to connect various SAN or LAN islands into heterogeneous converged or unified networks to simplify resource sharing and management.

Design of storage networks can be as varied as the environments and applications they support. Storage networking design involves having clear objectives, an understanding of business needs, assessing resources, analyzing information, documenting the design, and implementing it. As part of the storage networking design process, depending on the scope, you may decide to assemble a team of people from different groups including networking, storage management, server management, applications, database management, and security.

A storage network design consists of planning, understanding needs and requirements, indentifying what resources (people and technology) you have available, and technology awareness and trends. A poor storage networking design can lead to lack of stability, poor performance, unplanned outages for maintenance, and disruptions for future growth regardless of what hardware, networks, and software are used.

Some influences on storage networking design include:

- What are your business drivers and requirements?
- What are your availability objectives (SLO, QoS, RTO, and RPO)?
- What are applicable operating philosophies, paradigms, and principals?
- What existing technology do you have, and how long will you retain it?
- What is the scope of the network (how small, large, or complex)?
- What are your budget and project constraints or ability to justify them?

One of the benefits of storage networking is flexibility to meet various needs and support diverse applications both locally and over a wide area. Consequently, a storage network design needs to be flexible and adaptable to support changes in business requirements and technology enablement. Similar to traditional networks, a storage network can be built in a "flat" manner or a "segmented" manor. A flat approach would have all servers able to access all devices as one large SAN or fabric. The other approach is to segment the storage network into two or more subnets that may be physically isolated from each other but under common management, or physically interconnected, logically isolated, and under a common management schema.

The storage networking topology that is right for you is the one that works for you, one that enables scalability and stability, and one that enables your business to meet its needs. Topologies do not need to be complex; but they do need to be extendable to meet your complex and diverse requirements. From a physical networking and hardware standpoint, it is relatively easy to build storage networks consisting of thousands of ports. The need to manage that number of ports, however, will affect the design and implementation.

11.11.3. Cabling: Tools and Management

Tying I/O and networks together, in addition to adapters, switches, bridges, routers, and gateways, are cabling in the form of copper or fiber optics and associated transceivers. There are many different types of copper and fiber optic cable that have various price points and support for distance and performance. Similarly, there are different types of transceivers to match cable speeds and distances. Transceivers are the technologies that attach to copper or fiber optic network cables and interface with adapters, NICs, switches, or other devices. You may recognize transceivers by different names, such as GBIC, SFP, and XFP, or for attachment to twinax (copper) or SMF and MMF (optics). Some transceivers are fixed while others are removable, enabling switch or adapter ports to be reconfigured for different types of media. An example of a fixed transceiver is an Ethernet LAN port on your laptop or server.

Wireless networking continues to gain in popularity, but physical cabling using copper electrical and fiber optic cabling continues to be used. With the increased density of servers, storage, and networking devices, more cabling is being required to fit into a given footprint. To help enable management and configuration of networking and I/O connectivity, networking devices, including switches, are often integrated or added to server and storage cabinets. For example, a top-of-rack or bottom-of-rack or embedded network switch aggregates the network and I/O connections within a server cabinet to simplify connectivity to an end-of-row or area group of switches. Lower-performing servers or storage can use lower-cost, lower-performance network interfaces to connect to a local switch, then a higher-speed link or trunk, also known as an uplink, to a core or area switch.

Cable management systems, including patch panels, trunk, and fan-in/fan-out cabling for overhead and under-floor applications, are useful for organizing cabling. Cable management tools include diagnostics to verify signal quality and db loss for optical cabling, cleaning and repair for connectors, as well as asset management and tracking systems. A relatively low-tech cable management system includes physically labeling cable endpoints to identify how the cable is being used. Software for tracking and managing cabling can be as simple as an Excel spreadsheet or as sophisticated as a configuration management database (CMDB) with intelligent fiber optic management systems. An intelligent fiber system includes mechanisms attached to the cabling to facilitate tracking and identifying cabling. Another component in the taxonomy of server, storage, and networking I/O virtualization is the virtual patch panel, which masks the complexity by abstracting the adds, drops, moves, and changes associated with traditional physical patch panels. For large and dynamic environments with complex cabling requirements and the need to secure physical access to cabling interconnects, virtual patch panels are a great complement to IOV switching and virtual adapter technologies.

In addition to utilizing cabling that is environmentally friendly, another "green" aspect of cabling and cable management is to improve air flow to boost cooling efficiency. Unorganized under-floor cabling results in air flow restrictions or blockages, requiring HVAC and CRAC systems to work harder, consuming more energy to support cooling activities. Cabling should not block the air flow for perforated tiles on a cool aisle or block upward hot air movement in overhead conveyance systems. Newer, environmentally safe cabling that is physically smaller in diameter enables more cabling to be installed per footprint to help improve environmental issues. IOV and virtual connect technologies in blade centers for blade servers and high-density fan-in, fan-out cabling systems can further reduce the cabling footprint without negatively impacting networking or I/O performance for servers, storage, and networking devices. For cost-sensitive applications, shorter-distance copper cabling continues to be used, including for 10 GbE, while fiber optic cabling continues to increase in adoption locally and on a wide area basis.

11.12. Common Networking Questions

Are networks less reliable today than in the past? From capability, accessibility, and affordability standpoints, networks should be more flexible, scalable, and resilient than in the past. As is the case with many technologies, it's how they are deployed, configured, and managed to particular service levels, often under specific financial considerations, that cause networks to have different perceived or actual availability. Networks should and can be more resilient today, similar to servers and storage, when best practices are applied, even in cost-sensitive environments.

With a dependence on networks (local and remote) for cloud access, what happens if someone decides to turn the network off? Look for ways to prevent your network or access to public resources being a single point of failure. Networks can and do go down for periods of time, so design to eliminate points of failure, including having alternative connections or access points. With public clouds that depend on public Internet access, loss of Web access can be a disaster, so talk with providers about alternative options for accessing their services. For example, can you call a backup or archive service provider and, with appropriate security authentication, arrange to have your data returned via some physical medium if necessary?

How is a flat network different from how Fibre Channel SANs have been designed? If you are familiar with designing SANs, other than some terminology differences, you should be very comfortable designing flat layer 2 networks.

Why not just run everything over TCP/IP? Perhaps someday, IP in general may be the path; however, that will not happen overnight, due to support of legacy process and practices and for other reasons. For now, the stepping stone on the road to convergence is Ethernet.

Is FCoE a temporal or temporary technology? Depending on the timeframe, all technologies can be seen as temporary. Given that FCoE probably has at least a 10-year temporal timeline, I would say that, in technology terms, it has a relative long life for supporting coexistence on the continued road to convergence.

What comes next, after Ethernet? For at least another decade or two, I see Ethernet or the various forms of 802.x continuing to evolve, with faster speeds, more efficient encoding, QoS, and other capabilities. That's not to say that some other interface will not appear and become viable, rather that Ethernet continues to gain momentum and traction from consumer PDAs to enterprise servers and storage.

11.13. Chapter Summary

To keep pace with improvements and new functionalities being added to storage and servers and to boost efficiency, networks will need to do more than provide more bandwidth at a lower cost. This will require faster processors, more interoperability and functionality, and technology maturity. More intelligence will move into the network and chips, such as deep frame and packet inspection accelerations, to support network and I/O QoS, traffic shaping and routing, security including encryption, compression and de-duplication.

I/O and networking vendors include Adva, Avaya, Barracuda, Broadcom, Brocade, Ciena, Cisco, Dell, Emulex, Extreme, F5, Fujitsu, HP, Huawei, IBM, Intel, Juniper, LSI, Mellanox, NextIO, Network Instruments, PMC, Qlogic, Riverbed, SolarWinds, Virtual Instruments, Virtensys, and Xsigo, among others.

Action and takeaway points:

- Minimize the impact of I/O to applications, servers, storage, and networks.
- Do more with less, including improved utilization and performance.
- Consider latency, effective bandwidth, and availability in addition to cost.

- Apply the appropriate type and tier of I/O and networking to the task at hand.
- I/O operations and connectivity are being virtualized to simplify management.
- Convergence of networking transports and protocols continues to evolve.
- Fast servers and storage need adequate bandwidth and low-latency networks.

True convergence combines people, processes, products, and policies with best practices to realize business and technology benefits.

Chapter 12

Cloud and Solution Packages

In chaos and confusion there is opportunity: Rack 'em, pack 'em and stack 'em.

— Greg Schulz

In This Chapter

- Which type of cloud is best for your needs or requirements
- What is needed for accessing or using a cloud service
- What is needed for deploying a private cloud
- What is needed for building your own cloud
- What are solution and technology stacks or bundles

This chapter looks at public and private cloud services, products, and solutions and how they can be used to address various business or technology challenges. Key themes, buzzwords, and trends include public, private, and hybrid clouds. Additional topics, themes, and buzzwords include product, technology, and solution stacks or bundles.

12.1. Getting Started

I am commonly asked whether clouds are real or hype, what they are, and where to use them. There is plenty of hype; however, there are also real products, solutions, and services that you can leverage for different purposes. Clouds have different definitions that vary depending on who you talk to, which may in turn be influenced by what they have heard, seen, read, experienced, sell, or prefer. The definition of a cloud product, service, solution, or architecture that you subscribe to or prefer will determine its adoption or deployment.

Leveraging managed service providers (MSPs) and clouds enable organizations to focus on core business functions and to avoid costs associated with establishing an IT data center. Some business models rely extensively on outsourced or managed services, including contract manufacturing for virtual factories, managed payroll and human resource functions, or email services from other providers. Smaller businesses can offload or defer costs to MSPs for functions including data protection, email, and Web hosting. Large organizations can also leverage on-line, managed, and traditional outsourcing services as part of an overall IT virtual data center strategy. For example, legacy applications associated with aging hardware could be shifted to a MSP whose economies of skill and operating best practices may be more cost-effective than in-house capabilities.

By shifting some work to third parties, internal IT resources, including hardware, facilities, and staff, can be redeployed to support emerging applications and services. Similarly, new technologies and applications can be quickly deployed using MSPs, while internal capabilities, staffing, and associated technologies are brought up to speed prior to bringing applications in-house.

Part of not being scared of clouds is to understand them and their different variations, including public, private, hybrid, services, and solutions (Figure 12.1). This means looking before you leap and understanding where, when, why, how, and what type of cloud solution or service addresses your needs.

Figure 12.1 shows how physical resources combine with software, hypervisors, measurements, best practices, policies, and people to enable information services and information factories. Figure 12.1 also shows cloud resources, using the nomenclature

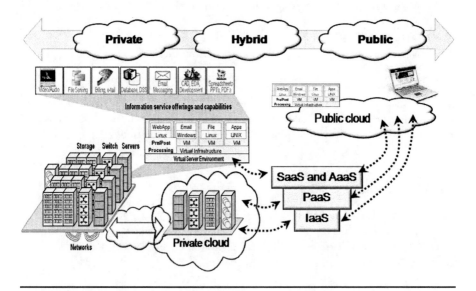

Figure 12.1   Various IT clouds.

of Infrastructure as a Service (IaaS), reflecting server, storage, networking, and I/O resources. In addition to IaaS, also shown are Platform as a Service (PaaS), also known as middleware, which provides environments for developing and deploying applications that run on a public or private IaaS. Application as a Service (AaaS) and Software as a Service (SaaS) are also shown where access to software is provided.

12.2. Clarifying Cloud Confusion: What Does Your Cloud Need to Do

Do you need a cloud (or do you want a cloud) and, if so, a public or private one? Take a step back for a moment and rethink what it is that you are trying to address and accomplish. What is the business or IT challenge that you are looking to solve or capability to enable? If you are a vendor, value-added reseller (VAR), or service provider, are you trying to sell a solution looking for a problem to generate revenue or find a means to help your customer in a new way? If you are in an IT organization, how will clouds fundamentally enable your organization?

Clouds can be

- Architecture, product, or service, for fee or free
- Management and operating philosophy
- Public, private, and hybrid
- Delivered on premises, remotely, or by a combination

So, do you want a cloud because you have been told, read, heard or watched a video that it is the thing to do? Or do you have a mandate from the corner office to do something with cloud because they have heard or been told to do something with a cloud? On the other hand, you may be in a situation where you do not think you need a cloud, but with more learning and research, you are starting to see where clouds can complement and coexist with what you are doing.

Clouds do not have to be seen as competitive to what you have been or are currently doing; instead, look at them to see how they can be complementary as an enabler. Also look at the different types of cloud from public to private and hybrid and the different variations such as SaaS, AaaS, PaaS, and IaaS. Some of the confusion about clouds stems from some vendors, service, or solution providers or consortiums trying to establish definitions around their particular capabilities. Be sure to look at the more diverse set of options; after all, if the value proposition of clouds is to liberate and enable your IT organization to be more agile, then why get locked into a model or approach that is not as flexible as you need?

12.3. IaaS, PaaS, SaaS, and AaaS

Clouds (public and private) are made up of physical servers, storage, I/O, and networking combined with software, management tools, metrics, best practices, policies, and people that are housed in a facility somewhere. Depending on the type of service being provided, the servers may be running hypervisors to support a given type of virtual machine or several different types, for example, a mix of VMware VMDK, Microsoft VHD, Citrix, and OVF. In addition to hypervisors, servers may be configured with database instances, networking tools, Web serving tools, PaaS or middleware tools, and APIs, along with storage management tools. Storage management tools range from basic file systems to object-based access with multiple protocol support including NFS, HTTP, FTP, REST, SOAP, and Torrent. In the PaaS layer, support could be for a particular environment such as .NET or VMware Spring Source.

In Chapter 1 some examples were given of cloud services and providers from a high level. Not all cloud service providers are the same; some focus on specific functionalities or personalities while others have diverse offerings. Cloud personalities mean what the cloud can do, such as enable email as a service or compute as a service or VMs as a service or storage or file sharing, backup and recovery, archiving or BC/DR.

Other personalities include social media, collaboration, and photo or audio sharing, which often get lumped under the SaaS or AaaS model. If you back up up your computer or smart phone to a service such as ATT, Carbonite, EMC Mozy, Iron Mountain, Rackspace Jungledisk, Seagate i365, or Sugarsync, you are accessing a SaaS or AaaS cloud. If you use a Web expense reporting tool such as Concur, you are using a cloud. If you use Google Gmail or Microsoft Live office, you are using a SaaS cloud. If you are developing a big data analytics application using hadoop and other open-source tools leveraging a site such as Amazon, Google, or Rackspace, you are using a cloud and a mix of IaaS and PaaS. If those same types of functionality are sourced from your own facilities or systems, you are using a private cloud. If others are using the same service but you are not sharing data or information, you are using a public cloud. If your private cloud relies on an IaaS public provider such as Amazon, AT&T, and Google, Rackspace, Iron Mountain, VCE, or others for remote storage or VM hosting, you are using a hybrid cloud. Figure 12.2 shows private, hybrid, and public clouds along with IaaS, PaaS, and SaaS layer focus.

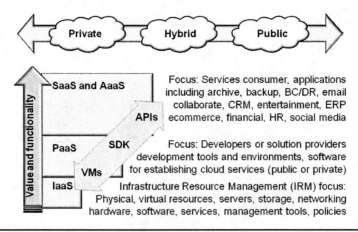

Figure 12.2   Various types of clouds, layers, and focus.

Something that is occurring with clouds is that, at the IaaS layer, different vendors and providers are maneuvering their tools to support environments such as physical servers and storage along with converged networking and hypervisors. At the IaaS layer the objective is to support both new and existing environments and applications. At the PaaS layer there is the need to support existing applications while establishing how new systems will be developed and deployed in the future. Consequently, at the PaaS layer, there is more of a focus on the tools, the development environment, APIs, and SDKs in order to manage and support what gets developed now and in the future. This is similar to decisions made in the past about what languages, development environments, and runtime bindings or environments would be selected. While some applications may be short-lived, and today's tools allow new applications to be deployed faster, many applications need to continue to run for many years or longer.

It is important to pay attention to what is going on with the PaaS or middleware layer for new development, as those applications are what will be needing support in your private or a public cloud on a go-forward basis. The golden rule of clouds is similar to the golden rule of virtualization: Whoever controls the management, which includes the development environment, controls the gold.

12.4. Accessing Clouds

Cloud services are accessed via some type of network, either the public Internet or a private connection. The type of cloud service being accessed (Figure 12.3) will determine what is needed. For example, some services can be accessed using a standard Web browser, while others require plug-in or add-on modules. Some cloud services may require downloading an application, agent, or other tool for accessing the cloud service or resources, while others provide an on-site or on-premises appliance or gateway.

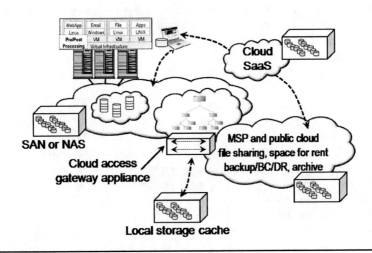

Figure 12.3   Accessing and using clouds.

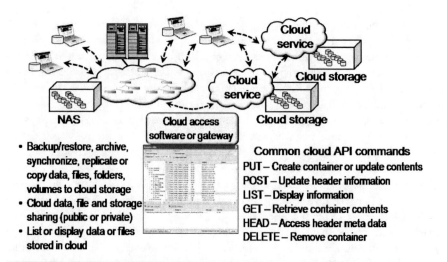

Figure 12.4 Cloud access tools.

Cloud access software and gateways or appliances are used for making cloud storage accessible to local applications. The gateways, in addition to enabling cloud access, provide replication, snapshots, and other storage services functionality. Cloud access gateways or server-based software include tools from BAE, Citrix, Gladinet, Gluster, Mezeo, Nasuni, Openstack, Twinstrata, Zetta, and others. In addition to cloud gateway appliances or cloud points of presence (cpops), access to public services is also supported via various software tools. Many IRM and data protection tools including backup/restore, archiving, replication, and other applications have added (or are planning to add) support for access to various public services such as Amazon, Google, Iron Mountain, Microsoft, or Rackspace.

Some of the tools have added native support for one or more of the cloud services leveraging various APIs, while other tools or applications rely on third-party access gateway appliances or a combination of native and appliances. Another option for accessing cloud resources is to use tools (Figure 12.4) supplied by the service provider, which may be their own, from a third-party partner, or open source, in addition to using their APIs to customize your own tools.

For example, I can access my Amazon S3 or Rackspace storage accounts using their web and other provided tools for basic functionality. However, for doing backups and restores, I use the tools provided by the service provider, which then interface with two different cloud storage services. The tool presents an interface for defining what to back up, protect, and restore, as well as enabling shared (public or private) storage devices and network drives. In addition to providing an interface (Figure 12.4), the tool also speaks specific API and protocols of the different services, including PUT (create or update a container), POST (update header or Meta data), LIST (retrieve information), HEAD (metadata information access), GET (retrieve data from a container), and DELETE (remove container) functions. Note that the actual behavior and API functionality will vary by service provider. The importance of mentioning the above example is that when you look at some cloud storage services providers, you will see mention of PUT, POST, LIST, HEAD, GET, and DELETE operations in addition to services such as capacity and availability. Some services will include an unlimited number of operations, while others will have fees for doing updates, listing, or retrieving your data in addition to basic storage fees. By being aware of cloud primitive functions such as PUT or POST and GET or LIST, you can have a better idea of what they are used for as well as how they play into evaluating different services, pricing, and services plans.

Depending on the type of cloud service, various protocols or interfaces may be used, including NAS NFS, HTTP or HTTPs, FTP, REST, SOAP, and Bit Torrent, and APIs and PaaS mechanisms including .NET or SQL database commands, in addition to XM, JSON, or other formatted data. VMs can be moved to a cloud service using file transfer tools or upload capabilities of the provider. For example, a VM such as a VMDK or VHD is prepared locally in your environment and then uploaded to a cloud provider for execution. Cloud services may provide an access program or utility that allows you to configure when, where, and how data will be protected, similar to other backup or archive tools.

Some traditional backup or archive tools have added direct or via third party support for accessing IaaS cloud storage services such as Amazon, Rackspace, and others. Third-party access appliance or gateways enable existing tools to read and write data to a cloud environment by presenting a standard interface such as NFS that gets mapped to the back-end cloud service format. For example, if you subscribe to Amazon S3, storage is allocated as objects and various tools are used to access or utilize. The cloud access software or appliance understands how to communicate with the IaaS storage APIs and abstracts those from how they are used. Access software tools or gateways, in addition to translating or mapping between cloud APIs, formats your applications including security with encryption, bandwidth optimization, and data footprint reduction such as compression and de-duplication. Other functionalities include reporting, management tools that support various interfaces, protocols and standards including SNMP or SNIA, Storage Management Initiative Specification (SMIS), and Cloud Data Management Initiative (CDMI).

12.5. Public Cloud Services

Public clouds provide services either for a fee or free. These services range from SaaS or AaaS to PaaS and IaaS along with variations of XaaS (Table 12.1). Variations of XaaS include Archive as a Service (AaaS), Storage as a Service (the other SaaS), Desktop as a Service (DaaS) (not to be confused with Disk as a Service), Compute as a Service (CaaS), Backup as a Service (BaaS), and Email as a Service (EaaS), among many other permutations. Some public services provide information or data sharing such as Flickr, while others provide a shared or multitenant service, with your data or information kept separate unless you chose to share it.

In addition to being used to complement local physical, virtual, and private cloud environments, public clouds can also be used to support other public clouds. For example, I use Rackspace Jungle Disk for cloud or MSP backup with the option of

Table 12.1 Cloud Characters, Functionalities, and Examples

	Characteristics	Functionality	Examples
SaaS	Application or information services that eliminate the need for you to buy and install your own software and infrastructure. Focus is on consumption	Archive, backup, email, office, payroll or expense, file or data storage, photo or information sharing services and others	AT&T, Boxnet, Carbonite, Dell medical archiving, Dropbox, EMC Mozy, Google, HP Shutterfly, Iron Mountain, Microsoft, Rackspace, Oracle, VCE, VMware, and others
PaaS	Environment for creating and deploying applications or services functionality	APIs, SDKs, tools for developing and deploying services	Amazon EC2 and S3, Facebook, Microsoft Azure, Oracle, Rackspace, VMware, W3I
IaaS	Resources provisioned to support processing (compute), storing (storage), and moving information (networks)	Metrics for E2E management and insight, abstracted elastic resources with varying SLOs or SLAs	Amazon Web Services (AWS) EC2 and S3, Dell, EMC, HP, IBM, Microsoft Azure, NetApp, Rackspace, Savvis, Terremark, VCE, Visi, Sungard

using Rackspace or Amazon IaaS storage. Some services give you a choice of which IaaS or PaaS environments or services you can use, while others mask that information from you, leveraging their own or others'.

An IaaS solution bundle, for example, can contain some number of VMs (standard or high-availability), firewall and VPN, storage, metered or unmetered network connectivity (bandwidth), some number of public and private dedicated IP addresses, VNICs and VLAN, FTP, RDP, and SSH access for a given fee. The service may be fully managed, partially managed, or not managed, with different tiers of networks, storage, and server performance capabilities. Optional fees may apply for upgrading from one type or tier of server (e.g., to get faster or more cores), or for more memory, storage capacity, and I/O and networking performance in addition to backups, BC/DR, and other add-on capabilities.

Keep in mind that a public cloud must provide security and access. You may lose access to a resource for a period of time; however, you should not lose any data or information. A best practice is to have another copy of anything important you put on a cloud. Your alternate copy of what you put into a cloud need not be current, depending on its value or importance, but unless you can live without it, have another copy even if at a different location. Another consideration, particularly with services where you are storing data such as backup or archive or in support of BC and DR, is how quickly you will be able to restore a large amount of data in a given amount of time. Individual files may be able to be restored from on-line service very quickly, but what about hundreds of megabyte- or gigabyte-sized files, or terabytes of data?

Look into what mechanism a service provider offers either as part of a base package fee or as an add-on cost to other services to support bulk data import and export and via what media. Also keep in mind that when sending data electronically to a cloud service, data footprint reduction (DFR) techniques including compression and de-duplication are usually employed on your systems or via a gateway appliance. What this means is that data may flow faster to a cloud than it does on a restore, even if your network supports faster download speeds, given that a full file may be restored instead of differenced or portions of data being protected.

12.6. Private Clouds

Private clouds are similar to public clouds except that they are intended for use or consumption on an internal to an organization basis. A private cloud can be built and located entirely internally or can leverage external and public resources. The lines between private cloud and traditional IT can be blurry, depending on different definitions or solution offerings. In general, a private cloud has the same tenants or operating principles as a public cloud, meaning agility, elasticity, effective resource usage, and metering for management insight. In addition, private clouds can be extended and evolved to support chargeback or billing where applicable, as well as self-provisioning or procurement of resources by information services consumers. Many of the same tools and technologies, from hardware to software and networking, are used for establishing both public and private clouds and traditional environments. For example, EMC ATMOS is an object-based storage system that supports multiple interfaces, including NFS for file-based access, along with built-in metering for accounting, management, and chargeback, and also provisioning tools like similar solutions from other vendors. EMC ATMOS can be used for deploying private as well as public clouds. In addition to IaaS solutions or products, PaaS and middleware products also support public and private deployments.

Server virtualization enables both public and private clouds by providing a mechanism for encapsulation of servers and of their applications and data. By being encapsulated into a VM, applications can easily be moved into a private cloud or migrated to a public cloud as needed. By decoupling data from the VM, similar to shared storage for physical servers, flexibility also exists in what storage to use. For example, a VM can be local yet point to remote cloud storage, or a VM can be moved to a cloud using storage provided by that service.

12.7. Stacks and Solutions

Cloud and solution stacks have variations from loose multivendor marketing alliances to integrated and tested interoperability technology reference architectures. Stacks (Figure 12.5) can include products from the same or different vendors, purchased separately or under the same SKU/part number.

Stacks can be focused on:

- Application functionality (database, SAP, EMR, PACs, email)
- Platform or middleware, including hypervisors

- Infrastructure (server, storage, networking)
- Data protection, backup, archive, BC/DR

Stacks can center on networking and servers such as Cisco UCS, storage, server, networking, hypervisor, and management tools such as EMC vBlocks, or other variations. Another stack is Oracle Exadata II, which combines server, storage, and software, including database tools. Oracle Exalogic, on the other hand, combines server, storage, operating systems, management tools, and middleware to support various applications. A value proposition of stacks and solution bundles is ease of acquisition, deployment, and interoperability.

The solution stacks or bundles can exist on your premises or at a co-location or hosting site. Some solution stacks are focused on IaaS in support of Citrix, Microsoft, or VMware server virtualization, combining servers, storage, networking, hypervisors, and management tools. Other solutions include database, middleware or PaaS, and email. Preconfigured data center solutions have been in existence for several years, with servers, storage, networks, and associated cabling, power, and cooling already integrated at the factory. What differs between existing preintegrated solutions, which have had various marketing names including data center or SAN in a can, is density and scale. Existing solutions are typically based on a cabinet or series of cabinets preintegrated and with all components prestuffed or ready for rapid installation once at a customer's site.

In general, the big advantage of these approaches is that they are bundled, which helps to take some complexity, and thus cost, out of the equation for the customer. These solutions help jump-start efforts for moving to a dynamic, converged, or virtual flexible abstracted environment with a ready-to-deploy solution. Cost savings can be in ease of acquisition, ease of installation, ease of configuration, and, if tools are provided, how well those tools enable automated provisioning. If there is a cost advantage to deploying technology that is the same or similar to what the customer has done in the

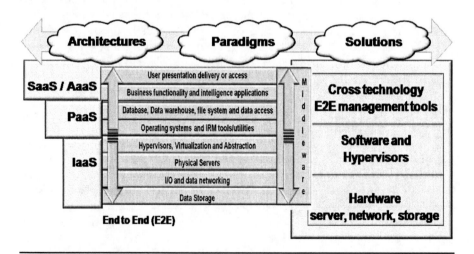

Figure 12.5   Stacks and integrated solutions.

past, there is a savings. However, if there is a premium price from the vendor for the packaged or bundled solution, then cost savings need to come from elsewhere.

Stacks and solution include:

- Cisco Unified Computing System (UCS)
- Dell Virtual Integrated System (VIS)
- EMC vBlocks
- HP Converged Infrastructure
- IBM Dynamic Infrastructure and Cloudburst
- NetApp FlexPods
- Oracle Exadata II and Exalogic
- Virtual Computing Environment (VCE)

Solution bundle and stack considerations include:

- What management tools and interfaces are included
- What optional add-ons are available?
- Are any hypervisor or operating system tools installed, and are licenses included?
- Who is responsible for maintaining the different components?
- How is management enabled across different technology groups?
- Can you reconfigure the individual components without violating warranties?
- What are the licensing and rights to use, as well as maintenance costs?
- What are flexibility options to interoperate with other solution bundles?

12.8. PODs and Modular Data Center Components

For large-scale environments faced with rapid growth or those that already have large-scale server, storage, and network deployments, a new approach to bulk resource installation and implementation is using large shipping containers. Using semi truck trailers as data centers is a practice that, over the past couple of decades, has been used by some vendors who provide "data centers on wheels" for DR needs. A growing trend is for IT resource manufacturers, particularly server vendors, to provide preconfigured, "pre-stuffed" data centers in a box, using standard 20-foot shipping containers as the "box." Instead of using shipping containers to transport the cabinets and server, storage, and networking components, cabling, power, and cooling components to a customer site, shipping containers are preconfigured as ready-to-use mini-data centers or modular computer rooms or zones for a larger data center.

The new generations of data centers in a box are based on the shipping industry standard intermodal container. These containers are called "intermodal" because they can be transported using different modes of transportation, including ship, rail, and truck, or by large cargo-carrying aircraft, without having to unload and repack the cargo contents. Given the diverse use of intermodal containers, standardization has resulted in robust and sturdy containers that are commonly used for shipping high-value cargos. Interior dimensions of a standard 20-foot intermodal container are approximately 18 feet

10 inches by 7 feet 8 inches wide and about 7 feet 9 inches tall. These intermodal containers are commonly seen in 20-, 40-, 45-, 58-, and 53-foot lengths on cargo container ships, railroad flat cars or intermodal double-stack (two containers high) and over-the-road tractor trailer trucks.

Benefits of using preconfigured large container-based data center modules include:

- The shipping container is a large field-replaceable unit for technology upgrades.
- IT resources including servers, storage, and networking are integrated.
- Installation and implementation time at the customer site is shorter.
- Rapid deployment of new or upgraded data center capacity is enabled.
- Units plug into facility power, cooling, networking, and monitoring interfaces.
- Power, cooling, and cabling are preintegrated in the large modular container.
- Overhead and other built-in conveyance and cabling schemes are used.
- Volume deployment of server, storage, and networking equipment is supported.
- Receiving, shipping, and equipment staging areas can be smaller.

12.9. Vendor Lock-in: The Good, the Bad, and the Ugly

Do clouds and virtualization eliminate or move vendor or technology lock-in? Is vendor lock-in caused by vendors, their partners, products, protocols, or by customers? In my opinion, it can be due to all, some, or may be a non-issue. Vendor and technology or service lock-in is a situation in which a customer becomes dependent or "locked in" by choice or other circumstances to a particular supplier or technology.

What is the difference between vendor lock-in, account control, and stickiness? Generally speaking, lock-in, stickiness, and account control are essentially the same or at least strive to obtain similar results. Vendor lock-in has a negative stigma, but vendor stickiness is a new term, perhaps even sounding cool, and doesn't have the same (or any) stigma. Using a different term, such as sticky instead of vendor lock, can make the situation seem different or better. Is vendor lock-in or stickiness a bad thing? No, not necessarily, particularly if you the customer are aware and still in control of your environment.

I have held different views of vendor lock-in over the years. These have varied from when I was a customer working in IT organizations to being a vendor and later as an advisory analyst consultant. Even as a customer, I had different views of lock-in, depending on the situation. In some cases lock-in was a result of upper management having their favorite vendor, which meant when a change occurred further up the ranks, sometimes vendor lock-in would shift as well. On the other hand, I also worked in IT environments where we had multiple vendors for different technologies, to maintain competition across suppliers.

When I was a vendor, I was involved with customer sites that were "best of breed," while others were aligned around a single or few vendors. Some were aligned around technologies from the vendors I worked for, and others were aligned with someone else's technology. In some cases, as a vendor we were locked out of an account until there was a change of management or mandates at those sites. In other cases where lock-out occurred, once our product was OEMd or resold by an incumbent vendor, the lockout ended. Some vendors do a better job of establishing lock-in, account management, account control, or stickiness compared to others. Some vendors may try to lock customers in, creating the perception that vendors lock customers in. There is also a perception that vendor lock-in occurs only with the largest vendors, but I have seen this also occur with smaller or niche vendors, who gain control of their customers and keep larger or other vendors out.

Vendor lock-in or stickiness is not always the result of the vendor, var, consultant, or service provider pushing a particular technology, product, or service. Customers can allow or enable vendor lock-in as well, either by intent via alliances to drive some business initiative or accidentally by giving up account control management. Vendor lock-in is not a bad thing if it brings mutual benefit to the suppler and consumer. On the other hand, if lock-in causes hardship to the consumer while benefiting the supplier, then it can be a bad thing for the customer.

Do some technologies lend themselves more to vendor lock-in than others? Yes, some do. For example, often it is expensive hardware that is seen as being vulnerable to vendor lock-in, but software is where I have seen a lot of stickiness. With virtualization solutions, vendor lock-in could occur around a particular hypervisor or associated management tools.

Locking or stickiness can occur in many different places: application software, databases, data or information tools, messaging or collaboration, and infrastructure resource management (IRM) tools ranging from security to backup to hypervisors and operating systems to email. In addition, hardware has become more interoperable, from servers, storage, and networks to integrated marketing or alliance stacks, making it more vulnerable to lock-in. Another opportunity for stickiness can be in the form of drivers, agents, or software shims, where you become hooked on a feature functionality that then drives future decisions. In other words, lock-in can occur in different places in traditional IT and in managed services, in virtualized or cloud environments if you let it.

Thoughts about vendor, service, or technology lock-in:

- Customers need to manage their resources and suppliers.
- Technology providers need to get closer to influence customer thinking.
- There can be a cost with single-vendor sourcing, due to loss of competition.
- There can be a cost associated with functioning as your own integrator.
- There is a cost in switching from vendors and or their technology.
- Managing suppliers may be easier than managing upper management.
- Virtualization and cloud can be a source for lock-in and a tool to minimize it.
- As a customer, if lock-in provides benefits, then it can be a good thing.

Ultimately, it's up to customers to manage their environment and decide if they will allow vendor lock-in. Granted, upper management may be the source of the lock-in and, not surprisingly, is where some vendors will want to focus their attention, either directly or via influencing high-level management consultants. While a vendor's solution may appear to be a locked-in solution, it does not become a lock-in issue or problem until a customer allows it to. Remember the IT "golden rule": Whoever controls the management tools (server, storage, networking, services, physical, virtual, or cloud) controls the gold!

12.10. Evaluating Cloud Servers and Solutions

One of the value propositions of public cloud services for many people or organizations is the low advertised cost compared to using traditional in-house capabilities. As part of evaluating a cloud service, understand what the advertised fee includes, along with the terms of service. For example, if the fee is shown with an asterisk or qualifier, then that cost is based on some volume of use or level of service. As with anything that is promoted on low price, look into what the fees are as more data is added or as access increases. Also look into whether the service at a particular fee is limited to a certain number of users or sessions (total and concurrent), amount of access using the service, how much network traffic is generated viewing information or sending data. For example, Amazon S3 storage prices are often mentioned by people in cloud discussions, but when I ask if they know the charges for bulk import or export, the fees for actually reading or writing data or generating reports, and the fees for location-based services, I often get a blank stare or an expression of surprise. There is the assumption that for a given price, service customers will get what they expect, not necessarily what the service price actually includes. Amazon, as an example, has a graduated pricing model for services: As you increase the amount of data stored, price per gigabyte or terabyte decreases (i.e., a volume discount), including some specified number of reads, writes, and status or inquiries. Note that Amazon is only being used as an example; other service providers have different subscription plans, SLOs, and SLAs to meet different needs.

Optional services include the ability to pick the availability level and the geographic region where your data will reside. Knowing what geographic region is important for data or applications that for regulatory compliance cannot leave certain jurisdictional boundaries. Also check to see if in the case of a regional disaster, your service provider, as part of your subscription package, will automatically move your data or access to a different region for a fee or free of charge. Additional fees may apply for different levels of service, including faster storage and network access, improved data resiliency, and availability or long-term retention. A service provider's financial and business stability should also be considered, including how data can be retrieved should the service cease to exist. As is the case with any emerging technology or solution provider, look for organizations that are flexible and that have a growing list of active customers. In some situations, a lower "a la carte" pricing model, where you determine what components or services and availability you need, may be a good option. For other situations, a package that has a higher fee but is more inclusive may be a better value. For services offering either free or very-low-cost services including all you can consume, look into the terms of services to see what the SLAs and SLOs are—particularly for information you may need in a hurry.

Additional considerations when evaluating cloud solutions or services include:

- What management tools are included or supported
- Capabilities for moving data, applications, and VMs into a cloud
- Security (logical and physical) along with information privacy
- Compliance and audit functionality reporting

- Interoperability with APIs or access tools (gateways, software)
- Metering, measurement, reporting, and chargeback
- Service management, including SLOs and SLAs
- Does the service maintain a copy of your data in different locations

12.11. Common Cloud Questions

What are some good uses for public and private clouds? At the risk of being labeled a cloud cheerleader, there are many good uses for both public and private clouds to access different services and functionality. I like using cloud-based backup to complement on-site data protection, because the combination adds resiliency while enabling agility in a cost-effective manner. Archiving is another good use of cloud resources, as is using public cloud storage as another storage tier. Email, office, collaboration tools or services, and traditional multifunction hosting sites are other good uses.

My hosting service is a cloud that I can self-provision and self-procure. I get charged a fee for some things, while others are free. The service has SLOs and SLAs, management and reporting dashboards, supports functionalities from email, word press, and other blogs to HTTP Web and many other functions that I do not have to buy, host, and manage in my own facility. Private clouds are a good fit for those who want to transit to a cloud operation and management model yet want to maintain control. Hybrids are a natural evolution, where public services complement private cloud and traditional functionality.

Some other great uses for clouds include supporting seasonal surge demand when more compute or server resources are needed. In addition to seasonal workload balancing, support for development, testing, quality assurance or regression testing, and special project activities are also good candidates. Does that mean everything should go to the cloud? Gain comfort with clouds by doing a pilot or proof-of-concept project to understand the benefits as well as caveats to establish best practices and new polices for usage. Look before you leap, don't be scared, have a plan, and know whether it makes sense from a functional and service-level support perspective, and not just in terms of bottom-line cost, to move to a cloud.

Do clouds have to be delivered via the Internet? Public cloud service may be rather difficult to access without using the Internet unless some type of private network is made available. For private clouds, a combination of public Internet and dedicated networks may be deployed.

Do clouds require chargeback? Clouds need measurements, metering or metrics, and associated reporting including usage or activity accounting tied to service management. Fee services need chargeback billing; other services may involve usage statements for information purposes. It is always good to have insight and awareness into services being delivered to meet SLOs, SLAs, and resource activity that are needed for enabling an information factory.

Is the traditional IT data center now dead? In most situations I would say no, although for some environments there may be more of a transition and reduction if not elimination of the actual IT data center presence. Some IT environments will continue as they have in the past, perhaps moving into some private cloud and over time leveraging public clouds as another tier of IT resources, to augment and complement what they are doing.

Are clouds best suited for new applications or legacy? That depends on the type of cloud you are considering and for what objectives. In some situations, moving legacy systems to a hosting or managed service provider can free up resources to support new systems deployed using a combination of public and private cloud approaches. In other situations it may make more sense to do new development using a mix of public and private clouds for deployment.

Is it true that if a salesperson is required or involved, something cannot be a cloud? The premise behind this idea is that real clouds are not products, only services available from the likes of Amazon, Google, or others, and that they do not have salespeople knocking at your door to sell you something. Keep in mind, however, how much marketing cloud services do, and, unless the service is free, someone has to close the sale and process the payment.

What is meant by "Don't be scared of clouds, but look before you leap"? Do your homework, including reading this book, to understand the variations of cloud services, products, and solutions and how they can complement what you are already doing.

12.12. Chapter Summary

It is important to determine whether moving applications or data to a cloud is simply moving a problem or is an opportunity to improve the overall business. It is also necessary to keep in mind that cloud-based services need to make a profit and need to rely on their own host or managed service providers to house their service or leverage their own facility, including equipment. Their goals are to keep costs as low as possible, spreading resources across multiple users or subscribers, which could lead to performance or resource contention issues. Performance and latency or delays in accessing information from a cloud or network service provider also need to be kept in perspective.

General action items include:

- Clouds do not have to be an all-or-nothing approach.
- Clouds can be complementary to what you are currently doing.
- Look at clouds as another tier of IT resources to deliver information services.
- Situational awareness is important for navigating your way around clouds.
- Don't be scared, but look before you leap.

Public and private cloud services and solutions along with management tools vendors, in addition to those mentioned in this chapter, include Amazon, Appistry, Aster, AT&T, CA (3tera), BMC, Cirtas, Cisco, Citrix, Cloudera, Cloudcentral, Cloud.com, CSC, Ctera, Enstratus, Eucalyptus, Fujitsu, GoGrid, HP, IBM, Joynet, Microsoft, Mezeo, Nasuni, NetApp, Nirvanix, Openstack.org, Redhat, Reliacloud, RightScale, Scality, Seagate i365, VCE, Verizon, and Xyrion.

Chapter 13

Management and Tools

If all you have is a hammer, everything looks like a nail.

– Greg Schulz

In This Chapter

- The different types of tools for accomplishing various storage network tasks
- The importance of metrics and measurements for situational awareness
- End-to-end and cross-technology management
- The value and importance of managing software licenses
- Tools are only as good as how and where they are used

This chapter looks at management tools for cloud, virtual, and data storage networks. Key themes, buzzwords, and trends include infrastructure resource management (IRM), end-to-end (E2E) management, public and private clouds, and best practices.

13.1. Getting Started

Software and management tools are interwoven with hardware, services, and best practices in a transparent manner. What this means is that, rather than considering hardware, software, and tools separately, they must be considered together because you can't have hardware without software, nor can you have software without hardware, which means that virtualization and cloud services rely on underlying physical resources, tools, people, and best practices.

One of the main ideas, as well as a value proposition, of clouds and virtualization is to enhance infrastructure resource management, IT service management (ITSM), and services delivery relative to traditional IT approaches. If the difference were simply the tools, then why not apply those to legacy environments and technologies, simply labeling them as private clouds, IT 2.0, or dynamic and optimized environments? Tools are just tools unless they are put to use in a way that leverages their benefit for achieving some goal or objective. What this means is that cloud resources and tools can be used in traditional manners to mimic standard IT and IRM activities. Similarly, various tools and technologies can be used in different ways to enable a converged, flexible, elastic, scalable, and resilient data infrastructure—often referred to as a cloud.

We have already looked at several different technologies, tools, techniques, and best practices pertaining to data and IRM in support of delivering information services. Although it is important to have a diversified IT toolbox, it is also important to know what to do with those tools. If all you have is a hammer, everything looks like a nail.

13.2. Software and Management Tools

Management tools can be software, hardware, a combination of the two, or be available as a service. For example Software as a Service (SaaS) is an example of how Web-based tools can be used for delivering business and information services and enabling IRM activities. An example of a hardware-based tool is an analyzer or probe for assessing server, storage, or networking health or troubleshooting. A combination approach might involve a hardware diagnostic or monitoring tool that provides information to software running on a server or virtual machine or via a cloud SaaS capability. Tools can be purchased, rented or leased, borrowed, or found on the Web as a free or contribution-shareware model.

Software and management tools pertain to:

- SaaS, Infrastructure as a Service (SaaS), and Platform as a Service (PaaS)
- Physical, virtual, and cloud resources
- Servers, storage, and networking hardware devices
- Application, middleware, and IRM software
- Operating systems and hypervisors
- Facilities, energy, power, cooling, and HVAC

Software and management tools address:

- Application, business functionality, and information services
- Service and help desk, incident, and trouble tickets
- Performance, availability, capacity, and change tracking
- Data movement and migration
- IT services delivery and IRM activities
- Testing, simulation, diagnostics, and benchmarking
- Security, compliance, and identity management

- Data protection, including backup/restore and high availability (HA)
- Business continuance (BC) and disaster recovery (DR)
- Data footprint reduction (DFR) and optimization
- Planning and analysis, forecasting, acquisition, and disposition of IT resources
- Configuration, provisioning, troubleshooting, and diagnostics
- Metrics and measurement for enabling situational awareness
- Activity and event monitoring, accounting, and chargeback

A case can be made that any form of software is a tool, just as many tools are hardware, being used for managing resources and services delivery. Some software or hardware technologies are focused on managing or supporting other tools in addition to enabling services. For example, a database is a software tool for organizing and managing data that can be used by other applications and tools for delivering information. Additional tools are used for configuring, tuning, securing, performing maintenance or updates, and protecting data in databases. Other tools are used for accessing the database to perform analytics, queries, support transactions, and to import and export data to other applications or tools, including data mart, data warehouse, and big data analytics systems.

Having a diversified toolbox (Figure 13.1), and knowing what to use when, where, and why, is important for enabling an information factory comprised of physical, virtual, and cloud resources in support of information services delivery. There is a caveat that having too many tools with too much focus on the toolbox can become a distraction from service delivery activities. This means that maintaining a balance of the right tools, best practices, people skill sets, automation, insight, and awareness of information services delivery is important.

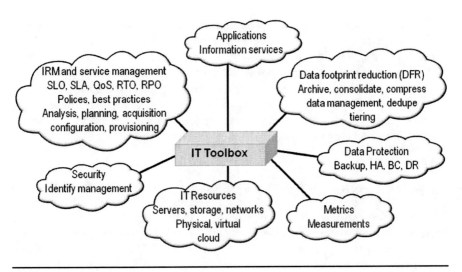

Figure 13.1   IT toolbox.

Returning to the information factory analogy that has been used throughout this book, tools and tooling are important for the transformation of resources into delivery services. Factories rely on tooling in the form of equipment such as printing presses, metal stamping or bending equipment, mixers and extruders, cookers, and packaging devices. These physical tools together with various techniques and equipment are managed with various other tools that enable collection of metrics for monitoring, management, troubleshooting, proactive or predictive analysis, quality control, configuration, and accounting, among other activities.

Tools in a factory can be a mix of automated activities, graphical user interfaces (GUIs), text printouts, and command line interfaces (CLIs), along with various alarms or event alert mechanisms. There are also tools or tooling that may be generic in nature, such as hammers, wrenches, screwdrivers and pliers, as well as custom tooling designed for specific tasks for specific factory technology. Information factories have the same characteristics in that there are various tools or technologies for delivering information services that have to be managed with a combination of automation and human intervention. Like a traditional factory, information factories have specialized tools for maintaining efficient service delivery as well as when maintenance, configuration, or repair need to be undertaken. For example, operating systems, hypervisors, and file systems are tools that in turn have either built-in or third-party-provided for free or fee utilities for managing them, including configuration, provisioning, or allocating resources, diagnostics and troubleshooting, monitoring, and reporting.

Public cloud services are also tools that leverage software running on virtual environments based on physical resources that in turn rely on various plug-ins, applets, drivers, shims, agents, dashboards, or utilities, all of which are tools. Virtualization hypervisors are tools for enabling abstraction, transparency, emulation, and agility, in addition to supporting consolidation. There are tools for managing hypervisors and their associated IRM activities, including provisioning, capacity planning, security, and data protection.

Tools and functionalities can be implemented as general-purpose software running on a standard off-the-shelf x86 server, natively on a physical machine (PM), or coexisting with other software or tools such as on an application, database, email, Web, or other servers. Tools or software can also run on dedicated hardware (open x86 or vendor proprietary), in what are often referred to as appliances. Appliances are also known as gateways, bridges, routers, and servers. Tools can be deployed running on a virtual machine (VM) or as firmware or microcode embedded within a physical server, storage, or networking device.

13.3. Management Tool Interfaces

What is the best management tool? Is it the one with the coolest GUI or the one that is so transparent and automated you forget about it? Depending on your role, the answer is, it depends. Some people prefer GUIs, while others like CLIs, and others a combination depending on the task or functionality. In addition to GUIs and CLIs, interfaces also include APIs and a mechanism for uploading or downloading information. For example, performance, event, or other information can be downloaded using XML and CSV, among other formats, to be imported to other tools or applications. Some tools are customer-facing (Figure 13.2), including service request and system status, while others are internally focused for manual intervention or analysis.

Other tools have interfaces yet leverage policies acting on data feeds from different sources such as event logs, usage, or activity to support automated operations. In Figure 13.2, element managers are shown for managing storage configuration, diagnostics, snapshots, and other device-specific and detailed functions. Also shown are SRM tools for monitoring and management and systems resource analysis (SRA) tools. These tools can also interface with each other and with framework tools.

Figure 13.3 shows various management tools and interfaces involved in using cloud services. Some of the images shown in Figure 13.3 include a Web-based SaaS provider's health status display (right), a configuration applet running on a client's or user's computer (center) and a Web-accessible management console for IaaS. Various technologies include network access, bandwidth, and data footprint reduction optimization, HTTP and REST. Event and performance information can be downloaded via CSV or XML to be imported into other tools for analysis or event correlation.

In addition to application, Web- or browser-based GUI and CLIs, other management interfaces for accessing or moving information include HTTP, FTP, XML, JSON, RSS, CSV, SOAP, and REST. Application program interfaces (APIs) and software development kits (SDKs) for vendor and industry, along with defector standards, include those from Amazon, GoGrid, Google, Open Stack, and Rackspace. Other management tools, interfaces, standards, and APIs include the Cloud Management Working Group (CMWG), Data Management Task Force (DMTF), Virtualization Management Initiative (VMAN), System Management Architecture for Server Hardware (SMASH), and Desktop and Mobile Architecture for Server Hardware (DASH). Others are the

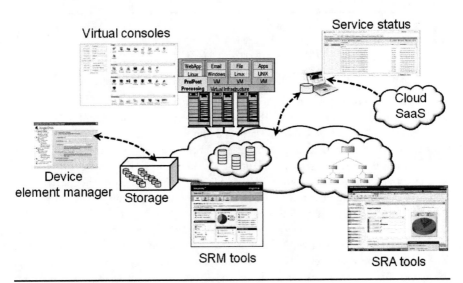

Figure 13.2 Management tool interfaces.

European Telecommunications Standards Institute (ETSI), Intel's Open Data Center Alliance, the National Institute of Standards and Technology (NIST), the Open Cloud Consortium (OCC), Open Cloud Computing Interface (OCCI), Open Grid Forum (OGF), Object Management Group (OMG), and Organization for the Advancement of Structured Information Standards (OASIS). Other initiatives and standards include Simple Network Management Protocol (SNMP), Management Information Bases (MIB), Storage Networking Industry Association (SNIA) Storage Management Initiative Specification (SMIS), and Cloud Data Management Interface (CDMI).

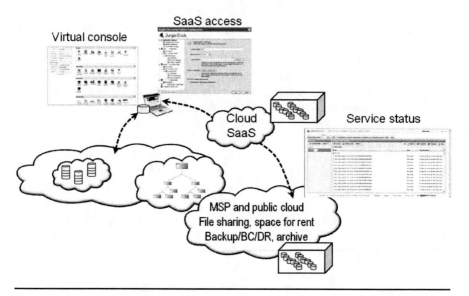

Figure 13.3   Cloud storage dashboards.

13.4. End-to-End Management

An important need when moving to a cloud or virtualized dynamic environment is to have situational awareness of IT resources. This means having insight into how IT resources are being deployed to support business applications and to meet service objectives in a cost-effective manner. Awareness of IT resource usage provides insight necessary for both tactical and strategic planning as well as decision making. Put another way, effective management requires knowing not only what resources are at hand but also how they are being used, in order to decide where different applications and data should be placed to meet business requirements.

Behind the layers of abstraction and virtualization are physical resources (servers, storage, networks, and software) that need to be managed in a coordinated manner. Key to managing resources effectively is being able to identify, track, and coordinate when and where those items are used for service delivery. It is also important to coordinate changes that occur across the different technology domains (servers, network, storage, appliances, and security) in a timely manner—for example, during physical-to-virtual (P2V), virtual-to-virtual (V2V), and virtual-to-physical (V2P) conversion, general IT resource consolidation, data center or storage movement, as well as for technology reconfiguration, refresh, and upgrades.

Common issues for managing physical and abstracted environments include:

- Finding, identifying, and tracking of logical-to-physical mappings
- Awareness of what resources are being used to deliver a given level of service
- Identifying where upgrades of hardware and software are needed
- Generating blueprints or documents to determine what to move where and when
- Facilitating task execution and workflow across technology management groups
- Error-prone manual interaction with various technology tools
- Resolving multiple-vendor, multiple-technology interoperability dependencies

The business benefit of virtualization and other forms of abstraction is providing transparency and agility. However, an additional layer of complexity is introduced that requires end-to-end (E2E) cross-technology management. Storage and networks are needed for IT organizations to effectively manage their resources and deliver applications services to business user and systems resource analysis (SRA) tools to support collection and correlation of data from servers.

Essentially, a new category of tools that provide E2E SRA and data protection management (DPM) are needed for planning and migrating while enabling ongoing management of either a virtualized environment or a traditional IT environment. Cross-technology domain SRA and discovery tools can help identify what is in place, what is needed, and where, when, why, and how to deploy those resources, as well as facilitate the effective delivery of IT services to the business. Three important capabilities that are needed for enabling IT and data storage transformation to a more dynamic cloud, virtualized, or other form of abstracted environment are migration automation, workflow, and configuration management.

Another important capability is visibility (or situational awareness) into common IRM tasks including BC, DR, DPM, resource tracking, change management, and performance capacity planning. Tools should provide situational awareness, including identifying resource usage and allocation, while providing insight into physical resource mappings in dynamic environments. In addition, tools should enable coordinated workflow management, including workflow generation, identifying areas in need of configuration change, and streamlining data and storage migration movement activities. E2E cross-technology management involves mapping service requests to service categories and templates to drive IRM and other functional tasks to enable information services deliver (Figure 13.4).

Figure 13.4 shows the importance and role of management in moving from service category requirements to specific tasks in support of services delivery. Streamlining service delivery and enabling efficiency involves working smarter as well as more effectively. Automation can be used for recurring routine tasks including resource provisioning, event correlation, and analysis, enabling IT staffs to focus on knowledge tasks and analysis.

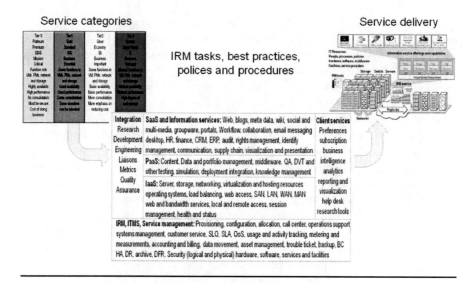

Figure 13.4   Management and service delivery enablement.

13.5. Licensing Topics

Licensing and fees apply to physical, virtual, and cloud resources and related services. How products and services are licensed varies, from capacity or performance to per-seat, -device, or -user, along with enterprise and site options. Software or tools may be licensed on a one-time, perpetual basis or on a time-duration basis. Perpetual-use licenses may be for a specific server or workstation or for a given number included in the fee, with updates or support also included for some amount of time.

Software and tools can be licensed by

- Flat fee per single or multiple copies, with or without support
- Perpetual (no time limit) until you buy a new version
- Limited time during which to use the software, get updates, and receive support
- Commercial, education, government, or personal use
- Enterprise or organization-wide and site-based
- Individual applications, systems, servers, or workstations
- Physical server or workstation instance
- Per CPU (single, multicore, or socket-based), physical or virtual
- Unlimited or on an hourly rate basis
- Per user, seat, or workstation (total or concurrent in use)
- Volume purchasing programs and tiered pricing

In addition to licensing fees, other fees cover maintenance and support. Consider tools with associated licensing and ongoing maintenance costs from a return-on-improvement basis. That is, does a tool help improve your environment [including supporting growth demands, maintaining or enhancing quality of service (QoS) and service-level objectives (SLOs)] while reducing per-unit costs? This requires insight and metrics to know how your environment is currently running and to determine the impact of a contemplated change. In addition to licensing application software, associated tools, and operating systems, virtualization adds another component or layer to be included. Depending on the hypervisor and tools being used, additional licensing fees and maintenance costs will probably apply. When using a cloud service for virtual machines or applications, licensing fees may be included as part of the package or subscription, or you may have to bring your own licenses as part of your VM.

Some hypervisors are available for free or at a lower price if they are not included with other software such as Microsoft Hyper-V and Windows Server. Management tools and additional functionalities may be required to be licensed to use with lower-cost or free versions of hypervisors. Hypervisor vendors including Citrix, Microsoft, and VMware, and third parties, have license management tools. Software licensing should not impede the value of virtualization or clouds to enable mobility and agility. This means making sure that your licenses are not restricted to running on a specific machine or given location. Also look into whether your current operating system and application tools licenses can be transferred as is, or if they need to be converted for free or a fee to be used in a VM or VDI environment. Server consolidation reduces physical hardware costs, but it does not by itself reduce software licensing fees. Depending on how you consolidate the number of VMs on a PM, the number of licensed guest operating systems may increase with their applications and VM fees. Consequently, tracking software or other services fees and licenses is as important as tracking IT resources. This means having reporting and metrics to show what tools you have, what licenses are in use, what are available for use, and what additional licenses may be needed.

A different approach that most software tool or service providers have been hesitant to embrace is a fee based on the benefit you receive from using the tool. This is a more complex model without clear metrics, and this complexity, along with the subjectivity of the returned value, is often cited as the reason for using a more straightforward fee model. However, there are opportunities for hybrid fee systems that combine some baseline or legacy fee with a bonus for the vendor if its tool is more productive. For the customer the benefit is lower initial cost, while any premium paid to the vendor is made up for by savings realized. Instead of profit sharing, think of it as "productivity sharing," with a vendor, supplier, or service provider benefiting by partnering with a customer. When or if this will happen is anyone's guess. However, part of what drives innovation is looking at things differently, so perhaps we will see someone enabling customers to do more by truly partnering with them instead of just delivering sales and marketing lip service.

Software, tool, cloud, and virtualization licensing consolidation involves the following considerations:

- Licensing for virtual environments should involve contracts and system administrators.

- Software licenses should be included as part of an IT resource capacity plan forecast process.
- When allocating VMs from templates, be sure there are provisional licenses available.
- Know how and when VMs are counted; is it an annual spot check or an average?
- Have a license review performed to ensure that you are getting the best ROI on those resources.
- Leverage tiered hypervisors from different vendors aligned to various service needs.
- Align the applicable tier of hypervisors and tools to the level of service needed.
- Per-VM licensing can be good fit for systems that do not lend themselves to consolidation.
- Per-physical-server licensing can be a good fit for applications that can be consolidated.
- If your organizations is concerned about hardware costs, then also focus on software fees

13.6. The Evolving Role of Management Tools

Management tools and software should help to reduce, or at least mask, complexity—as opposed to increasing complexity and activity for your environment. Tools can be used to help drive IRM or ITSM innovation by supporting growth demands, maintaining or enhancing SLOs, SLAs, and QoS while reducing per-unit costs. Part of innovation involves making better use of IT resources without negatively impacting QoS or SLOs. This innovation should apply to hardware, software, facilities, and people.

The primary objective of most business and organizations is not to support management. Businesses exist to transform and deliver services, leveraging various resources that are managed. Cloud, virtual, and data storage network environments should not exist to host or serve the needs of management; instead, management is there to make storage networks more effective and efficient. Management of resources including IRM, ITSM, and other activities should be focused on driving innovation, supporting demand, and maintaining or enhancing QoS and service delivery, while reducing per-unit costs including waste or rework. Management in the form of people, policies, best practices, and organizational boundaries and technology should not add to the complexity of information services delivery.

Management and tool considerations include:

- What is the focus or scope of the solution or service?
- Will you be able to use the tool, technology, or service across different products?
- How do tools work with other vendors' technologies, solutions, or services?
- What interfaces, protocols, and APIs are supported for free or fee?
- What metrics or measurements can the tool leverage from other sources?
- Is a tool integrated by name and branding or with actual technology?

- How is licensing of the technology along with plug-ins and maintenance priced?
- How does the technology feed information and results to other utilities?
- Does the solution or service reduce your infrastructure complexity or add to it?
- What are the scalability capabilities of the tool?

13.7. Hard vs. Soft Products

A *soft product* (not to be confused with software) is the result of how various resources including hardware or software are delivered as a service. A *hard product* is some technology such as hardware (server, storage, network, or workstation), software, or service, including network bandwidth, that can be used or deployed in different ways. Soft product refers to what you do with the hard product technologies to deliver various services combining best practices, personalities, or functionalities via configuration, look and feel, and other forms of customization.

Put a different way, soft product is how your services differ from someone else's using the same hard products. This means that different organizations can be using the same hardware, software, or networking and cloud services; it's what you do with those resources, and how you configure and manage them, that become the soft products. For example, two different airlines can buy a Boeing 737 jet airplane from the manufacturer at different prices, with the pricing difference based on volume discounts. The airplanes will be painted differently but have similar if not the same engines and basic components. How the two different airlines configure them with seat pitch and comfort, how they staff those planes once in service, and the in-flight service (or lack thereof) differentiates their soft products.

Building on that example, how two different airlines manage their fleet of aircraft, plan for new airplanes, forecast staffing and fuel, and manage customer service delivery using various tools is also part of their soft product. Going back to the factory theme used throughout this book, information factories such as cloud or managed service providers and hosting sites often use the same hardware or software tools—it's how they manage those resources and their service offerings that define their soft product.

Part of enabling cloud and virtual environments is to use different tools combined with service offerings and metrics as discussed earlier in this book to establish or deliver your particular soft product. The importance of understanding soft products is that what goes into making them has different costs or enables various services while using common components. Leveraging different metrics and measurements provides insight into how services are being delivered while reducing waste or rework that takes away from productivity while increasing costs. For example, focusing solely on reducing costs, driving up utilization without concern for service delivery along with QoS, SLOs, and SLAs, can result in poor customer satisfaction, rework, or other forms of waste (i.e., lost productivity). Maximizing resources is part of the objective for reducing costs, but so is reducing complexity, waste, rework, and other lost opportunities, including downtime or delays in enabling new services.

Automation can help to address time-consuming and error-prone common processes such as analysis of event logs, resource discovery, service-level monitoring, and change validation. Cross-domain systems resource analysis can help organizations manage resources more effectively by spotting trends through looking at various event or activity logs to identify issues before they become problems. Similar practices can also be applied to looking at various performances, usage, activity, events, and configuration information to monitor how resources are being used to meet service delivery.

In addition to basic monitoring and baseline comparisons, SRA and other tools can be used for proactively notifying staff or automated tools and policies managers to take corrective action to avert a service disruption or slowdown. As in traditional factories, reduced cost and improved customer service can be achieved while boosting activity via leveraging a combination of automation, tools, metrics for insight and situational awareness, as well as standard repeatable processes or procedures. In other words, maximize the main IT resource of skilled staff members' time by enabling them to work more effectively, and acknowledge specific tasks and occasional exceptions instead of addressing each service request as a custom undertaking.

13.8. The Other IT Resources: People, Processes, and Policies

Beyond the idea of combining multiple functions into a single product, the business objective and value proposition of converged technology includes reducing complexity, resulting in lower costs while, hopefully, boosting productivity and thus profitability. In some cases convergence can address ease of acquisition or product selection, while in others it's doing more with less, stretching budgets, consolidating, or enabling new functionality. Something to be considered before a convergence technology is deployed is how organizational processes, best practices, and staffing are aligned to support a given technology. For example, who owns the network, whether that is the physical cable, the switches, or protocols that are supported on those technologies? In some organizations the journey to convergence is well underway, while for others the technology may be in motion but with leveraging it to its full potential still a distance goal. For example, a converged network switch may be installed, but it is still being used as either a LAN or SAN box managed by either the network or storage group.

Building from the example of a network core switch, there are two things to consider. First, the switch is being managed as a box as opposed to a resource. Second, the box is being managed as either a LAN device by the networking group or as a SAN device by the server or storage group. Some organizations have taken an intermediate step of having combined groups managing connectivity devices; however, they are often still approached from either a LAN or SAN perspective or philosophy.

The barrier to leveraging converged technologies is not necessarily the people; it may be organizational boundaries, processes, procedures, and policies. Certainly, staff personal preferences and experiences are a factor to consider. For example, someone who has always worked with networking or LAN may be expected to see things differently than someone with a server or storage background. Similarly, someone with an open systems server and storage background might see and approach things differently than a person with mainframe experience.

While discussions or, in some cases, conflicts, may revolve around physical cables, boxes, management tools, configurations, or other tangible items, the real issue may be control. Another contributor to barriers is the organizational structure or politics of technology as a result of who reports to whom or whose budget is used. The net result is that a converged device, a network switch, a converged network adapter (CNA), management tools, server, storage, and other resources to support cloud and virtual environments are deployed as vertical or function-specific technologies. For example, a switch or adapter might be used for LAN or SAN, but not both.

It's necessary to look beyond the cable or box and identify what organizational process as well as technology culture barriers can be changed to realize benefits of converged technology. While it's important to know about the tools and technologies, it's also important to understand what to use when, where, and why and the associated best practices or policies so that they do not become barriers. In addition to preparing from a technology standpoint, it is important to consider how organizational structure, workflow, best practices, and processes are prepared to leverage the next step in converging network technologies. This means getting LAN and SAN as well as server people together to generate awareness of each others' respective wants and requirements while identifying common ground or objectives and areas that require remediation.

Leveraging converged technology means managing resources differently. Instead of managing the physical box, cable, or adapter, move to managing the processes, protocols, procedures, and policies that support the respective technology domain areas as well as those that are converged. Moving to a converged infrastructure for cloud, virtual, or physical environments means converged or unified management. Hybrid teams made up of professionals with server, storage, networking hardware, and software experience working together can identify existing process or procedural bottlenecks. Bottlenecks may be the result of a "that's how is been done in the past" mindset toward a particular technology area. SAN personnel, for instance, have traditionally had a focus on low latency, deterministic performance, and service delivery. LAN pros have had interoperability and ubiquity as common tenets. SAN people usually think in terms of block or files, while LAN people thing in terms of TCP/IP and associated technologies. Instead of debating who owns the cable or what the best cable is, converged management groups need to move beyond the physical to a logical and abstracted view. Who owns the protocols and associated processes as well as how are common technologies managed for effective service delivery? Think in terms of how workflows can be streamlined by leveraging the best of and experiences of different technology groups.

The initial deployment of converged networking solutions may initially be in a coexistent mode where, essentially, it is used for traditional LAN or SAN box-type functionality. The next step would be to leverage the converged capabilities, moving beyond the box with the technology as well as from an organization management approach. Break down organizational barriers to enable cross-technology domain and E2E management by establishing virtual teams. Over time, different groups should learn why their counterparts think and do things a certain way. Working as virtual teams in support of cloud, virtual, and physical technologies, new processes and providers, as well as best practices can be developed and deployed.

13.9. Common Management-Related Questions

With stacks and solution bundles, is storage or system management dead? Storage and systems management involves tools, people, and best practices. Some integrated solutions combining hardware and software tools can simplify certain tasks, while automation can be used for common time-consuming activities. By freeing up time from routine tasks, storage and system management staff resources can be made available for knowledge and value-adding activities.

Should I have a single management tool that does everything? A single pane of glass, which is a management tool that fits on a single physical or virtual display, may be a goal, but the cost along with the complexity associated with deploying various technologies remains a barrier to deployment. Federated as well as orchestration tools that support cross-technology domain activity across multiple resources can help to simplify and streamline management activities.

13.10. Chapter Summary

While virtualization, cloud, and other techniques or tools for enabling dynamic IT environments help abstract physical resources from applications, the need for E2E management tools providing situational awareness may be more important. Gaining insight into what you have, establishing a baseline, knowing how things are running, finding bottlenecks and issues, removing complexity instead of moving or masking it, and avoiding aggregation causing aggravation are all vital. Appropriate management tools can help identify and track configuration and interdependencies among various server, storage, and networking resources.

With abstraction comes some simplicity, but there is also additional complexity that needs to be managed by having a clear and timely view of how resources are being used and allocated. In addition to needing situational awareness via systems resource analysis tools, virtualized or abstracted environments also need to have streamlined common workflow management. Speed, agility, and accuracy are important to support dynamic IT environments. Consequently, tools that can identity, track, support automation, and enable workflow files for various vendors' technologies become essential for IT organizations moving to abstracted environments.

General action items include:

- Optimize your organization to leverage cloud, virtual, and converged technologies.
- Apply automation where it makes sense for common recurring tasks.
- Apply people power where it makes sense in knowledge-based activities.

- Make tools work for you, not the other way around, to avoid adding complexity.
- Have multiple tools in your IT toolbox and know when, where, why, and how to use them.
- Look at tool and licensing from a return-on-improvement, or return-on-innovation, basis.
- Manage your software licenses as diligently as your server, storage, and networking resources.

The following vendors, along with those mentioned in previous chapters, provide tools for managing cloud, virtual, and data storage networking environments: Amazon, Aptare, Autotask, BMC, CA, Commvault, Cisco, Citrix, Cloudera, Ctera, Dell, EMC, Enstratus, Fujitsu, Google, Gluster, HP, Hitachi, HyperIO, IBM, JAM, Joynet, Mezeo, Microsoft, Netapp, Network Instruments, Open Stack, Oracle, Quest, Racemi, Rightscale, SANpulse, Seagate, SGI, Solarwinds, Storage fusion, StoredIQ, Symantec, Teamquest, Veeam, Viridity, Virtual Bridges, VMware, Whatsupgold/ Ipswitch, and Zetta.

Chapter 14

Applying What You Have Learned

It's not what or who you know, it's how you use it that matters

— Greg Schulz

In This Chapter

- The importance of having a vision, a strategy, and a plan
- What to look for when evaluating and comparing various technologies
- Leveraging various approaches for effective information services delivery

This chapter ties together the various technologies, techniques, and topics covered in this book, to enable more efficient and effective information services delivery, including what can be done today and how to prepare for tomorrow.

14.1. Getting Started

So far this journey has spanned 13 chapters, considering the need and the opportunities for cloud, virtualization, and data storage networking along with various techniques and technologies for enabling efficient, effective, agile, scalable, and resilient data infrastructures. Back in Chapter 1, I made the statement that you probably didn't wake up one morning thinking, "I need to have someone buy or implement a cloud, virtualization, or storage networking solution." Another theme of this book is that there must be continued support to deliver information services while reducing costs and maintaining or enhancing quality of service, service-level objectives, and service-level agreements. This requires innovation—enabling your customers to do and be more effective or to facilitate new functionality. How you achieve innovation involves using various hard products (hardware, software, networks, and services) to create different soft products while leveraging best practices, policies, and people skill sets.

Innovation also means transforming how resources are acquired, deployed, managed, and disposed of when they are no longer cost-effective to use. Perhaps since we started this journey you have seen an opportunity for clouds, virtualization, and data storage networking technologies to play a role in your environment today or in the future. That role could mean coexisting with and complementing what and how your current environment functions, or replacing it. On the other hand, you may still be asking why you need a cloud, virtualized, or data storage networking environment.

14.2. Don't Be Afraid, but Look Before You Leap

A continuing theme of this book is "Don't be afraid, but look before you leap, and move beyond the hype." This means taking a step back and asking again: Do you want or need a cloud, and for what reasons? Do you need or want virtualization, and why? Can you reduce the number of software licenses and management complexity to support growth, reduce costs, while maintaining or enhancing QoS and SLAs? Is your staff or you able to manage more resources and services? Despite the hype, not all environments are ready to move to public, private, or hybrid cloud solutions or services. There are, however, public, private, and hybrid cloud services and solutions that are real and worth looking into.

Moving beyond hype and fud (fear, uncertainty, and doubt) also means testing the waters, so to speak, by doing proof-of-concepts (POCs) or trials of various solutions and services. The objective of a POC is to determine how the service or solution fits your current and future business requirements, SLOs, QoS, and SLAs and technical requirements. POCs also will help you gain comfort and confidence in the technologies and tools, as well as provide an opportunity to refine or develop new best practices for incorporating cloud services and solutions into your environment. Virtualization should be looked at beyond the context of consolidation, with an expanded view of how it can be used to remove complexity, enabling agility and flexibility for various IRM functions. Of course, there also needs to be consideration of the financial or commercial aspects, determining the return on investment (ROI) and the total cost of ownership (TCO) of different approaches, techniques, and technologies. Determining the ROI and TCO along with general cost comparisons should be on an apples-to-apples comparison basis, looking at functionality, SLAs, SLOs, resiliency, and other capabilities required to meet given levels of service. An informed buyer is an empowered buyer of traditional hardware and software as well as of cloud and virtualization services or solutions.

An informed seller whether a value-added reseller (VAR), a consultant, or a manufacturer, is able to adapt to different opportunities and react quickly to changing market dynamics. For example, if your competitors are all trying to sell the same server or desktop virtualization story to eliminate hardware yet are spinning their wheels due to customer resistance, change your approach—go to a different scenario or add a new one. For example, after your competition leaves in frustration because they cannot sell a solution such as consolidation to your prospect, sit down and find out the real resistance or, more likely, cause for concern. You might find out that it is QoS or performance or availability or security or some other issue that can be addressed with a different tool or technique. In the course of addressing those challenges you can spark the customer's interest in what you and your competitors were originally trying to sell them.

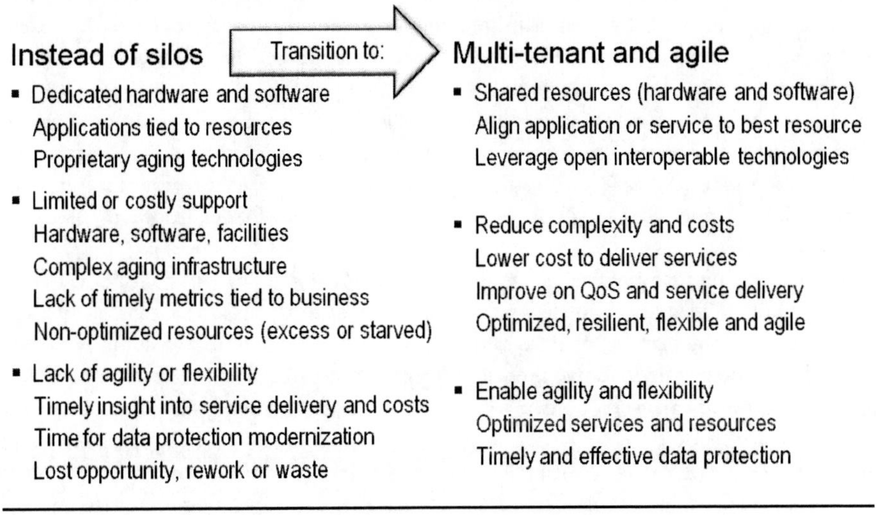

Instead of silos   Transition to: **Multi-tenant and agile**

- Dedicated hardware and software
  Applications tied to resources
  Proprietary aging technologies

- Limited or costly support
  Hardware, software, facilities
  Complex aging infrastructure
  Lack of timely metrics tied to business
  Non-optimized resources (excess or starved)

- Lack of agility or flexibility
  Timely insight into service delivery and costs
  Time for data protection modernization
  Lost opportunity, rework or waste

- Shared resources (hardware and software)
  Align application or service to best resource
  Leverage open interoperable technologies

- Reduce complexity and costs
  Lower cost to deliver services
  Improve on QoS and service delivery
  Optimized, resilient, flexible and agile

- Enable agility and flexibility
  Optimized services and resources
  Timely and effective data protection

Figure 14.1   Removing IT barriers and enabling delivery productivity.

14.3. Addressing Issues and Challenges While Enabling Opportunities

Many organizations have an interest in becoming efficient and effective in using their resources for information services delivery, regardless of whether they are or will be using cloud and virtualization techniques. As a result, some organizations will for now adopt what can be called cloudlike management or operating paradigms. Some environments will purchase private cloud solution bundles or stacks, while others leverage what they have and focus on processes, procedures, refining metrics, and aligning service-level expectations.

Either way, the journey will continue, with changes in technologies, techniques, plans, strategies, and visions. As a result, your vision, strategy, and plan should change over time to adapt to changing business requirements, challenges, and opportunities. As new technologies and techniques evolve, always look for opportunities to leverage those that canwork for you while providing a ROI or other benefit. Figure 14.1 shows on the left common issues and barriers that inhibit or add cost to information services delivery, with objectives or goals listed on the right.

Transformation (see Figure 14.1) can be enabled with different technologies, tools, and best practices in various combinations to meet your particular needs. Progress means more than a focus on boosting utilization to reduce cost while supporting growth. While boosting utilization is a part of transformation, reducing waste or rework in terms of lost staff time due to workflow and process complexities should also be considered. For example, as a means of reducing costs due to lost productivity of staff or clients and missed opportunities, streamlined workflows or templates aligned to service classes or categories can help speed resource provisioning. Another example is reducing the time required to migrate from an existing storage system to a new one or to a cloud or MSP by streamlining the workflows and processes across different server, storage, networking, hardware, software, data protection, and security technology domains or management groups.

As a consumer of information resources, the faster your request can be processed and resources made available, the sooner you can be more productive. As a provider of information services, by streamlining and enabling faster resource provisioning, your staff and other resources can do more in the same amount of time, improving per-unit costs and ROI.

Streamlining may involve use of automated tools to take care of routine recurring tasks, freeing skilled and knowledgeable workers to spend time with clients or users to guide them to the best fit for using various resources. For example, a combination of wizards can help guide a consumer or information services user on how to access or get resources and can be combined with pop-up live chat dialogues by which someone can assist with questions. Another variation is to enable skilled staff members to sit down physically or virtually with clients to work through adding value for larger, more complex scenarios, leveraging time that was made available by being more streamlined in workflow and other process.

14.4. What's Your Vision, Strategy, and Plan?

Unless you have the time and resources to just pick up and travel to whereever the pro-verbial wind takes you, most journeys involve some form of vision, strategy, and plan. The vision is where you are going, the strategy is how the journey will be accomplished, and the plan is what to do when, where, and how. Part of the plan involves determining your options for getting from point A to point B, what you can take with you and what you will have to leave behind, considering the logistics and the economics. Another part of the plan includes metrics and management tools for monitoring where you are, your current status, including finances, schedules, and other factors.

Your vision, strategy, and plan for your organization's networking should align business needs and opportunity with technology capabilities. Rather than starting with the technology or buzzword items such as storage, converged networking, dedupe, physical or virtual servers, clouds, chargeback, and frameworks, take a step back and ask how those elements fit into enabling your vision, strategy, and plan. Do they add cost and complexity or enable productivity and streamlining of information services delivery? Do you want those technologies, tools, and techniques, or do you need them? Can you afford to have them? If the tools, techniques, and technologies do not fit, is it because your vision, strategy, and plan need to evolve to leverage those items in the course of addressing business needs? Or do you have a situation where the solution is looking for a problem to solve?

Taking that step back can help set the appropriate level of expectation and avoid being disappointed or frustrated due to misperceptions of capabilities. It may be that today a cloud or virtualized or converged storage environment should remain on your wish list while you prepare your environment for the next step by gaining control, implementing metrics, reducing your data footprint impact, or modernizing your data protection to become more agile. In addition, you may do some initial POCs around cloud for backup/restore, BC, DR, archive, or general storage sharing, and virtualize some servers to prepare for the next phase of your journey while refining your business model.

The journey to enabling an information factory, regardless of whether you choose to call it IT 2.0, 3.0, 4.0, or cloud (public, private, hybrid), dynamic or virtual, involves a vision, a strategy, and a plan. The vision will evolve over time, the strategy will be refined to support new requirements or leverage opportunities, while the plan is in constant motion and will be updated as you go. Figure 14.2 shows a simplified "converged" vision, strategy, and plan that have been reduced to a single figure representing details that span more pages than are found in this book. It is, however, a path to enable a continuing journey that you can refine to meet your specific vision and strategy needs with a plan for what to do today, near-term, and long-term. Part of the plan should include revisiting the vision, strategy, and plan on a periodic basis.

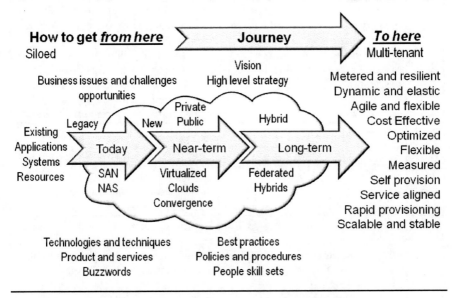

Figure 14.2   Enabling the information factory using a phased approach.

Clouds, virtualization, and data storage networks, along with convergence and other technologies and techniques discussed in previous chapters, can be used to meet various objectives and requirements of your vision, strategy, and plan. The solution for your environment will vary (see Table 14.1) based on your needs, requirements, budget, and business objectives and will involve various techniques, technologies, and services. Common objectives and requirements for IT services delivery, including traditional IT environments along with cloud and MSP, include boosting productivity, reducing costs, enhancing QoS and SLA, optimizing service delivery, and reducing complexity, waste, and rework while stretching budgets further. Additional objectives include reducing time and cost for data protection while enhancing coverage as well as business resiliency.

How various hard products (hardware, software, networks, and services) are combined with your best practices, policies, and service templates will determine your soft product. Your soft product or services being delivered may combine different types of public, private, or hybrid clouds to varying degrees, from all in (everything done in the cloud) to some lesser amount. Likewise, some of your resources may be virtualized, with the initial focus on consolidation expanding into enablement of agility and flexibility.

Table 14.1 When and Where to Use Various Public and Private Cloud Services

	Private Cloud	Public Cloud
	More control. May be cost-effective if demand can use the resources.	Less control. May be more dynamic with lower cost if aligned with SLO and SLA requirements.
SaaS	Migrate existing applications delivery to a Web services model, speed up and support new development. Free up internal resources for other critical applications or services.	Rapid access to new services or functionality or supplement existing capabilities. Some email from in-house to a public service, keeping critical or sensitive users on existing systems. Leverage cloud backup for remote offices/branch offices, workgroups, and mobile personal.
PaaS	Develop and deploy new applications that allow movement between private, public, and hybrid environments.	Develop and deploy new applications into public or private cloud environments. Deploy your applications using various development environments onto elastic platforms.
IaaS	Local and remote, virtual and physical servers, desktops, storage and networking resources delivered as an on-demand, measured service.	Pay for resources (or for free), various service levels, complement your data center and resources, balance peaks and demands, leverage your resources more effectively, rapid start-up.

14.5. What to Consider When Evaluating Technologies, Techniques, and Services

When considering cloud services and solutions, look beyond the cost per gigabyte for cloud storage to the level of service aligned with your service needs. Clouds and MSP services need to be trusted and have SLOs and SLAs to meet your requirements. Much like when buying servers, storage, networking hardware, and software, consider more than just cost as the definition of value. For some functionalities, free or very-low-cost on-line services can have value in their use or based on the value of the information to be stored or service accessed. In addition to base price, look into the fees for optional services and for exceeding your base resource. Some services allow you to store your information or access certain functions for free while charging for retrieving or accessing or using advanced features. Take a few minutes and read the on-line terms of services (TOS) agreement before clicking "yes." You might be surprised what some TOS contain, including how you can use the service, from what countries or locations to what types of information.

When deciding to move ahead with a virtualization, cloud, storage, or converged networking project or other optimization initiative, talk with other organizations similar to yours to see what worked, what didn't, and why. Keep in mind that what didn't work for one environment may work for another and vice versa. What I mean by this is that the same tools, technology, techniques, or hard products may be deployed differently to achieve various soft product results. The various services and soft products of one organization may differ from those of another even if they are in the same business or industry. As a result, understand why things worked and why other things did not, so that you can plan for those conditions or situations.

When you move your data and applications to a public cloud environment, you are trusting that you will be able to access those items when needed. This makes it important to consider the flexibility to move data and applications between cloud and virtualized environments in a timely, cost-effective manner to address changing business needs and leverage changing solution or service provider capabilities. Also look into how you will initially move data and applications into the new environment, and what existing tools will work and which will require an upgrade, along with associated costs. Explore the service provider's or, in the case of a product, the vendor's support capabilities, including having staff members contact the support center during off-hours to see how they help troubleshoot problems. Another technique is to have some of your less experienced staff contact the support center with a vague description of a problem to see how easily and quickly they can diagnose problems.

Another consideration when evaluating cloud and MSPs is to understand their HA, BC, and DR plan or capabilities, including what they will disclose publicly and what is under a nondisclosure agreement (NDA). If you are going to rely on a service or solution for part of your HA, BC, and DR, that resource should not become a single point of failure or weak spot in your environment. As part of understanding the service's capabilities, find out where on-line copies of data are kept, including foreign countries, to comply with regulations if applicable. Also determine if there are additional fees for your data to be copied to other locations, or the copy is free but access to the data has a fee.

14.6. Common Cloud, Virtualization and Data Storage Networking Questions

What are the most common questions I get asked? The most common questions from IT professionals are what service or vendor and product are the best, and whether clouds and virtualization are all hype or fud. My response to the latter is advice to look beyond the hype and fud to see what a given solution or service enables your environment to address or fix without adding cost or complexity. As to what is the best service, vendor, or cloud product, that will be whichever one meets or exceeds your requirements including SLAs in a cost-effective manner and is one that you are willing to trust your information or services to.

Are clouds for everyone? Clouds can be used by and have value for most people and organizations; however, not everyone is necessarily ready to use or leverage them.

Do virtualization and clouds add complexity? Yes, but depending on how they are deployed and with what tools, they can mask the added complexity, enabling additional benefits to your environment.

Can metering, measuring, reporting, and chargeback influence resource usage behavior? Yes, this is something to keep in mind. If, for example, you price a particular service high as a premium capability (regardless of whether you actually send an invoice or not), it can help direct consumers to a lower-cost capability. On the other hand, if the consumers are shopping or comparing yours or an external provider's service on price alone, they may be missing out on SLO and SLA factors. Another example is that if you want to force users to keep more data on disk instead of tape in archive, then make the tape-based archive a premium offering. However, when you find more data being stored on disk and less in a tape archive along with cost to deliver your services related challenges, it may be time to review your bill of materials, service categories, cost structures, and how you market or promote those.

Do clouds and virtualization automatically clean up or mask IT mistakes? Clouds and virtualization can abstract or hide problems, perhaps buying time until you can fix them. On the other hand, cloud, virtualization, or data storage networks can create problems if they are not deployed properly. This means getting ready ahead of time to use those resources, including cleaning up your data footprint impact or identifying bottlenecks and problems rather than simply moving them elsewhere.

Do clouds automatically provision and determine the best location to place or optimize data and applications for users? Some cloud services leverage templates, GUIs, or wizards that can automate the process of provisioning and making resources available to you. However, someone needs to set up and manage those service templates, guides, and wizards along with doing the analysis for more complex environments.

Does all of this IRM, service classes, templates, and workflow discussion mean that IT organizations should start thinking and operating like service providers? Yes, even if your environment is not planning on deploying or using cloud technologies or expanding your virtualization activities, reviewing and assessing your service categories is important. This means working with clients to revisit what their requirements are, what they want, and what they can afford. There is a common myth that clouds are clouds if and only if they support chargeback; this can be true for service providers generating invoices or billing for usage. However, what is needed are metering, measurements, and accounting of resources being used to map to services being delivered.

Is it really cheaper to go to the cloud? That depends on whether you are using a for-free or fee-based service, what level of service you are getting, what you need, and other factors. Look beyond the low-cost value proposition of clouds, expanding the focus to include value, trust, enablement, and considerations in your comparisons. For example, while writing this book I changed my cloud backup provider not because of cost—in fact, had I stayed with the previous provider, I would have saved money. I changed to gain additional functionality that enabled me to do more things which ended up having more value and hence a better ROI.

How do you get your data back when a cloud provider shuts down a service? This is a very important question, as there will be more shakeout and changes occurring in this area. Not all services will shut down, of course, and many of those that do will provide a period of time for you to phase out your usage and either get your data back or allow it to expire and be deleted as its retention ends. For other applications and data you may have to migrate your data by exporting it and then re-importing it elsewhere or using a cloud gateway, appliance, software, or cpop as a transparency or virtualization layer in front of your cloud service providers to move information around. For bulk restore and import, most services have offerings either included in packages or for optional fee to support shipping of data on various removable media.

What are the barriers to cloud, virtualization, and data protect modernization? There can be many barriers, ranging from lack of trust or confidence to limited budget resources to fund the projects. Working with VARs and consultants as well as vendors or service providers, you can establish a strategy and plan to find ways to implement changes that produce savings, which in turn help fund subsequent steps. Having the right metrics to know how your environment is running and the services being delivered is also important to provide baselines for building TCO and ROI models for comparisons or decision making.

14.7. Chapter Summary

I have mentioned it before and will say it again: Generally speaking, there are not bad technologies or techniques, but there are poor implementations, decisions, and deployments of tools or techniques used for the wrong task.

General action items include:

- If you do not have one, develop a vision, strategy, and plan.
- If you have one, continue to refine your vision, strategy, and plan.
- Do a proof-of-concept with clouds, virtualization, and storage networking.
- Gain experience; discover gaps to refine policies and best practices.
- Leverage metrics and measurements to be an informed buyer and service provider.
- Market and promote your information services capabilities to your consumers.
- Empower your users or consumers to be educated buyers who focus on value.

Chapter 15

Wrap-up, What's Next, and Book Summary

In This Chapter

- Where we have been, where we are going
- Efficiency vs. effectiveness
- What to do next
- What to look for in the future
- Closing comments

15.1. Wrapping up This Part of the Journey

Back in Chapter 1, I posed a question about clouds and virtualization. That question was whether you or your customer woke up that morning wondering about a cloud, virtual, converged, or data storage networking environment or solution.

If you are not a vendor, consultant, analyst, journalist, or someone responsible for IT-related solutions for your organization, typically the need to buy and deploy a new solution is tied to solving some business issue. You may wake up in the morning thinking about how to transform and evolve your information services delivery model into a more efficient, effective, cost-optimized, resilient, flexible, and scalable services-oriented environment. Rather than the question of do you need or want a cloud, virtualization, convergence, or data storage networking, turn the discussion around. Ask how you can enable your information services environment to become more agile, flexible, efficient, and cost-effective, and what tools, technologies, techniques, best practices, and people skill sets can help facilitate your specific objectives.

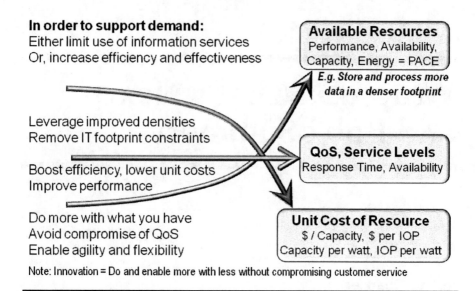

In order to support demand:
Either limit use of information services
Or, increase efficiency and effectiveness

Available Resources
Performance, Availability,
Capacity, Energy = PACE

*E.g. Store and process more
data in a denser footprint*

Leverage improved densities
Remove IT footprint constraints

QoS, Service Levels
Response Time, Availability

Boost efficiency, lower unit costs
Improve performance

Do more with what you have
Avoid compromise of QoS
Enable agility and flexibility

Unit Cost of Resource
$ / Capacity, $ per IOP
Capacity per watt, IOP per watt

Note: Innovation = Do and enable more with less without compromising customer service

Figure 15.1   Addressing information services delivery demand for innovation.

15.2. Where Have We Been, Where Are We Going: From Efficiency to Effectiveness

Through the various chapters in this book we have been on a journey of sorts, and now we have arrived at our destination. Granted, this destination may not be the endpoint of your journey; it may instead be way point, layover, or stopping-off point for some period of time. Similarly, the technologies, tools, and techniques discussed in this book may be for some the destination, while for others they will be vehicles or platforms for enabling continuing transformation and enablement. Your specific objective will vary depending on what you are trying to accomplish. Some people like to travel and enjoy the journey; some people like technology and are always looking for ways to use it. Other people tolerate travel as the price to pay to get to where they are going and have similar thoughts about technology.

The reason for using the travel analogies and the information factory examples is to help put the topics covered in this book into perspective while expanding your thinking. Some people are scared of flying or traveling, others tolerate it, and some, like me, enjoy it, albeit in moderation. Don't be scared of clouds, virtualization, data storage networking, and the idea of convergence; however, have a plan, look before you leap, and do your homework. By "doing your homework" I mean making applicable plans, arrangements, logistics, and packaging.

A common challenge in many organizations is exploding data growth and the associated management tasks and constraints, including budgets, staffing, time, physical facilities, floor space, and power and cooling. There will continue to be more data to move, process, store, preserve, and serve for decades to come. However, business and economic demands will continue for the foreseeable future to place limits on both capital and operating spending or budgets. The good news is that I am routinely hearing from IT organizations around the world that their budgets are increasing to varying degrees. The bad news, however, is that those same organizations have to do more with those budgets, including supporting growth, new applications, and functionality, while remaining competitive and maintaining or enhancing QoS, SLA, SLO, and reliability to meet compliance and other objectives.

Back in Chapter 1 there is a figure (see Figure 15.1) showing three curves, one aligned to supporting growth demands, another showing reducing cost per resource unit or service delivery, and the third tied to QoS, SLO, SLO, and other metrics related to the service delivery experience. Many IT organizations as well as service providers have been focused on improving efficiencies to reduce costs for business survival over the past several years. Some organizations have also expanded, or are in the process of doing, so their focus is on becoming more effective in addition to being efficient. Efficiency and effectiveness often are used interchangeably to mean reducing, conserving, consolidating, saving or avoiding, and/or increasing utilization to reduce costs. In reality, efficiency can be thought of as tactical and doing the right things, whether for conservation, reduction, saving, or avoidance.

Effectiveness should be thought of as doing the right things in the right place at the right time or aligning the applicable tool, techniques, or best practice to the task at hand with both a tactical and strategic objective. Where efficiency can be thought of as saving or reducing or driving up utilization, effectiveness takes into consideration reducing waste or lost opportunity from rework, retransmission, rebroadcast, poor response time, or lost availability. In Figure 15.1, innovation combines efficiency with effectiveness to support an increased amount of data and information in higher densities in terms of how much stored per cubic footprint, per watt of energy, or BTU of cooling, managed and protected per person and per software license, reduced overhead of data protection, and, of course, cost.

In Figure 15.1, effectiveness is supporting higher densities without introducing waste in terms of poor response time as utilization increases, retransmission of network traffic due to performance bottlenecks, downtime or lost availability while waiting for data to be restored or refreshed, or loss of goodwill or revenue due to information services not being available or accessible. Efficiency may mean consolidating underutilized storage capacity onto less large-capacity, lower-cost disk storage, either local, remote, or public cloud-based, where the focus is on cost per capacity per watt of energy. Effectiveness is consolidating I/O activity of underutilized storage capacity onto fewer high-performance devices, where the metric becomes cost per activity (transaction, I/O, page view, file access) per watt of energy.

During our journey, we have touched on many different technologies, trends, techniques, and best practices to help enable innovation to achieve the objectives of Figure 15.1 (support demand, maintain or enhance QoS, reduce per-unit and total cost to deliver service) in a balanced manner.

Speaking of energy, a common misperception is that Green IT is only about reducing CO_2 levels. The reality is that Green IT includes many other tenets, with a main theme of becoming more efficient, effective, and productive while supporting business and economic objectives with the side benefit of enabling environmental benefits. This has resulted in the "Green gap" (the disconnect between industry messaging and IT challenges and opportunities), where many IT organizations view Green IT as an environmental issue they would like be involved in but don't have sufficient funding for. Unfortunately, the Green gap results in missed opportunities to become more efficient, effective, and productive while helping the environment and sustaining business. I mention Green IT because there is a fog rolling in around clouds, where hype and messaging will cloud the themes around cloud computing (pun intended) and virtualization.

All popular technologies go through a hype cycle and then subside for a period of time in a trough of disillusionment. Technologies, techniques, and trends that have legs or lasting potential for the long term will reappear with new vigor, often after some additional technology maturity, ecosystem evolution, and increased education or awareness. Virtualization has gone from hype to trough and has since re-emerged, hitting its stride for consolidation and now expanding its focus to agility and flexibility. Consolidation is a fairly easy concept to grasp and a quick story to tell, so it has the initial focus. Agility and flexibility can have longer-term cost effectiveness benefits but take more time to understand and have a longer story. Now that story is being told and understood to help move virtualization beyond consolidation to the next wave for servers, storage, applications, networks, and desktops. Green IT has for the past couple of years been in the trough of disillusionment or at the bottom of the Green gap. Green IT is very much alive in the context of improving efficiency and effectiveness while helping the environment and boosting organizational agility and flexibility.

Clouds are currently at the top of the hype cycle and will go through some form of disillusionment; depending on how you view them, they may already be there. However, different variations of cloud products, technologies, services, and solutions will evolve, mature, and be around for the long haul in different shapes and forms. This is similar to how other information services delivery models, paradigms, and platforms (or stops on the IT journey) continue to live on as mainframe, service bureau, distributed minicomputers, time shares, PCs, outsourcing, client server, Web, insourcing, co-location, and hosting, among others.

15.3. What to Do Next

Optimize your data infrastructure (servers, storage, networks, facilities, services) and data as well as IRM activities (data protection, HA, BC, DR) from a performance, availability, capacity, energy, and economic (PACE) perspective. For example optimize performance with I/O consolidation to fewer, faster devices, including SSDs and 15.5K SAS as well as fast storage systems and performance accelerators, while finding and removing bottlenecks in the infrastructure and applications. Optimize availability to reduce, eliminate, or mask single points of failure, contain or isolate faults, and modernize how, when, and where data protection is done. This also means leveraging HA and

BC in an active manner so that resources are used proactively, in addition to traditional stand-by modes, resulting in improved utilization and lower costs. However, exercise care that for critical service categories the quest to drive down cost with increased utilization does not introduce bottlenecks or single points of failure. Position HA and BC as well as DR as your last line of defense as business enablers rather than as cost overhead.

Also look at optimizing capacity or space with an eye on both performance rates and reduction ratios across your entire environment. Part of storage capacity optimization ties back to performance and availability optimization, as they are strongly interrelated. Part of availability and capacity optimization involves revisiting service categories, retention cycles, and wants vs. needs or expectations. Also keep in mind that small percentage changes or ratios over a large basis have big benefits. While it is tempting to focus on tools that result in large percentage changes or ratios, if they make large changes only over small amounts of data, that is not where your tools should be focused. For example, if you have 100 TB of data, of which only 10% (10 TB) changes each day, a 10:1 reduction ratio results in about 1 TB of data using dedupe combined with the daily backup, or about the size of a high-capacity disk drive (depending on RAID and protection level of the device). What about the rest of the 100 TB of storage and data: How can that be reduced? Can it be deduped? The answer is "Perhaps," depending on the type of data, applications, time sensitivity, and other factors discussed in this book.

By using various techniques and tools, including real-time compression, archiving of databases, email, and file systems, and space-saving snapshots as part of your data protection modernization along with aligning the applicable RAID levels, thin provisioning, storage tiering, and data management, the overall environment can be enhanced. For example, assume that real-time compression can be applied to the entire 100 TB and assume no noticeable performance impact while achieving a simple reduction ratio of 2:1. Compared to the 10:1 reduction ratio in the previous backup example, 2:1 looks fairly small—perhaps even boring. However, keep in mind that the 10:1 reduction ratio was applicable to only a small subset of the environment that lent itself to that approach and yielded relatively small savings (e.g., from 10 TB to 1 TB). With the 2:1 reduction ratio similar to that seen on many streaming tape solutions, applied over 100 TB on-line (again assuming no performance impact), significant savings can be realized, or the amount of effective capacity increases.

The trick is not to see different data footprint reduction (DFR) techniques as competing, such as archive vs. compression or compression vs. dedupe; instead, consider how they can be used together in the most applicable location-balancing rates (performance and time) with ratios (space and capacity) to be most effective. DFR is an important consideration because addressing the expanding amount of data that needs to be protected, preserved, and served into a higher density using different techniques is a key enabler for becoming more efficient and effective.

If you are going to move data to a cloud, how will you get it there in an efficient and effective manner? Another way of looking at this question is how cloud resources can help house your information to help reduce your data footprint locally.

Part of what to do next includes revisiting your vision, strategy, and plan, making adjustments as needed. Conduct a readiness assessment or review of your existing information services delivery environment and data infrastructure to establish a baseline, including current activities, resource usage, and services delivery effectiveness. Understand seasonal or peak information services delivery workload demands and include those in your baseline and capacity forecast and services delivery plans. Develop a plan of action for both today and tomorrow, aligned with your vision and strategy, to apply various technologies, techniques, and best practices covered in this book and emerging items. Launch proof-of-concept (POC) tests using cloud services, products, and solutions. Apply lessons learned from POCs to develop new best practices, workflows, and service template processes for enhanced service deliver.

Items to consider include:

- Transform perception of IT from cost center to enabler.
- Learn to communicate IT resource in terms of business benefits.
- Identify staff time spent on routine reactive tasks that can be automated.
- Refocus staff time on value-added enablement tasks to become more effective.
- Measure staff based on effective service delivery instead of as overhead.
- Reduce your data baggage by reducing your data footprint.
- Big percentage changes or ratios can be good where they are applicable.
- Small percentage changes on a large basis should not be overlooked.
- Balance increased efficiency with the opportunity to become more effective.
- Expand focus from efficiency to effectiveness while balancing PACE.
- Empower your services consumers to become smart shoppers.
- Without metrics and end-to-end management, you are flying blind.
- Align metrics to business activity and services delivery.
- Implement metrics for comparing internal and external services.
- Have a capacity (server, storage, network, software, services) forecast.
- A capacity forecast enables more informed and effective decision making.
- Communicate service categories (SLOs and SLAs) with associated costs.
- Understand the full cost of using cloud services, including optional fees.
- Streamline organizational workflows, procedures, and best practices.
- To be effective, converged technologies require converged best practices.
- Invest in your facilities, hardware and software, and in your staff skill sets.
- Revisit service-level expectations with your customers.

Table 15.1 is a call to action of what to do for various audiences.

15.4. Futures, Trends, Perspectives, and Predictions

There is more current buzz around so-called big-data and big-bandwidth applications that focus on various forms of unstructured data used for event correlation, analysis, data mining, marketing intelligence, and simulation, among other applications. These include traditional analytics leveraging tools from statistical analysis software (SAS) operating on large amounts of data (a.k.a. number crunching) to processing text or log file streams. Newer solutions are being deployed that leverage cloud and grid architectures using Hadoop and map reduce technologies. The common theme is that

Table 15.1 Call to Action: What to Do, How to Do It

Who	What to Do	How to Do It
CEO, CFO, CIO, CMO, COO	Look at IT and information services as an asset and business enabler to differentiate between your organization and that of others. Information services should be seen as a tool or enabler so that your clients in turn can innovate.	Think of information services delivery in the context of an information factory, leveraging your own as well as other suppliers. Focus on productivity, reducing waste, and enhancing customer satisfaction in a cost-effective manner. Empower and engage your staff to understand how to achieve a more effective, agile, and enabling information services delivery environment. Generate awareness of your capabilities, and align service expectations and needs with business objectives vs. needs and wants. Develop a vision for where you want to go along with a strategy of how to get there.
IT admin, architect, manager	Refine your vision, strategy, and plan; apply the techniques, topics, and technologies discussed in this book. Communicate information services in your business context.	Develop and gather new metrics for those that do not exist while leveraging those that you have, including capacity baselines, forecasts, and plans. Optimize your data footprint using various techniques to enable easier migration to the cloud or other tiered storage environments. Conduct POCs, refining best practices and policies while streamlining workflow and establishing services categories where they do not exist.
Service provider	Educate and generate awareness of your services to customers and prospects.	Differentiate from those competing on low cost by focusing on providing value, including SLOs and SLAs, as well as establishing trust and credibility. Convey proposition of value vs. low-cost opportunity.
Student	Learn about various techniques and technologies for enabling flexible, scalable, and resilient infrastructures.	Become bi-lingual, speaking the language of business as well as that of technology. Learn about cross-technology topics where you may have a specialty focus; however, also acquire knowledge of servers, storage, I/O networking, hardware and software, and various IRM topics and best practices.
Vendors and value-added resellers	Differentiate and add value both near and long term. In the quest to sell a shiny new toy or technology, avoid the trap of missing out on legacy or mature products on which the customer continues to rely.	Look for opportunities to differentiate added value, including assisting customers or prospects in preparing vision, strategy, and plans for both short-term product or solution sales and longer-term annuity business. Expand the options in your sales playbook and develop dynamic scenarios to seize opportunities others neglect. Fill in gaps of coverage not being provided by your competitors, who may be more focused on the future, to enable current revenue and trust opportunities.

these applications require a large amount of compute resources, I/O bandwidth performance, and storage capacity. For some people the "big data" buzz is déjà vu all over again, because it's what they have been doing or working on and with for years; for others it's revolutionary, using new tools and technologies. There will also be increased awareness and maturing of end-to-end management tools along with single-sign-on digital rights and security tools.

There will be continued evolution of dynamic (RAM) and persistent nonvolatile memory (e.g., FLASH) for SSD and other uses as a complement, a device, and on server mother or main boards. Also watch for increased deployment of in-line compression for primary and secondary block, file, and object storage in addition to other DFR optimization technologies including dedupe, archive, CDP, and space-saving snapshots. There will be continued realization that archive is for more than regulatory compliance and provides a cure for many common IT storage or data management woes as well as being an enabler for Green IT, data footprint reduction, and cloud or to facilitate reducing the data footprint impact to get data to cloud.

From a connectivity or I/O and networking basis, look for improvements to PCIe to support more effective bandwidth and lower latency with more devices. Serial attached SCSI (SAS) will evolve from 6 to 12 Gb as a devise-to-controller or server interface. FCoE continues to evolve as an alternative for block-based access using common or converged networking adapters, switches, and cabling, as well as management tools based on Ethernet that also support IP and unified communications. Fibre Channel (FC) is going from 8 to 16 Gb and, probably, 32 Gb for those risk-adverse environments that need something beyond 16 Gb, or for those who will remain skeptical and have internal political (organizational) barriers to keep SAN and LAN separate. Ethernet should go to 40 Gb and become affordable, resulting in 10 GbE becoming a more prolific storage system-to-server interconnect supporting both block-, file-, and object-based access.

Converged E2E management tools from BMC, EMC, Dell, HP, IBM, Microsoft, NetApp, Solarwinds, Symantec, VMware, and others provide heterogeneous or federated support for various clouds (public and private) and different hypervisors.

Industry standards and initiatives pertaining to virtualization and cloud, such as SNIA CDMI, continue to evolve. The value proposition of CDMI and other standards or APIs when adopted by vendors and services providers and deployed by customers is to increase flexibility, transportability of data and applications, ease of management, and, hopefully, reduction in cost via less complexity. As with any new major technology and technique trend, there will be a shakeout of early solution providers and vendors as the ecosystem evolves and matures. Leveraging abstraction layers using federated or heterogeneous tools will help insulate your organization from change that is inevitable as well as facilitate future journeys.

15.5. Chapter and Book Summary

I hope that with this book I have been able to assist you in preparing for your next or current journey or, at least, given you ideas to get ready for one. I also hope I have answered some questions, stimulated new ones, and provoked thought into how different tools or technologies and best practices can be leveraged. After all, the best tool or technology is the one that works for you, not the other way around.

General action and takeaway items include:

- Broadly speaking, there is no such thing as bad technology, only inappropriate or poor implementation, deployment or usage, and promotional scenarios.
- Applying good money or budgets, staffing, hardware, software, facilitates, virtual, and cloud resources to problems may provide short-term relief or mask the underlying issues. You may buy yourself some time, but sooner or later those challenges, problems, or bottlenecks will need to be addressed.
- Cloud, virtualization, convergence, storage networking, and other technologies applied in the wrong way or for the wrong reasons can produce adverse results and increased complexity.
- Removing complexity should result in reducing costs, and in finding and fixing problems.
- Clouds should be seen as another IT resource tier, complementing existing technologies.
- You cannot manage effectively what you do not know about, thus the need for E2E management as well as situational awareness.
- Metrics and measurement matter as important enablers for management, along with accounting, performance capacity planning, and chargeback.
- Not all servers, storage, networks, or data centers can be consolidated, but many can be virtualized for agility and ease of management.
- There will be another stop or destination in the ongoing IT journey over the next decade or two, but what this will be is still foggy. However, we can use history and experience to see where we are going based on where we have been and applying lessons learned.

Regardless of whether virtualization or clouds are in your near-term or long-term future, becoming more efficient and effective should be in your future sooner rather than later. How you go about achieving efficiency and effectiveness will be a part of your own unique soft product and information services delivery manifest. Rome was not built in a day, nor are most information services and their delivery mechanisms. This means that information systems and their underlying infrastructures, including cloud, virtual, and physical resources, along with best practices, processes, procedures, and people skill sets take time to evolve to achieve targeted benefits. However, some benefits can occur within days, if not hours, leveraging the various techniques and technologies discussed in this book to help you do things today while preparing for tomorrow.

Return on investments (ROI) can only be realized once they are acted on, and the longer spent analyzing or planning, the longer will be the delay in realizing the benefits. On the other hand, jump too soon, incur a false start or aborted takeoff, and cost or services will be impacted and customers disrupted. As a result, find the balance in doing your homework, conducting analysis and investigation, and initiating pilot studies, proof-of-concepts, prototyping, and other activities to gain experience, prepare or refine best practices, and sharpen your skills for the future while evolving information services delivery.

Finally (for now), enjoy your journey regardless of whether or not it is to the cloud or a virtualized and green IT data center. Don't be scared, but look before you leap. Drop me a note, send an email, or mail a postcard to let me know how your journey progresses, as I would like to hear from you and provide assistance if needed. Best wishes, and have a safe and productive journey.

Appendix

Where to Learn More

Companion materials and resources for further reading—including additional technology, best practices, industry trends, perspectives, and other useful links—can be found at www.storageio.com/cvdsn. Additional information about clouds, virtualization, green and efficient IT and data storage networking is available in the author's others books, *The Green and Virtual Data Center* (CRC Press, 2009) and *Resilient Storage Networks—Designing Flexible Scalable Data Infrastructures* (Elsevier, 2004), found at www.storageio.com/books.

www.storageioblog.com	Author's blog
www.twitter.com/storageio	Author's twitter handle
www.storageio.tv	Author's video and related material
www.storageio.com/news	Commentary and interviews with the author
www.storageio.com/events	Author's calendar—speaking and other events
www.storageio.com/contact	Author's contact information
www.storageio.com/tips	Tips and articles by the author
www.storageio.com/links	Useful industry-related links to other sites
www.aiim.com	Archiving and records management trade group
www.dmtg.org	Data Management Task Force
www.cmg.org	Computer Measurement Group and capacity planners
www.communities.vmware.com	VMware technical community website
www.csrc.nist.gov	U.S. government cloud specifications
www.fcoe.com	Website pertaining to Fibre Channel over Ethernet
www.fibrechannel.org	Fibre Channel Industry Association
www.ieee.org	Institute of Electrical and Electronics Engineers
www.ietf.org	Internet Engineering Task Force
www.iso.org	International Standards Organizations

www.opendatacenteralliance.org	Alliance of data center and related technologies
www.pcisig.com	Peripheral Component Interconnect (PCI) trade group
www.scsita.org	SCSI trade association
www.snia.org	Storage Networking Industry Association
www.spec.org	Server and storage benchmarking site
www.storageperformance.org	Storage performance benchmarking site
www.t11.org	Fibre Channel and related standards
www.tpc.org	Transaction Performance Council benchmark site

Glossary

100 GbE	100-Gigabit Ethernet
10 GbE	10-Gigabit Ethernet
15.5K	15,000 revolutions per minute (RPM)
16 GFC	16-Gigabit Fibre Channel
1 GbE	1-Gigabit Ethernet
1 GFC	1-Gigabit Fibre Channel
24 × 7	24 hours a day, seven days a week; always available
2 GFC	2-Gigabit Fibre Channel
3G	Third-generation cellular broadband communications
40 GbE	40-Gigabit Ethernet
4 GFC	4-Gigabit Fibre Channel
7.2K	7,200 revolutions per minute (RPM)
8 GFC	8-Gigabit Fibre Channel
AaaS	Application or Archive as a Service
ACL	Access Control List
AES	Form of encryption
AFR	Annual failure rate measured or estimated failures per year
Agent	Software for performing backup or other IRM functions on a server
AIX	IBM open systems operating system
Amazon	Web services and e-commerce
AMD	Manufacturer of processing chips
ANSI	American National Standards Institute
API	Application Program Interface
APM	Adaptive power management; varies energy use to service delivered

ication blades	Server, storage, and I/O networking blades for different applications
Applications	Programs or software that performance business or IRM services
Archive	Identifying and moving inactive data to alternative media for future use
ASIC	Application Specific Integrated Circuit
ASP	Application service provider delivering functionality via the Internet
Asynchronous	Time-delayed data transmission used for low cost, long distances
ATM	Asynchronous Transfer Mode networking technology
Availability	The amount or percentage of time a system is able and ready to work
BaaS	Backup as a Service
Bandwidth	Measure of how much data is moved in a given amount of time
Base 10	Numbering system known as decimal
Base 2	Numbering system known as binary
BC	Business continuance
Blade center	Packaging combining blade servers, I/O, and networking blades
Blade server	Server blade packaged as a blade for use in a blade center
BOM	Bill of materials
Boot	Process of starting up and loading software into a server
BTU	British thermal unit; amount of heat from energy used
CaaS	Compute as a Service
CAD	Computer-assisted design
CapEx	Capital expenses
CAS	Content addressable storage
CBT	Change block tracking; or computer-based training
CD	Compact disc
CDMI	Cloud Data Management Initiative
CDP	Continuous data protection or complete data protection
CERT	Community Emergency Response Team for data security
Chargeback	Billing and invoicing for information services
Chiller	Cooling device to remove heat from coolant
Chunk	Storage allocation size for RAID and data protection
CIFS	Common Internet File system (NAS) for file and data sharing
CIM	Common information model for accessing information
CIO	Chief information officer
Citrix	Virtualization solutions provider

CKD	Count Key Data mainframe data access protocol
CLI	Command Line Interface
Cloud computing	Internet or Web-based remote application or IRM-related services
Cloud service	Information services provider
Cloud storage	Storage provided via a cloud service or product
Cluster	Collection of servers or storage working together, also known as a grid
Clustered file system	Distributed file system across multiple servers or storage nodes
CMDB	Configuration Management Database or repository
CMG	Computer Measurement Group; capacity and performance planners
CNA	Converged Network Architecture
CNIC	Converged Network Interface Card or Chip
CO_2 emissions	Carbon dioxide emissions
Cold aisles	Aisles between equipment racks or cabinets that are provided with cold air
Consoles	Management interfaces for configuration or control of IT devices
Cooked storage	Formatted, usable storage with a file system, or nonraw storage
Cooling ton	12,000 BTUs to cool 1 ton of air
COS	Console operating system, also known as a console or boot system
CP	Capacity planning
cPOP	Cloud point of presence or access gateway
CPU	Central processing unit
CRAC	Computer room air conditioning
Cross technology	Solution or tools that address multiple technologies and disciplines
CSV	Comma-separated-variable format used for spreadsheet data
D2D	Disk-to-disk snapshot, backup, copy, or replication
D2D2D	Disk-to-disk-to-disk snapshot, backup, copy, or replication
D2D2T	Disk-to-disk-to-tape snapshot, backup, copy, replication, or archive
D2T	Disk-to-tape backup, copy, or archive
DAS	Direct Attached Storage, either internal or external to a server
Data barn	Large repository for holding large amounts of on-line or off line data
Data in flight	Data being moved between locations, between servers, or to from storage
Database	Structured means of organizing and storing data
DB2/UDB	IBM database software

DBA	Database administrator
DBS	Dynamic bandwidth switching; varies energy use to performance
DC	Direct current electricity
DCB	Data center bridging
DCE	Data center Ethernet for converged I/O and networking
DCE	Data communications equipment
DCE	Distributed computing environment
DCiE	Data center infrastructure efficiency
DCPE	Data center performance efficiency
DDR/RAM	Double-data-rate random access memory
Dedupe engine	Software algorithms that perform de-duplication
De-duplication	Elimination of duplicate data
Desktop	Workstation or laptop computer, also known as a PC
DFR	Data footprint reduction (archive, compress, dedupe)
DFS	Distributed File Systems, for distributed and shared data access
DHCP	Dynamic Host Configuration Protocol for network management
DIO	Direct IO operations addressing specific storage addresses
Director	I/O and networking large-scale, multiprotocol resilient switch
DL	Disk library used for storing backup and other data; alternative to tape
DLM	Data lifecycle management
DLP	Data leak prevention
DMA	Direct memory access
DMTF	Distributed Management Task Force
DNS	Domain name system for managing Internet domain names
DoD	U.S. Department of Defense
DoE	U.S. Department of Energy
DoS	Denial-of-service attack
DPM	Data protection management
DR	Disaster recovery
DRAM	Dynamic RAM memory
DRO	Data replication optimization
DRP	Disaster recovery planning
DVD	Digital Video Disc
DVD Store	Transactional workload simulation
DVR	Digital Video Recorder
DWDM	Dense wave division multiplexing
E2E	End to end

EaaS	Email as a Service
ECC	Error-correcting code
ECKD	Extended Count Key Data
eDiscovery	Electronic search and data discovery
EH&S	Environmental Health and Safety
Energy Star	U.S. Environmental Protection Agency Energy Star program
EPA	U.S. Environmental Protection Agency
ESRP	Microsoft Exchange Solution Reviewed Program benchmark
Ethernet	Network interface
ETS	Emissions trading scheme
EU	European Union
Excel	Microsoft spreadsheet
FAN	File area network or file-based storage management
FC	Fibre Channel
FCIA	Fibre Channel Industry Association
FCIP	Fibre Channel on IP for long-distance data movement and mirroring
FCoE	Fibre Channel over Ethernet
FCP	Fibre Channel SCSI Protocol
FC-SB2	FICON Upper Level Protocol (ULP)
File data access	Accessing data via a file system, either locally or remotely
Firewall	Security device or software to block unauthorized network access
FLASH memory	Nonvolatile memory
FTP	File Transfer Protocol
FUD	Fear, uncertainty, and doubt
G&T	Generating and transmission network for electrical power
GbE	Gigabit Ethernet
Generator	Device for producing electrical power for standby or co-generation
Ghz	Gigahertz frequency measure of speed
Global namespace	Directory name space to ease access across multiple file systems
Gold Copy	master backup or data protection copy
GPS	Global Positioning System (or initials of the author of this book)
Green gap	Disconnect between messaging and core IT challenges and opportunities
Green grid	Industry Trade Group
Green IT	Efficient and effective information services delivery
Grid	Local or wide area cluster of servers or storage working together

Guest	Guest operating system in a virtual machine or logical partition, also known as an image
GUI	Graphical user interface
HA	High availability
Hadoop	Software tool for performing analysis on unstructured data
HAMR	Heat-assisted magnetic recording
Hash	Computed sum or key for lookup comparison
HBA	Host bus adapter for attaching peripherals to servers or storage
HCA	Host channel adapter for InfiniBand
HD	High-definition broadcast or video
HDD	Hard disk drive, such as Fibre Channel, SAS, SATA, or USB
HDTV	High-definition TV
HHDD	Hybrid HDD with RAM, FLASH, and/or magnetic media
Hosting	Facility or service provider that hosts IT components and services
Hot aisles	Aisles between equipment cabinets where warm air exhausts
HPC	High-performance computing
HSM	Hierarchical storage management
HTTP	Hypertext Transfer Protocol for serving and accessing Web pages
HVAC	Heating, ventilation, and air conditioning
Hyper-V	Microsoft virtualization infrastructure software
Hypervisor	Virtualization framework that emulates and partitions physical resources
I/O	Input/output operation, read or write
I/O rate	How many I/O operations (IOPS) read or write in a given timeframe
I/O size	How big the I/O operations are
I/O type	Reads, writes, random or sequential
IBA	InfiniBand Architecture
IC	Integrated circuit
IEEE	Institute of Electrical and Electronic Engineers
IETF	Internet Engineering Task Force
ILM	Information lifecycle management
IM	Instant messaging
Image	Guest operating system or workload residing in a virtual machine or logical partition
Index	Knowledge base or dictionary
Ingest	Data being read and processed by dedupe engine
Intel	Large processor and chip manufacturer
Iometer	Load generation and simulation tool for benchmark comparisons

IOPS	I/O operations per second for reads and writes of various sizes
Iostat	I/O monitoring tool
IOV	I/O virtualization including converged networks and PCI switching
IP	Intellectual property
IP	Internet Protocol part of TCP/IP
IPM	Intelligent power management; varies energy used to service delivered
IPSec	IP-based security and encryption
IPTV	IP-based TV
IRM	Infrastructure resource management
iSCSI	SCSI command set mapped to IP
ISO	International Standards Organization
ISV	Independent software vendor
IT	Information technology
JRE	Java Runtime Environment
JVM	Java Virtual Machine
Key management	Managing encryption keys
Knowledge base	Where dedupe meta, index, and pointers are kept
KPI	Key performance indicator
KVM	Keyboard video monitor
LAN	Local area network
Laptop	Portable computer
Linux	Open-source operating system
LiveMigration	Virtual Iron function similar to VMware VMotion
LPAR	Logical partition or virtual machine
LUNS	Logical unit numbers addressing for storage targets or devices
MAC	Media access control layer for networking interfaces
Magnetic tape	Low-cost, energy-efficient, removable media for storing data
MAID	Massive array of idle disks that avoids power when not in use
MAID 2.0	Second-generation MAID with intelligent power management
Mainframe	IBM legacy large server; generic name for a large frame-based server
MAN	Metropolitan area network
Metadata	Data describing other data, including how and when it was used
MHz	Megahertz frequency or indicator or speed
MIB	Management Information Block for SNMP
MLC	Multilevel cell
MO	Magneto-optical storage medium
MPLS	Multi-Protocol Labeling Switching WAN networking protocol
MR-IOV	PCI multi-root IOV capability

MSDS	Material Safety Data Sheet for products
MSP	Managed service provider
MTBF	Mean time between failures; measured or estimated reliability
MTTR	Mean time to repair or replace a failed item
MW	Megawatts, unit of power
NAND	Nonvolatile computer memory such as FLASH
NAS	Network attached storage such as NFS and CIFS Windows file sharing
NDA	Nondisclosure agreement
Near-line	Nonprimary active data storage that does not need fast access
NEMA	National Electronic Manufacturers Association
NFS	Network File System (NAS) for file and data sharing
Nfstat	Operating system utility for monitoring NFS activity
NIC	Network interface card or chip
NIST	National Institute of Standards and Technology
NOCC	Network operations control center
NPIV	N_Port ID Virtualization for Fibre Channel I/O networking
NVRAM	Nonvolatile random access memory
Object data access	Data access via application-specific API or descriptors
OC	Optical carrier network
Off-line	Data or IT resources that is not on-line and ready for use
OLTP	On-line transaction processing
On-line	Data and IT resources that are on-line, active and ready for use
OpEx	Operational expenses
Optical	Optical-based networking or optical-based storage medium
Orphaned storage	Lost, misplaced, or forgotten-about storage or storage space
OS	Operating system; also known or referred to as an image or guest
Outage	Systems or subsystems are not available for use or to perform work
Oversubscription	Allocating common shared service to multiple users to reduce costs
P2V	Physical-to-virtual migration or conversion of a server and applications
PACE	Performance, availability, capacity, energy, and economics
Para-virtualization	Optimized virtualization requiring custom software change
Parity	Technique using extra memory or storage to ensure that data is intact
PATA	Parallel ATA I/O interface
PC	Personal computer or program counter
PCFE	Power, cooling, floor space, EHS (PCFE)
PCI	Peripheral Computer Interconnect for attaching devices to servers

PCI IOV	PCI Sig I/O virtualization implementation
PCIe	PCI express is the latest implementation of the PCI standard
PCM	Phase-change memory
PDA	Personal digital assistant (e.g., Blackberry, Apple, Windows-based)
PDU	Power distribution unit
Physical volume	A disk drive or group of disk drives presented by a storage system
PIT	Point in time
PM	Physical machine, or a real physical server or computer
PMDB	Performance Management Database
pNFS	Parallel NFS (NAS) for parallel high-performance file access
POC	Proof of concept
POTS	Plain old telephone system
Primary	Storage, server, or networks used day to day for service delivery
Provisioning	Allocating and assigning servers, storage, and networking resources
Proxy	Backup server configured to off-load application servers for performing backup
PST	Microsoft Exchange email personal storage folder file
PUE	Power usage effectiveness measurement
QA	Quality assurance
QoS	Quality of service
Quad Core	Processor chip with four core CPUs
RAID	Redundant array of independent disks
RAM	Random access memory
RASM	Reliability availability serviceability management
Raw storage	Storage not configured or not formatted with file system or RAID
RDM	Raw device mapped storage, as opposed to file mapped storage
Re-inflate	Re-expand deduped data during restore
Reliability	Systems function as expected, when expected, with confidence
Remote mirroring	Replicating or mirroring data to a remote location for business continuance and disaster recovery
RFID	Radio-frequency ID tag and reader
RHDD	Removal hard disk drive
ROBO	Remote office/branch office
RoHS	Restriction of hazardous substances
ROI	Return on investment; return on innovation
Router	Networking or storage device for protocol conversion and routing
RPC	Remote Procedure Call for program-to-program communications

RPO	Recovery-point objective
RTO	Recovery-time objective
RTSP	Real-Time Streaming Protocol for streaming data
RU or U	Rack unit
RUT	Rule of thumb
S/390	IBM mainframe architecture now referred to as "Z" or "Zed" series
SaaS	Software as a Service
SAN	Storage area network
SAR	System analysis and reporting tool
SAS	Serial attached SCSI I/O interface and type of disk drive
SAS	Statistical analysis software
SATA	Serial ATA I/O interface and type of disk drive
Scheduled downtime	Planned downtime for maintenance, replacement, and upgrades
SCSI	Small Computer Storage Interconnect I/O interface and protocol
SCSI_FCP	SCSI command set mapped to Fibre Channel; also known as FCP
SDK	Software development kit
Semistructured data	Email data that has structured or index and unstructured attachments
SFF	Small form factor disk drives, servers, I/O, and networking blades
SFP	Small form factor optical transceiver
SHA-1	Secure Hash Algorithm
SharePoint	Microsoft software for managing documents utilizing SQLserver
SIS	Single-instance storage; also known as de-duplicated or normalized
SLA	Service-level agreement
SLC	Single-level cell
SLO	Service-level objective to manage service delivery towards
SMB	Small/medium business
SMIS	Storage Management Interface Specification
Snapshot	A picture or image of the data as of a point in time
SNIA	Storage Networking Industry Association
SNMP	Simple Network Management Protocol for device management
SoA	Service-oriented architecture
SOHO	Small office/home office

SONET/SDH	Synchronous Optical Networking/Synchronous Digital Hierarchy
SPC	Storage Performance Council benchmarks
SPEC	Performance benchmarks
SQL database	Structure Query Language–based database
SRA	System or storage resource analysis
SR-IOV	Single root PCIe IOV
SRM	Server, storage, or system resource management
SRM	VMware site recovery manager for data protection management
SSD	Solid-state disk device using FLASH, RAM, or a combination
SSP	Storage solution provider; also known as MSP or cloud storage
Storageioblog	Author's blog
STP	Spanning Tree Protocol
Structured data	Data stored in databases or other well-defined repositories
Supercomputer	Very fast and large performance-oriented server
SUT	System under test
SUV	System under validation
Switch	I/O and networking connectivity for attaching multiple devices
Synchronous	Real-time data movement communications
T11	ANSI standards group for Fibre Channel
Tape	Magnetic tape used for storing data off-line
TCP/IP	Transmission Control Protocol/Internet Protocol networking protocols
Thin provisioning	Virtually allocates or overbooks physical storage to multiple servers
Thumb drive	FLASH memory–based device with USB interface for moving data
Tiered access	Different I/O and network interfaces aligned to various service needs
Tiered protection	Different data protection techniques and RTO/RPO for service needs
Tiered servers	Different types of servers aligned to various cost and service needs
Tiered storage	Different types of storage aligned to various cost and service needs
TL	Tape library
TPC	Transaction Processing Council benchmarks
Transaction integrity	Ensuring write order consistency of time-based tractions or events
ULP	Upper-level protocol

UNIX	Open systems operating system
Unscheduled	Unplanned downtime for emergency repair or maintenance
Unstructured	Data, including files, videos, photos, and slides, stored outside of databases
UPS	Uninterrupted power system
Usable storage	Amount of storage that can actually be used when formatted
USB	Universal Serial Bus for attaching peripherals to workstations
V2P	Virtual-to-physical migration or conversion
V2V	Virtual-to-virtual migration or conversion of a server and applications
VAR	Value-added reseller
VCB	VMware consolidated backup proxy–based backup for virtual machines
VDC	Virtual data center
VDI	Virtual desktop infrastructure
VIO	Virtual I/O
Virtual Iron	Virtualization infrastructure solution provider
Virtual memory	Operating system or VM extended memory mapped to disk storage
Virtual office	Remote or home office for mobile or remote workers
Virtualization	Tools to abstract, emulate, and aggregate to IT resource management
VLAN	Virtual local area network
VM	Virtual machine or logical partition that emulates a physical machine
VMark	VMware benchmark and comparison utility
VMDK	VMware disk file containing the VM instance
VMFS	VMware file system, stored in a VMDK file
VMotion	VMware tool for migrating a running VM to another physical server
VMware	Virtualization infrastructure solution
VOD	Video on demand
Volume manager	Software that aggregates and abstracts storage for file systems
VPN	Virtual private network
VTL	Virtual tape library
VTS	Virtual tape system; same as a virtual tape librarya
WAAS	Wide area application services, similar to WAFS
WADM	Wide area data management, similar to WAFS
WADS	Wide area data services, similar to WAFS
WAFS	Wide area file services tools for remote data and application access
WAN	Wide area network

Web 2.0	Second-generation Web applications that are two-way or collaborative
WGBC	World Green Building Council
Wide area cluster	Server or storage cluster, also known as grid, spread over a wide area
Wi-Fi	Wireless networking for relatively short distances
WiMax	Higher-speed, longer-distance, next-generation wireless networking
Windows	Microsoft operating system
Workstation	Desktop PC or laptop computer
WWPN	World Wide Port Name used for power Fibre Channel addressing
x86	Popular hardware instruction set architecture designed by Intel
Xenmotion	VM movement utility for Xen, similar to VMware VMotion
XML	Extensible Markup Language
xWDM	Generic term for Dense Wave Division multiplexing
Y2K	Millennium or year 2000
Zen	Open source–based virtualization infrastructure used by Virtual Iron
zSeries	IBM legacy mainframe that supports zOS and open Linux and LPARs

Index